Refuge beyond Reach

Refuge beyond Reach

How Rich Democracies Repel
Asylum Seekers

DAVID SCOTT FITZGERALD

OXFORD
UNIVERSITY PRESS

OXFORD
UNIVERSITY PRESS

Oxford University Press is a department of the University of Oxford. It furthers the University's objective of excellence in research, scholarship, and education by publishing worldwide. Oxford is a registered trade mark of Oxford University Press in the UK and certain other countries.

Published in the United States of America by Oxford University Press
198 Madison Avenue, New York, NY 10016, United States of America.

Library of Congress Cataloging-in-Publication Data
Names: FitzGerald, David, 1972– author.
Title: Refuge beyond reach : how rich democracies repel asylum seekers /
David Scott FitzGerald.
Description: New York, NY : Oxford University Press, [2019] |
Includes bibliographical references and index.
Identifiers: LCCN 2018035437 | ISBN 9780190874155 (hc : alk. paper)
Subjects: LCSH: Refugees—Government policy—United States. | Refugees—Government policy—Canada. | Refugees—Government policy—Europe. | Refugees—Government policy—Australia. | Asylum, Right of—United States. | Asylum, Right of—Canada. | Asylum, Right of—Europe. | Asylum, Right of—Australia. | United States—Emigration and immigration—Government policy. | Canada—Emigration and immigration—Government policy. | Europe—Emigration and immigration—Government policy. | Australia—Emigration and immigration—Government policy. | International law and human rights.
Classification: LCC JV6346 .F57 2019 | DDC 323.6/31—dc23
LC record available at https://lccn.loc.gov/2018035437

For my parents, Dean and Dona

CONTENTS

ACKNOWLEDGMENTS

The first people called "refugees" in English were French Protestants who fled religious persecution in France in the seventeenth and early eighteenth centuries. Some of them found refuge in Britain's colonies in North America, including my 10th great-grandmother, Hester Mahieu Cooke, and the paternal ancestors of my wife. Today Marian pushes me to share the ideas and evidence from my scholarly work beyond the confines of the academy. Gabriela, our daughter, inspires me with her sharp instinct for what is just and what is unjust. My debts grow each year to them and the many other talented, generous, and energetic people who made this book possible.

The University of California, San Diego, has been my intellectual home for this project. I'm grateful for the support of the Center for Comparative Immigration Studies (CCIS), the Department of Sociology, and the Academic Senate. Ana Minvielle keeps CCIS running with her intense work ethic. Graduate students Angela Y. McClean, Michael Nicholson, Areli Palomo-Contreras, Henriette Ruhrman, and Yesenia Sánchez helped excavate the mountains of evidence for this book and read drafts. I have learned much from Rawan Arar's dissertation work on Syrian refugees in Jordan, our collaborative publications, and her archival research for this project in Canberra. Thanks also to participants in talks at the Center for U.S.-Mexican Studies, Department of Sociology, and the American Academy of Arts and Sciences San Diego Program.

On the road, colleagues have given feedback at talks or conferences hosted by the Centre for Refugee Studies at York University, International Association for the Study of Forced Migration, University of Connecticut School of Law, Columbia Population Research Center, El Colegio de la Frontera Norte, University of Zagreb Faculty of Law, Social Science History

Association, Canadian Association for Refugee and Forced Migration Studies, Monash University Faculty of Law, Sydney Ideas at the University of Sydney, Kaldor Centre at the University of New South Wales, American Historical Association, Loyola Marymount University, UCLA International Institute, Brooklyn Law School, Tel Aviv University Department of Sociology, Weatherhead Center for International Affairs at Harvard University, and NYU Abu Dhabi. I'm especially grateful to the Melbourne Law School and Susan Kneebone for hosting me as an academic visitor in April 2017.

Many people have shared their expertise and reactions over the years. In Australia, I thank Tamara Wood, Maria O'Sullivan, Madeline Gleeson, Amy Nethery, and Claire Higgins. At UC San Diego, Isaac Martin, Kevin Lewis, Akos Rona-Tas, and Kwai Ng shared their reactions to early pieces of the project. Several colleagues read chapters or the entire manuscript, including Asher Hirsch, Daniel Ghezelbash, Gabriela Díaz, Azadeh Dastyari, David Cook-Martín, Anita Casavantes Bradford, Maris Williams, and Maurizio Albahari.

I am fortunate never to have been a refugee. As a boy living in Jordan, the Gaza Strip, and Israel in the 1970s and 1980s, and later in Central America as a young journalist covering the waning days of the civil wars, I was reminded every day of the difference between being an expatriate and an exile. In 1970, my American parents and three older siblings were forced to flee Jordan as it descended into the civil war of Black September. Driving north through army and guerrilla checkpoints as machine guns chattered and mortar shells fell in the distance, they reached the Deraa border crossing. The Syrian guards opened the gates and waved them through. My family went on to live for six months in a peaceful Beirut. My final thanks are to the Syrian and Lebanese people who gave sanctuary to the FitzGeralds. Four decades later, Deraa became ground zero for the Syrian civil war that displaced 13 million people. To our new Syrian neighbors in San Diego, *ahlan wasahlan*. Welcome.

San Diego, California
July 2018

ABBREVIATIONS

ASICs	aliens from special interest countries
CA-4	Central America-4; El Salvador, Guatemala, Honduras, and Nicaragua
CAT	Convention Against Torture
CBP	Customs and Border Protection
CIA	Central Intelligence Agency
COMAR	Mexican Commission for Refugee Assistance
DHS	Department of Homeland Security
ECHR	European Convention on Human Rights
ECJ	European Court of Justice
ECtHR	European Court of Human Rights
EU	European Union
ICE	Immigration and Customs Enforcement
INA	Immigration and Nationality Act
INAMI	National Institute of Migration
INS	Immigration and Naturalization Service
IOM	International Organization for Migration
NGO	nongovernmental organization
OAS	Organization of American States
OECD	Organisation for Economic Co-operation and Development
PNG	Papua New Guinea
UNHCR	UN High Commissioner for Refugees
USINT	U.S. Interests Section in Havana

Refuge beyond Reach

CHAPTER 1 | The Catch-22 of Asylum Policy

THE GREEK ISLAND OF Kos lies just five kilometers off the coast of Asia Minor. The Roman historian Tacitus records that Roman citizens fleeing from a massacre on the mainland found shelter in Kos's temple in 88 BCE. As in other Greek communities, its religious sanctuary was considered an inviolable haven (*asylon hieron*) for victims of war and political persecution—a concept that gave birth to "asylum." Those seeking sanctuary had to appear and explain why they deserved protection through a formal rite. They sat on the altar and identified themselves by raising a freshly broken twig or strand of wool. Stepping outside the safe space of the temple was risky. Paintings depict pursuers armed with swords ready to attack rejected supplicants. Even in ancient Greece, asylum was restricted to delineated spaces. Athenian authorities in the fifth century BCE built a police station at the entrance to the Acropolis to prevent unwanted asylum seekers from entering the sanctuaries.[1] Measures to keep people from reaching sanctuary are as old as the asylum tradition itself.

In 2015 Kos became a major gateway for refugees from the Syrian civil war trying to evade policies that kept them out of the European Union (EU). Early on September 2, three-year-old Alan Kurdi and his family scrambled into an inflatable boat to make the short crossing from the Turkish town of Bodrum. The crowded dinghy capsized in minutes. Alan drowned along with his four-year-old brother, Ghalib, and mother, Rehana. At first light, a journalist photographed Alan's body lying face down in the wet sand with his palms turned toward the sky. He was still dressed in his red T-shirt, blue shorts, and black sneakers. Turkish gendarme Mehmet Çıplak cradled the body as he carried it away. Within hours, the images shone from screens around the world. Alan Kurdi became the drowned human face of the Syrian refugee crisis and the European response that tried to keep most refugees away from EU territory.

After the boat sank, journalists learned that Alan and his family belonged to Syria's oppressed Kurdish minority. Why did the Kurdis expose their family to such terrible risks? Why didn't they take a legal path to safety? Most countries do not allow asylum at their embassies, and it is not routine practice anywhere.[2] There are very few "humanitarian corridors" providing a legal way for refugees to travel to a safe country and ask for asylum. The programs that do exist are limited to a few hundred slots a year, while the need is in the millions.[3] The Kurdis were hoping to resettle in Canada, but the international refugee regime does not guarantee refugees protection in any particular country. Governments have discretion to choose whether to resettle refugees processed abroad. In 2017, thirty-five countries had some form of overseas refugee resettlement program. Together, they resettled 103,000 refugees, including 33,000 who moved to the United States, 27,000 to Canada, and 15,000 to Australia. Resettlements in Europe ranged from 6,202 in the United Kingdom to just 4 in Slovakia.[4]

The Kurdis had hoped to join their relatives in Vancouver. Canadian authorities said they had no record of receiving a refugee resettlement

FIGURE 1.1 Turkish gendarme Mehmet Çıplak carries the body of three-year-old Alan Kurdi on a beach in southern Turkey after a boat carrying Syrian refugees sank while trying to reach the Greek island of Kos in September 2015. Photo by Nilufer Demir/AFP/Getty Images.

application from Alan's father, but that Alan's uncle, Mohammad, had submitted an application that was rejected as incomplete. According to Alan's aunt, the Kurdis decided to head for Greece after receiving the news that Mohammad's application was rejected. Amid the publicity surrounding the deaths, the Canadian government offered to resettle Mohammad, his wife, and five children.[5] The gesture came too late for Alan, his brother, and mother.

The grim truth for almost all people fleeing violence is that overseas re-settlement programs are not an option. There is no legal line where they can register and wait as their number advances. Resettlement is like winning the lottery. At least since 1994, annual refugee resettlement flows as a percentage of the global refugee population have never exceeded 1%. Eighty-four percent of refugees live in poor and middle-income countries, mostly in countries such as Turkey and Kenya that neighbor the conflict. An even larger number of people, 40.3 million, are "internally displaced" by conflict and are not le-gally considered refugees for the single reason that they did not cross an international border.[6]

For 99% of refugees, the only way to find safety in a country in the pros-perous democracies of the Global North is to reach its territory and then ask for asylum.[7] If an individual investigation or group designation finds that they meet the statutory definition of someone who is fleeing persecution "for reasons of race, religion, nationality, membership of a particular social group or political opinion,"[8] they are granted asylum.

The core principle of the asylum regime is "non-refoulement," estab-lished by the 1951 UN Refugee Convention, which prohibits governments from sending refugees back to their persecutors. Of the world's 195 coun-tries, 148 have signed the 1951 Convention and/or its 1967 Protocol. An even stronger version of non-refoulement in the 1984 UN Convention against Torture, to which 162 countries are party, prohibits the forced return of an-yone facing torture.[9]

In 2016, the EU, United States, Canada, and Australia recognized asylum or a similar protected status for 734,961 people. Asylum recognition rates of applicants whose cases were adjudicated in 2016 ranged from 23.2% in the United States to 48% in the EU, 32.8% in Australia, and 62.2% in Canada. Increasingly, governments are granting some form of subsidiary protection that gives temporary refuge without the full rights of asylum, such as per-manent protection and the right to sponsor the admission of close family members.[10] However, the widespread acceptance of the principle of non-refoulement and the acknowledgment in the Convention that refugees may be forced to travel illegally are subverted by governments that try to keep asylum seekers at arm's length and penalize those who travel without official approval. Had Alan Kurdi and his family reached Kos, they stood a good chance of being granted asylum in Europe. Unfortunately for them, a system created to keep most refugees from reaching safety in the rich democracies of the Global North worked as designed.

Remote Control

Many border control measures are highly visible. My home city of San Diego is separated from neighboring Tijuana by fences made of steel plates, concrete barriers, barbed wire, and towers bristling with cameras and sensors— all patrolled by armed Border Patrol agents in pickup trucks and helicopters. When I fly over the border region at night in a commercial airliner, floodlights along the fence draw a shining yellow line across the desert that is obvious from cruising altitude. Donald Trump was elected president in 2016 largely on a platform of extending a wall the entire length of the border with Mexico. Governments have also built barriers to keep Africans out of Israel, Yemenis out of Saudi Arabia, Zimbabweans out of South Africa, Bangladeshis out of India, and Pakistanis out of Iran, to name but a few of the fortifications around the world.[11]

As important as these obvious barriers are for restricting mobility, most control of access by land, air, and sea takes place out of sight and far away from the national territory. Political scientist Aristide Zolberg coined the term "remote control" to describe the system of passports, visas, and passenger ship checks developed in the early twentieth century that kept people from leaving European ports for the New World unless they had passed an initial screening.[12] Since that time, border control has become even more distant from a state's territory—such that passengers flying halfway around the planet from Abu Dhabi to Los Angeles clear U.S. customs and passport control in Abu Dhabi. The notion of border has also become more diffuse. Asylum seekers trying to reach Sweden from Eritrea encounter a long series of hurdles put in their way by the Swedish government and the European Union working in concert with transit countries, rather than a single line drawn by the Swedish government.

Concepts similar to remote control further highlight the spatial characteristics of efforts to deter people from moving across international borders. Legal scholar James Hathaway described emerging policies of "non-*entrée*" to the territories of rich democratic countries in 1992.[13] Political scientists Virginie Guiraudon and Gallya Lahav influentially described how states shift migration policy "out" from their borders. Other researchers have described "non-arrival measures," "deterritorialized" control, "policing at a distance," and "externalization."[14] Government agencies portray their policies in catchphrases that echo academic terms. "Off-shoring our border control is the keystone of our border defence," the UK Home Office declares.[15] The EU conducts "pre-frontier" operations in third states, and its border control agency Frontex routinely acts "beyond the border."[16] The United States calls its long-range maritime interceptions in the Pacific a strategy of "pushing our borders out."[17] Citizenship and Immigration Canada touts the idea that "border control begins overseas."[18] The Australian Border Force considers "the border not to be a purely physical barrier separating nation States, but a complex continuum stretching offshore and onshore."[19] Governments and scholars alike agree that borders are being pushed out to keep the unwanted at arm's length.

The concept of "remote control" could be misleading if taken too literally. States do not have the capacity to turn migration flows on and off with the push of a button. Once a movement is channeled by social networks or a developed people-smuggling industry, it is especially resistant to government intervention. Neither are the rich governments of the Global North always the ones with the power to decide the composition and size of flows. As the case of Cuban movement to the United States in chapter 6 illustrates, the state of origin can exercise as much control as the state of destination.

Many remote control policies sweep up all kinds of people on the move, from tourists to terrorists, families reunifying with their loved ones, migrant laborers, and refugees.[20] Some remote controls specifically target people seeking asylum. Even when the policies were not intended to deter asylum seekers, the policies make it more difficult for persecuted people to find refuge. The UN High Commissioner for Refugees (UNHCR) and some advocacy organizations insist, for understandable political reasons, that "refugees are not migrants."[21] These organizations want to protect the special obligations that states have toward refugees and to defend those obligations against demands to restrict refugees based on the claim that they are merely "economic migrants" who do not deserve protection. This book uses "migrants" as an umbrella term for people who move across an international border regardless of the reasons or whether they have legitimate legal claims to protection. A "refugee" is a subcategory of migrant who moves across an international border to avoid violence or persecution.[22]

Non-refoulement of asylum seekers is a deeply institutionalized, international human rights norm that collides with governments' sovereign interests in controlling who can access their territory. All of these countries evade the spirit of the international refugee regime while variably complying with its letter. Their policies are marked by what legal scholar Claire Inder calls "hyper-legalism"—"a formalistic approach towards international law and international legality that allows States and other agents to benefit from the rhetoric of compliance with international law, without any constraint on their actions in practice, in order to both legitimize and depoliticize state policies."[23] Governments have developed increasingly elaborate techniques to keep asylum seekers away from spaces where they can ask for sanctuary. This architecture of repulsion is the parallel structure to what scholars of forced migration call an "architecture of protection"—a system in which humanitarians and legal advocates protect vulnerable people like refugees.[24] I use the medieval metaphors of cages, domes, buffers, moats, and barbicans to make visible a system of remote control that does much more to keep out refugees than the more obvious border walls.

A Medieval Architecture of Repulsion

Caging keeps refugees in their countries of origin or camps in other countries. Governments in the Global North work with the UNHCR and the International Organization for Migration (IOM) to fund refugee camps and centers for asylum seekers, usually in countries neighboring conflict zones, and to repatriate refugees who are willing or can be made to return home. Refugee camps are core elements in the architecture of protection as well as repulsion. They combine logics of humanitarianism, to provide basic services such as shelter and food, as well as logics of surveillance and control, to keep refugees from moving to the Global North.[25] Most caging takes place in the Global South in a "grand compromise" in which the Global North pays southern neighbors to keep refugees away from the North in return for limited resettlements and financial aid.[26] Eighty-eight percent of the UNHCR's $3.9 billion in voluntary contributions in 2017 came from government sources, led by the United States (37.2%), Germany (12.2%), EU (11.2%), Japan (3.9%), and UK (3.5%).[27]

Caging involves techniques that fall along a continuum of coercion. The softest tool is publicity campaigns to convince potential asylum seekers to stay home. Designating a country of origin as "safe" is a legal tool that governments use to create a rebuttable presumption that asylum seekers of particular nationalities are not refugees. The hardest tool of caging is military intervention. Since the 1990s, governments have established several "safe havens" with an explicit goal of preventing refugees from fleeing to

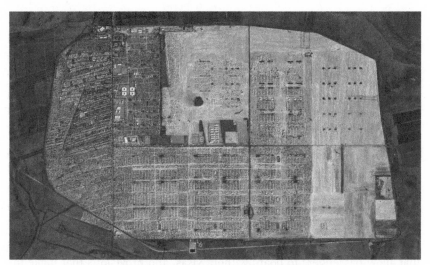

FIGURE 1.2 The Zaatari refugee camp in Jordan, seen in this 2013 satellite image, grew to host nearly 80,000 Syrian refugees by 2018. Camps funded by the rich countries of the Global North are key building blocks in both the architecture of protection, which provides shelter for refugees, and the architecture of repulsion, which cages them far from the Global North. Photo by DigitalGlobe via Getty Images.

neighboring countries and eventually the Global North. These caging efforts typically mix goals of migration control, humanitarian protection, and other foreign policy aims.[28] Following the 1990–1991 Gulf War, the UN Security Council passed Resolution 688 to create a safe haven that would protect hundreds of thousands of Iraqi Kurds fleeing the forces of President Saddam Hussein. Washington, London, and Paris used the resolution to justify two no-fly zones in Iraq to protect, and bottle up, Kurds in the North and Shiites in the South. Operation Provide Comfort air-dropped aid along the Iraqi-Turkish border and gave military cover to humanitarian operations on the ground.[29] Military interventions with similar rationales continued in Bosnia (1993), Haiti (1994), Kosovo (1998–1999), East Timor (1999), Sierra Leone (1999–2000), and Libya (2011).[30]

A virtual *dome* over national territories has become a primary technique of mobility control that restricts access via airspace.[31] The anchors of the dome are consulates across the planet where diplomats or their deputies decide whether to issue visas allowing travel to particular destinations. The global visa regime quietly keeps asylum seekers away from the Global North. Most member countries of the Organisation for Economic Co-operation and Development (OECD) have visa restrictions on most Asian and African nationalities. The restriction of African nationalities increased from 74% of all bilateral dyads (such as Canada-Somalia) between OECD countries and African countries in 1973 to 93% by the early 1990s.[32] In 2018 the thirty most restricted nationalities in the world could access forty-nine or fewer countries without visas. All the most restricted nationalities were in Asia or Africa, with the exception of Kosovo, which became a major source of refugees during the 1998–1999 war. All of the top-ten source countries of refugees were among these most restricted nationalities. At the extremes, Afghans could access only 30 countries without a visa, while Japanese could access 189 countries.[33] Visa requirements often have a "domino effect" as governments race to prevent the entrance of asylum seekers barred from other countries.

Smiling airline staff enforce visa controls. Sanctions against airlines that allow passengers to board without visas, and provisions that make the airlines responsible for transporting rejected passengers back to the point of embarkation, in effect deputize airline check-in agents to prevent asylum seekers from ever getting on an aircraft. Liaison officers from rich countries are stationed abroad to advise the airlines whom to prohibit from boarding. The United States has even established pre-clearance operations in fifteen foreign airports where passengers must clear U.S. passport control as far as 11,000 kilometers from U.S. borders. The 1944 Convention on International Civil Aviation, which predates the international asylum regime, required airlines to ensure that passengers have proper documentation. Revisions of the Convention imposed increasingly higher penalties for and stricter conditions on airlines to check passenger documents in a series of regulations beginning in 1990. The 2000 UN Anti-Smuggling Protocol required commercial carriers to ensure that passengers have the travel documents required for entry and impose sanctions if they do not.[34]

Governments of destination countries use their neighbors as *buffers* to repel unauthorized migrants, including asylum seekers. Common techniques include joint paramilitary patrols and funding and training to enhance control capacity. Legal tools include readmission agreements, in which the buffer states agree to take back rejected asylum seekers who passed through their territory, "safe third country" designations that deny asylum to applicants who passed through a named buffer country where they will not be persecuted, and pressure on buffer states to criminalize irregular migration.

Countries with maritime borders use the sea as a *moat* to keep out the unwanted by intercepting boats carrying passengers without visas. The U.S., Australian, and European governments have all used the high seas as a zone to intercept asylum seekers and keep them away from their coasts. Maritime interceptions sometimes take place thousands of kilometers from the home territory, such as when U.S. ships deploy in the Western Pacific and European ships patrol the coast of West Africa.[35] When the U.S. Coast Guard intercepts people on boats sailing from Caribbean islands, it engages in the most extreme form of the externalization of borders. These interceptions control both entry—to the United States—and exit—from Cuba or Haiti to any other country. Such policies turn an island into a cage.

Finally, governments design fortifications at the entrance to their territory where special rules apply. In medieval times, castle builders often constructed a *barbican* outside the main walls as an outer defense that was not part of the castle proper. In modern times, governments have created "anomalous zones" at the entrances to their territory that function as barbicans. For example, in 2001 Australia designated Christmas Island, the destination of many asylum seekers, as part of an "excised" zone with special restrictive rules. Many governments have experimented with designating international transit zones in their airports. These zones create the fiction that asylum seekers are not physically present in the state's territory, or at least not fully within its walls, where they would have greater rights like access to lawyers and independent review of their appeals. In Israel, a "hot return" policy elaborated in 2007 allowed the military to return asylum seekers caught within fifty kilometers of the Egyptian border under various conditions, employing the logic that they were being rejected at the border even if they were inside Israeli territory.[36] This medieval landscape of domes, buffers, moats, cages, and barbicans prevents the unwanted from finding refuge.

Catch-22

Governments jealously guard their discretion to select refugees from camps abroad and to admit mostly symbolic numbers through legal channels. The same governments put all kinds of remote controls in place to keep refugees from traveling legally. These controls vary, from visa policies that quietly repel most of those who have a legitimate claim to "safe third country" agreements that often suffer from serious humanitarian and rights problems in practice, but which in theory are a means of control that would not send refugees back into the hands of their persecutors, as discussed in detail in chapters 7, 8, and 10. The worst caging and buffering policies cynically use persecuting governments and even gangs as tools to close paths to sanctuary. Refugees who somehow evade these controls to reach a country in the Global North in theory should be protected by the principle of non-refoulement. The catch-22 for refugees is that rich democracies are essentially telling them, "We will not kick you out if you come here. But we will not let you come here."

Governments attempt to avoid the legal obligations of non-refoulement, to which they have explicitly agreed, by manipulating territoriality. A strategy of "extra-territorialization" pushes the control function of borders hundreds or even thousands of kilometers beyond the state's territory. Simultaneously, states restrict access to asylum and other rights enjoyed by virtue of presence on a state's territory, by making micro-distinctions down to the meter at the borderline in a process of "hyper-territorialization." The procedural rights to ask for asylum have varied a great deal depending whether one is inside or outside the door of an international transit lounge,[37] standing on the beach or dry land,[38] and climbing the first of several concentric border fences or stuck in the middle.[39]

For example, the U.S. Supreme Court heard a case in 2017 to decide whether Sergio Hernández, a Mexican citizen who was standing on the Mexican side of the border when he was killed by shots fired from a U.S. Border Patrol agent standing on U.S. territory, had rights under the U.S. Constitution that were violated by the shooting.[40] A similar issue lay at the heart of a 2011 case in which a U.S. agent shot dead a Mexican citizen, José Alfredo Yañez Reyes, during an altercation along the border. A surveyor hired by the U.S. Attorney's Office to determine where the body fell, and thus whether Yañez had U.S. constitutional rights, prepared a photographic exhibit with a yellow line drawn through his waist showing the bloody head in Mexico and the feet in the United States. "The majority of his body was in Mexico upon death," the U.S. government claimed, and thus his family had no right to sue.[41] Governments directly or indirectly project their control far beyond their territories at the same time they make micro-distinctions in space to circumscribe rights.

This book explains the catch-22 deliberately created by manipulating territoriality. It describes the origins of each building block in the architecture of repulsion, how they work together as a system of converging policies, and the conditions that enable or constrain their practice.

Cases and Methods

After establishing the historical origins of asylum and remote control, I examine four major contemporary cases—Australia, Canada, the United States, and the European Union.[42] These four cases fit two major selection criteria. First, they are signatory to international conventions establishing the principle of non-refoulement and in practice accept significant numbers of asylum seekers who make it past the obstacle course. Thus, they are "hard cases" for explaining the paradox of strict policies of remote control that subvert the spirit of international asylum law by manipulating territoriality.[43] Second, the cases vary over time in the type and intensity of remote control policies. While the overall trajectory is toward convergence to a similar package of policies, there is still important variation, which in turn suggests the conditions for constraints on particular strategies.

The book draws on multiple sources of evidence in each case, including the texts of asylum laws, formal policy statements around each type of remote control, landmark court cases, reports by government agencies and nongovernmental organizations, and academic studies that have primarily been elaborated by legal scholars. In a few instances my research assistant and I conducted interviews to fill in gaps, particularly in the discussion of Mexico as a buffer state, for which we conducted interviews with shelter directors on both the northern and southern borders and twenty-two asylum seekers at those shelters. I use policy process–tracing techniques based on a close reading of the documents,[44] as well as statistical evidence of asylum applications of particular nationalities, to determine whether asylum seekers were the targets of these policies and whether they were affected by them regardless of their primary intent. I also gather evidence of failed strategies, such as the UK's efforts within the EU in 2003 to promote offshore processing of asylum seekers. Unsuccessful efforts are important to analyze because they show the limits of remote control.

One shortcoming of official sources is that they do not provide information about hidden policies. Much remote control takes place in secret. A list of policies in each country cannot simply be tallied and compared because governments are unevenly successful at obscuring their activities. American diplomatic cables from the 2000s released by WikiLeaks and declassified CIA documents from the 1960s through the early 1980s provide an unprecedented window into policymaking behind the scenes. For example, preliminary analysis of electronically searchable diplomatic cables between the U.S. embassy in Mexico City and Washington, DC reveal previously unknown details of efforts to make Mexico a buffer state between the United States and third-country nationals. These documents also shed light on the remote control activities of Australia, the EU, and Canada, whose policies are monitored by the U.S. government. Internal government correspondence from the National Archives in Australia shows how Canberra modeled some of its policies on Canadian practices with the goal of promoting an equally humanitarian image abroad, and how it discarded some early remote control proposals in the 1970s because they would create reputational harms. While it is impossible to know what we do not know about secret policies, analysis of these documents provides a deeper understanding of the logic, techniques, and effects of efforts to push the border out.

Why Remote Control?

The political sociologist John Torpey has described how governments from the late eighteenth to early twentieth century invented passports and visas. States monopolized "the legitimate means of movement." In other words, states took away the authority to control their subjects' movement from private actors like feudal landlords, slave-masters, and employers of indentured servants. States have long deputized private actors to do the actual work of control at their behest, a phenomenon that has increased with the involvement of airline personnel in the dome and the processing of many countries' visa applications by private companies.[45] What is new about the system of contemporary remote control is that it involves governments reaching beyond their territories in extensive, routine collaboration to track and deter millions of individuals and particular groups trying to cross borders. As Torpey hastens to write of the earlier period, that does not mean states are always effective at controlling movement. Migrants find creative ways to slip past. A smuggling industry helps evade controls. But the interlocking system to control movement is gaining strength and deserves scrutiny.

Any system of territorialized asylum creates an incentive for governments to keep undesired asylum seekers away from those territories. Remote control policies predate the asylum regime that grew out of the 1951 Refugee Convention. Efforts to bottle up Jews fleeing Europe, whether through visa restrictions in the Americas or the British construction of a dome, moat, cages, and buffer states around Palestine, belie the notion that remote control of refugees began in the late twentieth century. What is undeniable is that remote controls have intensified and spread since the 1980s, with the basic set of techniques in place across North America, Europe, and Australia by the early 2000s. The following chapters will show that intensification is due to three main sets of factors that can be understood through institutionalist, realist, and constructivist perspectives.

The institutional story is that governments have developed ad hoc responses to perceived crises, such as irregular maritime arrivals of Haitians in Florida, Albanians in Italy, South Asians in Canada, and Afghans in

Australia. Policies created to deter specific groups have then become embedded for all groups. Laws, regulations, and practices accrete in local contexts as well as spread across countries through networks of experts and the idiosyncratic project of Europeanization.[46] The restrictiveness of the paths and their spread has been further reinforced by two international legal regimes—the 1951 UN Refugee Convention that inadvertently increased the incentives for states to keep asylum seekers away from their borders and the 1967 Protocol to the Convention that limited the utility of refugee policy as a tool of racial selection by expanding the definition of refugee beyond its 1951 limitation to Europeans displaced by World War II.[47]

At a realist level, the end of the Cold War reduced the realpolitik value of accepting asylum seekers as a means to publicly shame East bloc origin countries in the propaganda wars, bleed enemies of human capital, and seek firsthand information about conditions behind the Iron Curtain. There are other foreign policy rationales behind accepting asylum seekers, but Cold War rationales had dominated policy on refugees and asylum seekers throughout the West in ways that continued as a legacy—for example, in the case of special preferences for Cubans that lasted nearly three decades after the fall of the Berlin Wall.[48]

At a constructivist level, policies around asylum, refugees, and international mobility controls have become relentlessly securitized, both as a reaction to real incidents and a pretext for wholesale restriction fed by yellow journalism and political entrepreneurs.[49] Fears that asylum seekers will act as foreign agents are not new. They were activated to avoid admitting European Jews before World War II and to scrutinize defectors from East Bloc countries during months-long screening processes. The difference in the late twentieth and early twenty-first centuries is that security has become a master frame for public debates about asylum, especially in Europe.

Patterns of Remote Control

The countries of the Global North have divergent histories of immigration and providing protection from persecution. Many Europeans are opposed to granting asylum because they view it as a backdoor immigration policy and do not want to be settler societies. Historic settler societies such as the United States, Canada, and Australia are widely viewed as countries of immigration, which may help explain their high levels of participation in overseas refugee resettlement programs relative to other countries in the Global North. Despite these differences, the following chapters will show that all have converged on the widespread use of remote control of asylum seekers and irregular migrants.

The defining characteristic of modern remote control is that it has become a global system. The architecture of repulsion includes cages, domes, moats, buffers, and barbicans whose functions are all linked to one another. None of them can be understood in isolation because they rely on each other to be effective. Interceptions at sea work hand in glove with readmission agreements, buffering in coastal states, and caging refugees in offshore processing centers. The visa and air passenger inspection systems of the dome operate in conjunction with special barbican spaces in airports. The system of remote control has become globalized in similar ways because of the circulation of knowledge among governments and experts. Ideas about how to create effective controls, funding for caging and control capacity in other countries, joint operations to stop smugglers or intercept asylum seekers at sea, and the sharing of intelligence and biometric data take place every day.

Governments seek legitimacy—public acceptance that they have the authority to act the way they do. Remote control policies often include legal maneuvers to credibly stay within the narrow bounds of the black letter of asylum law. Claims to act legally generate legitimacy to state efforts to extend their control over people's movement into other territories and international waters. Governments are stymied in this effort by "embedded liberalism,"[50] but the degree varies widely over time and place. Countries that guarantee significant constitutional rights to everyone on their territory, such as the United States and Canada, provide stronger protections for asylum seekers than Australia, which lacks a constitutional bill of rights. European states are uniquely limited by the supranational courts of the European Court of Human Rights and the European Court of Justice. The degree to which international law restricts governments' room for maneuver is greater in Europe than in North America or Australia.

The most pervasive strategy is to build a dome. All the early movers for carrier sanctions were islands or quasi-islands—the United States, Australia, UK, and Canada, in which geographic isolation made creating a dome over the territory a particularly effective technique of remote control. By the 1990s, the United States, Canada, Australia, and European countries converged on ubiquitous visa policies, carrier sanctions, and liaison officers. The differences among the cases are fairly minor. The EU and Canada have most openly used visa policies to target asylum seekers, but generally the same nationalities are restricted under U.S. and Australian laws. Preclearance procedures in foreign airports are a U.S. phenomenon that reflect its status as a hyper-power that can convince other countries to yield spaces in their airports to U.S. agents in the interests of streamlining commerce, tourism, and other flows.

The United States, EU members, and Australia deploy their navies and other maritime forces at great distance from their territories to deter visa-less asylum seekers attempting to arrive by sea. Canada is generally an outlier in its lack of naval patrols to keep out asylum seekers, but that is the result of its remote geography and the thick buffering of the United States more than any institutional factors. Canada has the legal mechanisms and capacity to militarize its moat if it chooses to do so.

The major idiosyncrasies in maritime remote control relate to liminal barbican spaces. Australia alone has "excised" slices of its territory to reduce the rights of irregular maritime arrivals. On a smaller scale, other countries have created legal fictions of spaces where rights are restricted, such as Canada's designation of a military base in British Columbia for processing asylum seekers without access to lawyers. The United States stands out for its idiosyncratic "wet foot, dry foot" policy that applied to Cubans alone and extensive jurisprudence around the conditions under which arriving on a beach constitutes entering the United States. Barbicans at land borders are increasingly common in Europe, beginning in the Spanish enclaves of Ceuta and Melilla and spreading to Hungary. Special rules in airport transit zones are ubiquitous in Europe.

Caging mechanisms of keeping refugees or potential refugees in their places of origin are common to all the countries in this volume. All are major contributors to the UNHCR, whose camps and other services in mostly Global South countries provide humanitarian support as well as some control over refugees who might otherwise attempt to reach the Global North. All these countries have been involved in military interventions that were explicitly aimed at creating safe havens to prevent a mass refugee exodus, including Canada in the 2011 NATO military intervention in Libya, and Australia in Operation Provide Comfort in northern Iraq in 1991. The United States and several major European powers, including the UK and France, have been most muscular about using their armed forces in such interventions.

Softer forms of caging that use publicity campaigns to discourage departures are also ubiquitous. The United States stands out for using unbranded publicity campaigns to deter asylum seekers that are presented as if they originated in the countries of origin, unlike the clearly marked Australian and EU campaigns. The difference is likely the result of a backlash against the long history of U.S. intervention in Latin America. European powers obviously have a long history of colonialism and intervention in Africa, where anti-emigration campaigns are prevalent, but these campaigns bear the logo of the European Union in a way that does not directly invoke the colonial history of the metropolitan power. In 2013 Ottawa paid for six billboards in the Hungarian city of Miskolc, the origin of many Roma asylum seekers in Canada, warning, "Those people who make a claim without sound reasons will be processed faster and removed faster." The Canadian government has made less use of such publicity campaigns than the other cases, however, probably because the main way for people seeking protection is to enter Canada by air, and dome policies are much more effective.[51] The campaigns attempt to micro-target particular groups of potential asylum seekers to deter their departure, but the distribution of messages on mass media and social media make it difficult for governments to control the audience. The harshest dissuasion campaigns, such as the Australian government's video simulating an asylum seeker drowning, risk undermining a country's general humanitarian image and have been discontinued.

The greatest difference in caging is in offshore processing of asylum seekers. The governments of various EU members since the 1980s have proposed offshore processing of claims made by asylum seekers intercepted at sea, but, as of this writing, none of these plans have concretized. Australia and the United States have had the most robust offshore processing systems, centered in Guantanamo and the Northern Mariana Islands for the United States and Papua New Guinea and Nauru in the case of Australia. Offshore processing has not been a major issue discussed in Canada, likely because its remote geography sharply reduces the numbers of irregular maritime arrivals.

Some form of buffering is common to all the countries studied here, though techniques vary. Readmission agreements are a key part of the buffering legal structure for the EU and Australia while they are less so for Canada and the United States. Safe third-country designations are also key in Europe, less so in Australia, and only a side note in North America, where they only apply to the U.S.-Canada agreement that has numerous exceptions. Europeanization has driven the legal frameworks. The United States, European countries, and Australia invest extensively in building the migration-control capacity of buffer states, whereas Canada does not, given that its single buffer, the United States, already has such extensive capacity.

The effectiveness of remote controls varies across case. A study of nineteen rich democracies, including the United States, Australia, Canada, and most EU countries, found that policies tightening access to the territories between 1997 and 2014 reduced asylum applications by 17%.[52] Policies that make the journey physically dangerous disproportionately make it harder for anyone who is not an able-bodied male to seek asylum. For example, three-quarters of the Cubans directly reaching the United States in the 1991–1994 *Balsero* crisis were men, with those in their twenties highly overrepresented.[53] Adult men traveling by themselves comprised two-thirds of irregular maritime arrivals in Australia between 2008 and 2012.[54] In Europe, three-quarters of asylum seekers in 2015 were male.[55]

Geographic isolation promotes effective controls.[56] Islands such as Australia, New Zealand, and Japan are far from refugee-producing countries and are surrounded by large bodies of water that make control easier than in Europe with its long land borders and short distances by sea from North Africa and Turkey. Canada is a de facto island given that its only land border is with a giant buffer—the United States. Geographic isolation makes it possible to reduce visa-less maritime arrivals to nearly zero. Yet the creativity and determination of irregular migrants and a worldwide people-smuggling industry are barriers to full state control even for islands.

The Chapters Ahead

Chapter 2, "Never Again?" explains the origins of the modern asylum regime via the failure of the Allies to rescue European Jews from the impending Holocaust. British, U.S., Canadian, and other Allied governments developed techniques in the 1930s and 1940s to reduce the number of Jewish refugees reaching territories under their control. After the war, embarrassed by their moral failure, most countries in the Global North agreed to uphold the principle of non-refoulement, although the United States, Canada, Japan, and South Korea lagged. North American policies in particular were shaped by Cold War interests in using asylum to shame communist governments and in projecting a humanitarian image abroad.

Scholars have advanced many explanations for the emergence and convergence of remote control policies from the 1980s to 2000s. Chapter 3, "Origins and Limits of Remote Control," assesses these arguments. It shows that while explanations based on foreign policy shifts, security threats, improved transportation and communication technologies, and the expanded legal recognition of non-refoulement do explain the intensification of remote controls, any system of territorialized asylum creates an inherent incentive to keep undesired asylum seekers away from the territory. The major techniques of remote controls had already been developed to deter Jewish refugees from reaching the Americas and Palestine in the 1930s and 1940s, but controls intensified in the 1980s in North America, the 1990s in Europe, and the

2000s in Australia as ad hoc responses to domestic perceptions of asylum crises. Techniques converged through a process of diffusion as governments adopted policies from other countries.

The following seven chapters elaborate how remote controls work across the four main cases. Four chapters explain how these policies work in North America, where systematic research on remote control of asylum seekers has lagged. "The Dome over the Golden Door" shows how an interlocking system of visas, airline sanctions, airport pre-clearance arrangements, airport liaison officers stationed abroad, and anti-people-smuggling operations in foreign countries prevent most asylum seekers from reaching the United States or Canada. These policies are deeply rooted and not constrained. The actions take place abroad, the air travel system permanently puts security concerns above all others, and individuals who are persecuted after they are denied permission to travel are invisible and uncounted.

"The North American Moat" outlines the rise of intensive maritime interception policies that first targeted Haitians in the early 1980s and then spread to intercept Chinese asylum seekers in the Pacific. This history reveals the fragility of older U.S. legal standards of non-refoulement on the high seas, yet it points to other constraints based on looser humanitarian norms and civil rights advocacy in barbican spaces based on constitutional rather than international law. The flirtation with refoulement in Canadian policy was constrained by foundational Canadian law within its territory, and outside its territory, by the Canadian government's longstanding concern with avoiding harms to its international humanitarian reputation.

"Raising the Drawbridge to Cuba" examines the contrasting case of U.S. policy toward Cubans. The U.S. government time and again demonstrated the capacity to manage and accept large numbers of refugees when it had the political will. The case shows that during periods of restriction, remote control was made possible, but also limited, by the broader bilateral relationship with the government of the caging country. The destination state can also manipulate micro-distinctions of space to keep out unwanted foreigners even within its territorial waters as long as it maintains at least cursory asylum screenings that would not pass legal muster on land.

"Buffering North America" analyzes U.S. efforts to contain Central American refugees in Central America and how the U.S. and Canadian governments have increased their mutual buffering since the 1980s. "Transit states" are not always a separate class of countries distinct from countries of destination or origin. The United States is primarily a country of destination, but it is also a country of transit, along with Mexico, Morocco, Turkey, Indonesia, and other countries in the Global South usually discussed in the transit framework.[57] Mexico is the primary transit country in the hemisphere. Since the 1980s, the United States has successfully pressured the Mexican government to prevent asylum seekers from reaching the U.S. border. Strict border enforcement at the U.S.-Mexico border bottles up transit migrants in Mexico who otherwise would have passed through quickly. This dynamic creates an incentive for the Mexican government to adjust to the new pattern through a policy of deterrence, detention, and deportation enabled by weak rights of foreigners on Mexican territory. There are limits to the Mexican effort as the issue of transit through Mexico becomes linked to unauthorized Mexican emigration to the United States.

The next two chapters turn to the European Union, whose supranational structure has shaped remote controls in unique ways. Europeanization has crosscutting effects on remote control. It has promoted many legal tools of control and coordination among EU member states, yet its supranational courts and other institutions that have more autonomy from public opinion have constrained some EU coercive return policies. "Building Fortress Europe" examines the construction of the cage, dome, buffering, and barbicans. "The Euro-Moat" focuses on maritime interceptions and cooperation with coastal buffer states.

The final empirical chapter, "Stopping the Refugee Boats," analyzes the Australian case. The Australian government's policies since 2001 stand out for the detention of asylum seekers arriving by sea on remote islands that are formally sovereign powers but in practice are under Australia's regional dominance.[58] Australia's isolated physical geography is enhanced by idiosyncratically redefining its legal geography to restrict asylum rights in specific Australian territories. Australia's judicial system has weak rights of territorial personhood and shows little deference to international law. Of the four major cases, Australian courts limit remote control strategies the least. However, a robust civil society continues to press against state policies that thrive on secrecy.

The conclusion, "Protecting Access to Sanctuary," analyzes broader lessons from all the cases. I argue that a diffuse humanitarian mandate to help those in need is more difficult for governments to evade than enumerated legal rights alone.[59] Humanitarianism is not a panacea; indeed, by itself it carries many flaws. Nevertheless, strategies based on humanitarianism complement human rights approaches based on universal legal obligations. The strategies that states use to evade humanitarian norms are to cloak their activities by conducting them in spaces that are inaccessible to the public and contracting other state and nonstate actors to do the dirty work. It is difficult to know what happens behind the closed doors of airport terminals, on the high seas, and in remote wilderness areas. Transnational networks of advocates who monitor abuses limit some strategies of remote control, such as buffering, while leaving others, such as the dome, untouched. Any effective constraints on evasive government policies can only begin by sharing knowledge about what is done.

CHAPTER 2 | Never Again?

WHEN REFUGEES ARE NOT wanted, why don't border guards openly return them into the arms of their persecutors? Sometimes governments do ignore the non-refoulement norm, but in general, countries in the Global North and many others do not refoule refugees.[1] The explanation for the norm lies in a path-dependent process that has ancient roots but primarily grew out of the Allied powers' failure to protect Jewish refugees from the Holocaust.

The first major system of remote control specifically targeting refugees was aimed at keeping European Jews fleeing the Nazis from reaching the Americas and Palestine in the 1930s and 1940s. This history sheds light on remote control measures in several major ways that later studies ignore or underplay.[2] Most techniques predated their adoption in the rest of Europe, North America, and Australia by half a century. Well before World War II, the United States and Cuba used their maritime forces to keep refugees from landing on their shores. Many countries throughout the Americas openly or secretly used their visa policies to keep out Jewish refugees.[3] The British toolbox to keep Jews from reaching Palestine, which was controlled by Britain under a League of Nations mandate, included naval interceptions, visa restrictions, diplomatic pressure on buffer countries, stationing immigration liaison officers abroad, carrier sanctions, publicity campaigns, sabotaging vessels in countries of transit, crackdowns on people smugglers, vows to *never* allow irregular maritime arrivals to settle, and offshore island detention centers. The Palestine Patrol preceded the non-refoulement regime of the 1951 UN Refugee Convention, belying the argument that the protections of the Convention caused governments to externalize their borders for the first time.[4] This history also challenges the technologically determinist argument that states are pushing their borders out as a reaction to the extension of air routes from the Global South to the Global North and the cheapening of jet travel.[5] The entire drama of the 1930s and 1940s unfolded around lumbering ships. The states that became the Allies did not simply fail to act to open their gates to Jewish refugees. With popular support, governments actively worked to prevent Jews from reaching their territories. The murder of 6 million Jews showed the world the deadly consequences of repelling people fleeing for their lives.

After the war, a new asylum regime made non-refoulement a centerpiece of international treaties and domestic laws. There were several major laggards in joining the global regime, including the United States, Canada, Japan, and South Korea. Cold War politics strongly shaped national asylum policies in North America, mostly for the symbolic reason that granting asylum was a way to humiliate the governments of communist countries whose citizens had fled to the West. The institutionalization of the norm through law is critical for its reinforcement, but so too is the desire of signatory states to be seen as societies that promote humanitarianism and human rights. Visibly returning refugees into the hands of their persecutors does great damage to international reputations, which states avoid by keeping the refugees away from their borders in the first place.

A Failed System

The tradition of granting asylum to people fleeing persecution extends to ancient cultures around the world. The classical Greek tradition most directly influenced later norms that emphasized political persecution.[6] Among nation-states, revolutionary France led the way with a constitutional provision that granted asylum to strangers banished from their countries for the cause of liberty.[7] Belgium banned the extradition of political refugees in 1833 in a move that was widely copied.[8] After World War I, the League of Nations designated particular groups as refugees in ad hoc policies designed to deal with the disintegration of the Russian, Ottoman, and Austro-Hungarian Empires.[9] Eight governments signed the Convention Relating to the International Status of Refugees in 1933. The Convention included a non-refoulement provision, though three of the signing countries included reservations that maintained their sovereign right to expel foreigners.[10] The weakness of national laws and international agreements when Jews sought to escape Nazi persecution had devastating consequences.

Acting on popular support, governments put in place a system of laws and unwritten policies to deliberately restrict or repel Jews. The core of the system was built on visas, agreements with buffer states, and maritime interceptions. A U.S.-sponsored conference of delegates from thirty-two countries met in July 1938 to discuss how to help German Jewish refugees. The Evian conference produced handwringing and no meaningful solutions. In a typical response, an internal 1938 memo to the Canadian prime minister from officials responsible for foreign affairs and immigration wrote that while public opinion in Canada expected the government to do something to help redress "the problem which the Christian and civilised countries now find upon their doorstep," it was not possible to take large-scale action in a time of economic distress. "We do not want to take too many Jews, but in the present circumstances, we do not want to say so," the memo acknowledged.[11] The moment to provide sanctuary was not right, given the perceived need to put the economic fortunes of citizens first, regardless of what the actual economic effects of accepting refugees might be.

In the United States, 127,000 Jewish refugees were admitted between 1933 and 1940, but most applicants were rejected even though 110,000 more could have been admitted under the German nationality quota alone.[12] Public opinion stood firmly against accepting more Jewish refugees. A January 1939 Gallup poll found that two-thirds of Americans opposed a bill that would have admitted 20,000 German Jewish refugee children younger than fourteen.[13] Another plan to settle Jewish refugees as colonists in Alaska, and to give unused nationality quotas to refugees regardless of their nationality, failed.[14]

Otto Frank, a Jewish spice merchant living in the Netherlands after he fled his home in Germany, joined the thousands seeking a U.S. visa for his family. Frank appealed directly to U.S. authorities and to his personal connections in the United States. "I would not ask if conditions here would not force me to do all I can in time to be able to avoid worse," he wrote an American friend from college. "Perhaps you remember that we have two girls. It is for the sake of the children mainly that we have to care for. Our own fate is of less importance." When the chance for a U.S. visa closed after months of lobbying, Otto applied for a Cuban visa that was granted on December 1, 1941. Germany declared war on the United States ten days later, and Havana cancelled the visa. Otto, his wife, and two daughters stayed in Amsterdam. Three years later, they were arrested. The youngest daughter, Anne Frank, left behind a dairy chronicling their life in hiding. The mother and daughters died in Nazi concentration camps.[15] Visa policies had quietly caged hundreds of thousands who otherwise would have escaped.

Several thousand Jews had used Cuba as a backdoor to enter the United States since nationality quotas were imposed in the 1920s. Cuban authorities

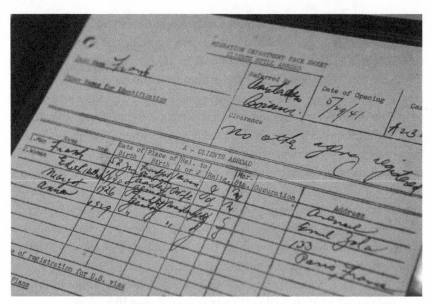

FIGURE 2.1 Otto Frank, the father of diarist Anne Frank, unsuccessfully tried to obtain U.S. visas for his family to escape from the Nazi-occupied Netherlands in 1941. Correspondence from the Franks desperately seeking help are on display at the YIVO Institute for Jewish Research in New York. Photo by Mary Altaffer, AP.

responded to U.S. pressure to close the door. Cuba's director of citizenship and migration wrote to the secretariat of the presidency in October 1938 to discuss privately how the Cuban government should react to the Evian conference. The letter noted that many of the Jews entering Cuba intended to migrate to the United States when their U.S. quota number became eligible for admission. Given the oversubscribed quotas, it was possible that Jews would become "forced residents [of Cuba] for long periods, or forever." The director suggested only admitting Jews in transit to the United States and settling on a number that could be negotiated with the U.S. government.[16]

In May 1939, the *St. Louis* passenger liner sailed from Hamburg to Havana carrying nearly 1,000 German Jews holding Cuban visas. Most intended to continue to the United States once they qualified for a U.S. visa. However, by the time the ship arrived in Havana, a growing populist movement in Cuba was demanding restriction. The Cuban authorities forced the captain to anchor in the harbor under the glare of spotlights and surrounded by armed patrols that prevented passengers from swimming ashore. Four days later, the government ordered the *St. Louis* to depart with its passengers, and the Cuban navy escorted the ship to international waters. The *St. Louis* idled twelve miles off the coast of Florida, where it was shadowed by a U.S. Coast

Guard patrol boat, the *CG-244*, "to prevent possible attempts by refugees to jump off and swim ashore," according to a contemporary *New York Times* account. Coast Guard sailors on the deck of the *CG-244* were close enough that they could see the refugees smiling in greeting. Aboard the *St. Louis*, passengers watched Miami shimmering in the distance as its captain cabled U.S. and Canadian authorities requesting permission to land. Rejected at every turn, the *St. Louis* sailed back to Europe, where the governments of France, Belgium, the Netherlands, and Britain agreed to admit the passengers. By all appearances, the refugees had found sanctuary in a safe third country. A quarter of them were later murdered by the Nazis when German forces overran Western Europe.[17]

The Palestine Patrol

The first sustained maritime campaign to interdict refugees and other irregular migrants took place off the coast of Palestine during the British Mandate (1920–1948). The logic and technique of these policies, particularly during World War II, echo contemporary practices in the Global North and belie the notion that remote controls in the moat began in the 1980s.[18] At the same time, there are important differences between policies then and now, such as the strong assumption then that intercepting irregular migrants on the high seas would violate international law.

British authorities attempted to control the numbers of Jews entering Palestine, whose native Arab inhabitants feared displacement and the establishment of a Jewish state at the expense of Arabs. Around 77,000 of the 485,000 Jews arriving between 1919 and 1948 entered illegally, in what was known in Hebrew as Aliyah Bet, including just under 19,000 clandestine arrivals between 1939 and 1942.[19] The first known instance of large-scale unauthorized entry by sea was the landing of 350 Jews from the Greek schooner *Velos* in 1934.[20] In response, Britain began a campaign of remote control throughout the countries of departure. It successfully pressured the Greek government to pass a law prohibiting anyone without a valid passport or visa from leaving Greece bound for Palestine.[21] In an early precedent for stationing liaison officers abroad, the Mandate government in Palestine sent immigration officers to the Italian port of Taranto to screen out passengers without visas.[22]

Even after war broke out in September 1939, the British government did not generally view Jews attempting to reach Palestine as refugees. "Illegal immigration into Palestine is not primarily a refugee movement," a confidential

FIGURE 2.2 Eastern Mediterranean, 1940

memo jointly prepared by the Foreign and Colonial Offices explained in January 1940. The memo suggested there were exceptions. "There are, of course, genuine refugees among the immigrants and the flow of refugees has recently increased owing to the flight of Jews from Poland to Roumania and other Balkan countries."[23]

British pressure on Germany to cage the Jewish population was not considered a realistic option. The Gestapo encouraged the emigration of Jews until the Nazi leadership elaborated an extermination plan between June 1941 and January 1942. "As it is obviously impossible to touch the main source of the traffic which is in German territory, the objective of the countermeasures must be to prevent the transit and embarkation of parties of Jews in countries bordering on Germany," the 1940 British memo continued.[24] An immediate goal was to keep 2,000 Jews who had fled Austria and were stuck on boats on the frozen Danube from reaching a sea port to embark for Palestine. British authorities blamed people smugglers for the situation of the refugees in a letter to the Zionist leader Vladimir Jabotinsky.

> It is understood that these unfortunate people were induced to embark upon their present journey by unscrupulous tourist agents who concealed from them the fact that persons not having immigration permits are prohibited from entering Palestine. His Majesty's Government have therefore taken steps to warn intending emigrants against the promoters of what is now generally known to be an illicit traffic.[25]

The goals of refugee deterrence and maintaining Britain's humanitarian image were inherently in tension. BBC broadcasts publicized the difficulties of illegal migration to Palestine.[26] Yet openly pushing forceful buffering appeared heartless when Jews were fleeing persecution from Germany, a country with which Britain was at war. The Foreign Office confidentially acknowledged in a February 1940 memo "what is at present a difficult and embarrassing, if not impossible, diplomatic task." The Foreign Ministry convinced the Romanian government to forbid the refugees on the Danube from coming ashore or continuing their journey overland. Under British pressure, the governments of Bulgaria, Greece, Romania, Turkey, and Yugoslavia discouraged shipping agents, captains, and crew from taking part in illegal migration to Palestine. Britain also discouraged countries of departure from allowing ships to sail under Panamanian registries that had been cancelled because of their involvement in unauthorized migration. In practice, buffering countries varied in the extent to which they enforced these measures.[27]

The greatest constraint on maritime controls was the British government's reluctance to establish precedents that would impinge on principles of free navigation that had long been critical to its military and financial fortunes as an island nation with a far-flung empire. Transit down the Danube did not require a visa from the countries passed along the way. "The status of the Danube (the main artery of this traffic) as an international waterway, impedes effective action by the Governments through whose territory it flows, and gives them a useful excuse for not interfering with a traffic which helps to rid them of their surplus Jewish population," lamented the Foreign and Colonial Offices. The principle of free transit through the Bosphorus was equally constraining:

> Practically every illegal immigrant ship has to pass through the Bosphorous on its way to Palestine. An attempt to stop them at this bottle-neck has,

however, been frustrated by the Montreux Convention. The most the Turkish Government can do is to delay ships on the pretext of sanitary inspection, etc.; they cannot refuse them passage through the Straits.[28]

The consequences of policies to evade the spirit of laws of free navigation were deadly. In December 1941, a converted cattle barge powered by a faulty engine sailed south from Romania carrying more than 750 Jewish refugees, including more than 100 children. At the request of the British government, Turkish authorities quarantined the disabled *Struma* and her passengers for two months in Istanbul's harbor. Turkish police finally boarded the *Struma* on February 23 and towed her back into the Black Sea. The *Struma* drifted through the night until a Soviet submarine torpedoed her in the morning. All but one of the passengers drowned.[29]

Treaties allowing free passage to ships did not apply to passengers when a ship sank. After the *Salvador* went down in Turkish waters in December 1940 with the loss of 231 of its 350 passengers, the British Foreign Office cabled the ambassador in Ankara to "press the Turkish government to do everything possible to prevent survivors from attempting to reach Palestine."[30]

During most of the Palestine Patrol, the high seas of the Mediterranean presented a gap in remote control. Legal experts initially concluded that the crews of unauthorized boats could be arrested for breaking Palestinian immigration laws only if they had entered its territorial waters.[31] It was not until January 1940 that the Colonial Office, Foreign Office, and Admiralty agreed "by way of experiment" to intercept a ship outside Palestinian territorial waters and then bring it to port using the Contraband Control law as a pretext to search the ship "in the hope that evidence of intent to commit a breach of the Palestinian immigration laws could be obtained." The passengers and crew would then be imprisoned and deported and the ship confiscated.[32] British officials considered it obvious that interception could not take place on the high seas without such legal fictions. "The patrol launches cannot, of course, operate outside territorial waters, but within these limits they have power to stop and search ships, and to order them to leave Palestinian waters if they are found to have illegal immigrants on board."[33] Reconnaissance planes, radar, and naval forces tracked ships suspected of carrying unauthorized passengers until they crossed into the Palestinian territorial zone three nautical miles from the coast.

The purpose of interception before refugees reached the beach was practical rather than legal. British authorities lacked the capacity to round up hundreds of passengers landing at once and sought to avoid violent encounters when the ships were welcomed by armed Zionists waging war against the

Mandate.[34] Interdicted ships were taken to the port of Haifa where the fates of their passengers varied. In April 1939, the British navy intercepted the Greek steamer *Assimi* with 240 Jews aboard. The ship and its passengers were taken to quarantine in Haifa harbor and then sent back to sea with an additional 160 people who had arrived on an earlier ship. After the British White Paper in May 1939 established a quota of 75,000 Jewish arrivals over five years, unauthorized "gatecrashers" were detained at the Atlit camp near Haifa and eventually admitted and charged against the legal quota.[35]

When large "mother ships" began offloading their passengers into small boats in international waters for the final dash to the beach, British authorities would not turn the small boats back. The Colonial and Foreign Offices agreed that knowingly placing the passengers in harm's way would violate the law of the sea.

> Even if the small boats are intercepted by the patrol launches they cannot be turned back as this would mean the death of the passengers from starvation and thirst . . . A sea patrol and coastguard service cannot therefore prevent landing of illegal immigrants, and can only ensure that most of them are detected and arrested on arrival.[36]

Countries of origin or last disembarkation generally refused to accept the readmission of deportees.[37] Without readmission agreements, where could unauthorized arrivals be deported? It was not even possible to determine the nationality of passengers who destroyed their travel documents in transit.

> Once an illegal immigrant has set foot on the Palestine coast, it is almost impossible to deport him. Illegal immigrants are commonly stateless, and those who are not take care to destroy their passports and all other evidence of identity before they approach the coast. It is, therefore, impossible to establish their country of origin for the purpose of deportation under existing international practice.[38]

The arrival of 3,600 unauthorized passengers on three ships in September 1940 prompted a new policy of deportations to offshore sites. The British High Commissioner in Palestine announced that irregular arrivals would never be allowed to enter Palestine.[39] "Short of sinking ships, which on many grounds is out of question, there is really only one way of putting an end to it," argued one official, "and that is by showing that all illegal immigrants, who succeed in reaching Palestine, can and will be deported elsewhere."[40] The Australian government rejected a British proposal to send the passengers to Australia.[41] The British governor of Mauritius, a 7,200-kilometer voyage from Haifa in the middle of the Indian Ocean, agreed to accept a group of Jews on the condition that they would not be allowed to settle permanently and that all costs would be paid by the Palestine government.[42] The "ultimate disposal" of the refugees would be considered at the end of the war.[43] The initial deportation to Mauritius was frustrated by the Haganah Zionist underground's botched bombing of a transport ship in Haifa harbor that resulted in the death of 267 refugees, crew, and British soldiers. Mandate authorities eventually deported around 1,600 refugees to Mauritius.[44]

The policy of only interdicting ships within Palestine's territorial waters allowed many to slip through the narrow interdiction zone and offload hundreds of passengers. In 1946, the Admiralty decided that it had the legal authority to interdict ships on the high seas that were not flying a recognized flag or that were flying the flag of a former Axis enemy. Passengers without a visa would be interned on the British colony of Cyprus 275 kilometers away.[45] Interdictions under these circumstances were considered extreme measures to be decided by high-level officials on an ad hoc basis. An appeals court in Palestine upheld the 1946 seizure of the unflagged *Asya* 160 kilometers off the coast. However, the lord chancellor strongly objected to interdictions on the high seas for fear that it would damage the international norm of freedom of navigation.[46]

Duplicity was the informal solution to this legal and political conundrum. Invoking Admiral Horatio Nelson's famous principle of turning a blind eye to unwanted directives, the lord chancellor observed that even if interdictions of immigrants on the high seas were not permitted, there was nothing improper about immigrant ship captains altering course for Cyprus under "peaceful persuasion by means of a strongly armed vessel." Neither was the actual spot where ships were interdicted as important as the appearance that they were within Palestinian waters. The Admiralty secretly increased the width of the interdiction zone to reach thirteen nautical miles into international waters.[47]

The policy of avoiding the appearance of interdiction on the high seas was illustrated most vividly in July 1947, when British aircraft and ships shadowed the *Exodus 1947* from the French port of Sète across the entire Mediterranean. The navy did not stop the ship on the high seas even though it had permission from Honduras to interdict any Honduran-flagged ship that was unlawfully transporting Jews to Palestine. The navy waited to interdict until it could plausibly, but falsely, claim that the *Exodus 1947* was in Palestinian waters. After forcing the ship to Haifa, British officials decided to return its passengers to France with the permission of the French government.

However, the 4,500 passengers refused to disembark at Port-de-Bouc near Marseilles. The British navy was reluctant to force them off under the gaze of the gathering world media and Jewish advocacy organizations publicizing every move. The navy eventually transported the passengers to Hamburg in the British occupation zone. British soldiers loaded the passengers into trucks and drove them under armed guard to refugee camps. The forced return of Holocaust survivors to refugee camps in Germany created a public relations fiasco for Britain. The French government fined the owners of the ship 10 million francs and cracked down on unauthorized sailings to Palestine, but all European governments refused later British entreaties to readmit intercepted passengers.

The British government relaxed its policy of avoiding interdictions on the high seas when it detected ships with very large numbers of unauthorized migrants. In December 1947, a naval detachment intercepted the *Pans Crescent* and *Pans York* off the coast of Turkey and forced the ships to sail directly to Cyprus, where their 15,000 Jewish passengers were interned.[48] Sabotage missions to foreign ports kept boats from ever leaving the docks. British intelligence agents crippled five ships in Italian ports in 1947 to

FIGURE 2.3 British troops in their occupation zone in northern Germany escort Jewish survivors of the Nazi genocide to the Poppendorf Reception Camp after intercepting their ship, the *Exodus 1947*, en route to Palestine. Photo by AP.

prevent their disembarkation to Palestine.[49] Efforts to cut off funding for the voyages were less successful. Many of the expenses, including the provision of forged documents and bribes, were paid by Jewish American groups.[50] According to a 1947 CIA report, financing of "the 'illegal' refugee traffic to Palestine" greatly concerned British officials and impaired the transatlantic relationship.[51] The Palestine Patrol continued until the end of the Mandate in 1948, when the remaining detainees on Cyprus were transferred to the newly established state of Israel.

The fact that the Allies were at war with the Nazi persecutors prevented Allied governments from cooperating with the Germans to cage Jews in their countries of origin. Instead, the British government pressured buffer states to prevent their passage and eventually created offshore detention sites in Mauritius and Cyprus. The logic of using these sites was to warehouse refugees as a deterrent, not because they were liminal barbican spaces with fewer rights. A strategy of using legal fictions to limit the rights of detainees in offshore sites was not developed until much later in the barbicans of U.S.- and Australian-controlled island facilities. In some ways, the Palestine Patrol represents the opposite of the U.S., European, and early Australian interceptions decades later, when great efforts were made to keep asylum seekers out of territorial waters and off the beach where they could ask for asylum and avail themselves of the rights of territorial personhood. In the 1930s and 1940s, even passengers intercepted on the high seas were brought to British-controlled territories such as Palestine, Cyprus, and Mauritius. Passengers were only considered to have broken immigration laws by entering Palestinian territory without papers, even if they were under armed guard when they crossed the imaginary line.[52] The Palestine Patrol also shows how strong the principle against interdiction on the high seas was in the 1930s and 1940s. The principle was undermined secretly until the scale of arrivals reached a tipping point and the navy began to openly interdict large ships in international waters. International norms that initially were taken for granted proved fragile.

The Modern Asylum Regime

The democracies' failure to protect European Jews from extermination and the displacement of millions of people by the war generated calls for new agencies and laws to manage refugee flows. The nonbinding 1948 Universal Declaration of Human Rights included "the right to seek and to enjoy in other countries asylum from persecution."[53] Several delegations, including the Australian and U.S. representatives, supported the 1948 provision only after ensuring that the declaration did not create any legal obligations for a government to admit asylum seekers. The UN General Assembly's 1967 Declaration on Territorial Asylum maintained the sovereign discretion of states to accept asylum seekers.[54]

The 1951 Refugee Convention created the first comprehensive international refugee regime and the standard definition of a refugee as a person who

> owing to a well-founded fear of being persecuted for reasons of race, religion, nationality, membership of a particular social group or political opinion, is outside the country of his nationality and is unable or, owing to such fear, is unwilling to avail himself of the protection of that country; or who, not having a nationality and being outside the country of his former habitual residence as a result of such events, is unable or, owing to such fear, is unwilling to return to it.[55]

Initially the Convention only applied to Europeans displaced by World War II. A 1967 Protocol extended its applicability beyond those temporal and geographic limitations. Most European countries and Australia joined the 1951 Refugee Convention by 1956.[56] Between 1968 and 1973, the biggest Western European countries, the United States, Canada, and Australia all signed the 1967 Protocol.

The core of the Convention is the prohibition of refoulement in Article 33. Interpretations over whether the principle of non-refoulement applies to those who are rejected at a border and never allowed to enter varied at the time the Convention was drafted and in subsequent jurisprudence. "If a refugee has succeeded in eluding the frontier guards, he is safe; if he has not, it is his hard luck," wrote legal scholar Nehemiah Robinson in 1953.[57] At least some of the drafters, including the U.S., Israeli, Belgian, and British delegates, intended the principle of non-refoulement to apply to those seeking entry at the border, while the Swiss delegate insisted it only applied to asylum seekers who were already inside the country. Controversies have continued about whether the non-refoulement provision applies outside a state's territory. Most legal scholarship argues that it does.[58] Similar non-refoulement provisions have been included in subsequent regional and international treaties. The 1984 Convention Against Torture explicitly prohibits refoulement of an individual to states "where there are substantial grounds for believing that he would be in danger of being subjected to torture."[59] The Committee Against Torture that interprets the treaty considers it to apply extra-territorially and "to protect any person, citizen or non-citizen without discrimination subject to the de jure or de facto control of a State party."[60]

A second core provision of the 1951 Refugee Convention is Article 31, which prohibits countries signing the Convention from penalizing refugees who used illegal means to enter if they come directly from a country where they are threatened.

> The Contracting States shall not impose penalties, on account of their illegal entry or presence, on refugees who, coming directly from a territory where their life or freedom was threatened in the sense of Article 1, enter or are present in their territory without authorization, provided they present themselves without delay to the authorities and show good cause for their illegal entry or presence.[61]

The drafters recognized that people fleeing violence may not have passports or visas. Individuals fleeing persecution by their government are especially likely not to have their papers in order, as they have often been denied the right to travel freely or fear that by applying for documents they will reveal their plans and be even more vulnerable to persecution. The idea of distinguishing "genuine refugees" from "illegal immigrants" is based on a false dichotomy. The possibility that refugees have unlawfully entered a country to seek asylum is explicitly recognized as legitimate under a binding international treaty.

Late Adopters

The 1951 Convention was not immediately accepted by all countries. The United States and Canada stand out from the other Western powers for not joining the 1951 Refugee Convention soon after it was negotiated. The United States never signed the Convention, but in 1968 it became party to the 1967 Protocol that removed the temporal and geographic limitations of who is defined as a refugee. Canada joined the Convention and Protocol in 1969. As a recently defeated Axis power, Japan was not part of the negotiation of the Convention. Japan did not accede to the Convention until 1981 and the Protocol until 1982. South Korea did not do the same until 1992. While the Japanese and Korean cases are not central to this volume because they accept so few asylum seekers who reach their territories, they illustrate a broader pattern of countries in the Global North that reap the international prestige of financing humanitarian refugee operations abroad. The policiesin practice pay other countries to cage refugees faraway from rich northern shores.

United States

During the first great wave of migration to the United States, from the nineteenth century to World War I, people fleeing violence or persecution entered under the same conditions as immigrants arriving to work or reunite with their family members. The United States did not have statutory provisions for refugees until 1917, when the Immigration Act exempted foreigners fleeing religious persecution from taking the literacy test that was applied to other immigrants.[62] White Russians on the losing side of the Russian civil war who had reached the United States were allowed to legalize their status in 1934 with simple requirements to show that they were in political exile and faced imprisonment or death if they were deported.[63] The first large-scale immigration of refugees took place after World War II through a series of laws that opened the gates for Europeans displaced by the war,[64] people fleeing communism or wars in the Middle East,[65] Cubans,[66] and Indochinese.[67] The 1965 Immigration Act reserved 6% of its "preference visas" for refugees fleeing communism, persecution in the Middle East, and natural calamities.[68]

Throughout this period, asylum was a policy backwater compared to the resettlement of refugees selected from overseas. Congress created the first general provision for asylum for foreigners in deportation proceedings in 1950. According to the 1950 law, "No alien shall be deported under any provisions of this Act to any country in which the Attorney General shall find that such alien would be subjected to physical persecution."[69] The Immigration and Nationality Act of 1952 adopted similar language.[70] In 1965, the grounds for persecution were changed to "persecution on account of race, religion, or political opinion," which are three of the five possible refugee criteria in the 1951 Refugee Convention.[71] The 1965 Act continued to leave the application of non-refoulement to the discretion of the attorney general and maintained that affirmative applications for asylum were not available to foreigners "at the border seeking refuge in the United States due to persecution."[72] The discretionary "parole" mechanism in the 1952 Immigration and Nationality Act, used to parole about a million refugees mostly from communist countries,[73] and the "conditional entry" mechanism in the 1965 amendments were the only other ways to gain asylum.[74]

The standardization of protections for asylum seekers was prompted by the highly publicized refoulement of a Soviet defector. On November

23, 1970, the U.S. Coast Guard cutter *Vigilant* moored alongside the Soviet trawler *Sovetskaya Litva* in U.S. territorial waters off Martha's Vineyard for a meeting to discuss international fishing issues. Lithuanian radio operator Simas Kudirka jumped from the trawler onto the deck of the *Vigilant* and asked for political asylum. The captain of the cutter called headquarters in Boston to ask for guidance and was ordered to return the defector. The U.S. captain allowed six Soviet crew members to board the cutter and chase down Kudirka, who was beaten into submission and tied in a blanket. The *Vigilant*'s lifeboat then ferried Kudirka and the boarding party back to the trawler as one of the captors sat on Kurdika's head punching him. A Soviet court later sentenced Kudirka to ten years of hard labor for high treason.[75]

In the wake of public outrage and a congressional hearing, the Nixon administration created the I-589 Application for Asylum form that is used to this day. Ironically, a group of Lithuanian-Americans later learned that Kudirka was entitled to U.S. citizenship because his mother had been born in Brooklyn. Soviet authorities commuted Kudirka's sentence and in 1974 allowed him to emigrate to the United States, where he became an anti-Soviet activist. "I come to U.S. not for stomach," he told a journalist. "I come for liberty."[76] Allowing dissidents to apply for asylum in the United States made for good domestic and international politics during the Cold War.

The United States signed the 1967 Protocol to the Refugee Convention in 1968 to demonstrate its compliance with international rights norms and to satisfy religious and ethnic lobbies advocating for refugees. At the time, there was little sense that signing the Protocol would significantly alter U.S. immigration law.[77] The Board of Immigration Appeals concluded in 1973 that ratification of the Protocol was not intended to change the non-refoulement provisions already in domestic law.[78] No federal court cases recognized claimants as refugees based on the Protocol between 1968 and 1980.[79]

The 1980 Refugee Act drew on the 1967 Protocol in three important ways. First, it wrote into domestic law a close variation of the UN statutory definition of a refugee, rather than relying on previous domestic versions that defined refugees as those fleeing communism, countries in the Middle East, or victims of designated natural disasters. Second, the 1980 Act created a legal framework for the United States to be not only a country of overseas refugee resettlement but also of first asylum. The Act created a statutory *right to apply* for asylum, with several enumerated exceptions, to "any alien who is physically present in the United States or who arrives in the United States (whether or not at a designated port of arrival and including an alien who is brought to the United States after having been interdicted in international or United States waters)." The decision to *grant* asylum remained at the discretion of the attorney general with the possibility of appeal to the federal courts under certain conditions.[80] Third, in keeping with most interpretations of the non-refoulement provisions of Article 33 in the Refugee Convention, the 1980 Refugee Act for the first time applied the principle of non-refoulement both to those already in the United States and those arriving at its borders.[81] Legislators and government officials did not anticipate that the asylum provisions would create significant changes in practice because so few people had asked for asylum in previous years.[82]

The U.S. Supreme Court has ruled since the late nineteenth century that foreigners do not have the right to admission into the United States and that only Congress and the executive can create the policies to decide whom to admit.[83] As the Third Circuit summarized in 2012, "An alien seeking admission to the United States through asylum requests a privilege and has no constitutional rights regarding his application, for the power to admit or exclude aliens is a sovereign prerogative."[84] Once foreigners are allowed into the United States, they acquire a bundle of rights by virtue of being on U.S. soil. These rights are not the same in all domains as those enjoyed by U.S. citizens, but they are nevertheless significant, which is precisely why the government has tried so mightily to prevent unwanted foreigners from entering the United States and claiming rights of "territorial personhood."[85]

Canada

Groups that might be thought of as refugees because they were fleeing persecution have arrived in Canada since at least the late eighteenth century, when Loyalists on the losing side of the U.S. Revolution fled to the British colony of Upper Canada. Around 30,000 European refugees were admitted between 1933 and 1944, though they were selected as much for their perceived economic potential as any other considerations. Postwar policies to select refugees from the displaced persons camps were motivated by the goals of publicizing Canada's humanitarian credentials while "skimming the cream of the camps" to get the most highly skilled refugees before other countries of resettlement took them.[86]

The Canadian government was an active participant in the organizations that managed Europeans displaced by the war, and its delegation chaired the committee that drafted the 1951 Refugee Convention. Like the United States, Canada refused to sign the Convention over concerns that it would open the gates to communist spies and constrain the government's ability to deport refugees. The Liberal government of Prime Minister Pierre Trudeau agreed to join the Protocol without public fanfare in 1969 based on the logic that the

Canadian government was already following the terms of the treaty in practice, having resettled Hungarians after the failed 1956 uprising and small numbers of Middle Easterners and Chinese. Ottawa did not want to continue to be a global outlier after the United States ratified the Protocol. Accession was seen as an inexpensive way to raise Canada's profile as a promoter of humanitarianism and UN multilateralism. Canada began resettling refugees from third world countries in 1969.[87]

During the Vietnam War, thousands of draft dodgers from the United States sought refuge in Canada by entering as tourists without visas and then adjusting their status to landed (permanent) immigrants. This legal device enabled the Canadian government to let them stay without granting asylum, which would have publicly antagonized the U.S. government.[88] Procedures for granting asylum to those who reached Canadian territory remained informal and discretionary until the 1976 Immigration Act.[89] The 1976 law adopted the 1967 Protocol's definition of a refugee and established formal procedures for refugee status determination for individuals already inside Canada or at its borders. Only several hundred claims a year were processed in the late 1970s.[90]

Like the United States, Canada has strong rights of territorial personhood in which individuals enjoy significant rights by virtue of their presence on the state's territory, regardless of their legal status. The Supreme Court ruled in its 1985 *Singh* decision that the 1982 Canadian Charter of Rights and Freedoms applies to everyone physically present in Canada and "anyone 'seeking entry at a port of entry.'" Asylum seekers thus have rights under the Charter when they reach the Canadian border.[91]

Japan and South Korea

Until the mid-1970s, Japan did not have a refugee policy. When the first Vietnamese "boat people" reached the port of Chiba on May 12, 1975, after being rescued by a U.S. ship, Japanese authorities received them under laws directed at victims of maritime accidents and sent them to the U.S. territory of Guam the next day. Between May 1975 and June 1979, 2,250 Indochinese refugees arrived in Japan or were born there to refugee parents. Most received temporary residency status while Tokyo searched for other countries willing to accept their resettlement. Of the 2,250, only 10 were given long-term residency status in Japan. As the Indochinese refugee crisis worsened, the United States and other countries of first asylum and resettlement began to pressure Japan to accept more refugees and provide relief assistance. While some domestic voices opposed opening the door to Indochinese refugees, the government's desire to develop a positive image in the international community led it to accept 11,319 Indochinese refugees between 1978 and 2005. Tokyo reverted to a restrictive policy after the Indochinese resettlements.[92]

Japan did not accede to the 1951 Refugee Convention until 1981, twenty-five years after it joined the United Nations. It signed the Protocol the following year. A 1981 amendment to the Immigration Control Law of 1951 included for the first time a system to legally regulate refugees following the Convention definition. However, the Japanese government recognized only 2.8% of the 22,599 asylum claims lodged between 1982 and 2014.[93] It gave some form of Convention or complementary protection to fewer than 1% of applicants in 2017.[94] Tokyo's strategy of maintaining a positive international image focuses on paying other countries to contain and support refugees. Japan was the world's fourth-largest government donor to the UNHCR in 2017, ranking eighteenth in per capita contributions.[95]

South Korea created a similar policy of accepting few resettled refugees and asylum seekers while paying the UNHCR to do its work elsewhere. Between 1977 and 1989, the South Korean government allowed Vietnamese arriving by boat to land and housed them temporarily in Busan until they were all resettled in third countries.[96] South Korea acceded to the 1951 Refugee Convention in 1992. Seoul did not grant asylum to a single applicant until 2001 and accepted fewer than 3% of the 22,792 asylum applications between 1994 and 2016.[97] Defectors from North Korea are not treated as asylum seekers, but rather, as Korean nationals who must pass a security screening and resettlement training before being allowed to live openly in South Korea.[98] Between 2015 and 2017, it resettled a symbolic number of refugees—eighty-six Burmese over three years—in partnership with IOM and UNHCR.[99] In 2017, South Korea ranked twenty-fifth in the world in per capita donations to the UNHCR.[100]

Scholars have developed several theories to explain Japan and South Korea's restrictive regime, beginning with the observation that most Japanese and Koreans consider and prefer their countries to be racially homogenous.[101] However, sociologists Dong-Hoon Seol and John Skrentny find that there is little evidence that strong, anti-immigrant public opinion drives restrictive policies there. Instead, they argue that the elite political culture of a "developmental state" that prioritizes economic growth over individual rights contributes to restrictive policies.[102] In both countries, policies relating to refugees are generally under the purview of a conservative Ministry of Justice that is insulated from foreign policy considerations and domestic, rights-oriented groups.[103]

South Korea and Japan, like the United States and Canada, were late adopters of the global asylum and refugee regime and are major financial contributors to the UNHCR. They are exemplars of the "grand compromise" in which the Global North pays the South to cage refugees.[104] Unlike the North American cases, however, the two East Asian countries have low rates of refugee resettlement and extremely low rates of granting asylum. In general, the Korean and Japanese governments do not practice the catch-22 of other countries in the Global North that provide sanctuary to people fleeing violence while systematically trying to prevent their arrival.

Conclusion

National asylum laws and the incipient international refugee regime prior to World War II failed to protect European Jews from the Holocaust. As a consequence, and to deal with the millions of people displaced by World War II, the victors of the war created an international refugee regime and passed domestic laws built around the principle of non-refoulement. The Federal Republic of Germany went the furthest in 1949 with a constitutional provision granting the right to asylum, not just the right to apply, to victims of political persecution. Most of the world's countries signed either the 1951 Convention or the 1967 Protocol, and many of those that did not recognized the principle of non-refoulement through other treaties and laws. Western powers such as the United States and Canada were especially keen to use asylum policy to project an image abroad of their countries as beacons of freedom as a contrast to communist countries whose citizens were leaving.

While the international legal instruments that emerged from the aftermath of World War II and the Holocaust provide some protection for refugees, the methods that governments used before and during World War II to trap Jews in Europe remain in place today. The following chapter modifies existing explanations for remote control and its limits in the late twentieth and early twenty-first centuries. Even if rich democracies typically do not refoule refugees, the vow to "never again" allow them to be slaughtered rings hollow for persecuted civilians from countries as diverse as the Congo, Bosnia, Rwanda, Syria, Myanmar, and Sudan.[105]

MANY THEORIES TRY TO explain why remote controls of asylum seekers proliferated in the 1980s and 1990s. Chapter 2 showed that most techniques of remote control were developed in the 1930s and 1940s. Chapter 4 on the dome explains how controls over air passengers were derived from controls over sea passengers dating back to the nineteenth century in the United States, and chapter 10 shows a similar dynamic in Australia. The stronger version of claims placing the advent of remote controls decades later, in the 1980s and 1990s, are untenable.

I argue that policies to push out the border were ad hoc responses to perceived crises that then spread as governments copied each other's policies. Europeanization took this process toward convergence the furthest of all the cases, as chapter 8 shows in detail. Over time, policies have tended to converge across the Global North as multiple forces, such as the end of the Cold War and the broadening of the refugee definition, incentivized further remote control. This chapter describes the broad factors that promoted the spread of remote control as well as where those impulses have been constrained by countervailing forces arising from the courts, transnational advocacy networks, and foreign policy interests.

Origins

Explanations for the intensification of remote controls in the latter decades of the twentieth century include an emphasis on asylum seekers as a security threat, the end of the Cold War that eliminated the foreign policy rationale for granting asylum, and a racist backlash against the broadening of the refugee definition to include non-Europeans. Other scholars emphasize negative media portrayals, a backlash against policies giving asylum seekers significant rights and access to public benefits, and the advent of cheap long-distance travel driven by new technologies that made it possible for them to travel farther afield.

Securitization

Many scholars emphasize that "securitization"—interpreting reality and creating policy through the master frame of protecting against violent threats to the state—has enmeshed controls over potential terrorists with controls of refugees.[1] While there is no question that policymakers made such a linkage in the 1990s and continue to do so, there is long historical precedent linking security and refugee policy. In January 1944, U.S. Secretary of the Treasury Henry Morgenthau presented a report to President Roosevelt that was originally titled "Report to the Secretary on the Acquiescence of this Government in the Murder of the Jews." The report charged that the State Department had kept Jewish immigration below the quota levels under the guise of protecting national security from subversives. "Now, of course, the refugee has got to be checked out because, unfortunately, among the refugees there are some spies," President Roosevelt told the press in June 1940.[2] Then, as now, restrictionists argued that security concerns trumped humanitarianism.

During the Cold War, the CIA reported that "Hungarian Communist agents pose as refugees" to take advantage of U.S. refugee resettlement programs. Security screening of refugees escaping from the Soviet bloc took two-and-a-half to three months.[3] One of the few grounds for refouling someone who meets the refugee criteria in the 1951 Convention is if there are reasonable grounds for regarding him or her "as a danger to the security of the country."[4] Fears that refugees might be a security threat, and procedures to manage that possibility, are nothing new.

Statistically, the chances of being killed in the United States by an asylum seeker in a given year between 1975 and 2015 was 1 in 2.73 billion. Of the 700,000 asylum seekers who entered the United States during that period, four killed a total of four people on U.S. soil in terror attacks. The annual chance of being murdered by someone born in the United States is 252 times greater than being murdered by foreign-born terrorists who entered under all visa categories combined.[5] However, media reports and political entrepreneurs stoke a fear of asylum seekers, and sometimes foreigners in general, in the public mind.

Several prominent incidents beginning in the 1990s generated intense public fears that asylum seekers might commit terrorist acts. In the United States, Kuwaiti-born Ramzi Yousef bombed the World Trade Center in New York City in February 1993. He had been detained when entering the United States five months earlier but was released before his asylum hearing. Yousef was linked to Omar Abdel Rahman, an Egyptian cleric, who was sentenced to life in prison for plotting a bombing campaign in New York City. Abdel Rahman had asked for asylum when facing deportation in 1992, and though his asylum application was rejected in 1993, he remained in the country during the appeals process.[6] In December 1999, Ahmed Ressam, an Algerian national affiliated with al-Qaeda who had been denied asylum in Canada but was never deported, took a car ferry from British Columbia to Washington State with the intention of blowing up the Los Angeles airport. Officers caught the would-be "Millennium Bomber" at the border before he was able to commit his crime.[7] In Europe, most of the attackers who attempted to bomb the London underground system in July 2005 had entered as asylum seekers.[8] Two of the Islamic State attackers in the November 2015 assaults in Paris that killed 130 people had hid among a group of 198 refugees arriving from Turkey by sea on the Greek Island of Leros the month before.[9]

All of these incidents contributed to the securitization of asylum policy. In Australia, Canada, the United States, and eight of nine European countries surveyed in 2016, majorities of adults believed that terrorists were pretending to be refugees.[10] Donald Trump fanned these fears in his 2016 election campaign. After taking office, he largely dismantled the world's largest refugee resettlement program. The number of resettled refugees declined from 97,000 in 2016 to 33,000 in 2017. The number of resettled Muslim refugees declined from 38,900 in 2016 to 22,861 in 2017 and plummeted further in early 2018.[11] During his presidential campaign, Trump called for a ban on Muslim immigration. As president, he issued executive orders targeting several Muslim-majority countries, putatively on security grounds.[12] The goal of screening out terrorists is easily conflated with the goal of keeping out all people seeking protection.

Realpolitik and Race

Many scholars date the beginning of remote control of asylum seekers to the early 1990s. The asylum system in the West was designed primarily to embarrass communist countries whose citizens defected in relatively small numbers. During the Cold War, the number of asylum seekers was limited by exit controls in communist countries that locked citizens behind the Iron

Curtain. Welcoming asylum seekers thus served Western propaganda at a low cost. Once the Cold War ended, Western countries no longer had the same foreign policy incentives to accept asylum seekers, so they sought new ways to deter their arrival.[13] This argument is broadly consonant with a neorealist theoretical perspective in the study of international relations. On this account, governments only comply with international norms like the refugee regime when it suits a coherent foreign policy interest.[14]

Yet remote control began decades before the Cold War ended. An underappreciated explanation for the increase in remote control of asylum seekers is that it grew out of the 1967 Protocol that stripped away the 1951 Convention's geographic and temporal limitations on who is considered a refugee. The 1951 Convention defined refugees as people displaced by "events occurring in Europe before 1 January 1951" (i.e., World War II).[15] By opening up the definition of refugees, it became more difficult for governments to selectively categorize refugees for foreign policy purposes. Governments of settler countries such as the United States, Canada, and Australia did not want to admit non-white refugees, such as Chinese who fled the People's Republic of China in the 1950s. The Protocol's opening of asylum to the persecuted throughout the world, including non-Europeans who had been excluded from mostly white countries of destination by racist immigration policies, stripped refugee policies in the Global North of much of their value as tools for realpolitik and racial selection. Thus, destination countries subverted the spirit of the Refugee Convention with remote controls.[16] This explanation is consonant with the neorealist approach and is not mutually exclusive with the Cold War story, but it points to deeper historical roots and the added issue of racial selection.

Media Hostility

Efforts to keep out asylum seekers work hand in glove with demands to bar all foreigners. Relentlessly negative media coverage and political attacks have smeared the term "asylum seeker" in many settings. In Europe, on the one hand, refugees are presented as deserving of protection; on the other hand, they are portrayed as a threat who bring with them cultural differences that are difficult to reconcile with prevailing national norms.[17] Media coverage of Syrian refugees in 2015 over time shifted from narratives of sympathy and empathy to suspicion and increasing hostility—although significant differences existed within the coverage of refugees across Europe, especially between receiving and non-receiving countries.[18] Most studies of media coverage of asylum seekers by the Australian media find that it depicts them negatively as an "uncontrollable danger,"[19] economically undesirable,[20] and a political problem.[21] Fears about the cultural and ethnic change introduced by immigration in general are expressed in attacks on asylum seekers who are portrayed as law-breaking criminals and cheats.

Compared with other Western countries, Canadians tend to hold more favorable attitudes toward immigrants and the effects of immigration. However, similar to other countries, Canadian media depictions of immigrants, and asylum seekers in particular, focus on the problems and threats they pose for Canadians.[22] Even though the 1951 Refugee Convention explicitly provides that governments cannot penalize people seeking asylum simply because they have arrived outside official channels, this nicety of international law is lost in the public debate.[23] Restrictionists invoke the principal of fairness to claim that asylum seekers are "queue jumpers" who should have waited to go through the proper legal channels to arrive.[24] At the same time, governments deploy remote controls to shut down almost all legal avenues to seek protection.

Rights Backlash

The expansion of the rights of asylum seekers and asylees in liberal democracies prompted a backlash that pushed governments to restrict their rights on arrival (to work, receive government benefits, or live outside detention facilities while their cases were adjudicated) as well as introduce remote controls. Efforts to protect the rights of those who have arrived on the territory may inadvertently be used as ammunition by restrictionists trying to keep out the next group.[25] However, chapter 2 showed that remote control predates the rights regime of the 1951 Refugee Convention and most relevant national and supranational laws. The logic of remote control is baked into territorial asylum and is not dependent on preventing access to a particular set of benefits.

Extraterritorial controls reduce the number of successful asylum applications, even if they allow some limited form of assessment aboard ships on the high seas or in special screening zones like the U.S. base at Guantanamo Bay where asylum seekers are denied access to lawyers. Asylum seekers without legal representation are less likely to be granted protection.[26] In a U.S. government study of asylum decisions in nineteen federal courts between 1994 and 2007, the grant rate was three times greater for those with representation. After controlling for the effects of the applicant's nationality, the period when the decision was made, the particular court, and other factors, asylum seekers without representation were still half as likely to be successful. Between 2007 and 2014, affirmative applicants with representation were 3.1 times more likely to be granted asylum and defensive applicants 1.8 times more likely.[27] Adjudicating claims in barbican spaces or at sea where asylum seekers are not given the rights to a lawyer, appeals, or other normal procedures reduces the number of asylees.

Technological Determinism

Many analysts argue that the rise of widely available technologies for potential migrants, particularly the advent of inexpensive jet travel in the 1960s, shrunk the insulating effect of geography and caused states to adopt remote control.[28] Until then, "the developed world was simply too distant, and jet-age travel too uncommon, for most Third World nationals to reach it."[29] Technological determinist arguments struggle, however, to explain the different timing of bursts of controls across cases. The United States established major controls in the 1980s, Europe in the 1990s, and Australia in the 2000s, even though technological advances were the same across cases. Earlier precursors such as British interdiction of Jews headed to Palestine on creaking ships in the 1930s are a reminder that many features of remote control predate mass air travel.[30]

The Missing Piece

Existing explanations for remote controls are incomplete. The timing, form, and effectiveness of controls vary across cases for reasons both internal and external to each country. Institutionalist perspectives developed by scholars to explain many kinds of policies help us understand the consolidation and convergence of the remote control regime. Ad hoc reactions to crises accrete and become path dependent, become taken for granted to the extent that their basic premise is no longer contested in mainstream domestic politics, and are then spread to other countries through policy diffusion.[31]

Government policies are highly reactive to crises generated by war and mass persecution. Governments initially saw visas as a temporary measure in World War I to prevent the entrance of subversives.[32] The crisis of refugees fleeing the Russian civil war in the early 1920s prompted the first international cooperation around passports for refugees—the Nansen passport.[33] The League of Nations then established a standardized passport regime for all international travelers during a series of conferences in the 1920s.[34] The global Cold War strongly shaped the policies of all the countries in this study, but specific wars had much greater effects on some countries than others.

The Indochinese War affected asylum policies in Australia more than any of the other cases. The wars in Central America in the 1980s shaped U.S. and Canadian policies. Turmoil in Cuba and Haiti in the 1980s and 1990s mostly affected U.S. policy. The Syrian civil war in the 2010s had much greater impacts on asylum policies in Europe.[35]

On the domestic side, right-wing governments generally push asylum policies that emphasize control and security. Left-wing governments have often expanded or at least maintained controls to deflate the right's use of asylum as a wedge issue.[36] Once policies are put in place in moments of crisis, they often become institutionalized and shape the options considered reasonable in subsequent crises, no matter the political stripes of the party in power.[37] The partisan color of a government is not a straightforward indicator of its asylum policies.

Neither are remote controls across the cases determined by whether the country is a long-standing "country of immigration," where sustained levels of permanent immigration were critical to nation-state building (the United States, Canada, and Australia) or a set of countries of mostly recent mass immigration or little immigration (the EU). The three countries with the largest sustained refugee resettlement programs (the United States, Canada, and Australia) have similar remote controls to Europe, which historically has resettled few refugees from outside the continent.

Australia, along with Canada, has historically been the most generous country for overseas refugee resettlement relative to the size of its population. However, shifting the point of comparison to include the countries in the Global South, where most refugees are hosted, shows that Australia's per capita hosting was only in fifty-seventh place and Canada's in forty-eighth in 2017.[38] Still, the idea that Australia is generous to refugees who properly wait in the queue resonates in the public sphere and has been a powerful rhetorical weapon against asylum seekers since the late 1970s.[39] Under the Humanitarian Program beginning in 1996, the issuance of protection visas became a zero-sum game in which the number of offshore spots was reduced by the number of successful onshore asylum grants. This move fed the public perception that asylum seekers are "queue jumpers,"[40] even though access to resettlement is more akin to winning a lottery ticket than a reward for waiting patiently in line.[41] The politics of how remote controls are justified thus varies across the cases, because of the prominence of refugee resettlement in the three Anglophone settler societies, but remote control policies themselves in North America, Europe, and Australia have tended to converge.[42]

Within Europe, both formal EU institutions and informal communities of experts shape controls and asylum policy.[43] The International Centre for Migration Policy Development was created in 1993 to Europeanize migration policy by constructing and spreading EU paradigms and by increasing the enforcement capacity of European states.[44] Many EU policies were transferred wholesale to former Warsaw Pact countries in the 1990s that had previously tried to keep citizens in rather than foreigners out.[45] European institutions have effectively promoted legal forms of remote control such as targeted visa policy, readmissions agreements, and safe third country and safe country of origin designations.

Even outside the unique structure of the expanding EU, policy in one country can affect policy in another. The EU, Australian, Canadian, and U.S. authorities are keen to copy each other's models outside formal treaties.[46] The Intergovernmental Consultations on Migration, Asylum and Refugees since 1985 has been a clearinghouse to share knowledge about migration-control mechanisms across sixteen countries in Europe, North America, Australia, and New Zealand. Informal groups of experts avoid public scrutiny as they share "best practices" that serve the control interest of states over the rights of those fleeing persecution.[47] Organizations such as the International Organization for Migration make remote control policies easier by facilitating repatriations from buffer areas and discouraging irregular migration through publicity campaigns.[48]

Existing theories help explain the intensification of remote controls beginning in the 1980s, but not its origins. Sources of intensification include the widespread adoption of the 1951 UN Refugee Convention that inadvertently incentivized states to keep asylum seekers away from their borders, the creation of a more universal definition of "refugee" in the 1967 Protocol to the Convention that limited the utility of refugee policy as a tool of realpolitik and racial selection, the end of the Cold War that reduced the propaganda value for the West of shaming East bloc origin countries, hostile media coverage, securitization, and improved communication and transportation technologies.

However, the stronger versions of these theories are inaccurate because the phenomenon of remote controls precedes these conditions. Any system of territorialized asylum creates an inherent incentive to keep undesired asylum seekers away from the territory. The deployment of particular strategies and their intensity is contingent on many other factors that include ad hoc responses to perceived crises that then become institutionalized and the diffusion of policies across countries through networks of experts.

Constraints

Researchers dispute how well states can control their borders. A 1998 review of every major migration system around the world called international migration "inevitable."[49] A 2004 survey of eleven countries highlighted the growing gap between the intent of immigration control policies and their failures in practice.[50] Surveying all these changes, theorist Saskia Sassen concluded that national governments are "losing control" over the flows of people across their borders.[51] Political scientists Virginie Guiraudon and Gallya Lahav disputed the conclusion that states were losing control to the forces of globalization. In their view, "globalist perspectives tend to overlook state responses" that shift policy from the national level to the supranational European level, down to the local level, and out from the geographical borders of a state.[52] The next step is to ask how successful governments have been at shifting control away from their borders. Governments do not have unchecked power to enforce remote control. Sometimes their attempts are unsuccessful.[53] Legal institutions, transnational advocacy networks, and linkages to other foreign policy issues can restrain the attempts of governments to externalize their borders.

Law

Legal scholars critically interpret how laws should govern the remote control of asylum seekers and identify practices that violate those laws. Guy Goodwin-Gill and Jane McAdam contend that for governments to contract out their obligations to buffer states "frustrates the goals of the multilateral treaty regime and is incompatible with the 1951 Convention's object and purpose" of protecting the fundamental rights and freedoms of refugees.[54] According to Thomas Gammeltoft-Hansen and James Hathaway, states practicing extraterritorial control of asylum seekers remain legally responsible for actions outside their territories.[55] Stephen Legomsky argues that a state that knowingly sends people to a buffer country where rights will be violated that otherwise would have been protected contravenes the "complicity principle."[56] For Maarten den Heijer, remote controls do not necessarily violate human rights, nor should they be abandoned completely. "The salient point, rather, is that European states cannot simply pretend that their policies do not entertain human rights concerns," he writes. "Policies must be embedded in a legal framework affording migrants *inter alia* access to a proper and fair status determination procedure, access to effective judicial oversight and adequate safeguards in relation to detention."[57]

The realist school in international relations, by contrast, dismisses the relevance of international human rights law such as the refugee regime. Without enforcement mechanisms, states act as they wish and only comply with treaties when it is in their interests. From this perspective, parsing jurisprudence does little to explain what happens in the real world.[58] "There is little evidence that human rights treaties, on the whole, have improved the well-being of people, or even resulted in respect for the rights of those treaties," claims Eric Posner.[59] Some scholars interpret the externalization of borders as evidence that human rights norms and law do not matter in practice because they are so fundamentally subverted. Liberal states contract private actors and illiberal governments to do their dirty work out of sight. Illegal practices such as pushing back asylum seekers from borders without hearing their claims calls into question the strength of legal norms.[60]

The election of Donald Trump to the U.S. presidency in 2016 raised great doubts about the strength of norms and government institutions. The Trump campaign and administration consistently and gleefully broke long-standing norms of political communication, U.S. foreign policy positions, deference to the independent judiciary, and immigration policies.[61] In June 2018, Trump called for depriving unauthorized immigrants of due process rights. "We cannot allow all of these people to invade our Country. When somebody comes in, we must immediately, with no Judges or Court Cases, bring them back from where they came," he tweeted.[62] The fact that Trump broke these norms does not mean they never mattered. It does highlight the extent to which norms are sticky constraints of taken-for-granted ideas but are not etched in stone. Norms matter as long as they are reinforced and survive periods of contestation. History is never over.

Despite the skepticism toward the importance of norms that has been articulated by the realist camp, immigration scholars since the 1990s have pointed to legal institutions as a key factor that explains why liberal states accept more newcomers than their publics say they want in opinion polls. Legal institutions limit governments' room to maneuver. The fact that governments take such extreme steps to shift control outside their borders reveals the power of the non-refoulement norm.[63] If law and norms were truly irrelevant, asylum rights would not be observed in practice even within national territories. In general, and in spite of important exceptions, asylum seekers within the territory or at its borders have their cases heard. Many are granted protection.[64]

The "embedded liberalism" of the Global North prevents governments from adopting the most restrictive policies that are hypothetically possible.[65] Market economies generate demand for the trade, tourism, and labor migration that drive economic growth. Political liberalism's emphasis on individual rights takes the most punitive policies off the table. Independent courts are the guardians of political liberalism that restrain the scope of the other branches of government to restrict the rights of immigrants.[66]

Scholars debate whether legal constraints are internal or external to the state. Some authors emphasize rights that are rooted in external norms of universal personhood divorced from a particular national citizenship.[67] Others emphasize norms rooted in the institutional design of national governments and political cultures.[68] The fact that so many countries have broadly similar asylum laws shows the importance of international treaties and norms in shaping domestic law. All states in the Global North are parties to the Refugee Convention and/or its Protocol. Language derived from the Convention is inserted into domestic laws, sometimes in ways initially meant to be symbolic but which later became more substantive. Policy feedback loops further incorporate international norms into domestic policies through regulations and bureaucratic practices outside of the statutes.[69]

The constraints on remote control created by both the economic and political aspects of embedded liberalism are illustrated in international maritime laws that facilitate global commerce and that obligate governments to protect lives at sea. The duty to help those in danger has long been part of maritime humanitarian culture and is a core principle of numerous treaties.[70] The international waters of the entire planet are divided into search and rescue (SAR) areas. These are not sovereign jurisdictions, but rather, zones in which a designated government is obliged to protect mariners and passengers in distress regardless of their nationality or legal status. For a government knowingly to allow people to drown in its SAR area just because they don't have visas to land is a major violation of international law and maritime norms. The precise obligations of governments to people after they are rescued are legally contested and vary across time and place, but refoulement of asylum seekers traveling by boat would unquestionably be more common in the absence of the law of the sea and the 1951 Refugee Convention.

Even if international law is sometimes effective, it does not inherently ease mobility. Passport conventions, treaties on anti-trafficking and anti-smuggling, and even aspects of the Refugee Convention promote restriction.[71] Under long-standing international law, governments may not interdict vessels on the high seas flying a foreign flag without the consent of that foreign government. At least since the Palestine Patrol, states have worked around this rule by signing agreements with one another that allow the interdiction of vessels suspected of carrying unauthorized migrants, even when they are flying the flag of one of the parties to the agreement. There is some legal controversy over whether states can detain passengers aboard vessels on the high seas that are not flying any flag. British and U.S. courts have long allowed this practice. The 2000 Palermo Protocol established extraterritorial jurisdiction over migrant smuggling, but traveling on the high seas as a passenger without identification documents or a visa does not violate the laws of most coastal states.[72] Interdiction of ships transiting the territorial waters or contiguous zone of a coastal state with the purpose of offloading passengers in violation of its immigration laws is permitted by the law of the sea.[73]

Transnational Advocacy

A psychological "proximity bias" generates feelings of greater responsibility toward people who are spatially close to us. The flipside of this bias is that humans historically have ignored suffering in distant places.[74] It wasn't until the nineteenth century that networks of long-distance humanitarians enjoyed major successes, such as ending the Atlantic slave trade and creating organizations such as the International Red Cross to attend to victims of war and natural disaster, even if those affected are socially and geographically removed.[75] "Transnational advocacy networks" are motivated by principled ideas, such as human rights and humanitarianism. They include nongovernmental organizations, media, researchers, foundations, and even agencies and actors within the state committed to upholding those ideals.[76] Scholars have studied all kinds of networks and organizations of advocates that operate across national lines to determine the strategies and conditions that produce effective pressure. Legal historian Samuel Moyn dates the rise of human rights as an actual external check on state action to the 1970s, when international nongovernmental organizations (INGOs) like Amnesty International, which won the 1977 Nobel Peace Prize, began to hold states accountable. His account suggests that while the groundwork of legal instruments such as the 1948 Declaration of Human Rights and the UN human rights treaties signed between 1951 and the 1960s were important, a transnational civil society needed to be built to actively promote those principles on the ground before they mattered in practice.[77] Table 3.1 shows the sharp rise in INGOs beginning in the 1970s.

When it comes to addressing remote control of asylum seekers, transnational advocates are most effective when they engage in "information politics" and "accountability politics." The goal of information politics is to quickly and credibly generate politically useful information and mobilize it to become accessible to audiences where it will have the most impact. Accountability politics uses that information to embarrass governments into

TABLE 3.1 Number of Human Rights International Nongovernmental
Organizations, 1953–2003

YEAR	NUMBER OF HUMAN RIGHTS INGOS
1953	20
1963	29
1973	26
1983	67
1993	124
2003	169

SOURCE: Jackie Smith and Dawn Wiest, "Transnational Social Movement
Organization Dataset, 1953–2003," Ann Arbor, MI, Inter-university
Consortium for Political and Social Research, http://doi.org/10.3886/
ICPSR33863.v1.

changing their policies by exposing gaps between governments' stated principles and their practices. Transnational advocacy networks work best when they provide accurate information that can counter government monopolies on information. In the public sphere, information that includes both technical details and dramatic personal testimonies are most effective. That information must then be spread through the press and among policymakers at different levels, from the local to the transnational, to be amplified. Networks can also channel credible information into the legal process where it becomes crucial for autonomous judicial oversight.[78]

Across transnational advocacy networks, one successful strategy is to call attention to "bodily harm to vulnerable individuals, especially when there is a short and clear causal chain (or story) assigning responsibility."[79] In the realm of remote control, it is much easier for advocates to tell compelling stories about asylum seekers drowning at sea or being beaten in detention than to tell narratives about the hidden effects of visa controls. Most asylum seekers repelled by the dome are faceless, testimonies of being turned back at a consulate are not as dramatic, there is a long causal chain between the goals and effects of policy, and it is not as easy to assign blame given competing explanations of security interests that enjoy broad legitimacy.

Some governments are more susceptible to effective pressure from civil society than others. States in which there is a wide gap between deeply institutionalized norms and practice, states that aspire to polish their international brand, and states that comply with human rights norms to get something they want from other countries are more susceptible to transnational advocacy. Like individuals, some states are more concerned with their international reputation than others. Governments' interests in their country's brand can change over time. The administration of Donald Trump has been uniquely indifferent to how its policies regulating foreign affairs, immigration, and refugees are perceived—a major departure from decades of U.S. practice.[80]

Advocacy groups such as Human Rights Watch and Amnesty International organize at both the domestic and international levels to monitor the treatment of asylum seekers. In Europe, migrant aid organizations in the 1990s focused their efforts primarily at the national level.[81] Over time, networks of experts and NGOs sympathetic to asylum seekers have increasingly organized at the European and transnational level, giving them greater visibility and influence than isolated national groups. European NGOs put anti-discrimination on the EU immigration agenda. Statewatch, since 1991, has conducted extensive investigative journalism into human rights issues in Europe and obtained leaked documents about efforts to keep out refugees. The German group Pro-Asyl since 1986 has expanded to campaign for asylum seekers around Europe. The Migrant Offshore Aid Station Foundation has carried out rescue operations of migrants in the Mediterranean since 2014 and monitored paramilitary interceptions that would otherwise be conducted in secret. By 2017, nine NGOs had ships rescuing migrants between Libya and Italy, including a ship from Médecins Sans Frontières (Doctors Without Borders). One of MSF's long-standing principles is *temoignage*—bearing witness. The goal is not simply to document abuses after the fact. An active presence itself limits the abuses that flourish behind closed doors, on the high seas, and in the darkness.[82] Investigative journalists play a similar watchdog role. Mass media outlets then amplify these reports.

Transnational civil society plays such an important role in monitoring states in part because there are limits to the UNHCR's willingness to criticize governments directly for their treatment of asylum seekers, given the agency's dependence on governments for funding and for gaining access to vulnerable populations.[83] The United States has long been the largest contributor to the UNHCR. Its contribution increased from 29% of the budget in 2007 to 37% in 2017. The EU, EU member states, and Japan are the other main contributors.[84] Yet the UNHCR does pose some constraints on policies of border externalization. Both the United States and EU have pushed for the UNHCR to become involved in buffer countries. Once the UNHCR is active on the scene, it promotes international norms and provides local governments with a set of policies off the shelf. The UNHCR tends not to publicly confront governments about abuses, but rather work behind the scenes.[85] One of its indirect influences is through the mechanism of information politics. The UNHCR is the world's primary source of credible information about the conditions of refugees and asylum seekers. This information is disseminated via media and often directly to agencies within national governments that are at least partly concerned with the integrity of the global refugee regime. UNHCR reports are then cited in government policy documents and court cases. A similar dynamic occurs when governments decide whether to designate a country as a "safe third country" or "safe country of origin."

One of the unsung features of the UNHCR is its influence in building the capacity of national NGOs working on refugee rights.[86] These organizations often have much greater autonomy to criticize policies that violate international and national law. The Global North's efforts to build control capacity in buffer countries is followed by NGOs building the capacity of rights-oriented groups, although the latter are not nearly as well financed. These rights-oriented groups conduct their own surveillance of the state and publicize abuses through accountability politics. For example, since 2008 the Asia Pacific Refugee Rights Network has brought together organizations and individuals from twenty-two countries with the support of the UNHCR. The network monitors conditions on the ground and amplifies the voices of national members up to a regional level.[87]

Foreign Relations

A focus by scholars on why legal institutions should limit the ability of states to push their borders out has obscured how foreign relations do the same in practice. This is especially true for the governments of would-be buffer states. Pressure from the Global North varies in its effectiveness. Weaker states are more easily coerced than stronger states, but even weaker states are often unwilling to fully cooperate when buffering is linked to their other interests. Rich liberal states are not the only ones with an incentive to open their borders to trade, tourism, and labor migration. Even poor, autocratic buffer states have incentives to keep their borders open enough to allow commerce and labor migration from even poorer states. Transit states like Mexico that are also countries of emigration are trapped in their own catch-22. Enforcement pressure from destination country governments bottles up transit migrants, creating an incentive for transit states to deter and expel them. Yet transit states often do not want to use openly harsh policies against transit migrants because they want to delegitimize harsh policies against their own emigrants abroad. The issue of acting as a buffer can also become linked to other interests in the bilateral relationship, including the appeasement of domestic constituencies by demonstrating sovereignty in the face of external pressure.

Caging potential asylum seekers in their regions of origin relies on co-operation with persecuting states in ways that can undermine other foreign policy goals around shaming governments that violate human rights. Oftentimes governments of refugee-generating countries have a hostile relationship with the governments of the Global North. They may even be at war with each other. Maritime interceptions are especially reliant on a caging or buffering country to be effective. Without the ability to send intercepted migrants back to their home country or place of embarkation, the only other solutions are admission or holding the intercepted in barbican spaces that are expensive and generate negative publicity about the conditions there. The "international brand" of countries in the Global North as enlightened places upholding the rule of law is threatened by remote controls that appear abusive or illegal.[88]

In the classical Westphalian view of sovereignty conventionally dated to the 1648 treaty that ended the Thirty Years' War, nation-states have the autonomy to govern within their territories without the intervention of other states. In practice, the international system has never functioned as neatly as the abstract principles. By the 1990s, decolonization and the breakup of the Soviet Union in some ways led to the most robust system of Westphalian sovereignty to date.[89] Yet even then, and continuing into the twenty-first century, there is a hierarchy of sovereignty. Powerful countries such as the United States are far abler to exercise their Westphalian sovereignty, and to impinge on the sovereignty of other states, than countries lower in the hierarchy. For example, Iraq and Afghanistan during the Bush administration in practice did not enjoy the same level of sovereignty as the United States.[90]

The notion of a hierarchy also applies to a second conceptualization of sovereignty—a state's ability to control flows of goods, capital, and people across international borders. Each government has the exclusive authority to control who comes in and out of its territory, but control over asylum seekers tells a more complex story about actual practice. Not only have most states voluntarily limited their sovereignty by signing the Refugee Convention and thus agreeing not to refoule refugees.[91] When it comes to remote control, powerful states are reaching into the territories of weaker states to control the nationals of the weaker state or third countries. The willingness of weaker countries to accept these interventions varies. The classical system of Westphalian sovereignty is still weak enough that powerful countries try to control people in other states, but the system is strong enough that dominant states cannot do so freely and must rely on cooperation that is not always forthcoming. No single entity monopolizes remote control.

Conclusion

Remote control of asylum seekers extraterritorializes the control function of borders while hyper-territorializing access to rights. Rights of territorial personhood and the territorialized right of non-refoulement increase incentives for states to practice remote control. These controls have quickly become taken for granted. Security concerns, as well as the use of security concerns as a pretext to prevent the entrance of asylum seekers, are part of the logic of remote control, but these fears are not new. Similarly, transportation and communication technologies have made it easier for people seeking asylum to learn of their options and travel long distances, which has engendered greater controls through the aerial dome, but remote control precedes the spread of these technologies. The decreased foreign policy utility of asylum as a tool for Western states to score propaganda points against communist countries and the universalization of the refugee definition in the 1967 Protocol in a way that undermines the selection of forced migrants by racial criteria have made asylum policy a less useful tool for many Western governments. Remote control policies in each country accelerated as ad hoc responses to movements portrayed domestically as "crises" regardless of their actual scale. These policies then accreted through a process of path dependency. Mutual modeling of policies among the countries of the Global North reinforced remote controls and contributed to the spread of new forms.

Efforts to push borders out do not operate in a vacuum. Courts, investigative journalists, and humanitarian and rights-based organizations often push back. Foreign policy considerations that link the issue of caging and buffering with other interests can also limit the effectiveness of contracting control to countries of origin and transit. None of these constraints are absolute. Their effectiveness varies by the country and particular type of remote control. Still, understanding the limits, as well as where the exercise of state power is unchecked, points to pressure points beyond jurisprudence for those who wish to open avenues to sanctuary.

CHAPTER 4 | The Dome over the Golden Door

THE STATUE OF LIBERTY is an icon of welcome to the millions who have found refuge in America. Emma Lazarus's 1883 poem beckons those "yearning to breathe free" to pass through the golden door lit by her lamp.[1] In the twenty-first century, a larger structure looms over the golden door. A dome stretches over the airspace of the entire continent to keep most potential refugees from reaching the threshold. Visa and air transportation policies created in Washington, DC, Ottawa, and Mexico City form an increasingly integrated system of remote control. This system does not produce dramatic images of paramilitary interceptions at sea, camps packed with refugees, or border walls. The dome can only be seen dimly where it is anchored—at consulates and airports across the globe.

The dome is the single most effective block in the architecture of remote control because it is pervasive, taken for granted, securitized, and barely constrained by independent oversight. The contemporary dome over North American airspace was derived from controls over transoceanic shipping passengers dating back to the nineteenth century. Its deeply rooted history makes the system seem natural and thus less vulnerable to challenges. The use and framing of mobility controls as a way to protect national security also has a history more than a century old. The spread of international skyjackings in the 1970s and the September 11, 2001, al-Qaeda terrorist attacks further generated a strong security rationale for strict passenger controls that states use to keep out all manner of unwanted foreigners. Many of these controls are exercised in spaces such as airport terminals and consulates that are difficult for watchdogs to access. The people harmed by the system because they are blocked from reaching sanctuary are uncounted and unseen. As a result of these characteristics, there are few institutional constraints on the system of visas, carrier sanctions, liaison officers, pre-clearance operations, and international anti-smuggling operations that together constitute the dome.

The Paper Curtain

Travelers boarding an international flight assume that they must first show a passport to an airline clerk. Depending on their nationality and itinerary, the passport must have a visa issued by the destination state. On arrival, travelers expect to wait in long queues as armed agents check their documents again. Yet immigration controls taken for granted today are relatively new. Until the late nineteenth century, when national immigration laws began to regulate newcomers in a sustained way, most immigrants arriving in New York or Halifax walked onto the docks with little scrutiny. Local governments sometimes tried to impose controls earlier, but it was not until World War I and its aftermath that national governments developed the documentary techniques of "the paper curtain" to keep unwanted people far from their gates.[2]

Decorous travelers were outraged by their subjection to new passport requirements as if they were common criminals.

> Affixed to this compulsory document was a photograph, a "most egregious little modernism" that shamed or humiliated those who loathed the idea of a banal likeness of themselves being on display; a reference to "Profession" that was an open invitation to self-casting and self-promotion, not to mention outright fraud, and a "Description of the Bearer" that presented unheard-of intimate details describing bodily features.[3]

What first seemed a shocking government intrusion on the right to free movement quickly became routine. The temporary wartime rationale for travel documents faded, and the institution accreted.

U.S. Visa Policy

Washington began requiring foreigners to obtain visas from consular offices abroad as a temporary security measure in 1917 when the United States entered World War I. By 1924, the war was long over, but the United States imposed a permanent visa regime. The visa system can be used to give positive preferences for designated nationalities or to subject others to extra restrictions. The U.S. Visa Waiver program began as a pilot in 1989 to facilitate the rapid passage of British and Japanese travelers. As of 2017, the program allowed nationals of thirty-eight countries to enter for up to three months without a visa. The composition of the list is limited to nationals of rich countries with low levels of visa overstaying and excludes wealthy Middle Eastern countries. Most other nationalities require visas.[4] Restrictions are thus not aimed explicitly at asylum seekers, as they are in Canada and many European countries, though amidst a general policy of restrictive visas, the effect is the same.

Canadian Visa Policy

Canada in theory has required visas for all nationalities since 1976 but exempts citizens of designated countries.[5] The Canadian government has often reimposed visa requirements with the open intent of reducing asylum claims from targeted nationalities. When a nationality makes up 2% or more of total asylum claims in Canada, the government considers imposing a visa requirement, regardless of the asylum recognition rate for that nationality. Such a policy does not just target asylum seekers without a convincing case—it targets all people seeking asylum. All the nationalities that have met the 2% standard since 1996 had visa restrictions imposed.

For example, Ottawa withdrew visa exemptions for Haitians in the late 1970s, Salvadorans in 1978, Chileans in 1980, and Guatemalans in 1984.[6] In response to the 1985 Supreme Court decision in *Singh* that asserted the Canadian Charter of Rights and Freedoms gives rights to asylum seekers on Canadian territory,[7] Ottawa imposed transit visa requirements on fourteen nationalities with the explicit intent of reducing asylum applications. By 1987, Canada required visas for visitors from ninety-eight countries. The same nationalities were required to have transit visas to "reduce the number of non-bona-fide visitors who abuse the transit privilege to claim refugee status."[8] Ottawa imposed visas on the Czech Republic in 1997 after an influx of more than 1,500 Roma asylum seekers holding Czech citizenship. The requirement was lifted in 2007 but reimposed in 2009 explicitly in response to the arrival of more than 1,800 Roma asylum seekers. Of the 900 Czech asylum cases finalized in 2008, 734 claims were withdrawn by the applicants, 90 were approved, and 76 were rejected. In 2001, Ottawa imposed visa requirements on Hungary and Zimbabwe, two of the top-ten source countries of asylum seekers in Canada, to dissuade Roma and Zimbabweans. Most Zimbabweans who had been able to reach Canada to ask for asylum before the visa restrictions were accepted.[9]

The goal of reducing the number of Mexicans applying for asylum openly motivated Canadian visa policy in the late 2000s. The number of Mexicans filing claims increased from 2,900 to 9,491 between 2004 and 2008. More Mexicans applied for asylum than any other nationality. The most common claims were based on gender discrimination and the risk of death, torture, or punishment if the applicant was returned to the drug violence wracking Mexico. The asylum-recognition rate for Mexicans ranged from 28% in 2006 to 8% in 2009, when the Conservative government of Stephen Harper imposed a visa requirement on Mexicans. A 2012 law gave the immigration minister the authority to designate safe countries of origin whose nationals would only be allowed to apply for asylum in an expedited process without the possibility of appeal. The minister placed Mexico on the list in 2013 despite the rampant violence of the drug wars, which resulted in the decrease of Mexican asylum claims to eighty-four that year. The UNHCR, Amnesty International, and the Canadian Council for Refugees sharply condemned the lack of transparency around the "safe countries of origin" process and its use to curtail Mexicans' access to asylum. In December 2016, the Liberal government of Justin Trudeau lifted the visa requirement to repair the damage done to the relationship with its partner in the North American Free Trade Agreement. However, immigration minister John McCallum said that the visas could be reintroduced if asylum applications from Mexico reached an unspecified level.[10]

Bilateral Pressure

Issuing visas is a sovereign prerogative, but the U.S. government uses its international dominance to try to convince other countries to create policies that serve U.S. remote control interests. Washington and Ottawa have quietly discussed coordinating their visa policies at least since the Canada-US Accord on Our Shared Border in 1995. In 2005, Secretary of Homeland Security Michael Chertoff met with Canadian Deputy Prime Minister Anne McLellan to raise the issue of harmonizing visa policies as part of the Smart Border Action Plan. A U.S. embassy cable described coordinated visa policy as "one of the most touchy [items] due to sovereignty and privacy considerations."[11] Visas are an even more sensitive issue for sovereign states when there is an obvious asymmetry, such as when Washington pressures Ottawa to follow the U.S. lead.

Sometimes pressure flows from Canada to the United States, however. In the first quarter of 2018, more than half of the 7,600 asylum seekers who entered Canada from the United States were Nigerian. Three-quarters of the Nigerians had a U.S. nonimmigrant visa. Ottawa asked Washington to tighten standards for issuing the visas and stationed three Canadian officials in Lagos to work with U.S. visa officials at the U.S. embassy, leading to a 10% increase in the U.S. nonimmigrant visa refusal rate for Nigerian applicants.[12]

Demands from the U.S. government are a sensitive issue in Mexico as well, as chapter 7 on buffering in North America explains, but in U.S. congressional hearings, the State Department has praised Mexican cooperation on visa policy:

> We have seen, under the rule of President Fox, that the Mexicans have taken steps to make the world see that it understands its obligations to control the flow of people across borders. They have . . . established a tighter visa regime, for example, requiring visas of individuals from certain countries who are suspected to be using Mexico as a transport point or a point of entry into the United States.[13]

A list of around forty restricted nationalities, mostly in the Middle East, Africa, and Asia, face heightened barriers for obtaining a visa to visit Mexico. Privately, Mexican migration authorities acknowledge effective U.S. pressure to shape Mexican visa policy that uses the threat of terrorism as a pretext. As one official explained to a researcher,

> We have an agreement with Brazil that we do not require visas for Brazilians. But [U.S. officials] are not allowing many Brazilians to enter the United States. So here, because they can enter legally, they walk to the border and enter the United States. So the United States starts to yell about that, "You are letting in too many!" and then what? They start saying that the problem is that there might be "terrorists." So we enacted visa restrictions [in 2006].[14]

Mexico has become so tightly linked to the U.S. visa system that foreigners with a visa to enter the United States can enter Mexico without obtaining a separate visa. These limitations reflect security concerns and efforts to reduce all types of irregular migration, whether or not people are seeking protection.[15]

Not all foreign governments are willing to cooperate consistently with the United States. Hurricane Mitch ravaged Honduras and Nicaragua in 1998 and generated expectations of large flows to the United States. Guatemala acceded to U.S. pressure to impose for the first time a passport requirement on its "CA-4" partners—nationals of El Salvador, Honduras, and Nicaragua.[16] The requirement aimed to bottle up Central Americans in the region. After a negative reaction from the other CA-4 states, Guatemala City reversed its position.[17] In June 2006, the CA-4 countries signed an agreement allowing their nationals to enjoy visa-free travel among the four member countries. Even in the deeply asymmetrical relationship between the United States and Guatemala, U.S. pressure has not always been successful. Visa policies are embedded in broader international relationships, and in this case, the Guatemalan government's self-interest in promoting favorable relations with other Central American states trumped U.S. pressure.

The Nicaraguan and Ecuadorian cases illustrate how transit states in hostile relationships with destination states have even greater room to resist pressures on visa policy. In 2009, Nicaraguan President Daniel Ortega relaxed visa requirements for seventy-three countries, predominantly in Africa, Asia, and the Pacific. In doing so, he undermined a 2005 accord among the CA-4 countries to follow common visa standards for third-country nationals. The U.S. embassy was alarmed at the weakening of remote controls. "We find it difficult to believe that the new visa regime will generate significant new legitimate tourism for Nicaragua," the U.S. embassy in Managua noted in a confidential cable to Washington. "A more likely and long-term result would be a persistent and increasing flow of third- and fourth-world 'tourists' whose true goal was northward migration." Ortega dismissed Nicaraguan critics of his decision as "boot-lickers of the gringos."[18] Similarly, the decision of Ecuadorian President Rafael Correa to relax visa restrictions in 2008 took place in the context of a confrontational relationship with the U.S. government. The shift led to a rapid increase of extra-continental arrivals, many of whom sought to use Ecuador as a springboard to North America.[19]

Carriers and Liaisons

Visas are only useful as a tool of *remote* control if they are checked before a passenger arrives at a port of entry. Governments force private airlines to carry out these checks by using the threat of sanctions to ensure compliance. Carrier sanctions are much older than is often recognized.[20] At the federal level, the 1882 U.S. Immigration Act required the owners of ships transporting inadmissible passengers to pay for their return.[21] In 1891, shipowners were made liable for the cost of caring for inadmissible foreigners. Owners who did not pay these costs could be charged with a misdemeanor and a fine of $300 for every offense, and their ships would be denied clearance out of any U.S. port until the fine was paid.[22] The 1924 Immigration Act made it a crime, punishable by a fine of $1,000 per passenger, for vessels to bring immigrants who did not have a proper visa. The shipping company also had to reimburse the excluded immigrants for their fare.[23] Carrier sanctions were extended to airlines in 1952 with a fine of $3,000 per inadmissible passenger, including those who required a visa but did not hold one.[24] Airlines must provide transportation back to the airport of origin. Canada's air carrier sanctions date to 1976, when a law required carriers to pay the detention and deportation costs of passengers without proper documents and fined airlines that knowingly allowed them to board. The sanctions were tightened in 1988.[25]

While private check-in agents do the lion's share of visa checks, they are trained and advised by North American migration officers placed in foreign countries. The Canadian government has deployed airport liaisons abroad since 1989.[26] Its network of fifty-five officers prevents an annual average of 5,500 passengers from flying to Canada.[27] "For us, a tremendous emphasis is placed on trying to screen out inadmissible persons before they get here, because we know that once they get there, they've got full access to our courts, and they can delay proceedings for a long period of time," explained a senior official from the Canadian immigration department.[28] The officers do not have legal authority to force the airlines to comply with their advice, but in practice, the airlines do the bidding of foreign agents stationed on their soil because of the threat of sanctions for transporting inadmissible passengers.

In the United States, the Clinton administration in 1993 confidentially ordered the State Department and U.S. Immigration and Naturalization Service (INS) to work with air carriers and embassies "to detect fraudulent documents and prevent boarding before departure to the U.S." According to the directive, "These measures will be undertaken subject to safeguards for those genuinely fleeing persecution."[29] There is no evidence that safeguards for asylum seekers exist in practice. Alternatives such as asking for asylum at embassies have been shut down in almost all cases.[30] Carrier sanctions, visas, and liaison officers operate together as an integrated system to "push the border out."[31]

The effort to prevent unwanted travelers from reaching North American airports, and even airports throughout the Western Hemisphere, has driven extensive collaboration between the United States and other countries. Much of the effort is aimed at preventing the entrance of terrorists and criminals. Governments also use the security framing to legitimate controls on a much broader set of unwanted travelers. Ottawa and Washington pledged to work together "to find solutions to immigration control problems offshore (i.e., closer to their source)" in a 1995 accord.[32] After the attacks of September 11, 2001, the U.S. government pressured the Canadian government to share information about air passengers and to establish a "common security perimeter."[33] President Obama and Prime Minister Harper in 2011 agreed to share their "no-fly lists" and enhance "perimeter security by systematically checking the other's visa and immigration databases for immigration and border related purposes, including visa and refugee resettlement applications, for third country nationals." The two governments began sharing biometric information, such as photographs and fingerprints, for refugee applicants and asylum seekers two years later, and in 2016 agreed to a coordinated entry and exit information system for all land and air movement between the two countries.[34] Ottawa implemented an Electronic Travel Authorization program in 2016 that was closely modeled after the U.S. systems used since 2008—the Electronic System for Travel Authorization for nationals from visa waiver countries, and the Advance Passenger Information System. The Canadian program allows prescreening for passengers who are exempt from Canadian visa requirements, except U.S citizens, and issues airlines messages advising whether to allow specific passengers to board flights bound for Canada.[35]

Mexico City shares information with Washington on air passengers arriving from outside North America as part of the Advanced Passenger Information System. Cooperation includes security protocols, such as sharing watch lists and common screening procedures "aliens from special interest countries" (ASICs).[36] All but three of the special interest countries have predominantly Muslim populations.[37] At a February 15, 2007, meeting between Department of Homeland Security (DHS) Secretary Chertoff and Mexican Ministry of the Interior officials, Chertoff urged Mexican authorities to broaden their collection and sharing of fingerprints collected from air travelers.[38] The U.S. military's Northern Command, State Department, and DHS then created the Biometric Data Sharing program with Mexico to put the plan into effect.[39] From the perspective of the Mexican government, sharing information with U.S. officials makes sense. Preventing terrorists from entering the United States via Mexico is paramount given that such a hypothetical event would surely be used by restrictionists in the United States to crack down on the immigration of Mexican nationals as well. However, the Mexican public's concerns over sovereignty have pushed these policies behind the scenes. As a U.S. diplomatic cable summarized:

[The U.S. government] would also like to encourage a closer relationship at the [Mexican] airports. This has been a sensitive issue, especially following inaccurate and sensational press reporting on U.S. law enforcement liaison in those airports during a heightened U.S. state of alert in late 2003. There is much we ([Customs and Border Protection (CBP) and Immigration and Customs Enforcement (ICE)]) can do in terms of liaison and training (e.g., with a CBP agent on scene to answer questions and offer insights and ICE training on fraudulent documents or smuggling practices) that need not involve a U.S. presence visible to the general public.[40]

The dome extends thousands of kilometers south as well. By 2016, DHS had forty agents operating full time in South America out of offices in Argentina, Brazil, Colombia, Ecuador, and Peru. The agents support the Biometric Identification Transnational Migration Alert program that trains officers and provides equipment in host countries to gather biometric and biographical information on "special interest aliens, gang members, and other persons of interest who may pose a potential national security concern to the United States." The program gives U.S. agencies access to this information. In 2016 the program was operational in Colombia and plans were afoot to expand it throughout South America. Guatemalan President Jimmy Morales promised to prioritize systems to share information with U.S. authorities about passengers at Guatemalan airports.[41]

While these programs are primarily motivated by security concerns, one effect is increased difficulty for passengers to enter North America and apply for asylum. The U.S. government attempts to monitor the passage of Asians, Middle Easterners, and Africans who fly to airports in Western Hemisphere countries like Brazil and Ecuador, and then head north to Mexico using air, land, and sea routes with the help of smuggling organizations. "While many citizens of these countries migrate for economic reasons or because they are fleeing persecution in their home countries, this group may include migrants who are affiliated with foreign terrorist organizations, intelligence agencies, and organized criminal syndicates," DHS Assistant Secretary Alan Bersin told a congressional committee. The U.S. government is aware that the same net used to catch terrorists will also keep out those "fleeing persecution in their home countries."[42]

Anti-smuggling

A people-smuggling industry has sprung up around the world to help travelers circumvent visa controls.[43] The United States has been especially active in long-range operations to disrupt the industry. In 1997, the INS began operation "Global Reach"—a "strategy of combating illegal immigration through emphasis on overseas deterrence." For the first time, the United States established a permanent group of investigators and analysts based in countries of origin and transit to accomplish these goals. Between 1997 and 2001, 150 agents based in forty offices around the world trained

45,000 foreign officers to detect fraudulent documents and arrested more than 74,000 migrants.[44] By 2016, ICE deployed 250 special agents, 11 deportation officers, and 176 support staff in sixty-two offices in forty-six countries around the world, from Thailand to Brazil to South Africa.

While Washington pressures Central American governments to crack down on the sale of travel documents to migrants from outside the hemisphere, the Honduran immigration service has been implicated in selling Honduran passports to foreigners. During the 1994 *chinazo* scandal, 2,000 Chinese nationals paid US$25,000 to $50,000 each for Honduran passports.[45] The chief agent of the INS based in Honduras, Jerry Stuchiner, was sentenced to forty months of jail in Hong Kong in 1997 after he was caught with fraudulent, blank Honduran passports he was planning to sell to Chinese trying to reach the United States illegally. Stuchiner worked with confederates in the Honduran migration agency to sell passports and Honduran entry and exit permits.[46] In 2005, the senior leadership of the Honduran immigration service was fired and briefly jailed for corruption. A reformer brought in to run the agency was also removed after publicly describing it as "a gold mine" of corruption. Senior Honduran officials allowed Cubans to transit through Honduras bound for the United States in the 2006 *cubanazo* corruption scandal as well. The U.S. embassy warned in a 2006 diplomatic cable of "the threat to U.S. national security from a near neighbor that issues passports without meaningful controls."[47] The migration industry, especially when it operates with corrupt officers, undermines the effectiveness of the visa regime.

The Global Reach initiative persuaded some transit countries to criminalize migrant smuggling. "Today, through the efforts of the United States working with governments who recognize the malevolent nature of the traffickers, Panama and Nicaragua have criminalized migrant smuggling," the Department of State reported to Congress in 1997. "Using as a guide a model law we have written, these countries now have the legal authority to effectively combat smuggling."[48] Note the conflation of smuggling and trafficking, even though the definition of trafficking depends on coercion, while smuggling does not. Anti-smuggling operations in practice are equivalent to efforts to control unauthorized migration of Latin Americans and others in transit. The U.S. government has effectively expanded the set of migrant buffer countries and cages by harnessing their law enforcement apparatuses and spreading its own agents across the planet. The diffusion of laws criminalizing migration without visas is based on U.S. leverage over much weaker countries in Central America.[49]

Anti-smuggling operations sometimes target people seeking humanitarian protection or prevent them from applying. In 2000 during Operation Forerunner, described by U.S. authorities as the largest anti-smuggling operation ever conducted in the Western Hemisphere, agents from the United States and six Latin American countries arrested 38 smugglers and 3,500 migrants. A group of U.S. Catholic bishops touring a detention facility in Honduras found that detained migrants were not able to ask for asylum. The U.S. government financed the deportations of at least some of the detainees. In December 2002, prosecutors in San Diego charged Salim Boughader Mucharrafille, a Mexican of Lebanese descent known as *el libanés*, with alien smuggling. Authorities believe he smuggled several dozen Iraqi Christians seeking asylum in the United States on the grounds that they were fleeing religious persecution in Iraq. At the time, two-thirds of Iraqi asylum applications in the United States were granted.[50] Operation Coyote in 2014 "was designed to stem the flow of illegal Central American migration, including that of unaccompanied children," according to DHS official Lev J. Kubiak. During the operation, DHS sent additional agents to Mexico and Central America who helped make more than 1,000 arrests, dismantled six human-smuggling organizations, and disrupted nine others.[51] Operation Citadel in 2015 tried to shut down routes in Central America, including routes from the Eastern Hemisphere using Central America as a transit point to the United States.[52] Similarly, the U.S. government has publicly taken credit for providing training, equipment, and technical assistance to law enforcement in Mexico, Guatemala, and El Salvador in Operation Lucero, which led to the arrest of thirty-six people who had smuggled hundreds to the United States.[53] The construction of the aerial dome has become intertwined with efforts to cage potential asylum seekers in their countries of origin and to turn transit countries into buffers.

Pre-clearance

The ultimate form of strong remote control of air passengers is the "pre-clearance" program, in which U.S. officers stationed on foreign soil conduct passport checks and customs controls of passengers bound for the United States. The pre-clearance spaces contain elements of barbicans with special jurisdictions. Washington began checking U.S.-bound passengers arriving in Canadian ports by ship in 1894. Canadian authorities and transport companies agreed to U.S. controls in their ports to avoid the imposition of checks on the U.S.-Canadian border that would have encumbered the flow of regular traffic and commerce.[54] Pre-clearance programs for air travelers began in 1952 at the Toronto airport at the request of American Airlines. From the perspective of the airlines, the advantage is that they can land in U.S. airports that have congested or no facilities for international arrivals and create more seamless connections at their hubs for travelers changing to domestic U.S. flights. The 1974 Canada-United States Air Transport Preclearance Agreement formalized the arrangement.[55] Through 2017, U.S. officials had to rely on Canadian officers to arrest or detain passengers.[56] The Preclearance Act authorized U.S. agents to carry weapons and conduct strip searches in the pre-clearance areas of Canadian airports.[57]

By 2016, 600 U.S. officers conducted pre-clearance procedures at eight airports in Canada, Vancouver's port and train station, and some ferry routes between Washington State and British Columbia, as well as designated airports in Aruba, the Bahamas, Bermuda, the United Arab Emirates, and Ireland. Eighteen million travelers, more than 15% of those arriving in the United States on commercial flights, were pre-cleared abroad.[58] Although the 1974 Canada-U.S. agreement and subsequent versions provided for the possibility of pre-clearance by Canadian officers on U.S. soil, pre-clearance programs were entirely asymmetrical as of 2018, with no foreign governments operating such a program at U.S. airports.

The absurdity of the legal fiction that passengers have entered the United States at a Canadian airport was highlighted in 2013 when an Air Canada flight from Toronto to New York was cancelled for bad weather after passengers onboard had been stuck on the tarmac in Toronto for more than an hour. When the plane returned to the gate, U.S. and Canadian officers argued whether the passengers had technically left Canada and entered the United States. In the end, passengers who decided to stay in Toronto were required to clear Canadian customs, and those continuing on a later flight to New York went through a second U.S. pre-clearance screening.[59]

Pre-clearance programs disadvantage asylum seekers, as a refusal to allow embarkation cannot be reviewed by an immigration judge. As with the entire system of air passenger controls, pre-clearance programs prevent asylum seekers from physically reaching the territory to lodge a claim. The U.S. government asserts that "pre-clearance is an area of special territorial jurisdiction of the United States." The Department of Justice brought U.S. criminal charges for cash smuggling in a pre-clearance area in the Bahamas, but it does not accept asylum claims in the area.[60] The authority for U.S. agents to search passengers in pre-clearance areas of Canadian airports is derived from U.S., not Canadian, law. The relevant sections of the U.S. federal code are posted in Canadian terminals. The manipulation of rights and jurisdictions in pre-clearance areas is one of many instances of the government playing a "sovereignty game" to pick where its laws apply.[61]

Conclusion

The dome does not always keep out asylum seekers. Seventeen-year-old Fauziya Kassindja fled her home in Togo on the day of a forced marriage when she was to have her genitals cut. After traveling to Ghana and Germany, she decided to join her relatives in the United States. Notably, there is no legal mechanism for an asylum seeker to apply for asylum in the United States from Togo. Kassindja's options were to travel to the United States illegally to apply for asylum or not apply at all. She bought a fake passport and flew to Newark, where she told airport immigration officials that she had phony documents and asked for asylum. Rights advocates took up her case and publicized it in the media. Kassindja was granted asylum on appeal in a landmark 1996 case that established the first precedent in the United States that a woman fleeing female genital cutting could be eligible for asylum.[62] Had the system of remote control based on identity documents worked as designed, she never would have been able to arrive at a U.S. airport to present her claim. Individuals like Kassindja are the exception that proves the rule.

There is no way of knowing how many people who are recognizable refugees are blocked by the dome. Visa policies in Canada have explicitly been used to deter asylum seekers. The visa system in the United States accomplishes the same end, but it does not explicitly target asylum seekers, perhaps because the political culture of welcoming refugees has deeper roots in the U.S. historical imagination. Washington effectively applies pressure on other governments in the Western Hemisphere, especially its land neighbors, to tighten visa policies. These efforts are generally effective except where relations are hostile or undermined by endemic corruption. A system of transportation company sanctions more than a century old enforces visa policy, backed by the deployment of liaison officers and extensive information-sharing and anti-smuggling operations in foreign countries. The United States has been a pioneer in pre-clearance policies dating back more than a century. A system designed to keep out all irregular migrants does not in practice make any accommodations for people fleeing persecution. In fact, it has features that deliberately foreclose paths to sanctuary in pre-clearance spaces. Together, these policies keep most potential asylum seekers living outside the hemisphere from flying over the vast Pacific and Atlantic moats.

CHAPTER 5 | The North American Moat

THE U.S. COAST GUARD intercepted more than a quarter of a million migrants, including an unknown number of refugees, between 1982 and 2015. It is the "oldest [ongoing] extraterritorial interdiction, processing and detention regime in the world."[1] Over time the U.S. government has dramatically shifted how it treats people intercepted at sea and now coercively repatriates them without any hearing. This practice puts the United States far outside the international norm.[2] There are few legal constraints because the U.S. Supreme Court has interpreted the strong rights of personhood in the Constitution to apply only to those present on U.S. territory or to U.S. citizens and, in some cases, legal permanent residents outside the territory. Constitutional law has limited actions within U.S. territorial waters. Neither domestic nor international law has directly constrained U.S. actions on the high seas. However, refugee advocates have used the legal process to uncover information about unsavory government practices that are then revealed to apply political pressure that yields modest restraints on the state.

The most radical move to externalize borders not only keeps asylum seekers from reaching the United States; the same patrols in the moat prevent people from leaving their own island countries to go *anywhere*, essentially turning their islands into cages. Effective interceptions are enabled by a wider constellation of remote control practices that include the designation of barbican spaces and caging on third-country territories, cooperation with states of origin to deter exit and to accept readmission, and even the threat of military invasion. This chapter focuses on the general contours of patrolling the North American moat, which was developed from the interception of Haitians in the Caribbean, comprising nearly half of all nationalities intercepted between 1982 and 2015, and was then adopted to intercept

Chinese in the Pacific. The following chapter examines interceptions of Cubans as a contrasting case in which the U.S. government alternated between lowering and raising the drawbridge across the Straits of Florida, depending on broader goals in the hostile relationship between Havana and Washington.

Compared with the United States, there have been far fewer landings of irregular maritime arrivals in Canada, and only one major known attempt to intercept migrants at sea and turn them back. The history of Canadian policy toward maritime asylum seekers shows that the barbican can simply be invented anywhere, and that it does not require a quasi-colonial territory. In the late 1980s the Canadian government considered pushing back intercepted migrants, without determining their refugee status, from Canadian waters as well as the high seas. However, the legal constraints in Canadian territory imposed by Canada's Charter of Rights and Freedoms in 1982 and international criticism of refoulement on the high seas have prevented the Canadian government from exercising the most draconian options.

Where Is the United States?

Where does the "United States" begin? What does it mean to "enter" the United States? The answers are not obvious, and they have serious implications for the rights of people arriving by sea to ask for asylum. Under the Immigration Act of 1917, the definition of the United States included "any waters, territory, or other place subject to the jurisdiction thereof."[3] The 1952 Immigration and Nationality Act (INA), which in amended form is still in effect, construed the United States to mean "the continental United States, Alaska, Hawaii, Puerto Rico, Guam, and the Virgin Islands of the United States."[4] Whether the lack of references to "waters" in 1952 means that the INA does not apply to territorial waters of the United States was disputed in landmark court cases and regulations defining the rights of foreigners intercepted in the U.S. territorial sea that extends twelve nautical miles from the coast.[5]

The INS position in 1980 was that a foreigner apprehended within U.S. territorial waters "does not appear to have a right to apply for asylum." At the same time, it suggested that non-refoulement provisions applied, because the government could handle such a case by towing the foreigner's vessel to a third country where he or she would not face persecution.[6] By contrast, a 1986 internal INS memorandum stated, "it is rather well settled that individuals within our territorial waters may not be forcibly removed to the high seas" and "individuals interdicted within the territorial waters of the United States are transported to a port of the United States for an adjudication of their immigration status.[7] By 1993, in the face of large-scale movements from Haiti, the State Department and Department of Justice came to disagree with the "rather well settled" 1986 INS position and supported the 1980 INS position. According to a 1993 memorandum by the Office of Legal Counsel at the Department of Justice, "Undocumented aliens interdicted within the twelve-mile zone that comprises the United States's territorial sea are not entitled to a hearing under the exclusion provisions of the Immigration and Nationality Act." In its view, "For purposes of exclusion under the INA, the ports of the United States—not the limits of its territorial waters—are functionally its borders."[8] The relevant statutes had not changed, but interpretations swung back and forth like a pendulum according to the expediency of managing maritime arrivals.

Until the Illegal Immigration Reform and Immigrant Responsibility Act of 1996,[9] U.S. law differentiated between the *exclusion* of foreigners outside the United States who were seeking admission and the *deportation* of foreigners already within the United States.[10] The distinction mattered because foreigners in deportation proceedings had several significant advantages compared with those in exclusion hearings. In deportation hearings, the government bore the burden of proof. The foreigner had the rights to hear advance notice of charges, to appeal directly to the Federal Court of Appeals, to seek suspension of the deportation order, and to choose the country of destination if deported. By contrast, "[o]ther than protection against physical abuse, the alien seeking initial entry appears to have little or no constitutional due process protection."[11] As the Second Circuit noted, "Ironically, this dichotomy [between excludable and deportable] conferred greater legal protection upon aliens who entered the U.S. illegally and secretly than those who attempted to seek refuge by presenting themselves unsuccessfully to the officials at ports of entry."[12]

In a doctrine called the "entry fiction," physical presence within the United States by itself did not constitute legal entry.[13] The Board of Immigration Appeals in 1973 formulated a three-part test to define entry that became known as the *Pierre* test.[14] An entry had to include all three prongs: (1) physical presence in U.S. territory, (2) either inspection and admission by an immigration officer or successfully avoiding inspection, and (3) "freedom from official restraint."

The *Golden Venture* court cases in the mid-1990s presented a major test of what constituted entry to the United States and the processual rights of asylum seekers in the liminal zone between sea and land. The *Golden*

Venture cargo ship and its nearly 300 visa-less Chinese passengers had sailed for over three months from Thailand through the Indian and Atlantic Oceans and was under Coast Guard surveillance as it approached New York. Around 2 a.m. on June 6, 1993, the captain deliberately ran the ship aground on a sandbar 100 to 200 meters off Rockaway Beach. Passenger Liu Ping recalls a man shouting in the dark, "Jump! Jump! Hurry Up! Jump into the sea! You are in America. Or they will send you back to China!"[15] Around 100 passengers dove into the frigid water and struggled through the high waves. Ten passengers drowned in the surf. The rest were picked up by law enforcement in the water or swam to the beach. Many passengers subsequently asked for asylum based on their fear of coerced abortions or sterilization if they were sent back to China. Thirty-five of the passengers were eventually granted asylum.[16]

The legal issues included whether the passengers had (1) "entered" the United States, and thus had the greater protections of deportation hearings, (2) were simply "physically present" in the United States and could be excluded, or (3) if they were in U.S. territory in any sense. The Fourth Circuit ruled that Chen Zhou Chai never "entered" the United States because he was picked up by a boat before he reached the shore.[17] The Second Circuit overturned a district court decision that presence in U.S. territorial waters constituted presence in the United States. "United States immigration law is designed to regulate the travel of human beings, whose habitat is land, not the comings and goings of fish or birds," the court argued. It ruled that Xin-Chang Zhang "was not physically present [in the United States] until he came to the beach."[18] However, in the court's view, Zhang never "entered" because he was under "official restraint" as he swam under the glare of circling helicopter and rescue boat floodlights and was met on the beach by law enforcement personnel who handed out blankets before detaining Zhang and the other asylum seekers.[19] In his dissent in *Yang v. Maugans*, Judge H. Lee Sarokin argued that crossing into U.S. territorial waters constituted physical presence in the United States and met the first prong of the "entry test." Sarokin rejected the 2-1 majority's opinion that physical presence was not achieved until a foreigner reached dry land:

> I believe it would be impossible to base a determination of physical presence in the United States on arrival on land because it is unclear precisely what "dry land" means. Does this mean touching shore that is not covered by any water at all? What is the effect of high and low tides? Has an alien reached dry land upon standing on a beach that is moist with ocean water, or does the sand need to be perfectly dry? These questions may seem absurd, but they demonstrate

how difficult it would be to premise these determinations on such a vague standard which changes as constantly as the tides.[20]

After 1996, "excludables" and foreigners who successfully entered illegally and were caught within two years were lumped together as "inadmissible aliens" and typically subject to the same kinds of removal proceedings, including a new form of "expedited removal" with fewer legal protections.[21] The rights of many of those who successfully entered illegally were reduced to the same level as those who never legally entered in the first place. In 2002, the attorney general extended expedited removal to foreigners who arrived illegally by sea and were caught within two years.[22]

The Department of Justice maintained its position that foreigners interdicted in U.S. territorial waters were not entitled to admission screening or the legal protections of proceedings around "removal"—the post-1996 official euphemism for deportations—unless the foreigners were brought to U.S. territory. It did not explicitly state whether the government should follow the principle of non-refoulement for those interdicted in U.S. territorial waters:

> Until the State Department's views on the matter are expressed, we defer to the State Department on the question whether United States treaty obligations would require it to implement non-refoulement protections if an alien apprehended in internal waters demonstrates that his life or freedom would be threatened on account of race, religion, nationality, membership in a particular political group, or political opinion if he is returned to his country.[23]

However, the Department of Justice memo noted in passing that even if there were a treaty obligation to apply non-refoulement in U.S. territorial waters, to the extent such a treaty-based obligation is in conflict with the provisions of the 1996 Act, the latter would prevail as the more recent law. The memo cited one of the nineteenth-century Chinese Exclusion Cases that established Congress's plenary power over immigration admissions law, even if it violates bilateral treaties.[24]

The U.S. Constitution, rather than international law, constrains the ability of the executive and Congress to limit rights in liminal barbican spaces in U.S. territorial waters and on its beaches. The hyper-territoriality of these discussions around questions such as whether the sand is wet and the difference between physical presence and entry highlight the significance of the territorial rights of personhood rather than universal human rights. At the same time, non-refoulement provisions introduced into U.S. law as a consequence of signing the 1967 Protocol are much stronger protections than the statutory right to apply for asylum, as demonstrated by the government's wild swings in its claims about whether foreigners in U.S. territorial waters are entitled by statute to apply affirmatively.

Haitians on the High Seas

The U.S. policy of intercepting migrants in international waters, including people seeking asylum, began in a sustained way in 1981 as an effort to keep out people fleeing Haiti. The U.S. State Department long described Haiti as the poorest and "most oppressive" country in the Western Hemisphere.[25] In September 1963, two years after kleptocratic President François Duvalier was re-elected by a vote of 1,320,780 to 0, the first Haitian asylum seekers to make the 1,000-kilometer clandestine sea passage landed in Florida. The Immigration and Naturalization Service (INS) denied their asylum claims and returned them to Haiti. Detected flows ended for the next decade, until Jean-Claude Duvalier succeeded his father as president-for-life.[26] By 1979, more than 7,500 visa-less Haitians had arrived on Florida's shores. Washington considered Haitians to be "economic migrants" rather than "political refugees." The U.S. government saw Haiti as a bulwark against communism and was reluctant to grant asylum to citizens of a friendly regime.[27] Few Haitian asylum claims were successful despite mounting evidence from the U.S. State Department, rights groups, and reporters that Haitian authorities persecuted repatriates. "Many [repatriated Haitian nationals] will go to prison, their sole offense having been an attempt to gain asylum. In prison, many will be beaten, perhaps even tortured, and some will die as a result," U.S. Judge James Lawrence King summarized in a 1980 asylum case.[28]

On March 15, 1980, President Jimmy Carter signed the Refugee Act that introduced a more universal category of refugees into U.S. law and replaced provisions that favored people fleeing communist countries. A month later, President Castro opened the port of Mariel to a massive boatlift that brought 125,000 Cubans to the United States (see chapter 6). More than 25,000 Haitians sailed for Florida to seek asylum around the same time. Under pressure from rights groups and their congressional allies to treat Cubans and Haitians equally, the Carter administration created a Cuban-Haitian entrants program for nationals of those countries who arrived before October 10, 1980. As public hostility to the arrival of Cubans and Haitians grew, Floridian officials successfully pressured Washington to stop the boats.[29]

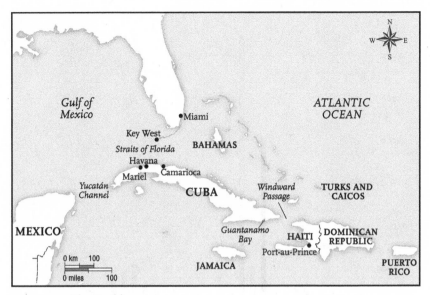

FIGURE 5.1 The Caribbean

"Walrus Courts"

The new administration of Ronald Reagan signed a bilateral agreement with Haiti in September 1981 that allowed U.S. authorities to board private Haitian vessels in international waters if they were suspected of carrying irregular migrants bound for the United States. The Haitian government agreed to accept the return of Haitian nationals and not prosecute them for illegal departure. Otherwise all repatriations would arguably constitute refoulement. Port-au-Prince also agreed to prosecute people traffickers and to seize their vessels. As is often the case, there was slippage in the usage of "trafficking" and "smuggling." In practice, trafficking was used to refer to smuggling. Six days after the bilateral agreement, the Reagan administration announced: "The entry of undocumented aliens from the high seas is hereby suspended and shall be prevented by the interdiction of certain vessels carrying such aliens."[30] The interdictions would be "given maximum publicity in Haiti" to deter further departures.[31] Initially, the program exclusively targeted Haitians. Through the early 1990s, the U.S. Coast Guard intercepted more Haitians than any other nationality, followed by Cubans. The largest spikes took place in 1992 and 1994, as shown in figure 5.2.

Three main rationales guided the decision to intercept Haitians in the Windward Passage near the Haitian coast rather than in U.S. waters or on U.S. shores, even though a third of the vessels carrying irregular migrants

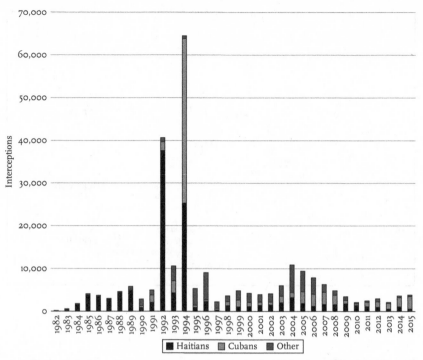

FIGURE 5.2 Maritime interceptions of migrants by the U.S. Coast Guard, 1982–2015.

SOURCE: U.S. Coast Guard 2016. http://www.uscg.mil/hq/cg5/cg531/AMIO/FlowStats/FY.asp. Accessed October 11, 2016. The database was subsequently removed from the link.

historically had been headed to countries other than the United States.[32] The U.S. government always cited the safety of passengers in transit as a primary reason for interceptions close to Haiti, and there is no question that sailing long distances in rickety boats was dangerous and led to numerous people drowning. On just one day in 1981, the bodies of thirty-three Haitian people washed onto a Florida beach after their boat hit a reef in high surf.[33] Rarely mentioned was that in the absence of legal paths to reach the United States to ask for asylum, a dangerous sea passage was the only way to travel. Another rationale for interception in the Windward Passage was technical. It was easier to concentrate U.S. forces in a geographic bottleneck before migrant boats dispersed at sea. The final rationale was not discussed publicly, but it lies at the heart of the hyper-legal logic of remote control. Under the provisions of the Refugee Act of 1980, foreigners "physically present in the United States or at a land border or port of entry" could ask for asylum.[34] The provisions in this section did not apply outside U.S. territory. By keeping asylum seekers away from U.S. land borders or ports, this avenue for protection was foreclosed.[35]

There is a second avenue for asylum in the 1980 Refugee Act that brought U.S. law into compliance with the non-refoulement provisions of the 1967 Protocol to the UN Refugee Convention.[36] The 1981 bilateral agreement included the understanding that the U.S. government did not intend to return Haitians who qualified for refugee status.[37] Thus, the agreement prevented Haitians from reaching U.S. territory where they could apply for asylum and have access to exclusion or deportation hearings, but it maintained the principle of non-refoulement in international waters. The agreement did not include details of how U.S. officials would determine at sea if an intercepted passenger was a refugee. Reagan's executive order simply stated that when the Coast Guard interdicted vessels outside U.S. territorial waters, "no person who is a refugee will be returned without his consent."[38]

According to a directive issued to the INS officials seconded to Coast Guard vessels, "To the extent that it is, within the opinion of the Commanding Officer of the United States Coast Guard vessel, safe and practicable, each person aboard an interdicted vessel shall be spoken to by an INS officer, through an interpreter." Every intercepted person would be asked, "Why did you leave Haiti?" and "Is there any reason why you cannot return to Haiti?" If "the interview suggests that a legitimate claim to refugee status exists, the person involved shall be removed from the interdicted vessel, and his or her passage to the United States shall be arranged."[39]

Sympathetic organizations on the U.S. mainland struggled to establish standing in court to act on behalf of the asylum seekers, but the Haitian Refugee Center in Florida eventually sued the federal government. The case revealed that INS officials conducting the interviews had extremely limited knowledge of political conditions in Haiti. In practice, many interdicted passengers were interviewed superficially, questioned as a group rather in private, where they could make sensitive claims, or not interviewed at all.[40] A Coast Guard document obtained through the Freedom of Information Act stated that the length of the interviews was determined not by the facts of the asylum seekers' cases but by the length of time until the cutter docked in Haiti to repatriate those onboard.[41] Haitians intercepted at sea did not have access to lawyers. There was no appeals process for decisions made by low-level bureaucrats. Between 1981 and September 1991, only 28 of the 24,600 Haitians intercepted were allowed to enter the United States to apply for asylum. The rest were repatriated.[42] A *New York Times* editorial criticized the interviews as "walrus courts—kangaroo courts at sea."[43]

The U.S. Court of Appeals for the Eleventh Circuit ruled 2-1 that INS officials had unreviewable discretion to make refugee status determinations and that the Immigration and Nationality Act does not apply outside U.S. territory:

> Plaintiffs contend that because the United States Government is reaching out into the Caribbean to interdict them, it is effectively extending the borders to that extent. We decline to interpret the statute this broadly. The plain language of the statute is unambiguous and limits the application of the provision to aliens within the United States or at United States' borders or ports of entry.[44]

In effect, the decision legitimated the extension of border control activities outside U.S. territory without extending rights to those affected by that control. Judge Joseph Hatchett's dissent criticized the majority for accepting "a pure legal fiction" that treated Haitians differently from other excludable foreigners because the Haitians had been forcibly kept away from U.S. territory.[45]

> At the bottom of this case is the government's decision to intercept Haitian refugees on the high seas, in international waters, to prevent them from reaching United States territory. If these refugees reach United States territory, they will have the right to insist, in United States courts, that they be accorded proper, fair, and adequate screening procedures. In addition, they will receive counseling from the Haitian Refugee Center (HRC) and volunteer lawyers who will ensure the proper application of United States immigration laws. The interdiction program is a clear effort by the government to circumvent this result.
>
> The United Nations Protocol on Refugees, and the United States immigration laws which execute it, were motivated by the World War II refugee experience. Jewish refugees seeking to escape the horror of Nazi Germany sat on ships in New York Harbor, only to be rebuffed and returned to Nazi Germany gas chambers. Does anyone seriously contend that the United States's responsibility for the consequences of its inaction would have been any less if the United States had stopped the refugee ships before they reached our territorial waters? Having promised the international community of nations that it would not turn back refugees at the border, the government yet contends that it may go out into international waters and actively prevent Haitian refugees from reaching the border. Such a contention makes a sham of our international treaty obligations and domestic laws for the protection of refugees.[46]

Hatchett's dissent neatly summarized both the logic of remote control and the historical origins of the non-refoulement provisions that the

U.S. government sought to circumvent. Even when a federal district court upheld the government's position on non-refoulement by agreeing that the 1967 Protocol was not a self-executing treaty, the judge excoriated the deeper logic of refoulement on the high seas. "The Government's conduct is particularly hypocritical given its condemnation of other countries [such as the British colony of Hong Kong] who have refused to abide by the principle of non-refoulement," Judge Sterling Johnson wrote. He called the non-refoulement provision in Article 33 "a cruel hoax and not worth the paper it is printed on" without congressional action to implement Article 33 or the Supreme Court's reinterpretation of earlier cases.[47] Civil rights organizations were unsuccessful at using the courts to stop the Haitian interdiction program, though by forcing the matter into court, they were able to expose the details of government practices that would have otherwise remained obscured.

Meanwhile, Washington pressured Port-au-Prince to keep its citizens from leaving. The 1982 Mica Amendment included Haitian cooperation "in halting illegal emigration" as a condition of U.S. foreign aid. Haitian critics of the regime argued that the government's deal with the United States on the interdiction program was "surrendering Haitian sovereignty" with little to show in return. "This criticism may induce Duvalier to limit Haiti's cooperation with the United States on this issue, especially if he sees no tangible increase in bilateral aid or security assistance," a CIA report warned.[48] After Duvalier was overthrown in 1986 and replaced by a series of short-lived dictatorships, Haitian authorities continued to cooperate with the U.S. interdiction program. CIA officials warned that in the event of estrangement with Washington, "the Haitian government might decide to reject repatriation of refugees intercepted by the US Coast Guard."[49] The National Security Council's internal documents from the period described Haitians trying to reach the United States as "refugees." It called for engagement with the military government and rejected a policy of "benign neglect" because growing chaos would likely lead to increased flows to the United States.[50]

After a military coup overthrew democratically elected president Jean-Bertrand Aristide on September 30, 1991, President George H. W. Bush imposed economic sanctions and suspended interdictions in a gesture to highlight the illegitimacy of the new regime. The departure of Haitians was portrayed as visible proof that the regime lacked popular support. Yet after thousands fled, Washington decided that what was meant as a symbolic gesture was too costly and announced on November 18 that it would resume interdiction and repatriation. Voice of America broadcasts urged Haitians not to attempt the dangerous journey. Many ignored the warning, and during the

FIGURE 5.3 Haitian refugees file off a U.S. Coast Guard cutter on March 2, 1992, after being forcibly returned to Port-au-Prince to be registered by Haitian officials. Maritime interceptions in the Caribbean became a model for later U.S. policies in the Pacific as well as Australia's "Pacific Solution" beginning in 2001. Photo by Ron Bull/*Toronto Star* via Getty Images.

six months following the coup, the U.S. Coast Guard interdicted over 34,000 Haitian passengers. Officials screened and allowed in 4,301 and brought them to the United States.[51] Another 550 were resettled in Belize, Honduras, Venezuela, and Trinidad and Tobago.[52] The rest were repatriated, even though a federal judge found that "repatriated Haitians face political persecution and even death on their return."[53] As the *New York Times* reported:

> In recent months, nearly every time the United States Coast Guard has returned fleeing boat people to Haiti, plainclothes agents have pulled returnees out of Red Cross processing lines and hauled them away for arrest. The disfigured body of one returnee, Yvon Desanges, was recently found near the airport, his eyes plucked out, a rope around his neck, his hands tied and a red handkerchief crudely marked "President of the Red Army."[54]

With its short-term capacity to conduct shipboard screenings overwhelmed, the Coast Guard transferred about 12,500 Haitian nationals to the U.S. naval base at Guantanamo Bay (discussed in detail in chapter 5). By May 1992, the navy decided that even Guantanamo was beyond capacity.[55] A system based on keeping most asylum seekers out of U.S. territory, but which at least recognized the principle of non-refoulement, was about to strip away that protection.

A "Floating Berlin Wall"

In one of the biggest shifts in the history of U.S. asylum policy, President Bush issued what became known as the Kennebunkport Order on May 24, 1992. It stated that the United States was not obliged under international law to apply the UN Refugee Convention's non-refoulement provision to "persons located outside the territory of the United States."[56] The Kennebunkport Order revoked Reagan's executive order that had specified that when the Coast Guard interdicted vessels outside U.S. territorial waters, "no person who is a refugee will be returned without his consent."[57] The May 1992 order made non-refoulement for persons outside U.S. territory flexible by providing that "the Attorney General, in his unreviewable discretion, may decide that a person who is a refugee will not be returned without his consent." Bush further ordered the State Department to create "cooperative arrangements with appropriate foreign governments for the purpose of preventing illegal migration to the United States by sea."[58]

The Coast Guard intercepted Haitians in international waters and immediately transported them back to Port-au-Prince, where they were turned over to the Haitian military for fingerprinting, interrogation, and in some cases, arrest.[59] Legal scholar Harold Koh describes the program as a "floating Berlin Wall" around Haiti that prevented its citizens from fleeing to any country, not only the United States, thus interfering with their internationally recognized right to exit.[60] Washington was not just shifting U.S. immigration control to the Haitian coast. At the same time, the United States was creating emigration control that prevented Haitians from fleeing anywhere beyond the neighboring Dominican Republic. This is the most extreme form of the externalization of borders because it includes control of both entry and exit.

The shift in U.S. policy in the short run was driven by its limited capacity to follow a model of interception, detention, and repatriation when faced with thousands of irregular maritime arrivals. In the long run, the shift was driven by political will. The United States could clearly develop the capacity to screen tens of thousands of people for asylum status if it were a major priority. The treatment of Cubans discussed in the next chapter shows that the U.S. government has routinely exercised that capacity when it has the political will rooted in foreign policy preferences for people fleeing communist countries. In the case of Haitian refugees, the Bush administration chose a more expedient solution.

Restrictive policies developed by the right often remain in place when the left takes power. As a Democrat presidential candidate, Bill Clinton announced his opposition to Bush's policy. "I am appalled by the decision of the Bush administration to pick up fleeing Haitians on the high seas and forcibly return them to Haiti before considering their claim to political asylum," Clinton said. "This policy must not stand."[61] Yet when Clinton took office as president in January 1993, he continued to follow the Kennebunkport Order and, indeed, between January 15, 1993, and November 26, 1994, the Coast Guard carried out "the largest single peacetime operation" in its history.[62] Operation Able Manner's fleet of seventeen cutters, nine aircraft, and five U.S. Navy ships interdicted more than 25,000 Haitians.[63] Although a reinstated President Aristide terminated the 1981 bilateral migration agreement in 1994, the Haitian government continued to permit repatriations and routinely allowed U.S. military aircraft to make shoreline flights at low altitude to deter Haitians from taking to the sea.[64] Port-au-Prince occupied a vulnerable place in the international hierarchy of sovereignty and played a critical role in facilitating remote control as a condition for U.S. economic and political support.

After lower courts rendered inconsistent decisions about whether non-refoulement provisions applied to U.S. interdictions in international waters, the Supreme Court issued a landmark ruling in *Sale v. Haitian Centers Council, Inc.* in 1993. By a vote of eight to one, the Court ruled that neither the Immigration and Nationality Act nor the 1967 Protocol to the Refugee Convention applied to Coast Guard action in international waters. The Court made this ruling even as the majority opinion strongly implied that Haitians interdicted at sea might well meet the definition of refugees:

> As the District Court stated in an uncontested finding of fact, since the military coup "hundreds of Haitians have been killed, tortured, detained without a warrant, or subjected to violence and the destruction of their property because of their political beliefs. Thousands have been forced into hiding."[65]

The majority also recognized that the goal of U.S. policy was to prevent refugees from reaching U.S. territory to access non-refoulement protections. "For 12 years, in one form or another, the interdiction program challenged here has prevented Haitians such as respondents from reaching our shores and invoking those protections."[66] The Court lamented that U.S. policy in international waters "may even violate the spirit of [non-refoulement provisions in] Article 33; but a treaty cannot impose uncontemplated extraterritorial obligations on those who ratify it through no more than its general human-itarian intent."[67]

Justice Harry Blackmun penned a scathing dissent. "What is extraor-dinary in this case is that the Executive, in disregard of the law, would take to the seas to intercept fleeing refugees and force them back to their persecutors—and that the Court would strain to sanction that conduct," he wrote. Blackmun noted that the executive branch had previously recognized that the non-refoulement provision of the 1967 Protocol applied in inter-national waters. The Department of Justice had reviewed the 1981 bilateral agreement between the United States and Haiti, and while it argued that the Immigration and Nationality Act provisions around asylum did not apply to "aliens who have not reached our borders (such as those on board interdicted vessels)," it did argue that they were protected by "the U.N. Convention and Protocol."[68]

In a case brought before the Inter-American Commission on Human Rights, which hears cases related to member countries of the Organization of American States, the Commission rejected the majority's argument in *Sale* that Article 33 did not apply to Haitians interdicted in international wa-ters. The Commission further ruled that U.S. interdiction policy violated the non-binding 1948 American Declaration of the Rights and Duties of Man by preventing Haitians from seeking asylum in other countries in the re-gion where Haitians had previously received asylum, such as the Dominican Republic, Jamaica, Bahamas, Cuba, Venezuela, Suriname, Honduras, and Turks and Caicos. The Commission held that the policy illegally discriminated against Haitians, in contradistinction to Cubans interdicted at sea, and pro-vided inadequate asylum hearings. The U.S. government refused to comply with the Commission's recommendation that the U.S. provide compen-sation to the plaintiffs in the case.[69] There is no supranational court that creates binding decisions on the U.S. government.

The Executive Committee of UNHCR criticized the *Sale* decision as "a setback to modern international refugee law which has been developing for more than forty years." Legal experts in the United States and around the world largely repudiated the majority opinion.[70] Maarten den Heijer notes the flaw in the argument that U.S. immigration law did not apply to the interdiction operation, when the operation was explicitly justified by a pres-idential order stating that U.S. immigration law was being violated simply by the *intent* to enter without inspection.[71] The Immigration and Nationality Act creates a smuggling offense out of the intent to bring foreigners into the United States without authorization and provides for its prosecution. The U.S. Court of Appeals for the District of Columbia has ruled that the smuggling provisions of the law apply outside U.S. territory, thus allowing for prosecutions even if the individuals do not reach U.S. territory. As with the prosecutions in pre-clearance zones in foreign airports discussed in chapter 4, the U.S. government prosecutes people for crimes committed outside U.S. territory without allowing asylum rights in those same spaces.[72]

The losing counsel in the *Sale* case, Yale law professor Harold Koh, argued in 1994 that international norms often work through diffuse mechanisms by becoming intertwined with domestic policymaking. This logic "predicts that in time, the United States will comply with the norm of 'extra-territorial' non-refoulement."[73] Koh's reasoning turned out to be prescient if not entirely fulfilled. Although the judiciary gave the executive carte blanche to ignore the non-refoulement principle in international waters, in practice, the U.S. government continued to conduct some form of screening, which ranged from systematic assessments of intercepted Cubans to a passive and cursory process for intercepted Haitians.

On May 8, 1994, the Clinton administration announced that it would resume asylum screening for Haitians intercepted at sea. The shift came not because of any court decision or change in the law, but rather as a result of concerted pressure by civil rights interest groups and their congressional allies. Deposed President Aristide joined the U.S. Congressional Black Caucus in decrying as racist the policy of not screening Haitians while screening Cubans, who were more likely to be white. Clinton's shift in policy remained discretionary, however, and did not change the Kennebunkport Order.[74]

The following month, the U.S. and Jamaican governments signed an agreement allowing the United States to process refugees in Jamaican waters for six months and an unimplemented agreement to do the same in the British dependency of Turks and Caicos.[75] The Coast Guard began taking interdicted Haitians to the harbor of Kingston, Jamaica, for asylum screenings aboard the 1,000-bed U.S. Navy hospital ship *Comfort*. Rejected applicants were transferred to a rented Ukrainian cruise ship, the *Ivan Franco*, for later repatriation by U.S. Coast Guard cutters.[76] The Clinton administration announced in July that up to 10,000 recognized Haitians asylees would be housed on U.S. military bases in Panama and eventually in the Caribbean countries of Antigua, Grenada, St. Lucia, Dominica, Suriname, Panama, and the Dominican Republic. Asylees would be given protection until conditions improved in Haiti and they could be repatriated.[77] The Turks and Caicos agreement stands out for requiring the islands' government to pass a law that excluded the Turks and Caicos courts from jurisdiction over any civil suit connected to the operation against the U.S., British, or Turks and Caicos governments.[78] Only the agreements to detain asylum seekers at the U.S. base in Panama and to conduct screenings in Jamaican waters were implemented. Most intercepted Haitians were taken to Guantanamo Bay.[79]

The immense paramilitary effort to repel the thousands who clearly met the refugee definition generated a countervailing political incentive to create an alternative path that a symbolic handful of refugees could access. The U.S. embassy had processed refugee claims at its embassy in Port-au-Prince since 1992 in one of four in-country processing programs active at the time, including programs in Cuba, the Soviet Union, and Vietnam. Initially, eligibility to apply in-country was limited to those who were likely targets of prosecution because of their professions or memberships in associations. Eligibility was expanded to all Haitians in May 1992 when the United States stopped shipboard asylum screenings. Two more refugee processing centers in Haiti were opened by May 1993. A total of forty-five to sixty U.S. and International Organization for Migration (IOM) staff processed applications. The embassy urged Haitians to apply at the processing centers, claiming that Haitians had an equal chance of proving their case in Haiti and offshore. However, only 2% of the 58,000 who applied in-country were recognized, compared to 30% of those processed off Jamaica. Many Haitians were leery of applying at a processing center in Haiti. By lining up on the street outside a U.S. office in Haiti, they would call attention to themselves as dissidents and exacerbate their vulnerability.[80] Human rights organizations documented multiple cases of Haitians who faced serious persecution after they applied to the program and were waiting for a decision. Washington cancelled in-country processing as it ratcheted up pressure on the dictatorship to leave office.[81]

On September 15, 1994, Clinton announced on television that a U.S. fleet was en route to Haiti to remove coup leader Raoul Cédras. After detailing the brutality of the regime, Clinton announced that stopping the flow of refugees was an explicit goal of the United States.

> Thousands of Haitians have already fled toward the United States, risking their lives to escape the reign of terror. As long as Cédras rules, Haitians will continue to seek sanctuary in our Nation. This year, in less than 2 months, more than 21,000 Haitians were rescued at sea by our Coast Guard and Navy. Today, more than 14,000 refugees are living at our naval base in Guantanamo. The American people have already expended almost $200 million to support them, to maintain the economic embargo. And the prospect of millions and millions more being spent every month for an indefinite period of time loom ahead unless we act. Three hundred thousand more Haitians, 5 percent of their entire

population, are in hiding in their own country. If we don't act, they could be the next wave of refugees at our door. We will continue to face the threat of a mass exodus of refugees and its constant threat to stability in our region and control of our borders.[82]

Four days later, as two U.S. aircraft carrier groups sailed toward the island and the 82nd Airborne Division was on its way to parachute into Haiti at midnight, Cédras stepped down and avoided a full-scale U.S. invasion. Operation Uphold Democracy turned into a relatively nonviolent occupation that lasted until March 1995. The motivations for the operation were mixed, but the U.S. government had demonstrated its willingness to deploy the full force of its military to cage refugees away from its shores. The mobilization inadvertently belied the U.S. government's claim that it did not have the capacity to screen thousands of Haitians for asylum claims. A state that could seize a foreign country and its population of 7.6 million overnight could surely process asylum claims if it had the political will.

The "Shout Test"

After Operation Uphold Democracy, discussions of remote control shifted from the public spectacle of a threatened invasion to negotiations in the back rooms of Geneva. In 1996, the U.S. delegation to the UNHCR forced its Executive Committee to water down non-refoulement provisions in its official Conclusions that state the position of the UNHCR on the interpretation of the Refugee Convention. The Conclusions are not legally binding, but they provide guidance for how the UNHCR believes the convention should be applied. The statements require unanimity among the Executive Committee, in which the United States plays a strong role as a consistent donor of more than a third of the UNHCR budget.[83] The U.S. delegates pushed the 1993 *Sale* case logic that the non-refoulement principle does not apply in international waters, and even assailed the idea that it applied at borders. In the face of U.S. pressure, the UNHCR Conclusions in 1996 and 1997 struck the language on non-refoulement found in the 1977 Conclusions, which had said that refugees arriving at borders would not be expelled, and from the 1981 Conclusions, which said that "asylum-seekers at sea should not only not be forcibly returned, but rather disembarked at the next port of call, or in the case of mass influxes, should be admitted, at least on a temporary basis."[84] An internal e-mail from a leading official at the UNHCR explained, "[t]he bottom line is that the Europeans are aghast at the U.S., but aren't going to take them on, and agree that we mustn't have a floor fight."[85]

The State Department eventually agreed to the "humanitarian" but not "legal" principle of proscribing refoulement at borders.[86] The discretionary quality of humanitarianism is a major reason for its bad odor among many legal advocates. The avoidance of recognizing a legal obligation was consistent with the U.S. government's position in front of the Inter-American Commission on Human Rights following the *Sale* case.

> Any United States action to provide additional asylum avenues to interdicted Haitians—such as the safe haven at Guantanamo Bay and the refugee screening that was conducted for Haitians at different times on Coast Guard cutters, at Guantanamo Bay, on the Naval Ship *Comfort* in Jamaican territorial waters, and even within Haiti itself—has been and continues to be wholly discretionary under both U.S. domestic and international law. These additional benefits that have been provided to interdicted Haitians over the years are just that—additional benefits, and not the source of binding legal obligation or standards.[87]

By 2003, the U.S. position appeared to soften. The Executive Committee Conclusion upheld "the principle of nonrefoulement without geographic limitation, whether at frontiers of states, in territorial waters, the high seas, or within the territory of a state where embarkation is prevented." By acquiescing to this language in the Executive Committee Conclusion, the United States apparently reverted to its position before the Kennebunkport Order and the *Sale* case and brought it back into line with the international norm that had developed in previous decades. Refugee rights advocate Bill Frelick attributes the shift to U.S. diplomatic engagements with the UNHCR and the issue linkage with the Palermo anti-smuggling and anti-trafficking protocols pushed by the United States, which included strong non-refoulement provisions in return for international cooperation on otherwise tightened mobility controls. The limitation on U.S. remote control came not from the courts, but from more diffuse international pressure articulated through the U.S. State Department. The State Department is generally more concerned with foreign policy ramification of U.S. practices, and indeed in 1978 unsuccessfully tried to convince the INS to include a notice on the I-589 asylum application form of a right to have one's case reviewed by the UNHCR.[88]

In 2007, however, the Bush administration responded to a UNHCR advisory opinion on the extraterritorial application of Article 33,[89] and it reverted to the *Sale* position that Article 33 only applies "within the territory of the Contracting States."[90] The State Department maintained that it "has been the longstanding policy of the United States to take actions outside the United States consonant with non-refoulement obligations that apply to individuals within U.S. territory under the Refugee Convention, as well as under the Convention Against Torture" but described these as a matter of humanitarian policy rather than legal obligation. Thus, Washington insisted on its discretion to apply Article 33 outside U.S. territory.

The U.S. position on non-refoulement swung back toward a more generous interpretation during the Obama administration. The United States had signed the Convention Against Torture (CAT) in 1988 and ratified it in 1994. Article 3 of the CAT obligates its signatories not to "expel, return ('refouler') or extradite a person to another State where there are substantial grounds for believing that he would be in danger of being subjected to torture."[91] The Committee Against Torture that interprets the treaty considers the CAT to apply extraterritorially "to protect any person, citizen or non-citizen without discrimination subject to the de jure or de facto control of a State party."[92] While the U.S. position under the George W. Bush presidency in 2007 was that the CAT did not apply to U.S. actions outside U.S. territory,[93] in 2014, the Obama administration moved toward accepting CAT in "all places that the State party controls as a government authority," including the U.S. naval station at Guantanamo and "U.S.-registered ships and aircraft."[94] Given that interdicted migrants are taken aboard U.S. ships, the pendulum of non-refoulement thus swung back toward the international norm. The norm of extraterritorial non-refoulement is not deeply institutionalized in the United States and could be reinterpreted by a different president or courts. The practical question after *Sale* became not so much whether the United States would simply return migrants intercepted in international waters without screening, but the quality of that screening given that applicants are denied lawyers, appeals, and other rights.[95] The parameters of the U.S. debate over non-refoulement outside U.S. territory are set by accreted responses to crises rather than a coherent interpretation of law.

Following mass departures from Haiti during an outbreak of violence in 2004, Bush announced that "we will turn back any refugee that attempts to reach our shore."[96] Bush's statement was remarkable for its open pledge to interdict "refugees." Under Operation Able Sentry, the thinnest level of non-refoulement screening was applied. Haitians were not told they had the right to seek asylum, interpreters were not always available, and the Coast Guard only screened those who passed "the shout test." As Frelick describes the test, "Only those who wave their hands, jump up and down, and shout the loudest—and are recognized as having done such—are even afforded, in theory, a shipboard refugee pre-screening interview."[97]

In an institutionalized version of the hear-no-evil principle, the Coast Guard trains its sailors not to elicit information from people seeking asylum unless ordered to do so and to limit their communication with interdicted migrants to what is "necessary to accomplish embarkation, initial briefing, security, safety, medical care, food distribution and disembarkation."[98] Unlike Cuban nationals, Haitians and other non-Cubans were not read a statement offering them the chance to ask for a shipboard protection interview. The systematic minimization of opportunities to ask for asylum on board U.S. ships captures in miniature the macro-logic of remote control policies. The policies are designed to prevent U.S. authorities from hearing pleas for asylum.

Of the 905 Haitians intercepted by the Coast Guard in February 2004, only three passed the shout test, and they were rejected in the "credible fear" test onboard the cutter. The Coast Guard forcibly returned all 905 during a chaotic weekend when the Haitian president was forced into exile. The Coast Guard dumped the group, some of whom were shackled, onto the dock at Port-au-Prince where they were met by a taunting crowd that was forced back at gunpoint to allow the returnees to pass. By 2005, the State Department appeared to have at least cursory monitoring in place for repatriates at the docks in Port-au-Prince. A new Coast Guard training regime included provisions that asylum seekers could show fear of being returned in a variety of ways, including "withdrawal, sadness, panic, screaming, and passing notes." Only one of the 445 Haitians intercepted at sea in 2013 passed the test, even though roughly half of Haitians able to present their claim in a full asylum process in the United States were recognized as refugees.[99]

Washington increasingly relies on cooperation with buffer states to patrol the Caribbean. Since 2004, the U.S. Coast Guard had collaborated with Bahamian authorities to interdict migrants sailing through the Windward Passage bound for the United States or the Bahamas. By placing Bahamian "ship riders" on board U.S. vessels, the United States can conduct operations in Bahamian waters. One advantage of this arrangement from the Bahamian government's perspective is that Washington finances the expense of repatriation. Haitians are the primary intercepted nationality. A second advantage for the Bahamas is that by availing itself of U.S. interdiction capacity, it can prevent migrants from reaching Bahamian territory. As a U.S. diplomatic cable explained, "Intercepting migrants before they hit the beaches of New Providence or other islands [in the Bahamas], to become the targets of law enforcement and repatriation efforts, and attendant publicity, reduces and simplifies the government's work in many respects."[100] The 2004 U.S.-Bahamas Agreement prohibits refoulement and does not make any exceptions for extraterritorial interceptions.[101] However, "UNHCR has no evidence that these provisions are monitored or enforced or that penalties have been assessed for failures of compliance."[102]

The Dominican Republic is a secondary conduit for Dominicans and third-country nationals trying to enter the United States by crossing the Mona Passage to Puerto Rico on homemade wooden boats called *yolas*. Under the dry foot policy in effect until January 2017, Cubans reaching Puerto Rico were "assured of an asylum hearing once their feet touch American soil," as explained in chapter 6. Cubans paid three times the smuggling fee charged to Dominicans. Groups that a State Department cable called "exotic aliens, such as Chinese" paid up to ten times the Cuban price. Washington strengthened the Dominican navy's capacity to stop flows of people and drugs by providing Zodiac inflatables, computer equipment to track trafficking cases, payment for fuel and sailors' rations, and by placing Dominican patrols in the Mona Passage "under U.S. Coast Guard operational control." Under the Mérida Initiative, the Dominican Republic and Haiti became eligible for further funding to build migration-control capacity.[103] In 2016, the Obama administration requested US$600,000 for the Dominican government to combat transnational organized crime, including migrant smuggling and human trafficking.[104]

Capacity building is accompanied by publicity campaigns and readmissions agreements. In 2004, the U.S. embassy began sponsoring "an intensive public information campaign emphasizing the hazards of yola travel, the untrustworthy nature of smugglers, and the difficulties of life as an illegal immigrant in the United States."[105] A formal memorandum of agreement is not necessary for effective interdiction. The Dominican Republic routinely allowed repatriation in the 1990s even in the absence of a formal agreement.[106] By 2003, the U.S. and Dominican governments had signed a readmissions agreement that included repatriation of third-party nationals intercepted at sea. As with the Bahamian agreement, it included a non-refoulement provision without a monitoring mechanism.[107] The policies of patrolling the moat and turning coastal states into buffers overlap in practice.

The U.S. Pacific Solution

The U.S. government adopted the model for intercepting Haitians in the Caribbean to keep irregular Chinese migrants away from U.S. territory. In April 1993, the U.S. Coast Guard intercepted a ship 200 miles off Honduras carrying 200 Chinese people trying to reach the United States. Honduran authorities allowed the U.S. Coast Guard to force the ship to a Honduran port, where it was met by two INS officers who interviewed the passengers to determine whether they had political asylum claims. While the INS concluded that five passengers were refugees, the local UNHCR office determined that none met the standard. The Honduran government repatriated the entire group at U.S. expense.[108]

The Clinton administration issued a confidential directive on June 18, 1993, that the United States would "attempt to interdict and hold smuggled aliens as far as possible from the U.S. border."[109] Over the next decade, U.S. forces intercepted thirty-two ships carrying more than 5,000 Chinese nationals.[110] In a Coast Guard procedure that uniquely applied to citizens of the People's Republic of China (PRC), interdicted migrants were given a questionnaire in which they were asked why they left. The answers were transmitted to Washington where asylum officers remotely decided whether to conduct an in-person asylum prescreening interview before repatriation.[111]

The U.S. government has worked with several countries to intercept irregular migrants at sea. These policies are most effective when they are done secretly. In July 1993, the U.S. Coast Guard intercepted three Taiwanese ships carrying 659 PRC nationals bound for California. It held them 100 kilometers off the coast of the Mexican port of Ensenada.[112] Emboldened by the *Sale* ruling two weeks earlier, the Clinton administration decided that rather than conducting asylum screenings, it would ask the Mexican government to give the Chinese temporary asylum in exchange for U.S. payment for their eventual deportation. Although over the previous three years, the U.S. embassy in Mexico City had quietly paid Mexico to deport third-country nationals bound for the United States, this time the Mexican

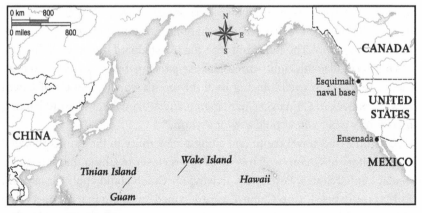

FIGURE 5.4 Pacific Rim

government refused the U.S. offer because of the publicity surrounding the standoff and the open implication in the media that Mexico City was doing Washington's dirty work.[113] After more than a week of negotiations while the Chinese passengers sweltered on their ships eating military rations and rice delivered by U.S. authorities, the Coast Guard forced the boats to Ensenada. The Mexican government did not consider requests for asylum and summarily deported the passengers by air from Tijuana. "They wanted to go to the United States. We don't want people coming here thinking they can use Mexico as a platform," Mexican diplomat Andres Rozental announced.[114] At the time, Mexico was not a party to the UN Refugee Convention.[115]

"Snakehead" people-smugglers continued to bring several hundred Chinese by cargo ship to the coast of Baja California or Sinaloa and disembark them for travel by land to the U.S. border. In 1999, Mexican authorities intercepted almost 400 Chinese nationals on the Baja route. Surveillance of the Mexican coast redirected landings further south. Between 1999 and 2001, a ring smuggled Chinese nationals through Ecuador and Mexico to the United States for a fee of US$20,000–30,000. In 2000, authorities uncovered a route that offloaded Chinese passengers without visas on sandbars off the Pacific coast of Guatemala and then transported them in tractor trailers on a forty-hour journey across Mexico.[116]

The U.S. government took extreme steps to ensure that intercepted Chinese nationals being repatriated through U.S.-controlled spaces were not able to ask for asylum. For example, in April 1993, when Washington paid the costs of Mexico City to deport 300 Chinese nationals, the U.S. government refused to allow the charter flight to land in Alaska to refuel so that passengers could not ask for asylum on U.S. soil. The plane eventually arrived in China after refueling in Europe.[117] In 1995 the U.S. military used Wake Island as a stopover point to repatriate 147 Chinese interdicted 1,600 kilometers southeast of Hawaii. Wake is an incorporated territory administered by the U.S. military in the remote Western Pacific where the Immigration and Nationality Act does not apply. The following year, the Coast Guard intercepted the *Xing DA* off Bermuda with eighty-three Chinese passengers aboard who had been hiding in the ship's hold during its three-month transit. The Coast Guard flew them back to China via Guantanamo and Wake Island to avoid landing on territory where they could ask for asylum.[118]

Unauthorized travel continued along a new route to the unincorporated U.S. territory of Guam, which is three times closer to China than the continental United States. Foreigners arriving on Guam could apply for asylum. By May 1999, nearly 600 Chinese were detained on Guam in tent cities while U.S. authorities screened them. Even those who passed their credible-fear interviews and were not detained were prevented from traveling to the U.S. mainland, where many of their lawyers were based. Under strong pressure from the Guamanian governor, whose nonvoting delegate to Congress unsuccessfully filed a bill to prevent future asylum seekers from filing applications on Guam,[119] the Clinton administration ordered U.S. authorities to detain Chinese interdicted at sea on the neighboring island of Tinian in the Commonwealth of Northern Mariana Islands. Most provisions of U.S. immigration law did not apply in the Commonwealth until 2008.[120] Foreigners physically present or arriving in the Commonwealth, including people brought there after being intercepted in international or U.S. waters, did not have a statutory right to ask for asylum. Intercepted Chinese were detained in a tent complex at North Field, best known as the airfield used by the *Enola Gay* to launch its atomic bomb attack on Hiroshima in 1945.

The effort to prevent Chinese from reaching Guam was highlighted most vividly in 1999, when a U.S. Navy surveillance plane spotted a thirty-five-meter fishing trawler with 102 Chinese passengers on board heading toward Guam. As the trawler's captain apparently tried to ground the ship on a reef, a landing party from a Coast Guard inflatable boat seized control of the trawler and steered it back out to sea at the last minute. A Coast Guard cutter then towed the trawler and its passengers to Tinian. Although Tinian was not a U.S. territory, the INS sent forty officials to conduct credible-fear interviews there. Eighty-nine Chinese asylum seekers were eventually sent to the mainland after passing the initial screening.[121] Most provisions of U.S. immigration law were extended to the Commonwealth beginning in 2008. The right to seek asylum in the Commonwealth under U.S. immigration law is scheduled to begin in 2020, at which time the logic of detention on Tinian would presumably end.[122]

As in Guantanamo and aboard U.S. Coast Guard cutters, the U.S. government used the barbican space of Tinian to conduct discretionary screenings without providing asylum seekers the rights they would have enjoyed on U.S. territory. The norm of non-refoulement continued to moderately constrain state practice even when the government rejected any formal legal obligation.

Canada's Coasts

Canada is essentially an island surrounded by two enormous oceans and a high-capacity U.S. buffer. Few asylum seekers have tried to cross these seas. When they have, the Canadian government has intercepted them and considered refoulement. As in the United States, the activities of the authorities in territorial waters are limited by the protections of foundational domestic law. Canadian authorities have been far more deferential to international laws and norms than their U.S. counterparts, however, presumably because the Canadian government has long sought to maintain a positive image at home and abroad as a humanitarian country that plays by international rules. So few asylum seekers have attempted to arrive by sea compared with the United States that the strength of this norm has not been fully tested.

The first irregular maritime arrivals asking for sanctuary in Canada were a group of 987 mostly Estonian refugees who had been living in Sweden and who faced possible repatriation to the Soviet Union. Frustrated by delays in negotiations over their resettlement to Canada, the Estonians took matters into their own hands and sailed to Canada in nine vessels that landed between August 1948 and November 1949. A third of them arrived on the SS *Walnut* in the largest irregular maritime landing of people seeking refuge on Canada's eastern coast in the twentieth century. Canadian authorities detained them and set up an ad hoc screening process. All the maritime arrivals were admitted, except for twelve who were deported for failing to meet Canadian requirements or for posing a security risk. The notion that the Estonians were "fleeing the Reds" and their European origins generated favorable media coverage that helped their cases.[123]

Few asylum seekers since then have arrived by sea. The small numbers who manage to make it to Canadian coasts stir a great deal of political excitement. In August 1986, 152 Sri Lankan asylum seekers who had sailed on the *Aurigae* were rescued in lifeboats off Newfoundland and given temporary residence status based on their Sri Lankan nationality. Sri Lanka was on a "B-1 list" of presumed unsafe countries to which Canada would not deport. It was later discovered that the group had traveled via West Germany, a presumably safe country for asylum seekers, and hidden that fact from Canadian authorities. The following year, 174 Sikhs from the *Amelie* arrived on the coast of Nova Scotia and asked for asylum. The conservative government of Prime Minister Brian Mulroney recalled Parliament for an emergency session to try and push through the Refugee Deterrents and Detention Act, which would have given immigration officials the discretionary power to interdict ships with unauthorized immigrants in Canadian or international waters and turn them away without hearing any asylum claims. The Senate rejected the bill.

Senator Jerahmiel S. Grafstein (Liberal, Ontario) laid out the objections based on Canada's non-refoulement obligations in the Refugee Convention and the costs to its international humanitarian brand:

> If a boat is turned away, how will we ever know if that boat contained real refugees or not? Was not this exactly what Canada accused others of when the Vietnamese boat people fled their land? Canada protested when Thailand did precisely that, and now Canada, humane Canada, generous Canada, is proposing laws to do what we preached to others would be wrong. Is this leadership? Is this the international example Canada wishes to give?[124]

A compromise maintained the principle of non-refoulement by specifying that ships with asylum seekers could be prevented from entering Canadian waters only if the vessel could safely return to another country that protects refugees from persecution.[125]

In a rare case of Canadian involvement in refouling asylum seekers after interception at sea, U.S. and Canadian authorities in 1998 collaborated with the Senegalese navy to intercept the *African Queen*, which was transporting 192 Tamil asylum seekers from Sri Lanka through Senegalese territorial waters on a roundabout route to North America. After the Tamils were returned to Sri Lanka with the assistance of the IOM, they were arrested, many were abused, and one was severely tortured.[126]

Canadian policymakers during this period did not typically pursue interception on the high seas because of both logistical and legal challenges that limited their options compared with U.S. and Australian policymakers. Canada did not have the same naval forces in place or quasi-colonial territory readily available for offshore processing as the United States. As Martha Nixon, a high-ranking Canadian immigration official, summarized in a November 1999 parliamentary hearing:

> It's my understanding that the U.S. has a considerable capacity, particularly in the south Pacific, to be available and aware of boats that are passing. They often have the capacity to intercept those boats and direct them toward an island that is a protectorate as opposed to a U.S. territory. This makes it easier for them to actually do the processing of people, because they are not on U.S. soil and so they do not have the right to make a refugee claim.[127]

Compared with Australia, Canadian options were limited by its Charter of Rights and Freedoms, as Greg Fyffe from the immigration department explained to the committee:

We certainly are looking at the experience of the U.S. and Australia for best practices. We're involved in a lot of conversations with them. I think our situation is probably closest to that of Australia, although they do not have a charter of rights, so they have more flexibility in some ways. But their basic practice is similar to ours. They intercept the boats on the high seas, escort them to land, and give the people refugee hearings, although they have a detention facility at Port Hedland in which they keep all people before removal. They have worked extensively with the Chinese to assist in removal, and we are interested in learning some of the lessons from there.[128]

Only a handful of boats reached Canada in the 1990s, but the boats that made it were large. Over a span of six weeks in 1999, four boats carrying 599 Chinese passengers reached the coastal waters of British Columbia. The federal government detained the passengers and created a temporary barbican on the Esquimalt naval base that was designated as a "port of entry" in which the asylum seekers were denied access to lawyers until processing was finished. The liminal space on Vancouver Island was briefly transformed into what geographer Alison Mountz calls "not Canada."[129] More than 500 of the passengers asked for asylum. Many abandoned their claims when released and were presumed to have traveled to New York City's Chinatown.[130]

The Canadian government puts little effort into patrolling its moat for reasons of geography, political institutions, and foreign policy. The vast Pacific and Atlantic cannot be crossed by tiny craft like those traversing the Straits of Florida and the Mediterranean. When faced with the few instances of large ships arriving with asylum seekers, Canadian authorities considered refoulement but were deterred by Canada's strong rights of territorial personhood in its Charter and the non-refoulement provisions in the Refugee Convention it signed in 1969. Political elites have been more deferential to the judiciary and have not constantly probed the boundaries of the law to the extent of the other cases studied in this volume.[131] Ignoring international law would incur reputational costs to an international brand based on multilateralism and humanitarianism. The small scale of irregular maritime arrivals has never been high enough to override those international interests, but the fact that refoulement was proposed by the conservative government in 1987 suggests that the international constraints are shaky. When asylum seekers do arrive by sea, Ottawa has shown its willingness to carve barbican spaces out of its mainland that function as temporary, miniature Guantanamos.

Conclusion

Forty-two years after the U.S. Coast Guard shadowed the *St. Louis* to keep it from landing European Jews in Florida, it began a sustained operation in the same waters that has intercepted a quarter of a million migrants. Many of them sought greater economic opportunity or family reunification. Many plainly were refugees. Bracketing the issue of the mixed causes that often motivate international movements, it is impossible to know the balance of refugees and other types of migrants because of shortcomings in the screening measures. Incontrovertibly, Washington effectively pushed control over its borders hundreds of kilometers into the Caribbean and thousands of kilometers into the Pacific while simultaneously trying to avoid extending legal obligations.

The United States is often an outlier among Western democratic countries in its refusal to join widely adopted international treaties.[132] The 1993 *Sale* decision stands out amid a much larger body of international law clearly stating that the principle of non-refoulement applies outside a state's territory.[133] There is no supranational court that provides binding oversight over U.S. practices. Other governments have flirted with the majority interpretation in *Sale*, including Canada, but they have typically been reeled back by greater deference to international law and the concern that openly flouting it would potentially damage their international reputations.

Practices developed in moments of supposed political crisis, such as the arrival in South Florida of Haitians around 1980, were then transported to other contexts such as preventing Chinese asylum seekers from crossing the Pacific. Similar policies of patrolling the moat, establishing barbican spaces, and relying on the cooperation of origin and buffer countries became part of the system of remote control. Policies are often implemented by conservative governments and continued under progressive governments until they are eventually taken for granted. The U.S. Coast Guard routinely intercepts vessels on the high seas even though such a practice was considered anathema by world powers in the 1930s, as shown in chapter 2, because it violated cherished principles of freedom of navigation.

The main story of remote control in the North American moat is its huge scale and the normalization of patrolling policies, but it is also important to consider the institutional limitations on state action. The U.S. Constitution and Canadian Charter ensure strong rights of territorial personhood, which is why Washington and Ottawa have been so creatively cynical about defining what constitutes "entry into the territory." The United States is a world leader in defining military bases strewn across the globe as territories under its control but not its sovereignty and thus where asylum seekers have limited rights. On the high seas, the executive branch practices some self-restraint despite the wide latitude offered by *Sale*. The fact that there are screenings at all, whatever their serious inadequacies, is evidence of diffuse international pressure articulated through the State Department and the influence of civil society. There is a robust network of rights organizations in the United States that has not been effective in directly restraining most extraterritorial practices of the U.S. government. However, taking the cases to court has yielded embarrassing details of cynical government interceptions and screening practices. Rights groups, journalists, and elements within the State Department concerned with human rights have revealed the grim consequences of refoulement. These facts then become part of subsequent court cases and the public record. Their primary effect is not to legally constrain what the government does, but rather to apply modest political checks that prompt the government to continue at least cursory screenings and not openly refoule refugees.

CHAPTER 6 | Raising the Drawbridge to Cuba

ONLY 150 KILOMETERS SEPARATE Cuba from Florida. As I stood on Havana's *malecón* in 2009, a young man sauntered past singing in Spanish, "I'm going to Miami / I can't take it anymore." Cuba has been a major source of refugees and other types of immigrants seeking greater economic opportunity and family reunification since the 1959 socialist revolution. The degree to which the U.S. government labels individual Cubans or all Cubans on the move as refugees has varied over time. Few have been part of a formal refugee resettlement program. Yet Cubans arriving in the United States, particularly in the 1960s, have often been described as refugees or exiles by themselves, scholars, advocates, and the U.S. government.[1]

The Cuban-U.S. case reveals three lessons for the study of remote control. First, extensive "antagonistic cooperation" with the government of the country of origin shows that remote control is made possible, but also limited, by the broader context of bilateral relationships. The willingness of Havana to cooperate, rather than legal constraints on U.S. policies, has strongly shaped flows.[2] The best explanation for the timing of major migration episodes is Cuban policies of exit and repatriation. Washington and Havana quietly began cooperating as early as 1965 to deter Cubans from crossing the Straits of Florida. This cooperation is not unique, but it is rare because, historically, one of the main goals of refugee policy has been to shame states of origin. The U.S.-Cuba relationship has been hostile for decades. The U.S. economic embargo beginning in 1960, rupture of diplomatic relations from 1961 to 2015, armed invasion by U.S.-sponsored exiles at the Bay of Pigs in 1961, the Cuban Missile Crisis in 1962, and a litany of other confrontations have characterized the relationship. Havana has oscillated between promoting and restricting emigration, and within that framework, shaped the characteristics of those it allowed to leave. These decisions have been based on the state of the island's economy, its political stability, and the broader context of U.S.-Cuban affairs. Havana has used its ability to moderate the outflow as a tool to force the United States to negotiate and create more normalized relations between the two countries.[3] The United States has often promoted outflows from Cuba by giving Cubans special admission preferences, but Washington's ability to control those flows has also depended on Havana's willingness to restrict exit and accept readmission of Cubans intercepted at sea. In a reversal from the typical notion of remote control by Washington, Fidel Castro often pushed the buttons that opened and closed the doors of the cage.

Second, U.S. policies toward Cubans demonstrate the vast capacity of the U.S. government to manage and accept large numbers of refugees when it has the political will. The more generous treatment of larger numbers of Cubans shows that the harsher treatment of other nationalities, particularly Haitians, was not a question of overwhelmed state capacity, but rather a political choice. While there are many historical examples of U.S. laws that favor designated nationalities for refugee admission, preferential policies toward Cubans have endured more than half a century, first because of a general preference for people fleeing communist countries, and then as a response to the anti-Castro Cuban-American lobby that has enjoyed disproportionate influence on national policy because of its base in the electorally strategic state of Florida.[4] The size of the resulting flows—approximately 1 million from 1960 to 1980—is unusually large. The recurring availability of legal channels to migrate, particularly for political refugees, has provided an alternative to irregular migration that has not been available to the vast majority of potential asylum seekers from other parts of the world. The United States also has clearly demonstrated the capacity, at least in the long run, to accommodate large flows of maritime asylum seekers. What varies is whether the balance of political power within the country supports accommodation.

A formal agreement in 1994 openly extended functional U.S. border control all the way to Havana's waterfront, even as it hyper-territorialized where rights to enter were activated through a "wet foot, dry foot" policy that applied only to Cubans. Until January 2017, Cubans without visas whose feet reached U.S. soil were allowed to enter. Those interdicted at sea were expelled back to Cuba after a cursory asylum screening. The result of this policy was a series of Kafkaesque controversies about just where U.S. land begins that involved measuring high tides and squabbling over the territoriality of bridges and lighthouses. The general lesson of the wet foot, dry foot policy is that even within its sovereign territory, the government can create micro-manipulations of space to keep out unwanted foreigners as long as it maintains at least cursory asylum screenings.

Welcome to Miami

A triumphant Fidel Castro initially allowed a mass exit of Cubans. The flow was encouraged and facilitated by Washington, which had supported the dictatorship of Fulgencio Batista during the revolution. Even after the break in diplomatic relations on January 3, 1961, Pan American and KLM continued to fly between Havana and Miami. Cuban passengers could no longer obtain U.S. visas, but the airlines forwarded requests for visa waivers to the U.S. government and allowed only Cuban nationals with waivers to board the aircraft. Only about 1% of the 96,000 passengers on flights in 1961 and 1962 were denied a waiver.[5] In effect, the U.S. government suspended the standard remote control system of air carrier sanctions and visas to benefit Cubans wishing to leave the island. By the time regularly scheduled commercial travel from Cuba to the United States ended in October 1962 during the Cuban Missile Crisis, more than 200,000 Cubans had already flown to the United States since the revolution.

Minor illicit flows by boat began as early as July 1959. By June 1965, the U.S. Coast Guard had rescued or assisted 6,862 Cubans clandestinely attempting to reach Florida.[6] In October 1965, Castro opened the port of Camarioca so that Cubans living in the United States could pick up their family members by boat. A CIA report interpreted Castro's motivations in terms that would resonate into the 1990s:

> In agreeing to permit Cubans to come to the US, Fidel Castro has both short- and long-range motives. For the short run, he is further strengthening the Communist regime in Cuba by permitting malcontents and socially non-productive elements to depart. These people were contributing little to the revolution and will not be missed. In the longer run Castro probably desires to achieve a basis for establishing a dialogue with the US which could lead toward some kind of normalization of relations.[7]

The U.S. Coast Guard warned Cuban Americans bound for Camarioca that their activities were illegal and dangerous, but it cooperated with the boat captains in practice. The Coast Guard rescued and brought to Florida 1,970 of the 2,979 Cubans who made the transit during the five weeks the port was open.[8]

Unregulated arrivals by sea always stir greater public anxiety of "invasion" than the same or greater number of arrivals by air. The Johnson administration grew concerned by the scale of the boatlift and secretly negotiated the closure of Camarioca in exchange for an airlift. Under the terms of the 1965 migration agreement, the first formal agreement of any kind between Castro's government and Washington, U.S.-financed "Freedom Flights" brought more than 265,000 Cubans to the United States until the program ended in 1973. The Freedom Flights included a kind of ad hoc pre-clearance. Officials from the United States screened passengers at the Varadero airport in Cuba before their departure, as they had done in a smaller program in 1963.[9] The main rationale for conducting the screening in Cuba was that there was no provision for repatriation if the U.S. government decided that a Cuban national was inadmissible. Washington did not want to pay the political price of forcibly repatriating someone to a communist country. Havana did not want to accept repatriates whom it considered traitors and counterr evolutionaries.[10]

Once Cubans arrived in the United States, they were "paroled" into the country by the attorney general under the terms of the 1952 Immigration and Nationality Act.[11] Federal assistance for Cubans began in 1960. The following year, the Cuban Refugee Program started providing a wide range of social services in the first known U.S. program for refugees who had not been previously screened abroad.[12] After they were present in the United States for a year, Cubans became eligible for lawful permanent residency under the terms of the Cuban Adjustment Act of 1966. While the 1966 law did not use the terms "refugee" or "asylee," it is clear from congressional debates that lawmakers considered people fleeing Cuba refugees under international law. Undersecretary of State George Ball argued that by passing the bill, the United States would "be demonstrating to the world our sympathy for peoples who do not want to live under totalitarian regimes."[13] In 1980, Castro would severely test the resolve of the U.S. government to continue to accept Cubans heading north.

Mariel

Castro opened the Cuban port of Mariel on April 20, 1980. The immediate motivation was an embarrassing incident in which some 10,000 Cubans sought asylum in the Peruvian embassy after the Cuban government removed its guards around the compound. The asylees were eventually allowed to fly out via Costa Rica. The level of public discontent revealed by the incident stunned the Cuban leadership.[14] Deeper background disputes included the U.S. welcome of Cubans who had hijacked boats to Florida and negotiations over the departure of political prisoners, including the 9,000 who had been allowed to travel to the United States from 1979 to 1980.[15] The Cuban government wanted the United States to accept more Cubans in an orderly fashion. In a scaled-up reprise of the Camarioca boatlift, Castro publicly invited members of the "Cuban Overseas Community" to come to Mariel by boat and pick up any of their relatives who wished to leave. "We have removed the guards protecting the Florida peninsula," the government declared. By the end of April, a flotilla of 1,500 boats from Florida packed the harbor.[16]

The initial U.S. response was incoherent. The Carter administration had ordered U.S. diplomats to oppose the opening of Mariel, and, once it occurred, Washington publicly stated that the informal boatlift violated U.S. law. Yet the administration did not immediately take measures to prevent flows across the Straits of Florida and touted widespread demand by Cubans to leave as a sign of the revolution's failures.[17] In the early days of the crisis, the National Security Council argued that the U.S. government should stop the boatlift. The State Department warned on April 23 that anyone traveling illegally to Cuba to pick up relatives was subject to felony prosecution and up to five years in prison, civil fines, and forfeiture of the vessel. The White House vacillated between calling for Cuban Americans to "respect the law and avoid these dangerous and illegal boat passages" on April 27 and ambiguously pledging on May 5, "We'll continue to provide an open heart and open arms to the refugees." The Customs Service initially seized three commercial vessels arriving in Key West with visa-less Cubans and served captains of such vessels with the government's intent to fine them $1,000 per passenger. However, by April 20, seizures of boats had been suspended based on negative reactions from Cuban Americans involved in the boatlift and fears that returning boats would simply unload their passengers at other locations in Florida that would be difficult to police.

Amid conflicting signals about whether Cubans were to be embraced or repelled, the Coast Guard reverted to its search-and-rescue mandate. One of the first two civilian boats that reached Mariel broke down on the way back to Florida and was towed to Key West with its passengers by a Coast Guard cutter. At night, Coast Guard ships created a corridor between Mariel and Key West by using their flashing blue lights to guide boats safely north. The Coast Guard assisted 363 vessels in the first week alone and was credited with saving hundreds of lives at a time when twenty-seven people died at sea.[18]

On May 6, 1980, INS Acting Commissioner David Crosland sent a memorandum to the Office of Legal Counsel at the Department of Justice arguing that a foreigner apprehended within U.S. territorial waters who has not landed "does not appear to have a right to apply for asylum" under the terms of the 1980 Refugee Act and could be towed to a third country where he or she would not face persecution.[19] However, the White House announced that arriving Cubans would be considered asylum seekers. A new "Cuban-Haitian Entrants" temporary status was created the following month for undocumented Cubans who had arrived between April 19 and June 19 and Haitians who had arrived before June 19. At the same time, Carter announced a new plan to stop the boats. The Treasury Department amended the Cuban Assets Control regulations to prohibit the transportation of Cuban nationals without visas and banned the kinds of financial transactions that had been taking place in the port of Mariel between U.S.-based vessel owners and Cuban authorities.

The day after Carter announced his plan, Customs officers seized seventy-five boats. The Coast Guard issued 1,600 citations for infractions of maritime safety law. It issued hourly marine broadcasts warning vessels not to travel to Cuba or return with Cuban nationals. Small Coast Guard boats watched over the harbor at Key West. Two large cutters supported by helicopters patrolled the Straits, and the navy began to support the Coast Guard for the first time. In practice, interceptions were limited to boats southbound for Mariel. Boats headed back north to Florida were allowed to pass.[20] "We are unwilling to risk the death of those 100 to 200 people at sea daily," Attorney General Benjamin Civiletti told the Senate Judiciary Committee on September 19, 1980. "The judgment of the Navy and the Coast Guard is that an attempt to return at sea a boat . . . does great risk to their safety."[21]

During the summer of 1980, several organizations attempted to use large ships capable of carrying hundreds of people in a single trip. The use of large ships prompted stricter control measures. The U.S. government worked with authorities in Panama and the Cayman Islands to strip the registry of any commercial ship attempting to transport Cubans to the United States. Externalization of U.S. borders thus took place both behind the scenes as well as through highly visible actions by the U.S. military. Yet definitive measures to stop even large commercial ships were not taken when they had passengers in medical distress on board. When humanitarian and enforcement interest collided during the Mariel saga, humanitarianism prevailed.

Washington's efforts to end the Mariel boatlift were ineffectual. It was not until the Cuban government closed the port on September 25 that the flow stopped overnight. The CIA concluded that Castro had become worried that the departures were creating too much political damage to Carter's re-election effort and that a loss to anti-communist hardliner Ronald Reagan would harm Cuba's interests. The size of the flow also created domestic turmoil in Cuba and hurt Cuba's reputation by showing the world how many citizens wanted to leave. Castro retaliated against some of those who registered to leave, but who were not able to get out before the door closed, by taking away ration cards, housing, and education benefits for their children—leading some to survive on charity. The CIA estimated that a further million would have left the island if given the chance and that further opportunities would arise. "The Mariel experience has taught Castro how sensitive and vulnerable Washington is to a massive, uncontrolled influx of refugees," the agency concluded, "and he can be counted on to resume the exodus—or simply threaten to do so whenever he believes it politically useful."[22] Castro's finger was firmly on the buttons of the remote.

Selecting Refugees

The bipartisan U.S. consensus that Cubans should be allowed into the United States had begun to break down in the 1970s. Some opponents of preferential treatment argued that the exodus of opposition figures and discontented citizens in Cuba was an escape valve that eased political pressure on the communist government. Others argued that many Cubans were leaving for economic rather than political reasons and thus did not deserve protection. The specific features of the Mariel boatlift also generated a negative reaction among the U.S. public. The inflows were large and sudden. Around 125,000 Cubans and 25,000 Haitians arrived in just five months. The social characteristics of a substantial minority of those who entered through the boatlift were distinct from previous waves. New arrivals were more likely to be black than the predominantly white flows of the 1960s and were more likely to be met with racist hostility.[23] The CIA estimated that about a third of the Mariel arrivals had been convicted of crimes in Cuba.[24] In an effort to rid the island of undesirables and tarnish all exiles as "common criminals, lumpen, and other anti-social elements," Castro had offered prisoners the choice of staying in prison or leaving for the United States. For every family member allowed to leave on a boat from Mariel, the Cuban government designated four other passengers that the captain had to accept as a condition of departure.[25] A CIA report described Castro's policy as using the United States as a "dumping ground" for those disaffected with his revolution and an effort to force the United State to negotiate a new bilateral relationship.[26]

Washington's approach toward irregular Cuban migration became openly restrictionist for the first time in the wake of the Mariel boatlift and the strong backlash in Florida. In July 1981, the State Department announced that boats carrying Cubans and Haitians interdicted on the high seas would be turned back to their countries of origin.[27] Less than a year after Attorney General Civiletti had testified that returns at sea were too dangerous, enforcement would now trump humanitarianism. The major goal became to wrest control and selection from Castro's hands. The foreign policy price for the shift was that Cuban refugees became a less potent symbol in the Cold War propaganda wars to point out the deficiencies of the revolution and the allure of the West.

Havana's refusal to readmit the Mariel "excludables"—those rejected by U.S. authorities because of their serious criminal records—posed a dilemma. "Any attempt to return undesirables covertly to Cuba would—if detected in advance—be met with force by Cuba's military establishment," predicted a CIA report. "Havana would have a propaganda field day if there were, for example, confrontations on the high seas or incidents that resulted in loss of life."[28] The CIA drew up a list of options. They ranged from internationalizing the issue through the UN Security Council, freezing Cuban assets in the United States, restricting the travel of Cuban diplomats in the United States, bribing the Cuban government through schemes such as sending "a tractor for each prisoner 'resettled' in Cuba," and admitting prescreened, legal Cuban refugees into the United States in exchange for Cuba accepting the return of the excludables.[29] The Reagan administration picked the last option.

Cuban and U.S. authorities signed a new migration accord in December 1984 that would annually provide a maximum of 20,000 preference immigrant visas to Cubans screened by U.S. officers in Havana, allow political prisoners and their families into the United States, and return the 2,746 excludables from the Mariel boatlift. With the exception of the political prisoners, Cubans were no longer to be treated as refugees, but rather as regular immigrants.[30] The move was consistent with the 1980 Refugee Act, which had removed fleeing from communist countries as the central criterion for establishing refugee status. Defining Cubans as migrants, rather than refugees, served the Cuban government's interest in avoiding the appearance that Cubans were leaving because they were politically dissatisfied. Both sides wanted to avoid mass irregular crossings.[31]

The 1984 migration agreement collapsed in May 1985 when it became linked to a dispute over Washington's anti-communist radio broadcasts to the island. A U.S. intelligence report in 1982 had predicted that if "Radio

Marti causes significant discontent in Cuba, Castro could threaten another mass refugee exodus to punish the U.S."[32] The U.S. government accused the Cuban government of "facilitating illegal migration to the United States" and refused, with narrow exceptions, to issue exit visas to Cubans. A provision to suspend entry into the United States of Cuban nationals traveling from third countries, unless they were immediate relatives of U.S. citizens, in effect turned the rest of the planet into a buffer zone.[33] The bilateral migration agreement was revived in November 1987, but Cubans continued to trickle into Florida, mostly on rafts, and were paroled into the United States.[34] Between 1987 and 1994, 13,275 unauthorized Cubans arrived.[35] Washington's ability to control the flows continued to be limited by Havana's lack of cooperation in limiting exit and accepting readmission, combined with the willingness of many Cubans to risk their lives at sea.

The 1994 Balsero Crisis

The implosion of the Soviet Union, Cuba's patron during the Cold War, unleashed a serious economic and political crisis for Cuba in the early 1990s. By 1994, increasing numbers of rafters (balseros) took to the sea. Others hijacked boats. Dozens entered embassy compounds and diplomatic residences seeking political asylum. Riots broke out in Havana. Castro blamed Washington for promoting illegal migration and squeezing the Cuban economy through its boycott. On August 12, he ordered police to allow the departure of balseros, in open violation of Cuban law regulating exit, and called on Cubans in Miami to come pick up their relatives as they had during the Mariel boatlift. "We cannot continue to act as border guards for the United States," he announced in a televised address.[36] The number of balseros rescued at sea by the U.S. Coast Guard surged to 21,300 in August.

Under pressure from Floridian officials to stop the politically unpopular flows, Attorney General Janet Reno announced the administration would "demagnetize" the United States by denying entry to the balseros.[37] The new policy toward Cubans followed the model applied to intercepted Haitians. Clinton announced that Cubans rescued at sea would be indefinitely detained at the U.S. naval base at Guantanamo while the United States negotiated with third countries for their resettlement. Americans who tried to pick up Cubans would be prosecuted and their vessels seized. "The Cuban government will not succeed in any attempt to dictate American immigration policy," Clinton said. He referred to the targets of the policy as "illegal Refugees from Cuba." This was a curious term to use in a formal policy announcement, given that according to Article 31 of the UN Refugee Convention, legal status upon arrival is not to be taken into account for the purposes of refugee status determination.[38] Over the course of Operation Able Vigil in 1994, the Coast Guard rescued/interdicted more than 30,000 Cubans.[39] After Guantanamo filled to capacity, the U.S. military transported 8,600 people to U.S. bases in Panama. The Coast Guard and Department of Defense spent nearly half a billion dollars interdicting and housing Cubans on bases in the Caribbean between August 1994 and the end of 1995.[40]

Both the Cuban and U.S. governments quickly concluded that the tumultuous spectacle of the balseros and the interdiction campaign was against their interests. On September 9, 1994, they reached a migration accord framed as a way to preserve safety at sea and prevent "alien smuggling." Washington pledged to continue the policy in effect since August 19 that "migrants rescued at sea attempting to enter the United States will not be permitted to enter the United States, but instead will be taken to safe haven facilities outside the United States." The U.S. side noted that it had "discontinued its practice of granting parole to all Cuban migrants who reach U.S. territory in irregular ways." The statements subtly maintained U.S. discretion to allow in selected asylum seekers. In a remarkable about-face from Castro's declaration that Cuban officials would not be the border guards of the United States, Havana pledged to "take effective measures in every way it possibly can to prevent unsafe departures using mainly persuasive methods." Both countries agreed to cooperate on anti-smuggling measures and to prosecute those who used violence to leave the island.[41] Most importantly from the perspective of enabling remote control, Havana agreed to accept the return of Cubans intercepted at sea. In a subsequent agreement in May 1995, the Cuban government agreed not to punish anyone who had sought to leave legally or illegally and to allow U.S. diplomats to monitor the treatment of returnees. The readmission agreement was the cornerstone of an effective U.S. interception policy.

In return for Cuba's help cracking down on irregular flows, Washington agreed to admit an annual minimum of 20,000 Cuban immigrants selected by lottery, in addition to sponsored relatives of U.S. citizens. The guarantees for Cubans were unique in U.S. immigration policy, as were the details of a "P-2" in-country refugee processing program. Eligibility for P-2 visas was restricted to Cubans who were former political prisoners, members of persecuted religious minorities, human rights activists, forced laborers from the 1965 to 1968 period, persons deprived of their professional credentials or subjected to other disproportionately harsh or discriminatory treatment resulting from their perceived or actual political or religious beliefs, and persons who experienced or feared harm because of their relationship to someone who fell under one of the preceding categories. More than 44,000 P-2 visas were approved between 1995 and 2008. Most refugee admissions from Latin America and the Caribbean have come through the P-2 program in Cuba.[42]

Cables to Washington from the U.S. Interests Section (USINT) in Havana, which functioned in lieu of an embassy until the reestablishment of diplomatic relations in 2015, relayed how officers from the section promoted the lottery and political refugee program to repatriates at the docks in Cuba:

> USINT officer transferred 12 Cubans from the U.S. Coast Guard cutter *Knight Island* to Cuban authorities on November 14 without incident. The cutter docked in the Cuban port of Cabanas at approximately 10:00 am local time to transfer the migrant. USINT officer briefed the returnees and provided standard information packets on legal immigration methods. Officer advised the returnees that USINT officers would attempt to contact them in the next several months to assess their well being, including visiting some Havana-based returnees in their homes. Returnees were also advised that they could meet with a U.S. official at the Refugee Annex Fridays 10 am to discuss specific claims of harm, including retaliatory acts such as being unjustly dismissed from one's job, being frequently detained by police, or being the target of public acts of repudiation.[43]

These policies allowed the U.S. government to control irregular migration from Cuba while providing alternative legal pathways to dissidents. The logic of the policy contained inherent tensions and could not be easily reproduced in other contexts. In-country processing only makes sense if a government that is persecuting its citizens allows them to leave and does not further persecute them for attempting to leave.

Guantanamo

One of the major U.S. techniques for controlling the moat is using the U.S. naval base at Guantanamo Bay as a barbican for offshore detention and processing asylum seekers. Washington leased the base in 1903 and negotiated an indefinite extension in 1934 that can only be broken by mutual agreement or if the United States abandons the site. According to the terms of the lease,

> While on the one hand the United States recognizes the continuance of the ultimate sovereignty of the Republic of Cuba over the [leased] areas of land and

water, on the other hand the Republic of Cuba consents that during the period of the occupation by the United States of said areas under the terms of this agreement the United States shall exercise complete jurisdiction and control over and within said areas.[44]

The base was a backdoor to the United States after the revolution. Around 3,200 Cuban "fence jumpers" entered between 1964 and 1973, but after the Cuban government installed barbed wire, dug a mine field, and deployed naval patrols, only twenty-nine Cubans succeeded entering the base in 1974.[45] The fence jumpers were flown to the United States and granted permission to remain.[46] The Clinton administration closed the back door in 1994 when it announced that Cubans held at Guantanamo and Howard Air Force base in Panama would not be allowed to apply for asylum as long as they were held at the bases. Cubans held at the bases could choose to repatriate, but the Cuban government refused to readmit all of them, and many refused to return.

The U.S. government has intermittently screened intercepted Haitians at Guantanamo since at least 1977.[47] The site was chosen not because it was geographically convenient, but because its liminal territorial status could be manipulated to prevent asylum seekers from accessing their full rights. As Sen. Robert McLory (R-IL) told a congressional hearing in 1981 following an influx of Cubans and Haitians, "the processing and the screening should be done before any of these refugees reach our shores. Once they have reached our shores the problem becomes extremely difficult as far as repatriation or deportation."[48]

Until 1991, U.S. officials and courts had considered U.S. constitutional rights to apply to anyone on the base.[49] Under the asylum-processing scheme, however, refugee status decisions at Guantanamo could not be appealed, and applicants typically did not have access to a lawyer.[50] In October 1994, Cuban Americans' rights organizations and some Cuban nationals being held at Guantanamo filed a class-action suit in a federal district court asking for an injunction that would prevent the government from denying the rights of the detainees and their lawyers to communicate with each other. While a district court agreed that Guantanamo Bay was a "United States territory," and thus the detainees had rights under the U.S. constitution, the Eleventh Circuit appeals court overturned the district decision. "We disagree that 'control and jurisdiction' is equivalent to sovereignty," the Eleventh Circuit ruled.[51] As a result, "these migrants are without legal rights that are cognizable in the courts of the United States."

Finding third countries willing to take the thousands of Cubans in the offshore processing centers proved impossible. Panama rejected asylum requests from Cubans detained at Howard Air Force Base. Rioting broke out on the base in December and was squelched by U.S. troops. The U.S. government eventually transported the Cuban detainees back to Guantanamo, having spent $170 million on the Panama detour.[52] Cuban and U.S. officials announced an agreement on the fate of the 33,000 Cubans encamped at Guantanamo in May 1995.[53] They would be eligible for "humanitarian parole" into the United States, unless they were ineligible for admission under the Immigration and Naturalization Act, in which case they would be repatriated. Since then, when the U.S. government decides that individual Cubans held at Guantanamo have legitimate protection concerns, it tries to resettle them in third countries. The process is slow and typically takes place in diplomatic negotiations behind the scenes. A confidential cable from the U.S. embassy in Panama City to Washington about the effort to resettle two Cubans from Guantanamo explained:

> The acceptance of any refugees—particularly Cuban refugees—is an extremely sensitive matter for Panama, a country that across administrations has posited its foreign policy on sustaining friendly relations with all who seek friendly relations with it, including Cuba. The Torrijos Administration does not wish to draw the ire of the Cuban regime for accepting these migrants. It is for this reason that the GOP [Government of Panama] is highly appreciative of the discrete manner in which these cases have been handled.[54]

Of those who were interdicted between May 1995 and July 2003, about 170 successfully claimed asylum and were resettled in eleven different countries, including Australia, Spain, Nicaragua, and Venezuela.[55] Of the 100 individuals detained at Guantanamo from 2009 to 2014 whom the U.S. government concluded had protection needs, only five were admitted or paroled into the U.S. mainland. The rest were resettled in Latin America, Europe, Canada, or Australia.[56] As of 2009, Guantanamo housed twenty to forty migrant detainees at any one time in addition to the more famous detainees from the "war on terror."[57]

Guantanamo is central to Washington's contingency planning for a massive interdiction campaign called Operation Vigilant Sentry. The Coast Guard patch for the operation features a bald eagle sweeping down from the north with its talons hanging between the Caribbean islands and the United States. The Coast Guard is responsible for preventing vessels from departing from the United States en route to Caribbean countries "for the purpose of illegally transporting migrants," which is clearly an effort to avoid a repeat of the Mariel boatlift carried out by Florida-based Cuban-Americans. The Coast Guard is also in charge of migrant interception operations and will "deliver migrants ashore to [as yet undesignated] locations in the event non-domestic migrant processing centers are unavailable or at their capacity." The U.S. Army provides mass detention facilities on Guantanamo.[58] The plan contemplates at least perfunctory fulfillment of non-refoulement obligations in international waters. Under the plan, the Coast Guard supports shipboard screening carried out by Department of Homeland Security (DHS) agents aboard their cutters and takes those who pass an initial screening to offshore processing centers. DHS conducts secondary screening at those centers and initial "credible fear" interviews when shipboard screening is suspended.[59] However, Guantanamo has hypothetical vulnerabilities. During the Mariel boatlift, for instance, the CIA worried that Castro might encourage a large refugee influx at the base.[60] The utility of the barbican still relies on the Cuban government's assistance in sealing it off from the rest of Cuba.

Wet Foot, Dry Foot

Under the wet foot, dry foot policy from the mid-1990s to 2017, most Cubans intercepted at sea were returned to Cuba, while only those who reached dry land were allowed into the United States. The policy only applied to Cubans. The "wet foot" part of the policy was derived from the 1994 and 1995 bilateral agreements. When the U.S. Coast Guard interdicted Cubans at sea, they were informed of their right to a credible-fear interview and given information about alternative ways of entering the United States. A protection screening officer read a Spanish translation of the following passage:

> You are being taken back to Cuba. You will not be taken to the United States. U.S. Government officials in Havana will meet the ship and will provide information to you if you wish to apply to go to the United States through established migration programs. The government of Cuba has provided a commitment to the United States that you will suffer no adverse consequence of reprisals of any sort for illegal departure or for making applications for legal migration to the United States at the US Interests Section. Only those people who are approved by the US Interests Section in Havana can be assured of entry to the United States. (I) or a (U.S. Government official) will be available to speak with you if you have any concerns about returning to Cuba. This will be done in a completely confidential setting and no information regarding your

concern will be given to the Cuban authorities. If you would like to speak with (me) or (this officer) please let me (or this officer) know.[61]

When intercepted Cubans asked for an interview, and the protection screening officer decided they had a credible fear of persecution or torture, the Coast Guard transferred them to Guantanamo for further screening.[62] Only 425 of those intercepted between 1996 and 2014 were transferred to Guantanamo for a full refugee status determination process.[63] The vast majority of intercepted Cubans were repatriated under the wet foot provisions.

Although the 1994 bilateral agreement stipulated that the U.S. government would not allow automatic entry to Cubans arriving by sea, it left an opening for Washington to continue the unilateral dry foot policy that the Cuban government criticized for encouraging illegal migration.[64] In his August 19, 1994, press conference, Clinton stated that Cubans who made it to the United States would "not simply be released into the population at large" and their cases would be reviewed "in light of the applicable law, including the Cuban Adjustment Act."[65] By January 1995, Cubans who reached U.S. territory were temporarily detained and then quietly paroled into the country with strong support from the Cuban-American community in South Florida.[66] Doris Meissner, the INS commissioner, issued a memorandum in 1999 clarifying that Cubans arriving at "other than a designated port-of-entry" would be considered eligible for adjustment of their status under the 1966 Cuban Adjustment Act, provided that they met its other provisions. The 1999 memo formalized the dry foot part of the wet foot, dry foot policy.[67] Between 1995 and 2004, the Coast Guard intercepted 8,675 Cubans at sea and 10,314 reached land.[68]

Word of a wet foot, dry foot policy quickly spread. Between 1998 and 1999, visa-less Cubans stopped trying to elude the authorities as soon as they reached the beach.[69] Those who had nearly reached the shore lunged for it. On June 30, 1999, a Coast Guard aircraft spotted six Cuban men in a wooden rowboat 400 meters from Surfside Beach in the Miami area. After using a water cannon to sink the rowboat, four Coast Guard vessels circled the men to keep them from swimming ashore. A Coast Guardsman doused a swimmer in the face with pepper spray. Eventually, four of the migrants were captured and hauled aboard a Coast Guard vessel. Two others managed to make it ashore as some fifty bystanders cheered them on.[70] The incident was broadcast live on local television and incited angry protests in Miami at the treatment of the men in the water.[71] Two days later, the INS released all six Cubans and paroled them into the United States. One of the men, Carlos Mirabal Fumero, said federal officials confirmed their release was triggered by political pressure from protestors.[72] The wet foot policy evidently was subject to discretion. Had the same incident taken place outside the view of the public on the high seas, the men almost surely would have been forcibly returned to Cuba.

An even greater controversy broke out in November when a five-year-old Cuban boy, Elián González, was found floating in an inner tube five kilometers off the coast of Ft. Lauderdale after his mother drowned. As in other cases of medical emergency, the Coast Guard took Elián to a hospital in Florida. Elián became the center of a bitter international custody battle between his maternal relatives in Florida, who were backed by many in the Cuban-American community in Miami, and his biological father, who was supported by the Cuban government in demanding Elián's return. In the predawn hours of April 22, 2000, armed federal agents stormed the house in Miami where Elián was staying. A federal appeals court upheld the executive's authority to deny Elián an asylum hearing, and on June 28, he was repatriated to be reunited with his father.[73] Like the wet foot policy, the dry foot policy was subject to discretion.

Establishing where dry land begins turned out to be a controversial exercise in hyper-territoriality. According to the Coast Guard's Maritime Law Enforcement Manual:

> Migrants interdicted in U.S. internal waters, U.S. territorial sea or onboard a vessel moored to a U.S. pier are not considered to have entered the U.S. Migrants located on pilings, low-tide elevations or aids to navigation are not considered to have come ashore in the U.S. Migrants who reach bridges, piers, or other structures currently and permanently connected to dry land have not, as a matter of law, reached dry land; however, they are generally treated as if they had reached dry land in order to have a workable, operational standard from a policy perspective.[74]

These standards were put to the test on January 5, 2006, when the Coast Guard found fifteen Cuban nationals on the abandoned Old Seven Mile Bridge in the Florida Keys.[75] The Coast Guard held the Cubans on a vessel offshore for five days while legal experts debated whether the group should be forcibly repatriated or paroled into the United States. The section of bridge was indisputably in U.S. territory. The main question was whether the section of the abandoned bridge counted as U.S. dry land. If it did, then the Cubans could stay. The Coast Guard's legal office and Immigration and Customs Enforcement decided that the section of old bridge did not constitute dry land because it had been severed from the rest of the bridge and it was impossible to walk to the nearest island.[76] The Coast Guard announced the Cubans were therefore "feet-wet" and returned them to Cuba on January 9.[77]

Three days later, U.S. District Judge Federico Moreno suggested in court that the U.S. government might have erred in forcing their repatriation. Calling the abandoned bridge "as American as apple pie," the judge said the average person would call the line between the bridge and U.S. soil "a ridiculous distinction."[78] On February 28, Judge Moreno ruled that the Old Seven Mile Bridge was "part of the U.S. despite its present lack of use," and therefore, "the Coast Guard's decision to remove those Cuban refugees back to Cuba was not a reasonable interpretation of present executive policy."[79] While expressing sympathy for the Coast Guard's difficulty in making split-second decisions at sea, Moreno stated it "acted unreasonably" when it repatriated the fifteen Cubans, and that "those Cuban refugees who reached American soil in early January 2006 were removed to Cuba illegally."[80] Moreno noted that "even the Coast Guard's own website states, 'If [migrants] touch U.S. soil, bridges, piers, or rocks, they are subject to U.S. Immigration processes for removal'" rather than immediate repatriation or exclusion. The judge ordered the federal government to "use their best efforts" to give the Cubans "the due process rights to which they were entitled when they landed on the Old Seven Mile Bridge."[81] As of December 2006, the U.S. government had issued visas to fourteen of the fifteen Cubans, but the Cuban government had not granted them exit permits.[82] Cuban officials told members of the original group that they would not be permitted to leave Cuba for another four years because of the publicity around their case. By the end of the year, six out of the original fifteen had reached Florida in a make-shift boat and were paroled into the United States.

On May 20, 2016, a group of twenty-four Cubans being pursued by the Coast Guard jumped off their boat in the waters of the Florida Keys. All but three swam to the American Shoal Lighthouse eleven kilometers south of Sugarloaf Key. The Coast Guard detained them, and after its legal team decided that they were in a "wet-foot situation" due to the location of the lighthouse, transferred them to a cutter. Meanwhile, several of the Cuban men and their family members in the United States, aided by a Cuban-American advocacy organization, filed an injunction seeking a declaration that they had reached dry land and should be allowed into the United States. Everyone agreed that the lighthouse was in U.S. territory. Once again, a federal judge decided what constitutes dry land.[83] The lighthouse is constructed on a submerged reef covered by 1.3 meters of water at low tide. The U.S. government maintained that the lighthouse was not dry land, because it is part of the "pilings, low-tide elevations or aids to navigation" exempted by the Coast

Guard's Maritime Law Enforcement Manual. Judge Darrin Gayles accepted the government's position. "Because the Migrant Plaintiffs here would necessarily require transportation from the Lighthouse to the mainland in order to survive, landing on the Lighthouse is essentially no different than having been interdicted at sea," he wrote. Because the Cuban men had not legally "entered" the United States, he ruled that they did not have constitutional rights either.[84] Immigration authorities conducted "manifestation of fear" interviews and concluded that twenty had "credible fears of persecution" and were sent to Guantanamo for further screening. The remaining four were returned to Cuba. In August 2017, seventeen of the Cuban refugees were resettled in Australia, apparently as part of an opaque U.S.-Australia swap of refugees discussed in chapter 10.[85]

The re-establishment of diplomatic relations between Cuba and the United States in 2015 was the precursor to the end of the dry foot policy in January 2017 during the final days of the Obama administration.[86] As relations normalized, there was less incentive for Washington to try to humiliate

FIGURE 6.1 A group of Cuban nationals pursued by the U.S. Coast Guard stand atop the American Shoal Lighthouse off Sugarloaf Key in the Florida Keys on May 20, 2016. A federal judge ruled that although the lighthouse was in U.S. territorial waters, it did not constitute "dry land" for the purposes of the wet foot, dry foot policy that until 2017 allowed most Cubans who reached U.S. dry land to enter the United States. Photo by WSVN-TV via AP.

Havana by accepting those who reached dry land. The Trump administration began deporting Cubans from the U.S. mainland and continued to repatriate Cubans intercepted at sea. In the first four months after the dry foot policy ended, the Coast Guard repatriated 113 Cubans intercepted at sea, a decrease from 939 during the same period in 2016. It is not clear if the Coast Guard conducted asylum screenings, but the hyper-territorial debates about just where dry land began were over.[87]

"A Springboard to Enter the U.S."

One unintended consequence of the wet foot, dry foot policy until 2017 was to redirect irregular flows from Cuba to the United States via third countries. Cubans quietly arriving at the U.S. border were quickly paroled into the country. No images of rafts or hyperbolic talk of invasion generated loud public calls for restriction. Consequently, U.S. authorities applied only light and uneven pressure on Mexico to act as a buffer against Cubans and sometimes even encouraged the back door to remain open. As early as the mid-1990s, the director of the Department for Asylum and Refugees in the Mexican Interior Ministry said that Mexico City was complying with a U.S. State Department request to permit unauthorized Cubans apprehended in Mexico to remain there for up to six months or until they could continue their travel to the United States.[88] At the same time, the U.S. Border Patrol grew increasingly concerned with Cuban arrivals at the border with Mexico—highlighting the diverging interests regarding Cubans among the different agencies of the U.S. government.[89]

By 2005, more Cubans without a U.S. visa reached the United States through Mexico than arrived by sea. The distance between Cuba and the Yucatán Peninsula is similar to the distance between Cuba and Florida. The minimal Mexican navy presence in the Yucatán Channel made the route through Mexico much easier. Mexican fishermen charged between USD$8,000 and USD$15,000 per passenger.[90] Many of the Mexican smugglers were caught and imprisoned in Cuba. They were soon replaced by Florida-based smugglers using faster boats.[91] In 2007, fifty-six percent of the 20,697 Cubans attempting to reach the United States without visas passed through Mexico.[92] The increased flows led Washington to quietly apply pressure on Mexico City to reduce the numbers without refouling dissidents. "As Mexico looks to discourage Cubans from using it as a bridge to enter the U.S. in the future, we will need to stress the importance we attach to its exercising due diligence not to return detainees who risk facing political persecution," the embassy in Mexico City cabled Washington.[93] The U.S. Coast Guard and Mexican navy discretely coordinated their planning to manage a mass outflow from Cuba. Around the same time, U.S. diplomats suggested they would ask Central American governments to prevent the transit of unauthorized Cubans.[94]

According to a 2008 U.S. diplomatic cable, "Mexico regards Cubans using its country as a springboard to enter the U.S. as an irritant in its relations with the U.S. and Cuba."[95] Under an informal 2005 agreement that created Mexico's own version of a wet foot, dry foot policy, Cubans interdicted at sea were detained up to three months while the government sought their repatriation.[96] If the Cuban government refused to accept the return of the detained migrants, they were fined, ordered to leave Mexico within ninety days, and released inside Mexico. By contrast, Cubans arriving by land from Central America were fined and given a departure order without begin detained. In January 2008, the Mexican government began detaining all Cubans for fifteen days and seeking their repatriation except for the "extremely rare instances" when they asked for, and were granted, asylum in Mexico. Most of the released Cubans made their way to the U.S. border where they were admitted under the U.S. dry foot policy.[97] A Mexican immigration official explained to a researcher, "All Cubans can stay here, but no one else can. We keep our door closed to everyone else, but open it to the Cubans. This is strange, is it not? What is so special about Cuba? This is the migratory policy of the United States." He went on to lament, "We are in the middle. Everything is done for the United States. We are their border."[98]

President Felipe Calderón pursued an improved relationship with Cuba across a range of issues, from trade to migration, and negotiated a bilateral memorandum of understanding in November 2008.[99] The agreement set out procedures for deportation and cooperation between the Mexican navy and Cuban border guards to combat "illegal migration, illegal trafficking, commerce, and associated crimes."[100] Havana agreed to accept the repatriation of most categories of unauthorized Cubans in Mexico but refused to accept those who posed a danger to Cuba.[101] According to a confidential State Department analysis,

> Mexico posits its newly embraced policy on Cuban repatriation as an effort to stem the flow of Cubans through Mexico in large measure to appease U.S. concerns about Cuban migration and make the case it is being responsive. Mexico is serious about reaching an agreement that produces a legal frame- work for dealing with a potential mass migration of Cubans. In the meantime, however, as Mexico regards Cuban migration to the U.S. through Mexico as

more a U.S. problem, it is unlikely it will sacrifice its desire for improved relations with Cuba by pressing Havana to repatriate significantly greater numbers of migrants.[102]

Mexico remained an ineffective buffer for Cubans heading to the United States during most of the wet foot, dry foot policy. Only 39% of detentions of Cubans led to deportations in 2009, falling to 4.1% in 2015.[103] In 2010, more than 5,500 Cubans arrived at southwestern points of entry, increasing to more than 56,000 in 2016.[104]

Havana eased exit visa restrictions with a new policy that went into effect in 2013. A new route emerged in which Cubans flew to Ecuador, which had eliminated its visa requirements, and then traveled through Colombia, Central America, and Mexico to reach the U.S. border.[105] With the end of the dry foot policy in January 2017, Cubans who had previously walked across the border became bottled up in Mexico. In April 2017, only 191 "inadmissible" Cubans arrived at a U.S. land border.[106] The Cuban government also continued to restrict irregular flows to the United States through its requirement that departing citizens prove they had a visa to enter the destination.[107] The drawbridge was raised and the gates closed as the U.S. government combined its strategies of caging, patrolling the moat, and strengthening control of buffer countries.

Conclusion

The U.S. Coast Guard patrols the moat between Florida and its Caribbean neighbors. Yet the treatment of people seeking to enter has differed dramatically depending on their island of origin. Policies toward Haitians and the small numbers of other nationals have been consistently restrictive. Policies toward Cubans have oscillated between periods of welcome and restriction embedded in an overall trajectory of restriction. The biggest difference between the treatment of Haitian and Cubans was that only Cubans seeking protection were granted realistic legal paths to enter the United States, such as the visa waivers for air passengers in the 1960s, the 1966 Cuban Adjustment Act that allowed most Cubans who reached the United States to stay, relaxation of enforcement of immigration laws around episodes such as the 1965 Camarioca and 1980 Mariel boatlifts, the Freedom Flights in the late 1960s and early 1970s, more robust asylum screening on the high seas, and various in-country processing programs for dissidents and other programs guaranteeing slots in the immigration stream. By January 2017, these advantages had fallen away except for the guaranteed minimum of 20,000 immigrant visas and the in-country refugee P-2 visa program. Ironically, the easing of hostilities between Washington and Havana *raised* the drawbridge over the moat.

The Cuban case challenges the conceptualization of "remote control." Fidel Castro, rather than a succession of U.S. presidents from Kennedy through Clinton, controlled the remote as much as they did. Cycles of antagonistic cooperation when it served the perceived interests of each government were punctuated by periods of crisis prompted by the Cuban government's decisions to stop serving as the de facto border guards of the United States. That is not to say that Castro simply acted as he pleased, given the enormous political and economic pressures that shaped his policies, and U.S. preferences that created opportunities for Cubans. However, the caging and out-migration policies of Cuba strongly shaped U.S. options. Cooperation was consistently higher after the mid-1990s. The contrast with the earlier period shows just how dependent the destination state's interception programs are on the willingness of the origin state to admit repatriates and to discourage departures. Remote control is relational, rather than simply imposed. Its efficacy is highly dependent on collaboration among governments.

Most importantly, the history of U.S. policy toward Cubans shows what did not happen. Even after more than a million Cubans fled to the United States, including 125,000 who arrived by sea without documentation during the five months of the Mariel boatlift, government services were not overwhelmed in the long run. The temporary crunch was concentrated in Miami, and the long-term effect on native-born wages was negligible.[108] As recently as 2016, more than 56,000 Cubans without visas were arriving at the Mexican border and let in without fanfare or a sense of crisis. The favorable treatment of Cubans shows that even tens of thousands of asylum seekers arriving over the course of a few months did not threaten the capacity of the United States to provide sanctuary for those facing persecution at home. The question was, and remains, whether the political will exists to mobilize the resources necessary to distinguish and welcome those who fit the refugee criteria.

| Buffering North America

WHEN TRAVELERS ARRIVE AT a U.S. port of entry, they encounter agents from Customs and Border Protection (CBP). By law, foreigners who ask for asylum must be turned over to another unit within the Department of Homeland Security (DHS) where an asylum officer with specialized training conducts a "credible fear" interview. Advocacy organizations along the border have found many examples of CBP agents summarily expelling people asking for asylum without allowing them to make a claim, sometimes by falsely stating that they require permission from Mexican migration authorities to ask for asylum in the United States. These pushbacks, by definition, are illegal according to both U.S. and international law. Pushbacks are also a direct threat to U.S. constitutional rights of territorial personhood. Related techniques of hyper-territorialization include hiring private security guards to keep asylum seekers from entering the gate marking U.S. territory around its asylum office in San Ysidro, California, and by using officers to physically block the exact borderline on binational bridges. In 2018, a reporter observed CBP agents standing directly on the line on the bridge between the Mexican city of Ciudad Juárez and the U.S. city of El Paso to prevent Central American asylum seekers from stepping on U.S. soil and asking for asylum.[1] Secret pushbacks and patrols right on the line of a 3,145-kilometer border are difficult for the government to sustain, which is why it systematically deploys remote controls instead.

Since Central Americans began fleeing to North America during the civil wars of the 1980s, Washington and Ottawa have tried to contain most of them in Mexico and Central America using the dome techniques discussed in chapter 4. Central America and Mexico buffer the United States, which in turn buffers Canada by preventing most asylum seekers from ever reaching their shared 8,891-kilometer land border. The U.S. government has also propped up client states, paid for refugee camps, and collaborated with migration control agencies thousands of kilometers away to create what one high-ranking State Department official called "a defense in depth."[2] Providing training and equipment, financing deportations, and pushing neighbors to restrict visas are major techniques of remote control. Mexico has weak rights of territorial personhood, so rather than strictly controlling entry across its southern border, its entire territory has become a "vertical frontier" with the United States.

Aggressive U.S. enforcement at the Mexican border traps transit migrants in Mexico and creates an incentive for the Mexican government to deport them. But the unilateral character of U.S. enforcement, and the fact that it targets Mexicans as well as third-country nationals, then impedes the bilateral cooperation that would make Mexico a more effective buffer with countries further south. The essential paradox for Washington's efforts to use Mexico as a buffer derives from the fact that Mexico is a country of both transit and mass emigration. Buffering is linked to a wide range of issues in the bilateral relationship and Mexico's own interests in allowing the kinds of mobility that generate economic growth.

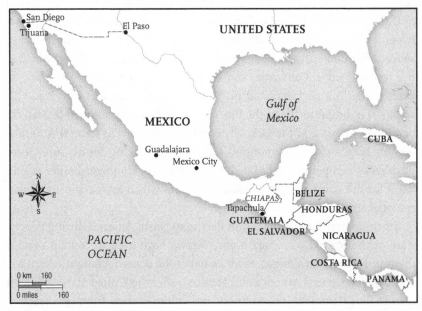

FIGURE 7.1 Mexico and Central America

"Feet People" and "Bus People"

Containment of refugees was a central goal of U.S. foreign policy during the waning years of the Cold War. The U.S. government spent $5 billion from 1984 to 1989 to prop up client states in Guatemala, El Salvador, and Honduras during civil wars that were framed as Cold War proxy fights with the Soviet Union.[3] High-ranking U.S. officials repeatedly justified U.S. intervention as a way to keep potential refugees at bay. President Reagan warned in 1983 that if Democrats blocked his Central American policy, the United States faced "a tidal wave of refugees—and this time they'll be 'feet people' and not 'boat people'—swarming into our country."[4] Using less dehumanizing language, he told a national audience in 1984, "Concerns about the prospect of hundreds of thousands of refugees fleeing communist oppression to seek entry into our country are well founded." A year later Reagan claimed that unless the United States took decisive action, "We face the risk that 100 million people from Panama to our open southern border could come under the control of pro-Soviet regimes and threaten the United States with violence, economic chaos, and a human tidal wave of refugees."[5]

Internal CIA reports initially used more circumspect language but made the same broad point. The CIA estimated in 1981 that small numbers of Nicaraguans fleeing the Sandinista regime might reach the United States via Mexico and that more significant flows would come from El Salvador.[6] Internal documents show concern about refugee flows increasing through the mid-1980s. "Should Central America fall to Communism, experience indicates that a flood of sudden emigrants would pour out of the region," the National Security Council concluded in 1983. "The best estimates indicate that at least 1.5 million and probably 2.5 million would flee. We can avert this tragedy by helping our neighbors resist the Soviet-Cuban assault."[7]

A 1984 CIA report acknowledged that "illegal immigrants" from Central America were refugees:

> Central American refugees will continue to be of direct concern to the United States for more than purely humanitarian reasons. The refugees contribute to political instability in the region and heightened tensions between neighboring countries. Continuing political upheaval may turn today's refugee within Central America into tomorrow's illegal immigrant in the United States.[8]

At the same time as U.S. officials acknowledged that abstract people leaving Central America were refugees, most flesh-and-blood Central Americans who reached the United States were denied asylum and called economic

FIGURE 7.2 The family of Jerónimo Sojuel Sisay, age ten, mourns his death in 1990 at the hands of government troops in Santiago Atitlán, Guatemala. During the civil wars in Central America, the United States spent billions of dollars to prop up client states and to prevent what President Ronald Reagan called a "human tidal wave of refugees" from reaching the United States. Photo by David FitzGerald.

migrants.[9] From 1984 to 1990, the recognition rate was just 2.6% for Salvadorans and 1.8% for Guatemalans. Both groups were nationals of U.S. client states. Nicaraguans, whose country was controlled by the socialist Sandinistas, enjoyed a much higher recognition rate of 26%.[10] Deportations from the United States carried real consequences. Rights groups documented more than 100 murders of Salvadorans deported from the United States in 1981.[11]

Canada was much more likely than the United States to accept Central Americans fleeing right-wing regimes. For example, the Salvadoran asylum grant rate in Canada during the 1980s was 80%. Canadian consulates in the United States began issuing visas in 1981 to Salvadorans who faced deportation and extended the policy to Guatemalans in 1984. The Canadian government also resettled almost 21,000 Central American refugees through the UNHCR and allowed Guatemalans to apply for resettlement while still in Guatemala through a special program. Canada's relatively welcoming stance toward controlled resettlement of Central Americans was a means of promoting its international brand as a beacon of humanitarianism.[12]

As the numbers of Central Americans attempting to enter Canada increased, however, Ottawa tried to shut off access to most asylum seekers by using the United States as a buffer and requiring visas as described in chapter 4. Ten thousand forced migrants, mostly Central Americans, entered Canada between December 1986 and February 1987. The Canadian press dubbed them "the bus people." In February 1987, the Canadian government responded by issuing asylum seekers who arrived at the U.S.-Canadian border a preliminary hearing date, usually many months in the future, and then forcing them to return to the United States to wait. In some cases, U.S. authorities then immediately deported Central Americans to their countries of origin. Others were forced by the Immigration and Naturalization Service (INS) to sign a "voluntary departure" form so that if their case in Canada was denied, the INS could quickly deport them back to Central America. By April, the monthly number of Central Americans arriving at the Canadian border had fallen to 191. The U.S. buffer prevented thousands of people who were likely to be recognized as refugees from accessing Canadian territory, where a refugee status determination process characterized by high levels of judicial autonomy followed Canadian and international norms against refoulement.[13]

Safe Third Country?

Buffering works in both directions but is primarily south to north. Forty-four times as many people passed through the United States to seek refuge in Canada as those who sought refuge in the opposite direction between 1990 and 2004.[14] "We can afford to be a bit smug, but it's not because of anything we're doing right, but because of geography and an aggressive neighbor," a Canadian immigration ministry employee told geographer Alison Mountz.[15]

The United States and Canada buffer each other in the form of a "safe third country agreement" based on European models.[16] In 1988, Canada's Parliament gave the Cabinet the authority to designate a "safe country" list to which asylum seekers could be returned without having their claims heard in Canada. Rights groups effectively pressured the government not to create a list unless it could ensure that those countries met Canadian asylum standards. The list was never made.[17] A stricter 1992 law provided that arrivals from safe third countries could not file an asylum application in Canada and would be returned. A safe third country was defined as a state with a positive human rights record that had signed the Refugee Convention and observed its Article 33 ban on refoulement. An exception was made that allowed people who had only made connecting flights in a safe third country to claim asylum in Canada. The 1992 law was not put into effect for more than a decade because Washington refused to guarantee that asylum seekers returned to the United States under the provision would be given a hearing.[18] For its part, the U.S. Department of Justice released new regulations in 1994 that gave the attorney general discretion to deny asylum to persons who had entered the United States from a third country where they would not face persecution and where they would have access to a full and fair asylum claim "in accordance with a bilateral or multilateral arrangement with the United States."[19]

By late 2002, forty asylum seekers a day were applying at the Lacolle border crossing between New York and Quebec. On January 30, 2003, Canadian border agents began to implement a policy of "direct backs" in a reprise of the 1987 policy directed against Central Americans. Rather than interviewing applicants on the spot, they were given an appointment for a later interview and sent back to the U.S. side.[20] A UNHCR report found that of the 129 direct backs in 2005, approximately 25 were detained by U.S. authorities and 6 were deported back to their countries by the United States before an asylum decision was made in Canada. Based on strong criticism from the UNHCR that direct backs could potentially result in chain refoulement, the Canadian government pledged in 2006 to limit their uses to "extraordinary situations."[21]

The Safe Third Country Agreement whose groundwork was laid in the early 1990s was signed in December 2002 and took effect in 2004. Asylum seekers in Canada or the United States must make a claim in the first of the two countries where they arrived, unless they qualified for an exception. The agreement does not apply to U.S. citizens, those who have family members in Canada, or nationals of a country to which Canada had suspended deportations because of generalized risks in that country. The agreement only applies to individuals who arrive at a land border. It does not apply to arrivals by air or sea or applications made in the Canadian interior.[22]

The Federal Court of Canada struck down the agreement in November 2007 for violating the equality and life, liberty, and security of person provisions of the Canadian Charter of Rights and Freedoms, but the Canadian Federal Court of Appeal reversed the decision in June 2008 and allowed the agreement to stand.[23] More than 80% of the asylum seekers at the land border between 2004 and 2005 were not subject to the agreement because they met one of the exceptions. Still, the number of asylum applications at the Canadian land border side dropped from 8,896 to 4,033. The Canadian government turned back 303 individuals to the U.S. side. The agreement had little effect on claims made at U.S. border crossings with Canada. During the first year of the agreement, sixty-six asylum seekers presented claims at U.S. northern points of entry, up from an annual average of fifty-eight over the previous five years.[24] The Safe Third Country Agreement makes the United States a buffer for Canada much more than it makes Canada a buffer for the United States.

After the Trump administration took office in January 2017, it initiated harsher policies toward asylum seekers, sharply curtailed the in-flow of refugees, banned the admission of several predominantly Muslim nationalities, ended temporary protected status for several nationalities, and consistently deployed a hardline rhetoric against immigrants and refugees. In response, the number of asylum seekers crossing from the United States and apprehended by Canadian authorities between its border posts increased from just under 2,500 in 2016 to more than 20,000 in 2017.[25] Between June and August 2017, an estimated 8,000 Haitian nationals fled the United States to Quebec after the Trump administration signaled it would end temporary protected status for Haitians in January 2018. By circumventing border controls and walking through the woods to present an asylum claim in the Canadian interior, the Haitians were not subject to the agreement. However, the effect of the agreement forced them to enter illegally, which then undermined the public perception of the legitimacy of their claims. At the same time that Canadian refugee advocates called on their government to scrap the agreement because the United States was not a safe third country in practice, Canadian officials in Washington sought to make the agreement more restrictive by removing its exemption for asylum seekers who crossed between legal ports of entry.[26]

Strict U.S. remote controls have kept some potential asylum seekers out of North America altogether, but, in the short run, U.S. policies within its borders pushed more asylum seekers into Canada. The paradox of transit states is that their policies can have countervailing effects. On the one hand, knowledge of buffering can deter some potential migrants from ever attempting to enter the buffer's territory. Repatriations and other expulsions drive migrants further away. On the other hand, migrants already in the buffer country who face hostile policies have an incentive to keep moving to a safer and more welcoming country. Canada's relatively high asylum recognition rate and refugee resettlement rate, like features of Canadian immigration policy that are generous by international standards, are likely derived in part by Canada's geographic isolation and ability to rely on the United States

FIGURE 7.3 An asylum claimant and her daughter cross the border into Canada from the United States on March 17, 2017, near Hemmingford, Quebec. By circumventing border controls to present their claim in the Canadian interior, they were exempt from the Safe Third Country Agreement, under whose terms they would otherwise have been returned to the United States. Photo by Paul Chiasson/ The Canadian Press via AP.

to reduce the numbers of asylum seekers.[27] If Canada is buffered less effectively, its policies may become more hostile and resort to barbican strategies that arguably violate domestic and international law.

The Mexican Buffer

As the sole southern land border with the United States, Mexico is the most important buffer country in the Western Hemisphere. Migrant advocates have long argued that Mexico City does Washington's "dirty work."[28] Yet research on Mexico as a buffer state is highly fragmented and ambiguous. Manuel Ángel Castillo, the leading scholar of Central American migration to and through Mexico, summarizes that while Mexico is a "filter" for Central Americans, "it is difficult to prove the influence of U.S. national security policy on the increase in mechanisms of migration control on Mexico's southern border."[29] Pressure from the U.S. government is a highly sensitive political topic given the long history of U.S. intervention in Mexico and the resulting nationalist backlash. Buffering policies are often secret.

Mexican authorities have regularly denied collaborations with the United States that have been verified by independent researchers.[30] Releases of diplomatic cables through WikiLeaks, budget records, congressional testimony, interviews, and other sources must be pieced together to reveal the extent of remote control policies and to show that the Mexican government deliberately acts as a buffer state.

Standing on the border between Mexico and Guatemala, the idea that Mexico is a buffer for the United States seems risible. The borderline with Guatemala and Belize runs 1,100 kilometers through barely patrolled forests and jungles. At the major crossing point of Ciudad Hidalgo, ferrymen pole travelers across the muddy Suchiate River on inner tube rafts in plain sight of the checkpoint on the bridge. "The migrant crosses without any problem; there is no one watching," admitted a Mexican border official.[31] Unlike in the United States or Europe, Mexican migration enforcement is not concentrated on the border. There is no constitutional tradition of strong rights of territorial personhood. Mexican authorities are not particularly concerned if foreigners touch the Mexican side of the riverbank, because, as shown later in this chapter, the Mexican constitution gives the executive wide latitude to expel foreigners. Hyper-legal debates about what rights apply in particular territories are not part of the Mexican discussion as they are in Australia, Europe, Canada, and the United States.

A Vertical Frontier

Despite the appearance of an open southern border, at least since the 1980s, Mexican authorities have used other techniques to keep migrants away from the United States. The main strategy is to patrol and establish detention centers on transportation routes leading north in a *frontera vertical* across Mexico's entire territory from south to north.[32] Mexico has become a thick buffer for Central Americans, a thin buffer for Cubans during the wet foot, dry foot era as described in chapter 6, and a cactus-like buffer for people from outside the hemisphere that is sharp on the outside but supple on the inside.

The earliest efforts to control movement across the border targeted security threats. Declassified State Department and CIA documents show that in the early stages of the Guatemalan civil war in the 1960s and 1970s, U.S. and Guatemalan officials worried about Mexico's lack of control over its southern border. A 1966 cable from the U.S. embassy in Guatemala City informed the State Department that if need be, the Mexican government would "place surveillance on known and more dangerous subversives and take steps to prevent their approaching [the] border area."[33] In 1972, the Mexican military responded favorably to a request from the Guatemalan government to boost border control during a major Guatemalan military operation in the region. These early security policies were not aimed at refugees.

Until around 1981, the Mexican government did not have a policy toward the small numbers of Central Americans in transit. Relatively weak U.S. controls on the border with Mexico meant that Central Americans could cross into the United States without getting stuck in Mexico. From the Mexican government's perspective, people quickly passing through did not pose a problem.[34] The intensification of the civil wars in the early 1980s propelled the first large movement of Central American refugees. During the first half of 1981, the Mexican government deported thousands of Guatemalans. Officials assumed the rest would not stay long.[35] The Mexican military boosted its forces along the Guatemalan border to interdict Guatemalan guerrillas and to discourage incursions by Guatemalan troops into refugee camps in Mexican territory.[36] Yet the Secretariat of National Defense in 1984 acknowledged its lack of capacity to control new flows of refugees. "It will not be possible to control the more than 800 kilometers of border with Guatemala," an internal report concluded.[37] In addition to its limited capacity, the Mexican government was under pressure from businesses to keep the border open to facilitate commerce and access to Guatemalan agricultural labor.[38]

Pressure from Washington and the growing realization that refugees were not leaving prompted Mexico City to allow the UNHCR to open an office, register refugees, and meet their basic needs in camps in the southern state of Chiapas. Of the 200,000 Guatemalans who fled to Mexico in the 1980s, 46,000 were registered and assisted by the UNHCR in ninety-two camps patrolled by armed Mexican Migration Service agents.[39] Guatemalans who arrived after the first wave had greater difficulty finding refuge. By 1989, only about 20% of Guatemalans in southern Mexico were protected by the UNHCR, leaving around 100,000 to fend for themselves.[40] The situation was even grimmer for Salvadorans. "Anyone who leaves El Salvador at this time deserves the status of refugee," declared the UNHCR representative in Central America in 1981.[41] However, only about 3,500 Salvadorans were allowed into the camps in Mexico.

The arrival of the UNHCR institutionalized the promotion of international rights norms to protect refugees in Mexico. It set benchmarks and provided staff to patrol the boundaries of acceptable national policy. Mexico's foreign ministry was eager to maintain its positive international image as a country with a history of welcoming political exiles.[42] Diplomats used the

UNHCR as a resource to counter pressure from other government agencies for a paramilitary response of mass deportations. The UNHCR was instrumental in consolidating the Mexican Commission for Refugee Assistance (COMAR) and even paid its budget in 1981. Over time, the UNHCR indirectly promoted human rights norms as well by contracting with partner NGOs such as Sin Fronteras and the Casa del Migrante Scalabrini, which, in addition to providing services to refugees, monitored rights violations in Mexico and amplify their findings through reports to media and other NGO outlets in Mexico and abroad. Mexico City resisted UNHCR pressure to join the Refugee Convention, but in 1982, the government agreed not to refoule refugees, even as it continued to insist that Guatemalans did not qualify for asylum because they were economic migrants. Only 100 Central Americans received a Mexican asylum visa in the early 1980s and none from 1986 to 1990.[43] Washington contributed to the containment of Guatemalans in the camps in Chiapas, but, in the long run, its successful pressure on Mexico City to allow in the UNHCR indirectly constrained the harshest potential tactics of buffering by putting more independent observers on the ground who had the ear of the international community.

Mexico's military and immigration control bureaucracy understood this dynamic and tried to restrict the activities of the UNHCR. They promoted mass deportations and forced relocations within Mexico. Most government officials were "alarmed by their loss of jurisdiction over recognized refugees and their inability to revoke refugee status."[44] By the late 1980s, the government tried to limit UNHCR operations to Mexico City and the camps in Chiapas. The military relocated thousands of refugees away from the border into isolated camps in the Yucatán Peninsula in 1984, ostensibly to protect them from cross-border incursions by the Guatemalan military that had killed and wounded numerous refugees. The military argued that only subversives hiding among the refugees opposed relocation and that "people who really fled the country to save their lives" would not resist. According to internal documents from the Secretariat of National Defense, "it is recommended that strict measures of control be taken, such as breaking the social structures of the Guatemalan refugee population in Mexico . . . for this structure is currently being preserved practically intact through the ties of family, language and culture, as well as due to pressure from the subversive organizations."[45] The relocation camps in the Yucatán Peninsula were designed to destroy refugees' social networks and cultural autonomy.

Historian Rodolfo Casillas asserts that the United States did not try to control Central American transit migration through Mexico in the 1980s because it did not want to take away the pressure valve that allowed Washington's

Central American allies to shed excess labor.[46] However, other researchers show more convincingly that the Reagan administration urged the Mexican government to bottle up Central Americans because many were presumed to be heading for the United States. The Reagan administration wanted Guatemalans in Chiapas to be repatriated but understood that conditions were not ripe given the ongoing conflict. It provided USD$105 million to the UNHCR and International Committee of the Red Cross to assist refugees, repatriates, and displaced persons in the region. Administration officials could then argue that Guatemalans who came to the United States did not merit U.S. protection because they had bypassed camps in Mexico that had been set up to protect "legitimate" refugees.[47] The camps effectively kept refugees far from the United States.

Mexican authorities increasingly tried to keep Central Americans out of Mexico and contain in the south those who managed to cross its border. The CIA noted this was part of Mexico City's effort to "maintain its image" as a country of refuge while keeping out refugees.[48] In 1983, the Mexican government tightened visa requirements for nationals of Central American and Caribbean countries. Airlines could no longer issue tourist permits. Intending visitors now had to apply at Mexican consulates in their home countries and prove their financial solvency—two requirements unfriendly to the needs of refugees fleeing civil war and dissidents escaping persecution.[49] In 1987 Mexico City further tightened the documentary standards for Central Americans to prove their solvency.[50] Salvadorans who previously could have flown to Mexico joined other Central Americans in crossing the land border without papers.[51]

Mexican authorities tried to keep Central Americans who had already entered Mexico away from the U.S. border in the north. Refugees recognized by the UNHCR were given Mexican documents identifying them as "border visitors" who had to stay within 150 kilometers of the Guatemalan border. In 1981 and 1982, many Mexican visas for Salvadorans prohibited the bearer from traveling further north than Guadalajara, 850 kilometers south of Texas. The main migration official in Tijuana, the principle crossing point with California, declared in April 1981 that Central Americans would be detained if "the purpose of their visit to Mexico was with the main objective of crossing the U.S. border."[52] The Secretariat of the Interior issued a circular in 1982 prohibiting Central Americans with tourist visas from traveling to the U.S.-Mexico border area and ordered the detention of Central Americans intending to enter the United States. The government concentrated its control efforts in airports and on train and highway routes in the north.

Checkpoints generated opportunities for extortion. Central Americans typically paid police USD$20 to USD$100 to pass. Amid a brisk trade in false documents and in the absence of biometric identification systems, authorities relied on racial profiling and informal tests to distinguish Central Americans. Officials quizzed suspects about the names of towns in Mexico or asked them to sing the national anthem. Refugee networks spread word about how to prepare for the most common questions. One man who successfully passed the first round of questions was finally tripped up when he failed to correctly define a *molcajete*, a uniquely Mexican term for a volcanic mortar and pestle.[53]

Mexican and U.S. authorities informally collaborated to process Central Americans who attempted to enter the United States. Central Americans applying for asylum in Nogales, Arizona, were told by U.S. agents that they had to return to Mexico while their cases were adjudicated. American agents then turned them over to their Mexican counterparts.[54] Central Americans who attempted to enter the United States with false papers or by making false claims of U.S. citizenship were immediately turned over to Mexican border police. The head of the migration service in Tijuana revealed in February 1981 that Central Americans apprehended by the U.S. Border Patrol in the immediate vicinity of the border were summarily returned to Mexico as well. No formal agreements governed these arrangements, but as he explained, "This has become a customary practice. As you know, customary practice becomes the law."[55] A UNHCR report concluded, "It is obvious that there is an agreement between the border patrols on both sides which allows massive expulsion of the illegal foreigners from the USA toward Mexico, from where they are deported."[56] Mexican agents bused Central Americans to the Guatemalan border and pushed them across, even if they were from countries further south. The deportation of Salvadorans to Guatemala partly protected the Mexican government from claims it was engaging in refoulement. The Guatemalan government ignored Salvadoran deportees unless they were suspected of subversion.[57] Many immediately headed back north in an expensive, arduous, and sometimes deadly game of human pinball.

One of the legacies of the 1980s refugee crisis in Central America was greater regional cooperation around controlling all kinds of mobile people, including refugees, migrant workers, tourists, and drug runners.[58] Washington quietly pressured Mexico City to deport Central Americans beginning in the late 1980s. A network of U.S. liaison officers monitored flows of Central Americans and other third-country nationals in Mexico and Central America, trained Mexican authorities to detect fraudulent documents, and coordinated U.S. policy on the ground.[59] Mexico and Guatemala created the Binational

Subcommission on Migration Issues in 1989 to discuss unauthorized transit migration. The same year, the UNHCR and the governments of Mexico and Central American countries launched the International Conference on Central American Refugees.[60] More than 40,000 Guatemalan refugees in Mexico eventually returned home in the early 1990s after a long negotiation among the refugees, UNHCR, and the two governments. About a third of the recognized refugee population settled in Mexico. Beginning in 1996, the multilateral Puebla Process brought together representatives from Mexico, Central America, Canada, and the United States to discuss how to manage a broad range of regional flows. Pronouncements following the meetings always included references to safeguarding human rights of migrants, but their most important effect was to create a regional cadre of experts dedicated to managing migration and sharing techniques of control.

Thickening the Buffer

The end of the civil wars in Nicaragua (1989), El Salvador (1992), and Guatemala (1996) did not end outmigration. The world's highest levels of peacetime violence, the growth of powerful gangs initially formed by deportees from the United States, and persistent poverty continued to propel Central Americans north.[61] Behind the scenes, U.S. pressure on Mexico to become a more effective buffer grew throughout the 1990s. The U.S. Border Patrol's 1994 long-range strategy included enhancing Mexico's control of its southern border to keep out "OTMs" (other-than-Mexicans) or at least contain them in Mexico away from the United States.[62] Mexico City tried to establish greater control as a result of several interactions with U.S. policy, including direct U.S. diplomatic pressure, the fact that Central Americans were becoming bottled up in Mexico by increased U.S. border enforcement, and Mexico City's effort to link U.S. policy toward Mexican immigrants with Mexico's policy toward foreigners in transit.

The U.S. government began to further strengthen its border with Mexico following the 1986 Immigration Reform and Control Act. Enforcement intensified with Operation Hold the Line in El Paso (1993) and Operation Gatekeeper in San Diego (1994). Aggressive U.S. border enforcement aimed in the first instance at deterring unauthorized crossers from Mexico who dominated the flows made it politically more difficult for Mexican authorities to openly collaborate with their U.S. counterparts. "Finding the political will for closer collaboration may be compromised if the Mexican public perceives that the [U.S.] border is being militarized," a senior Mexican official explained.[63] At the same time, it became even harder for Central Americans to cross into the United States illegally. They became stuck in Mexico for long periods and increased the incentives for Mexican authorities to conduct large-scale deportations.[64]

Applying conditions to financial aid is one U.S. technique to extend its border control on to Mexican territory. In January 1995, the Clinton administration proposed USD$40 billion in loan guarantees to Mexico to support the collapsing peso. The public rationale for the bailout included preventing "an increase in the flow of illegal immigrants across our borders."[65] Supporters of the bailout publicly framed it as necessary to stabilize the Mexican economy so that Mexicans would not migrate to the United States. Within days, Mexican officials agreed to control transit migration through Mexico as well. On February 15, the U.S.-Mexico Binational Commission issued a report agreeing to cooperate on migration issues, including policies toward migrants from third countries. The Mexican delegation agreed to let U.S. authorities train Mexican migration police and confirmed the formation of a special surveillance unit to enforce migration laws along the southern border.[66] Mexican press reports at the time characterized the agreement as a condition for the bailout, which had been announced just two weeks earlier.[67] Public U.S. budget documents do not refer to an explicit requirement to buffer third-country nationals. Regardless of the explicit conditions imposed in the bailout, Mexico City's efforts to build up its southern border throughout the period were consistent with its growing intimacy with Washington following the North American Free Trade Agreement (NAFTA) going into effect in January 1994.

President Vicente Fox (2000–2006) wanted a comprehensive migration agreement with Washington as a pillar for even greater regional integration inspired by the EU model. In return for an expanded temporary worker program and legalization of the unauthorized population living in the United States, Fox would restrict unauthorized emigration from Mexico and Central American transit.[68] "We want to put a brake on the growing problem of Central American migration bound for the United States," he announced.[69] The bilateral talks collapsed after the September 11, 2001, terrorist attacks as security considerations overwhelmed the broader agenda. Fox increased transit migration control even in the absence of U.S. concessions on the immigration of Mexican nationals. Between 2001 and 2003, the National Institute of Migration (INAMI) launched a USD$11 million *Plan Sur* (Southern Plan). The administration fired border agents accused of corruption and abuses and sent hundreds of new agents and the military to operate checkpoints along highways leading north from the Guatemalan border. The goal was to establish two belts of control. The first belt ran close to the southern border between the states of Chiapas and Tabasco. The second belt ran across the Isthmus of Tehuantepec where Mexico's territory narrows to 200 kilometers.[70]

Despite increased buffering actions, the Mexican government's deployments remained limited. In 2005, an average of only 32 INAMI agents patrolled the entire southern border at any time, in addition to 226 agents posted along roads in the interior of the southern states. By 2010 there were still only 130 agents to patrol eleven points of entry. In the view of the U.S. State Department, fewer than 100 of the INAMI agents were properly trained. Customs agents at remote checkpoints in the jungle along the Guatemalan border were unable to communicate with their headquarters daily because of poor mobile phone reception. Corruption among the agents was endemic. In 2008, 49 out of the 100 agents in the sector were replaced after failing background checks.[71]

The Mexican government lacks the capacity to seal the 1,100-kilometer border, but it also lacks the political will. Between 2007 and 2010, Mexico's southern border was crossed by an estimated 1.9 million foreigners, of whom 17% were Central Americans bound for the United States.[72] The rest were engaged in commerce, labor migration, family visits, and tourism. Keeping the border open allows access to cheapened labor. The Mexican government issues border-crossing cards to Guatemalans that allow them to remain up to three nights within 100 kilometers of the border. Mexico shares many similarities with states in the Global North whose border control policies are constrained by the demands of market economies.[73] The government does not want to hermetically seal the border even as it tries to control the movement of foreigners through the country.

Securitization 2.0

The U.S. embassy has confidentially characterized Mexico's border with Guatemala as its "vulnerable underbelly."[74] The securitization of transit through Mexico reached new heights and developed new targets following the September 11 terrorist attacks. Mexican Foreign Minister Luis Ernesto Derbez publicly stated that after the attacks, anti-terrorism became "the number one issue" in the bilateral relationship.[75] President Fox promoted the idea of a "North American security perimeter" to face a common threat and unveiled *Plan Centinela* (Sentry Plan), which deployed 18,000 troops on transportation routes and at the southern border to prevent any attacks on the United States or its interests in Mexico during the U.S.-led war in Iraq. Two years later, the United States, Canada, and Mexico launched the

Security and Prosperity Partnership of North America to counter external threats to North America and build efficient border controls within the continent. Since 2005, Mexico's migration agency, INAMI, has been legally incorporated into Mexico's National Security Council. The Mexican navy took charge of southern border security and since 2010 has constructed a dozen naval bases, each staffed with detachments of 54 to 108 marines, on rivers that cut through Chiapas and Quintana Roo. At a regional level, the High-Level Group on Border Security involving officials from Mexico and Central America began meeting regularly in 2002 to discuss the smuggling of people, arms, and drugs across borders. The goals of the Puebla Process shifted toward the same set of issues. Securitization reduced public access to information about INAMI's activities.[76]

Government documents illustrate the slippage between fighting terrorism and controlling unauthorized migration, including refugees without papers. For example, the 2004 State Department "Reports on Terrorism" praised Mexico not only for its security operations clearly related to anti-terrorism, such as guarding critical infrastructure, but also for actions targeting unauthorized migration. "The Mexican Government continued in 2004 to step up efforts to address the flow of illegal migrants into Mexico, many of whom sought eventually to reach the United States."[77] Increasing control of Mexico's southern border continued to be a major goal of the U.S.-Mexico diplomatic agenda when President Felipe Calderón took office in 2006.[78] The U.S. secretary of Homeland Security and officials from the Mexican Secretariat of the Interior met in 2007 to discuss how to speed the repatriation of Central Americans detained in the United States and Mexico. They agreed "to work together closely in shaping and implementing a strategy to control Mexico's southern border."[79] Washington had discretely provided the Mexican government with equipment used for migration and border control at least since Fox's *Plan Sur*, when it gave Zodiac inflatable boats to patrol rivers in the area.[80] As chapter 4 describes, U.S. pressure on the Mexican government to restrict visas to around forty nationalities and share air traveler information put Mexico under the North American "dome" as well.

In October 2007, the two governments publicly announced the Mérida Initiative, a package of U.S. financial and technical assistance mostly given to Mexico with smaller components for Central America and eventually the Dominican Republic and Haiti. The Mérida Initiative included efforts to combat organized crime, particularly drug trafficking, and to reform the criminal justice system in Mexico. The creation of a "21st Century Border" was a pillar of the program. The border plan aimed to prevent undesired people and goods from ever reaching the U.S. border. As explained by the

State Department's Roberta S. Jacobson, "In some cases, the most effective approach to security is to redistribute law enforcement resources to screen people and cargo before they near the actual border, or even arrive in North America."[81] Between 2010 and 2015, the State Department spent $130 million on Mexican border security, of which half was directed at Mexico's southern border.[82] The Consolidated Appropriations Act of 2016 included USD$139 million for Mérida-related projects such as the modernization of Mexico's northern and southern borders. Funding for different parts of the initiative is notoriously difficult to track over time and with any detail, but there is no question that it increased the migration control capacity of the Mexican government. Alan Bersin, assistant secretary for policy in the Department of Homeland Security, bluntly declared in 2012, "The Guatemalan border with Chiapas is now our southern border."[83]

The United States paid to upgrade Mexico's migration control databases in return for access to the information. Mérida initially included more than US$91 million for INAMI to upgrade and expand an electronic system to keep computerized records of entries, exits, repatriations, residence permits, naturalizations, and other migration documents.[84] Thanks to Mérida funding, between 2008 and 2014, the percentage of Mexico's international transit points without electronic entry registries declined from 66% to 4%. The percentage without electronic exit registries declined from 79% to 17%.[85] Passport and fingerprint readers digitized biometric data. The goal was to "track all persons entering and exiting Mexico, via air, land and sea." The data would then be integrated in a way that would "enable appropriate information sharing" with U.S. law enforcement agencies, including the DHS; FBI; Drug Enforcement Administration; Marshals Service; and the Bureau of Alcohol, Tobacco, Firearms and Explosives.[86] The State Department asked Congress for a further USD$3 million in 2016 to develop a shared biometric standard for exchanging data among U.S. and Mexican law enforcement agencies.[87] While the dominant focus of border funding is enforcement, the Mérida Initiative included communication equipment and medical supplies "to assist Mexican immigration authorities in rescue operations along Mexico's southern border." [88] The communication equipment would presumably be useful for both rescue and control operations. The U.S. Department of Defense gave aid outside the scope of the Mérida Initiative to Mexican military units stationed along the southern border.[89]

In addition to building up border infrastructure, the U.S. government provided extensive training to Mexican agents. The U.S. Agency for International Development sponsored training in eight areas, including people trafficking, to more than 10,000 Mexican officials between August 2009 and March 2010 and 200 prosecutors and investigators between September 2009 and March 2010.[90] By 2014, sixty-nine Mexican customs officers had received training at the U.S. Immigration and Customs Enforcement's ten-week academy in Glynco, Georgia.[91]

Binational cooperation has become increasingly open in the era of NAFTA and the post–September 11 security landscape. Agents from DHS based at the U.S. embassy coordinate support along the U.S.-Mexico border, conduct intelligence work, and consult with U.S. diplomats.[92] In July 2014, President Enrique Peña Nieto declared the start of *Programa Frontera Sur* (Southern Border Program). The program called for three concentric cordons across southern Mexico up to 160 kilometers into the interior. More than 100 agents of the militarized Gendarmerie joined INAMI agents and 400 federal police in the region to focus on border security.[93] A new government agency, the Coordinator for Southern Border Issues, was created with a MXN$102 million budget.[94] The U.S. government supported *Programa Frontera Sur* by training INAMI agents, buying scanning units, and paying for mobile migration control kiosks and canine patrols.[95] During President Peña Nieto's visit to Washington in January 2015, President Obama praised his visitor for taking measures to reduce Central American transit. "In part because of strong efforts by Mexico, including at its southern border, we've seen those numbers reduced back to much more manageable levels," Obama told the assembled press corps.[96] In 2016, U.S. Deputy Assistant Secretary of State Juan Gonzalez praised Mexico for its U.S.-financed enforcement efforts "in particular at its southern border and along common routes toward the United States."[97] The willingness of U.S. officials to discuss Mexico's buffering more openly during the Obama administration was a sign that the topic was becoming less politically sensitive in Mexico. Officials in Mexico did not want the country to become "a closed sack" as entry to the United States became more difficult.

The Trump Challenge

Donald Trump began his 2016 presidential campaign by calling Mexican immigrants criminals and rapists, challenging the legitimacy of the decisions of a U.S.-born federal judge of Mexican heritage because he was "Mexican," and calling for the construction of a wall along the entire U.S.-Mexico border.[98] In the face of his hostility to Mexicans, it became much more controversial within Mexico for the government to control transit in ways that seemed to do the bidding of the Trump administration.

In April 2018, a "caravan" of 1,500 Central Americans, mostly Hondurans, left the Mexican city of Tapachula near the Guatemalan border and headed north. A significant contingent intended to ask for asylum in the United States. A local NGO, Pueblo Sin Fronteras, had organized smaller caravans of Central Americans since 2010. They traveled together for protection from the predations of gangs and corrupt police and to raise public awareness of the dangers faced by migrants crossing Mexico. The 2018 caravan was large and scrutinized by journalists so the migrants were able to publicly pass internal migration checkpoints without stopping, but international media coverage of the event turned the caravan into a major issue in U.S. politics. Goaded by coverage on the conservative Fox television network, Trump threatened to deploy the U.S. National Guard to the border and publicly urged Mexican authorities to stop the group.[99] As the caravan continued north, Trump linked migration control with trade policy. "Mexico, whose laws on immigration are very tough, must stop people from going through Mexico and into the U.S.," he tweeted. "We may make this a condition of the new NAFTA Agreement. Our Country cannot accept what is happening!"[100] The linking of migration control to the bilateral economic relationship echoed the 1994 U.S. bailout of the peso discussed earlier, but Trump's loud and overt threats to the Mexican government over this issue were unprecedented.

The Mexican government responded by quietly issuing *oficios de salida* travel permits to around 900 of the migrants seeking to reach the U.S. border, apparently in the hope that the migrants would disperse and stop attracting the attention of the media and Trump. However, around 400 continued to travel together and reached Tijuana a month later. Claiming that the government did not have the capacity to process and detain asylum seekers at the federal facility in San Ysidro, California, U.S. border officials limited the number of asylum seekers who could enter on a given day. Mexican officials prevented some of the group from reaching the borderline until U.S. authorities were willing to allow them to present a claim. Within a week, 228 asylum seekers had crossed the border to ask for asylum. Of 216 known to have been screened, 205 passed their credible-fear interview.[101]

The Mexican government prefers to buffer surreptitiously and certainly does not want to be portrayed domestically as acting on behalf of U.S. interests. In 2018 the Trump administration urged Mexican authorities to sign a safe third-country agreement so that the United States could return asylum seekers who passed through Mexico. The idea of an agreement with Mexico has been floated periodically since the 1994 Justice Department regulations that eventually led to the U.S.-Canada agreement. According to press reports, Mexican President Enrique Peña Nieto was willing to entertain such an agreement, presumably in return for leverage in the renegotiations of NAFTA, but pulled back in the wake of Trump's antagonism toward Mexicans and aggressive demands for Mexico to pay for a border wall with the United States.[102] Andrés Manuel López Obrador, Mexico's leftist president elected in July 2018, said during his campaign that Mexico's "neighbors in the north want us to continue doing the dirty work and to detain Central Americans who flee because of violence and misery."[103] Cooperation with U.S. authorities during the Trump administration became even more circumspect than during previous administrations.

Deportations

Mexico's mass deportation machine shows its importance as a buffer state between the United States and Central America. The Mexican government carried out nearly 3.5 million deportations from 1985 to 2016. Ninety-three percent were from the Northern Triangle.[104] Figure 7.4 shows that Mexico deported more Central Americans than the United States from 1990 to 2008

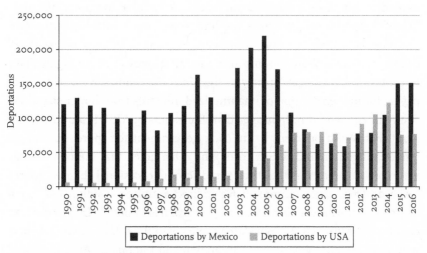

FIGURE 7.4 Deportations of Guatemalans, Salvadorans, and Hondurans by Mexico and the United States, 1990–2016

SOURCES: The "Boletín Estadístico" issued every year from 2001 to 2016 by Secretaría de Gobernación, Unidad de Política Migratoria, http://www.politicamigratoria.gob.mx/es_mx/SEGOB/Boletin_Estadistico_2017; Rodolfo Casillas, "Las rutas de los centroamericanos por México, Un ejercicio de caracterización, actores principales y complejidades," *Migración y Desarrollo 10* (2008), pp. 157–174; *Yearbook of Immigration Statistics* issued every year from 2003 to 2017 by Office of Immigration Statistics, Department of Homeland Security, https://www.dhs.gov/immigration-statistics/yearbook; INS yearbook issued every year from 1992–2002 as:

U.S. Immigration and Naturalization Service, *Statistical Yearbook of the Immigration and Naturalization Service*, U.S. Government Printing Office: Washington, DC.

and again from 2015 to 2016. Surveys of Central Americans deported from Mexico in 2014 found that 48% of Guatemalans, 92% of Hondurans, and 86% of Salvadorans intended to reach the United States.[105]

The Mexican government has denied accepting funds from the U.S. government to pay for deportations from Mexico, despite abundant evidence to the contrary.[106] In 1990, Mexico City asked Washington to help pay for Mexico's enforcement efforts against third-country migrants, traffickers, and smugglers who illegally entered the United States through Mexico. From 1991 to 1997, "Project 057" spent USD$2 million to pay Mexico and other countries in Latin America to repatriate third-country nationals. Senator Barbara Mikulski (D-MD) raised questions about how those funds had been used in 1994. According to the State Department's response, "We did not help repatriate any third country national from a refugee-producing country. Consequently, we did not help the Government of Mexico repatriate Central Americans." The State Department said the funds were used to repatriate Chinese, Brazilians, Dominicans, Ecuadorians, Indians, and Peruvians after they had been interviewed in Mexico by the UNHCR.[107]

Project 057 was expanded to other countries in the Western Hemisphere in 1997 to reduce unauthorized migration and "border dumping," the practice of deporting people across the line to become another government's problem. According to a cable from the U.S. embassy in Tegucigalpa, third-country nationals "border-dumped in Central America . . . are highly likely to continue their illegal journey to the U.S." The embassy calculated that paying for the repatriation of unauthorized migrants from buffer states was twelve to eighteen times cheaper than the estimated USD$30,000 per migrant that would be spent by the U.S. government for apprehension, detention, litigation, and return costs. The cable noted that the cost savings were considerable even after taking into account occasional "higher airfares resulting from the requirement for indirect routings avoiding U.S. territory when returning a [third-country national] from another Latin American country." [108] Although it is not stated explicitly in the cable, avoiding contact with a U.S. airport, where the Immigration and Nationality Act applies and the U.S. Constitution affords territorial rights of personhood, would prevent someone being repatriated from being able to ask for asylum in the United States.

At least since 1998, the U.S. government has paid for the rental of buses to repatriate Hondurans and Salvadorans apprehended near the Mexico-Guatemala border.[109] Washington also paid for Mexico City to deport about 1,000 Indians, Pakistanis, Sudanese, Chinese, Colombians, and Ecuadorians to Guatemala.[110] In the most notorious incident involving a group of Indian nationals detained in Guatemala for more than six months, detainee Kanu Patel hung himself. After a lawsuit was filed against the Guatemalan government for maintaining inadequate standards in the detention facilities, the other Indians were released. Some headed north only to be detained a second time by Mexican authorities.[111] The Guatemalan government then successfully appealed to the U.S. State Department to finance the costs of detention and flights back to their countries of origin.[112] The U.S. government also indirectly funds repatriate reintegration centers in Central America. The State Department gives the funds to the IOM, which then transfers the money to NGOs in Central America that provide services.[113] The activities of the IOM thus include a caging function as well as facilitating reintegration.

Mexico and Guatemala began collaborative chain deportations for nationals of other Central American countries beginning in 2001. More than 200 police officers spent several weeks combing the parks, brothels, and hotels of border towns and detained more than 1,200 unauthorized migrants, many of whom had previously been deported from Mexico. The two governments then deported them on guarded buses to the Salvadoran-Guatemala border. The Mexican government went on to sign memoranda of understanding with several Central American governments to manage deportations by land and air that are closely based on U.S.-Mexico agreements.[114]

The Mexican government deports almost all the Northern Triangle nationals it detains. By contrast, most detained Africans and Asians are released to continue their journey to the U.S. border. [115] Of the 12,401 Asians and 11,118 Africans detained between 2007 and 2016, 12% of Asians and 6% of Africans were deported. Although the Mexican authorities often arrest extra-hemispheric migrants in southern Mexico, many are not deportable because their consular agents in Mexico do not coordinate with Mexican authorities or recognize the migrants as their nationals. The fact that Mexico deports far fewer Africans and Asians than it detains may be an artifact of screening with U.S. collaboration that satisfies both countries' security concerns about extra-continental travelers. At least since 2012, Homeland Security Investigations, an agency within DHS, has staffed an office in Tapachula, Chiapas, to screen travelers, especially those from outside the region, who are flagged as suspicious. Between October 2015 and August 2016, U.S. agents screened more than 640 people from outside the Americas who were detained by Mexican authorities in Tapachula.[116]

Asad, a twenty-four-year-old Somali man in Tapachula who said he left Somalia because of the civil war and the deaths of several family members, described the security screening, which was conducted using interpreters dialing in to the interview when necessary:

They will take you into interview; they will ask you a lot of questions. You fill out forms, from square one they will ask where you started your journey and how long. Most people from Muslim countries are supposed to go into camp, because they are supposed to get the information from that person because they never know if this person was in a group or worked with terrorist people, so they ask you such questions. We are not terrorists. They treated us very well. We were there almost seven to eight days in the camp. The ninth day I came out.[117]

The U.S. government also trained migration control authorities in Central America in "screening and processing special interest aliens."[118] If a handful of extra-hemispheric migrants who pass the security screening then reached the United States to ask for asylum, the numbers were so small that they were not a major policy concern. The cactus-like buffering for extra-continental migrants was thus sharp on the outside, but for the few who reached Mexico and got past the U.S. security screening, buffering became suppler. The rates of detained Asians and Africans being deported sharply increased in 2016, however, suggesting a more restrictive turn was underway.

Containment in Central America

Central American governments historically have devoted few resources to controlling unauthorized migration from and through the region. For example, in 2004 the Guatemalan government deployed one helicopter and five pick-up trucks to patrol its 800-kilometer border with Mexico. The government lacked the basic electronic infrastructure of modern migration control such as comprehensive databases, biometric scanners, and linked computer systems. Little information was shared between Mexican and Guatemalan officials.[119] The U.S. government began a sustained build-up of the migration control capacity of Central American governments in the mid-2000s that aimed to both cage Central Americans in the region and use it as a "valuable buffer zone," in the words of a U.S. State Department cable, to prevent the transit of other nationals.[120]

Between 2008 and 2015, Washington allocated almost USD$1.2 billion to Central American countries under the Mérida Initiative and the related Central American Regional Security Initiative.[121] Washington helped Central American governments create central databases for the biometric information collected at far-flung airports and border posts.[122] The U.S. government regularly conducts operations in Central America to break up human smuggling networks that facilitate the outmigration of

Central Americans and the transit of people from outside the region.[123] By 2016, the DHS had attachés permanently assigned to Panama, Costa Rica, El Salvador, Honduras, and Guatemala and sent officers on a temporary basis to Nicaragua and Belize.[124] The DHS trains border and Coast Guard units in Guatemala, El Salvador, and Honduras and collects shared biometric data through the Biometric Identification Transnational Migration Alert Program. The priorities for U.S. funding suggest that the U.S. government in practice accepts that many of those leaving Central America are fleeing violence. The first of its "regional security development objectives" was "mitigating undocumented transmigration and displacement due to insecurity."[125] The budget request prioritized U.S. funding of programs to prevent crime by "strategically targeting at-risk communities identified as primary sources of outward migration."[126] Additional funding would be given to "border units charged with protecting the integrity of Central American frontiers and disrupting the traffic in narcotics as well as smuggling of migrants."

Several men who were able to circumvent the border controls in Central America described their experience in 2016. Ishmael, a forty-five-year-old man from Ghana who said he left because he was being persecuted by opponents after being named leader of his village, spent five months traveling north from Brazil to Mexico with the hope of reaching the United States because he could not get a visa to fly. Asad, the Somali man fleeing the civil war who had been interrogated by DHS agents in the Mexican border city of Tapachula, described how he flew to Ecuador and then spent two months evading controls to reach Tapachula.

> When I came to the border of Colombia, I walked through the jungle through Panama because I was not in a legal way. That's why I started walking through the jungle. So, I was in the jungle for about eleven days, and it was horrible. It was very hard and dangerous. It was a very bad place. But Allah was steadfast. The jungle was horrible.
>
> In Nicaragua, we were there for a few hours. We walked by night because soldiers would catch you and deport you. So, we starting walking at night; we walked around four hours. We then went inside a truck. It was very big. There were many people—190 people. A few were African, mostly were Haitian. It was a very hard journey, some of the people almost died inside the truck. The truck didn't stop at all . . . There was no oxygen, it was very hot. Outside it's raining, so the oxygen [that] come out, it's hot. When it reaches the roof, outside its cold and inside its hot, so it will become like water. It would rain down. Some people were reaching the water from the roof. I thought it was my last day; I was going to die. Everyone who came out, if they were Muslim

or Christian, said thank God, praise to Allah. We didn't see any Nicaragua; it was six hours.

It is very hard. Some of our friends who we traveled with, died in the jungle. Some of the children died also. Especially in the river, children are very [endangered]. River was very strong. Four men were gone with the river. They drowned. It was a very hard place. No one got food; everyone was very tired. So even if your brother is very tired, you cannot help him. You have to go. It is sorrow, you cannot remember all the time. That is when we pass a country; we leave the things behind. If you remember all the things, you cannot move on. You have to forget the past and move on. That's how we are trying to go.[127]

An increase in the arrival of unaccompanied children at the U.S. border in the mid-2010s prompted Washington to put new resources into containing Central Americans in the region. The number of unaccompanied minors from Northern Triangle countries encountered by U.S. authorities rose from 10,146 in 2012 to 51,705 in 2014 and was still running at 37,714 in 2016.[128] Congress in 2016 appropriated up to $750 million to Central American governments "to address the key factors in such countries contributing to the migration of unaccompanied, undocumented minors to the United States." For the three Northern Triangle countries, 25% of the funds were to be withheld until the secretary of state certified that the governments were taking effective steps to inform their citizens of the dangers of unauthorized migration, combating human smuggling and trafficking, improving border security, and cooperating with the United States on readmission of deportees.[129] Controlling migration to the United States became the master frame for wedging in all kinds of U.S. funding. For example, the USAID budget for Honduras included USD$5.5 million for Global Climate Change Adaption. Conservation and water management was framed as a means to "help keep the rural areas productive, thus lessening the push to migrate to the cities, which is often the first step to emigration."[130] Under U.S. pressure, the Northern Triangle countries passed new laws that prohibited children from leaving without parental permission.[131]

Campaigns financed by the DHS use television, radio, and billboard advertising to warn potential unauthorized migrants against trying to reach the United States. Campaigns such as *No Más Cruces* (No More Crosses) are unbranded, meaning it is not evident to the viewer that the U.S. government is the source of the campaign. One poster depicts a man lying in the burning desert sand on his stomach with his hand stretched out for help. He is dying or already dead. "To chicken out is manly," reads the text in conversational

Spanish. "Before crossing to the other side, remember: the cemeteries are full of the daring and big macho types."[132] In 2014, DHS began running thousands of radio and television advertisements in the Northern Triangle warning of the dangers of trying to reach the United States without papers.[133] One song, *La Bestia* (The Beast), is set to a catchy pop beat backed up by traditional marimba. It evokes the dangers of riding the freight train north that the railroad company in Mexico had sped up at the behest of Washington to make boarding more difficult.[134]

Migrants from everywhere
Entrenched among the rail ties.
Far away from where they come,
Farther away from where they go.

Waiting for earth's shaking
And the wheels' screeching.
Behind the mountains
The menacing snake appears,
Her scales are made out of iron
Her womb of iron as well,

They call her The Beast from the South
This wretched train of death,
With the devil in the boiler
Whistles, roars, twists and turns.

Hanging on the railcars
Of this iron beast
Migrants go as cattle
To the slaughterhouse
Taking hell's route
Within a cloud of pain.
This shuddering thunder
Does not know about favors
It wears three sixes tattooed
On her wheels and her head.

They call her The Beast from the South
This wretched train of death,
With the devil in the boiler
Whistles, roars, twists and turns.

Mara Salvatrucha feud,[135]
Coyotes' payday.
A crushing mortar,
A slicing machete.

They call her The Beast from the South
This wretched train of death,
With the devil in the boiler
Whistles, roars, twists and turns.[136]

There is no evidence that these publicity campaigns deter departures. A survey of Hondurans in 2014 found that most people were well informed about the dangers of unauthorized transit but that such awareness did not significantly affect their intentions to leave.[137] A major limitation on U.S. efforts to cage most potential asylum seekers in the Northern Triangle is that the governments of those countries do not simply lack the capacity to control migration flows. They face far more fundamental challenges from criminal organizations.[138] People flee the generalized violence of unstable states, who are then pressured by Washington to control the outflow of people when they cannot even effectively control all their territory. The cage has big gaps in its bars.

The U.S. government routinely acknowledges that both violence and economic distress propel people to leave Central America. Washington pledges to provide the protections that are compelled by U.S. and international law. In the face of domestic and international criticism that U.S. policies were making it impossible for those fleeing violence to access U.S. protection in practice, the Obama administration launched initiatives in 2014 and 2016 that combined the refugee and unaccompanied minor issues. In the initial version of the Central American Minors Program announced in December 2014, nationals of Guatemala, El Salvador, and Honduras who were legally living in the United States could request refugee resettlement for their children living in their home countries. Children who met the refugee criteria would be resettled in the United States with their parents. Children who did not meet the refugee criteria, but who were still at risk of being harmed, would be considered for parole. Under this version of parole, residence in the United States was temporary and did not open a pathway to citizenship.

In January 2016, the State Department announced that it planned to expand its refugee admissions program by working with the UNHCR to screen small numbers of Salvadorans, Guatemalans, and Hondurans fleeing violence at processing centers in Central America. Costa Rica agreed to host temporarily up to 200 of the most vulnerable Central Americans awaiting processing once they had passed security screenings in their countries of origin. Up to 9,000 Central Americans would be eligible to enter the United States annually under the program. The stated goal was to reduce unauthorized migration by opening a legal path to seek refuge. As of April 2016, more than 7,000 applications had been filed, but only 162 individuals had arrived in the United States, of whom 64 were considered refugees and 98 parolees. In July 2016, the program was expanded to include family members of minors from the Northern Triangle countries who met the refugee or parolee criteria. Amy Pope, a deputy Homeland Security adviser, explained that the policy was a reaction to the failure to provide broader legal channels of protection. "What we have seen is that our current efforts to date have been insufficient to address the number of people who may have legitimate refugee claims," she told the media, "and there are insufficient pathways for those people to present their claims."[139]

The programs highlight the gap between immense efforts to prevent people in distress from ever reaching U.S. territory with micro-gestures toward a legal path to protection. The Trump administration eliminated the Central American Minors Program in August 2017.[140] It was unwilling to sustain even this mostly symbolic program given its overall project of dismantling refugee admissions and creating more restrictive immigration and asylum policies in every sphere.

Asylum in the Buffer?

The use of Mexico as a buffer state to deter and filter asylum seekers would be less controversial if Mexico enjoyed a robust system of refugee status determination and protection. This has not been the case in practice despite increasing protections for asylum seekers in the black letter of the law. Mexico is an upper-middle-income country with the world's fifteenth-biggest economy, but its government has not developed the resources to provide asylum for more than symbolic numbers of people. The Secretariat of the Interior historically has enjoyed an extremely high degree of discretion to control the movement of all types of foreigners. Article 33 of the 1917 constitution authorizes the executive to deport foreigners without any judicial hearing. Mexico was not a party to the 1951 Refugee Convention until 2000, though it signed several regional conventions and declarations on asylum, including the 1954 Organization of American States (OAS) Convention on Territorial Asylum with a provision for granting territorial asylum to individuals who fled *past* persecution based on political beliefs.[141] In 1969, Mexico signed the OAS American Convention on Human Rights that recognizes "the right to seek and be granted asylum" if the person "is being pursued for political offenses or related common crimes," and which includes the principle of non-refoulement. However, Mexico exempted itself from the jurisdiction of the Inter-American Court of Human Rights that ruled on compliance with the treaty.[142] Mexico signed the nonbinding Cartagena Declaration on Refugees in 1984 that broadly defines refugees as persons fleeing civil war, foreign aggression, or other situations of generalized violence.[143]

Mexico amended its General Law on Population in 1990 to become the second country in the Western Hemisphere to adopt the Cartagena Declaration's definition of refugees in its domestic law.[144] The regulations of the statute required an asylum seeker to file a claim immediately upon entering Mexico and to wait at the port of entry while the application was processed. The regulations did not allow for individuals who entered the country illegally or who had other types of visas (such as the "border visas" held by Guatemalans in UNHCR camps) to apply for asylum.[145] Four years after the law passed, not a single application had been transferred from a local government office to the central asylum division for determination.[146] Mexico finally signed the 1951 Refugee Convention and its 1967 Protocol in 2000. It signed with reservations to Article 33, so it could maintain the executive's power to expel any foreigner without judicial process. Mexico City withdrew the reservations in 2014.[147]

Since the 2000s, Mexico has become a world leader in framing its migration laws to emphasize migrants' rights and protections. The reform of the General Law of Population in 2008 decriminalized illegal entry, reentry, and overstaying visas. It eliminated formal arrest for those offenses and left only administrative fines as a sanction.[148] Suspected unauthorized migrants who are detained appear in government statistics under the euphemisms of *alojados* (housed) or *presentados* (presented to the authorities). Detention facilities, which more than doubled between 2000 and 2011, are called *estaciones migratorias* (migrant centers).[149] The first principle of the 2011 Law of Migration is the "unconditional respect for the human rights of migrants, regardless of origin, nationality, gender, ethnicity, age, and migratory situation, with special attention to vulnerable groups such as minors, women, indigenous, adolescents and seniors, and crime victims."[150] It prohibited INAMI agents from checking migration status in private shelters for migrants.[151] The 2011 Law of Refugees and Complementary Protection bans refoulement and adopts the UN statutory definition of refugees as well as the broader Cartagena criteria.[152]

The United States was one of the main intended audiences of these statutory reforms and rights language. Mexico City took the high moral ground by showing that it had improved its treatment of unauthorized migrants in Mexico with the implication that Washington should do the same for Mexicans in the United States. As President Felipe Calderón explained in a speech celebrating the enactment of the law on May 24, 2011, "The Mexican government is doing what we have requested for many years; for example, from the United States: decriminalize migration and pay attention more sensibly and sensitively to the complex reality we live."[153]

There is always a gap between the law on the books and the law in practice. When it comes to Mexican migration law, the gap between the official language of rights and actual practice opens like a crevasse. Transnational advocacy networks highlight the most abusive practices. Human rights monitors have found that in reality, INAMI agents treat detained migrants like arrested criminals and routinely abuse and extort them.[154] Agents use racial profiling to pull aside suspected foreigners for further interrogation.[155] A 2017 survey of Central Americans in transit through Mexico suggested that refoulement is common.[156] An increasingly robust group of national organizations monitors buffering policies, including Sin Fronteras, Instituto para las Mujeres en la Migración, and the Centro de Derechos Humanos Fray Matías de Córdova. Organizations often have direct ties to broader global networks, such as the chain of migrant shelters run by the Scalabrinian order of the Catholic Church. The UNHCR maintains an active presence and works with organizations such as Sin Fronteras. Civil society foundations based in the United States, such as Ford, MacArthur, and Open Society, help fund national and transnational rights organizations and boost their reports up to an international level. International NGOs such as Amnesty International, Human Rights Watch, and the Washington Office on Latin America also monitor the externalization of border control, as do journalists, academics, and a growing number of smaller organizations. Within government, autonomous agencies, such as the Comisión Nacional de los Derechos Humanos, uncover information about abuses of people in transit. The work of these networks and the publicity they have generated about how the buffer works in practice make it more difficult for states to operate with a free hand and for their publics to pretend that they do not know what happens in their name.

People in transit are vulnerable to predation. In the most gruesome crime to date, the Zetas drug gang murdered seventy-two migrants, mostly from Central and South America, whom it had kidnapped in the northern border state of Tamaulipas in August 2010. A further 193 bodies in forty-seven clandestine graves were later found on surrounding ranches. The killings were not an isolated incident.[157] One survey documented at least 198 cases of collective kidnappings of a total of 9,758 migrants during the six months between September 2008 and February 2009. The average ransom was USD$2,500.[158] A second survey documented 214 collective kidnappings involving 11,333 migrants over six months in 2010.[159] In 2013, twelve percent of Central Americans deported by the United States said they had been extorted by gangs or the authorities while crossing through Mexico.[160] Sexual violence is a particular threat for women. The Inter-American Human Rights Commission found that many Central American women take a prophylactic injection of Depo-Provera before they start their journey to prevent pregnancy if they are raped. Migrants call this three-month contraceptive the "anti-Mexico shot."[161] The risks of violence to people crossing Mexico may deter some from entering the country, but once in Mexico, the risks are an incentive to keep pushing north.

By law, any migrant held at a detention center must be informed in writing of the right to apply for refugee status.[162] The Mexican Commission for Refugee Assistance (COMAR), makes refugee status recommendations for a final determination by the secretary of the interior. A 2010 survey of the detention center in Tapachula found that 90% of the children had not been informed of their right to ask for asylum.[163] After the UNHCR interviewers explained to unaccompanied Central American children that they had the right to ask for protection in Mexico, more than a quarter expressed an interest in applying. A 2014 UNHCR study found that 48% of Central American children in Mexico had international protection needs.[164] A 2013 survey of adult detainees at eleven migration centers found that only 39% had received the legally required information.[165]

The numbers of people applying for or gaining protection have historically been low. Between 2002 and 2016, only 3,847 foreigners were recognized as refugees in Mexico. An additional 6,075 people were given temporary humanitarian protection visas between 2012 and 2016 under the provision of a 2011 reform.[166] Arif, a Pakistani man in his mid-twenties who said he fled bombings in his hometown of Lahore and who was stuck in Chiapas trying to reach the United States, explained why he didn't ask for asylum in Mexico.

No, we don't agree for asylum. Here there is too much street crime. The mafia. We cannot walk at night. Too much mafia. They kidnap you and call your family on the phone. Twenty-five thousand dollars [ransom]. Same problem in

Pakistan. That's why we go to the U.S. Here in Mexico, no religious problems. But the mafia is the same problem.[67]

The Mexican government is also complicit in preventing foreigners along the northern border from making humanitarian protection claims in the United States. In 2016, several thousand Haitians arrived in Tijuana seeking humanitarian protection in the United States. Long lines formed on the Mexican side of the border as people waited to enter the U.S. border post. When the queue became longer than the number who could be processed each day, a migrant took it upon himself to create a handwritten notebook of appointments. The Tijuana municipal authorities then decided to rationalize the system by issuing tickets to leave Mexico and enter the United States at a designated time. Entrepreneurs quickly manufactured and sold fake tickets. Grupos Beta, the migrant aid division of INAMI, took over the appointment system and asked the Casa del Migrante Catholic shelter in Tijuana to issue appointments. When the director declined, Grupos Beta opened a post on the grounds of another migrant shelter. Initially it only issued appointments to Haitians. Later it included any migrant who had an exit permit from INAMI. The agency rarely gives the permit to Central Americans, so in practice Mexican authorities controlled which nationalities could approach the U.S. border to ask for humanitarian protection. Slight variations of this practice took place in the border cities of Nogales and Mexicali. INAMI agents have told Mexicans and Central Americans that the United States is not giving asylum to these nationalities and prevented some asylum seekers from approaching the U.S. border. People turned away rarely applied for asylum on the Mexican side of the border. The nearest office of COMAR, the Mexican asylum agency, is 2,300 kilometers away in Mexico City. Migrants being deterred by INAMI officers usually did not trust them to hear an initial claim that could then be referred to COMAR.[168]

As the Trump administration made even greater attempts to deter asylum seekers when it took office in January 2017 and the UNHCR boosted the refugee status determination capacity of COMAR, the number of people seeking and receiving protection in Mexico rose. Nearly 15,000 people asked for protection in Mexico in 2017. Of the 4,475 completed cases, 43% were recognized as refugees and 21% were given complementary protection.[169] Yet, given endemic violence in Mexico that targets migrants, including extortion at the hands of law enforcement, it is not surprising that relatively few ask for asylum in Mexico or wish to stay. At the same time as Mexican migration law turned toward rights-based framing to make the case for better treatment of Mexican nationals in the United States, it also became explicitly securitized, to enable more secretive cooperation with U.S. authorities. The result is a system that on paper would appear to make Mexico a safe space for refugees fleeing violence and persecution, but which in practice focuses its efforts on deterring groups that the U.S. government does not want.

In Central America, few ask for asylum, and access to legal procedures has often been sharply limited or ignored.[170] For example, a confidential 2009 U.S. diplomatic cable outlined the policy in Panama:

> [T]he unofficial policy of the [government of Panama] is simply to deny asylum requests and not accept economic migrants from Africa. As most migrants apprehended in Panama appear to have been headed for the United States, the issue has implications for the effort to secure our extended borders.

The cable referred to the recent detention by Panamanian police of ninety-six unauthorized Africans, seventy of whom where Somali. They had each paid between USD$3,000 and USD$10,000 to fly to Brazil and then travel through Ecuador and Colombia. Smugglers then ferried them in small boats along the isolated shores of the Darien Gap. In one instance, the smugglers left the migrants on the beach and told them they had reached Canada. Panamanian authorities denied asylum to eighty-nine of the ninety-six, but Colombia would not accept their return, and Somalia did not have a functioning government to accept repatriation. The Panamanian government detained them indefinitely while seeking resettlement options elsewhere in Latin America.[171]

De facto policies in Mexico and Central America typically do not make the region a safe alternative for asylum seekers trying to reach North America. Stuck in the buffer zone, they become prey for gangs and corrupt officials. Many continue to try to reach the United States or Canada.

Conclusion

The Mexican government has been deeply involved in buffering the United States from asylum seekers and other migrants since the early 1980s. Central American governments are increasingly involved in caging their citizens at home and preventing transit through the region. Canada and the United States have increased their mutual buffering, though this overwhelmingly works to keep asylum seekers out of Canada rather than the other way around. Then, as now, people are leaving for many reasons, including fleeing violence, seeking greater economic opportunity, and family reunification. Neither is the issue of security in the context of border control new, though fears and justifications for control have shifted from communist subversives to terrorists.

Mexico is the primary buffer in the Americas. One of the features of control in the Mexican case that makes it stand out from the United States, Canada, Europe, and Australia is the lack of concern with territoriality. While governments of the Global North go to elaborate lengths to define to the meter what constitutes the national territory for the purpose of asylum law and the provision of constitutional guarantees of territorial personhood, the Mexican government is apparently indifferent to such questions. The border with Guatemala and Belize is open. Enforcement takes place along a "vertical frontier" instead. One transportable lesson from this contrast is that what legal scholar Claire Inder calls "hyper-legalism" around territoriality is only relevant in contexts in which the rule of law is regularly practiced.[172] Where the rule of law is ignored on a routine basis, there is no need for recourse to hyper-legalism. The point is not that the law is always upheld in the democracies of the Global North, but rather that it tends to have a much greater meaning in practice there. Mexican authorities do not particularly care if an asylum seeker touches Mexican soil, because despite the increasingly generous formal law around asylum, the law is rarely applied in reality and is marked by extreme discretion.

Policymakers in the United States are deeply concerned with keeping undesired foreigners away from its border. They have pressured Mexico using a variety of techniques. Diplomatic pressure behind the scenes is a constant. There is also evidence for conditioning financial aid on a buildup of Mexican migration control. The U.S. government has sought to make Mexico more of a filter than a complete buffer, however. The Mexican government has read those signals and consequently has targeted different nationalities with different policy tools. Buffering is thick for Central Americans and ultimately results in mass deportations. Buffering was thin for Cubans as long as the United States maintained its idiosyncratic Cold War policies that favored Cubans above all other nationalities. Buffering toward Asians and Africans takes on the character of a cactus. The sharp spikes of restrictive visa policies keep most potential asylum seekers from ever getting on a plane for Mexico. For the small numbers who do arrive, quiet security screening in collaboration with U.S. authorities leaves them to go free while they make their way to the U.S. border. One of the most important mechanisms through which U.S. policy shapes Mexican policy is by changing transit patterns. Strict enforcement at the U.S.-Mexico border traps transit migrants in Mexico who otherwise would have passed through quickly. This dynamic creates an incentive for the Mexican government to adjust to the new pattern through a policy of deterrence, detention, and deportation. The Mexican government is not simply doing the bidding of the northern colossus. It aims to control a growing foreign population stuck in Mexico.

There are limits to the effectiveness of buffering, however. Just as states in the Global North do not try to hermetically seal themselves, Mexican authorities try to balance migration control with commerce, tourism, and employers' demands for foreign labor. Unlike the countries of the Global North, achieving the capacity for effective control is more difficult for Mexico, both because of limited resources and because the corruption that undermines effective control is more widespread. Some of the limits to effective buffering are inherent to migration systems in which states are simultaneously countries of origin, transit, and destination. Buffer countries such as Mexico, Morocco, and Turkey are often sources of emigration as well as transit migration, and the destinations are the same for both emigrants and transit migrants. The contradiction begins with the fact that Mexico is a country of mass emigration whose government is seeking better treatment of Mexicans in the United States and policies that make it easier for its nationals to legally migrate there. Thus, the Mexican government since the 2000s has attempted to set a higher standard of policy toward foreigners through soft, discursive strategies of generous rights-based lawmaking and public pronouncements. The logic is that by taking the high moral ground, the Mexican government will shame the U.S. government into improving the conditions of Mexicans in the United States. At the same time, Mexico City has tried to make a hard deal with Washington in which Mexican access to an expanded U.S. temporary worker program and legalization of unauthorized migrants are exchanged for a crackdown on Central Americans and other seeking to cross Mexico into the United States. The soft and hard goals are at odds with each other.

The second contradiction of buffering is that the greater the militarization of unilateral U.S. enforcement on its border with Mexico, which negatively affects Mexican migrants, the more politically difficult it becomes for Mexican authorities to cooperate openly with U.S. authorities to control third-country nationals. Finally, some buffering activities oriented toward control bring with them countervailing human rights pressures. The UNHCR was invited to help operate camps to bottle up refugees in southern Mexico, but, in doing so, it became an actor within the Mexican political sphere that advocated for limitations on deportations and became an ally of civil society watchdogs and sectors of the Mexican state oriented toward rights and international prestige rather than paramilitary responses. The migration control capacity building of the Mérida

Initiative is also bundled with some level of oversight by members of the U.S. Congress who insist that the resources not be used in ways that violate human rights. While human rights abuses may continue, buffer states and their patrons do not have carte blanche to deploy the full range of coercive policies. The Mexican government's solution to the limits and contradictions of buffering thus far has been to exercise its discretion quietly away from the eyes of the media and NGOs. It combines lip service to human rights with harsh practices in action. Effective buffering inherently relies on secrecy.

CHAPTER 8 | Building Fortress Europe

EUROPEAN GOVERNMENTS HAVE HISTORICALLY been reluctant to resettle refugees from overseas.[1] With very few legal routes, an estimated nine out of ten asylum seekers enter without visas.[2] The recognition rate of asylum seekers for refugee status or complementary protection averaged around one-third between 1982 and 2015, with a great deal of variation by nationality of origin and period.[3] Efforts to control those flows and manage asylum seekers who make it past the gauntlet in many ways resonate with the North American and Australian experiences.

However, the supranational structure of the European Union, in which member states and different EU institutions share responsibility for migration and asylum policies, has shaped remote controls in unique ways. EU states have not excised their territorial seas or overseas territories from spaces where domestic migration and asylum law apply. An EU Commission study found that EU asylum laws apply in the territorial waters of member states.[4] Strong rights of territorial personhood are built into European law, even if they are not observed in practice by all member states. The following chapter shows how Europeanization has cross-cutting effects on remote control in the cage, the dome, buffering, and the barbicans. Chapter 9 then analyzes the extensive effort to patrol a moat around Europe in cooperation with coastal buffer states.

Escape to Europe?

European politicians routinely harangue European courts for restricting member states' ability to control migration and their borders.[5] The leading political scientists of EU immigration and asylum policy take the opposite view. They argue that national governments shirk domestic constraints on policymaking through an "escape to Europe." In this account, national capitals are not losing their sovereign scope of maneuver to Brussels. Rather, national governments, and the executive branch in particular, are strategically shifting some of their policies up to the European level. This shift enhances executive power vis-à-vis national courts, parliaments, and domestic constituencies. Moving policy to the European level is also a way of escaping the constraints of national political culture and norms. Member states strategically play with the interaction between the national and European levels of policymaking.[6]

There is extensive evidence for the escape to Europe thesis during the initial ramp-up of European remote controls beginning in the 1980s. The security agencies of member states shifted their policies to the embryonic European level, where they could frame migration as part of a broader security agenda. Europeanization disempowered some domestic actors, such as foreign ministries, between 1985 and 1990 during the drafting of the Schengen Implementation Agreement. The Schengen agreement established freedom of movement within twenty-six countries, twenty-two of which are in the EU, and became part of EU law in 1997. Shifting policy upward reduced the influence of foreign ministries that are typically more sensitive to international norms and foreign relations than justice and interior ministries. Europeanization circumvented the constraints of national courts on member governments' ability to prevent family reunification of immigrants and to deport foreigners. The EU then became a major driver of externalization as it took on new members. It required Central and Eastern European candidate countries to adopt restrictive EU visa policies, border controls, and remote controls as part of the *acquis*—the body of EU law binding on all countries formally seeking to join.[7]

While the escape to Europe thesis was accurate at the time scholars formulated it in the late 1990s, the EU since then has become both a significant constrainer and enabler of remote control.[8] The two European supranational courts have become increasingly active in their oversight of asylum policy. Since 1959, the European Court of Human Rights (ECtHR) based in Strasbourg has been the court of the Council of Europe. All twenty-eight EU member states belong to the forty-seven-member Council of Europe. The Strasbourg court has made many rulings on member state violations of the 1950 European Convention on Human Rights (ECHR) that affect remote control of asylum seekers, most importantly by prohibiting refoulement on the high seas as discussed in the next chapter.[9] The second supranational court is the European Court of Justice (ECJ) based in Luxembourg. The

FIGURE 8.1 EU and Schengen Member States

ECJ has had a mandate since 2009 to review the legality of the actions of EU agencies and has become an increasingly important court on asylum issues.[10] Gregor Noll argues that the ECHR requires its signatories to protect basic rights in the treaty even when acting outside of their territory.[11] Case law establishes some limitations on state extra-territorial action.[12] Frank McNamara is less sanguine that supranational courts will find the EU liable for actions that take place on a third country's territory.[13]

Strong supranational courts have contradictory effects on the externalization of borders. The courts can constrain such policies, but they can also inadvertently create incentives for further externalization. For example, the UK incorporated the ECHR into its domestic law in 2000. This further motivated the British government to keep asylum seekers away from its territory so that they would not be able to seek protection by petitioning the Strasbourg court.[14] On the other hand, the same court limited the UK's applications of the safe third-country provision in the *TI v. UK* case, ruling that transfers to third countries do not absolve the transferring country from the obligation to avoid refoulement. The transfers are only legal where the asylum seeker will have access to an adequate hearing in the third country.[15]

EU policymaking is the product of discordant interests across EU institutions, member states, and agencies within each government.[16] The supranational institutions of the EU that have a mandate to represent the interests of the entire Union, such as the ECJ, European Parliament, and European Commission, have included human rights approaches in designing migration and asylum policies. Intergovernmental EU institutions, in which member state governments advocate for their own state's interests in coordination with other member states, such as the Council of the European Union, do not ignore human rights, but they are more likely to emphasize control.[17] The supranational institutions have strengthened over time. Their greater autonomy from national publics than the intergovernmental EU institutions creates space for a relatively greater consideration of rights concerns.[18] As the EU has moved its externalization agenda into its foreign policy, its enabling and constraining features have reappeared. Effective externalization of borders requires the cooperation of third countries, but when those third countries act in ways that obviously abuse the rights of asylum seekers to an intolerable degree, other parts of the EU apparatus object and insist on softening controls or avoiding the most draconian options.

Europeanization has had contradictory effects on specific techniques of remote control of asylum seekers. The following pages will show that it has enabled the spread of restrictive visas, carrier sanctions, stationing liaison officers abroad, and readmission agreements. The EU has had a mixed effect on designations of safe third countries and countries of origin. It encourages the policies while also expanding the monitoring of conditions in those countries that often questions their designation as safe. The EU has been a major vehicle for increasing the buffering capacity of transit countries, but in doing so, it has introduced the legal and political grounds for greater scrutiny of human rights violations. The EU border agency Frontex has been a leader in expanding maritime interceptions, but the Strasbourg court has insisted that ECHR members remain responsible for observing the principle of non-refoulement even on the high seas. European institutions have been a partial constraint in two areas—the redefinitions of territory to restrict the rights of asylum seekers in barbican spaces, such as in airport transit zones and in liminal border spaces, and, at least as of 2018, in member-state efforts to forcibly divert asylum seekers arriving in Europe to offshore processing centers.

The Euro-Dome

European governments and the EU as a whole have been instrumental in the construction of an aerial dome over the continent. Visa policies often specifically target asylum seekers. Carrier sanctions and liaison offices stationed abroad on paper make some provision for allowing asylum seekers to pass but simply block them in practice. These policies are not seriously constrained by other institutions.

Visas

European governments quickly followed the Canadian model discussed in chapter 4 of using visa policy with the explicit intent of keeping asylum seekers from ever reaching their borders. Germany was Europe's major destination of asylum seekers in the 1980s and led the way in imposing visa restrictions on Afghans in 1980 after the Soviet invasion sent refugees fleeing abroad. Germany placed visa restrictions on Bangladeshis, Indians, and Sri Lankans the same year and Ethiopians in 1982.[19]

Among European countries, in subsequent years the UK most consistently and explicitly used visa policies to prevent the arrival of asylum seekers. The Conservative government imposed visa requirements on Sri Lankans in May 1985 during the Sri Lankan civil war after a rise in asylum applications from Tamils.[20] Several Labour members of Parliament warned that strict visa policies would keep some people with a legitimate claim from seeking asylum. "It is difficult in an East European country, a dictatorial state in South America or a dictatorial state in the Far East to pop into the British embassy and get the necessary visa," MP Gerald Bermingham told Parliament. "The minute that one pops into the British embassy one tends to get arrested when coming out, because countries of that ilk do not wish to see their citizens flee from their territories."[21] Britain imposed asylum-related visa restrictions on Turkish nationals in 1989, in response to an increase in claims from Kurds living in Turkey, and on nationals of the former Yugoslavia in 1992, Sierra Leone in 1994, and Colombia in 1997 during their civil wars.[22] A representative of the British government openly stated in court that visa restrictions targeted asylum seekers: "When, for example, Colombia and Ecuador were included as visa States, this was directly in response to an increase in the number of those nationals coming directly to the United Kingdom in order to apply for asylum."[23] In 1998 to 1999, the UK, along with Ireland and Finland, imposed visa restrictions on Slovakia to reduce the arrival of Roma asylum seekers. The number of nationalities requiring visas to travel to the UK increased from 19 to 108 between 1991 and 2008.

British visa policies reduced asylum claims. For example, after Britain imposed visas on Zimbabweans during a wave of political repression, asylum applications fell from more than 7,600 in 2002 to just over 2,000 in 2004.[24] The British government openly linked the imposition of airport transit visas to a reduction in asylum claims. "We have substantially increased the nationalities that require visas just to pass through the UK," an official declared in 2005. "This has had a significant impact on unfounded asylum application."[25]

Visa policies create concentric rings of interactive buffers. During the civil war in the former Yugoslavia that killed 140,000 people and displaced 4 million more, Western European governments imposed visa restrictions on Bosnians. For example, Sweden imposed visas in 1992. Applications per week quickly dropped from 2,000 to fewer than 200.[26] The governments of Poland, the Czech Republic, Bulgaria, Hungary, Slovakia, and Slovenia followed suit to avoid becoming a "closed sack" for asylum seekers in transit who could enter but not leave.

In addition to this reciprocal adjustment mechanism, in which governments autonomously adapted to each other's policies, formal co-ordination shifted visa restrictions up to the European level.[27] In 1987 the European Community agreed in principle to create a list of fifty countries whose nationals required visas to prevent abuse, "notably in the domain of asylum," and to mitigate security risks.[28] The first "black list" in 1993 required 73 of the world's 183 non-EU nationalities to obtain a visa for short-term stays.[29] "The EU is replacing the Iron Curtain with a paper curtain across Europe," observed Ukrainian president Leonid Kuchma.[30] The black list expanded to 110 nationalities in 1995 and 134 in 2001, before falling to 107 in 2017.[31] The black list included every country in Africa and most of the Middle East, Asia, the Caribbean, and Pacific. In 1995, additional requirements for airport transit visas were slapped on nationals of ten countries with large numbers of asylum seekers—Afghanistan, Ethiopia, Eritrea, Ghana, Iraq, Iran, Nigeria, Somalia, Sri Lanka, and Zaire.[32] The exact number of nationalities requiring transit visas and their composition changes over time and increased to twelve by 2009.[33]

A "white list" included forty-five countries whose nationals do not require visas. Its composition was overwhelmingly countries in the Americas, Europe, and the rich parts of East Asia and the Antipodes. The white list reached sixty countries by 2017 with the addition of several Pacific and Caribbean islands and countries in Europe.[34] If policymakers meant to stop bogus asylum seekers, as they routinely claim, they would not slap visa restrictions on the very countries that are the world's major sources of recognized refugees. The fact that Syrians, Afghans, and Eritreans who made it past the obstacle course usually received asylum is strong evidence that the main goal of the visa policies is not to restrict asylum seekers without valid claims, but to keep out people even if they are refugees.[35]

Carrier Sanctions

Assessing fines on passenger carriers, in conjunction with tighter visa policies and the de facto targeting of asylum seekers, has marked the European carrier sanctions regimes since their inception. In the UK, the Immigration Act of 1971 allowed an immigration official to direct a carrier to return at its expense any passenger denied entry.[36] Tightened sanctions in 1987 added a fine of £1,000 for carrying an alien without a valid passport or visa. The fine doubled to £2,000 in 1991.[37] The government openly intended to use carrier sanctions to reduce arrivals of asylum seekers. "The immediate spur to this proposal has been the arrival of over 800 people claiming asylum in the three months up to the end of February," explained Home Office Minister Douglas Hurd when he introduced carrier legislation. Around 500 of the asylum seekers were Sri Lankans, who had been targeted with visa restrictions two years earlier.[38] Several members of Parliament objected to the sanctions because they would incentivize airlines not to allow asylum seekers with legitimate claims to board and because authoritarian governments in practice would be making boarding decisions. "Officials of the KGB involved in the working of Aeroflot will be interpreting and implementing British law, not simply in the case of their own nationals, but in the case of passengers from other countries who have stopped over in Moscow and wish to fly on to London," cautioned Labour MP Gerald Kaufman.[39] In the 1990 *Yassine* decision, the High Court noted that someone seeking asylum in the UK in effect only had three choices: lying to British authorities at a post abroad to get a visa under some pretense like tourism, obtaining a fraudulent visa, or buying an airline ticket that included a stopover in the UK.[40]

The immediate effect of introducing the carrier fines was a 50% reduction in asylum applications at UK ports of entry.[41] By 2000, the British government had levied more than £120 million on airlines for violating the 1987 Act. There is little documentation available about what happens to intended asylum seekers denied boarding. In one case in 1990, British Airways staff, hoping to avoid a £3,000 fine, held three Tamils from Sri Lanka against their will on a flight from Rome to London and then flew them back to Rome without ever telling the UK immigration authorities. Italian authorities expelled the three Tamils to Bombay, where Indian police beat two of them before sending them all back to Sri Lanka.[42] Between 1987 and 2001, 400 passengers who boarded British Airways flights with false documents were granted asylum in the UK. If airline personnel had scrutinized the documents more carefully, people later recognized as refugees would have been denied protection. As Lord Justice Simon Brown pointed out in a 2003 appeals case, "the combined effect of visa requirements and carriers' liability has made it well-nigh impossible for refugees to travel to countries of refuge without false documents."[43] The House of Lords ruled in 1993 that an individual who traveled to the UK with forged documents and applied for asylum on arrival had not entered illegally. The use of visas to deter asylum seekers continues.[44]

Sanctions regimes grew throughout continental Europe in the 1980s, though there are historical precedents dating at least as far back as a 1634 statute in the Dutch city of Medemblik that established a twenty-five-guilder fine for any ship captain transporting Danish or Norwegian "vagabonds" and that made the captain liable for the cost of their care and return.[45] Belgium imposed carrier sanctions in 1980.[46] Some EU member states used Europeanization to advance stricter immigration measures than they could accomplish at the national level. The French government pushed the European directive to harmonize carrier sanctions as a way to tighten its own border control. When the Dutch government's attempt to implement carrier sanctions encountered resistance in Parliament, it helped negotiate the Schengen Implementing Agreement in 1990 that required all Schengen member states to introduce sanctions.[47] By 1999, all the Schengen countries, as well as Norway and Iceland, had adopted some form of carrier sanctions.[48] EU policies spread east as Central and Eastern European countries looked ahead to joining the Union and brought their policies into compliance with EU norms. A conference of immigration ministers from around Europe in 1993 called for training airline personnel to check immigration documents and to sanction carriers that transported passengers without the necessary documents. The following year's Berlin Declaration by Central and Eastern European governments pledged to pass carrier sanction laws.[49]

Schengen regulations and some EU member states include provisions that carrier sanctions must comply with the 1951 Refugee Convention.[50] Recall that Article 31 of the Convention prohibits states from penalizing refugees who have entered illegally, with several enumerated exceptions. In practice, laws that exempt carriers from sanctions if they transport irregular travelers who make successful asylum claims are ignored. For example, Dutch law exempts airlines from fines for transporting undocumented passengers who wish to claim asylum if the airlines first obtain permission from Dutch authorities by calling the general phone number of the Dutch Ministry of Justice, which then forwards the call to immigration authorities at Schiphol airport. An audit of practices in 2007 found that airlines had never used this procedure to ask to transport undocumented asylum seekers.[51] As legal scholar Tally Kritzman-Amir argues,

> While carriers are threatened with sanctions if they err and allow entry to un-documented migrants, they are not subject to any sanctions if they effectively deny entry and admission of asylum seekers. There are thus incentives to err on the side of caution which in this case means to refuse to transport asylum seekers who wish to enter clandestinely . . . It renders those who were refused faceless, nameless, and absent from the country to which they wish to enter, unable to attain remedies in courts and—perhaps most importantly—not in-cluded in any official statistics that could later on be used against the state as proof of incompliance with the [1951 Refugee] Convention.[52]

The spirit of the carrier sanctions and the asylum regime are clearly at odds even if the carrier sanctions laws do not directly violate the letter of the 1951 Convention.[53] The Administrative Court in Frankfurt ruled in 1987 that even though the right to asylum that was then part of Germany's Basic Law could not be activated until the asylum seeker was on German territory, Germany could not prevent access to asylum procedures through administrative meas-ures like carrier sanctions.[54] The Federal Administrative Court in April 1992 agreed that visa requirements and carrier sanctions could not be used to nul-lify the right to seek asylum by cutting off access to the territory.[55] The 1993 reform of the Basic Law abrogated the right to asylum and thus circumvented the German judiciary's effort to maintain access to protection. The UNHCR (1995), European Council on Refugees and Exiles (1988, 1999), Council of Europe (1991), European Parliament (1991), and parliamentary commissions in the British House of Lords (1994) and French Senate (1991) denounced the use of carrier sanctions to deny access to asylum. The practice remains the norm across Europe.[56]

Officers Abroad

Liaison officers are stationed abroad to advise airlines which passengers to allow onboard an aircraft bound for their country. The UK began deploying carrier liaisons in 1983, and the EU did the same beginning in 1996.[57] By

2008, the UK had officers in thirty-two countries credited with preventing nearly 180,000 passengers from boarding between 2003 and 2007. How could someone facing persecution fly to the Global North? In theory, when asylum seekers are intercepted in a country that is not party to the 1951 Convention, they are supposed to be referred to the local UNHCR office, diplomatic mission, or an NGO.[58] Yet a 2000 UNHCR study that inspected operational manuals used by airline liaison officers and government reports of their activities found "no reference to possible refugee protection issues or other human rights concerns."[59] The EU's 1999 Afghanistan Action Plan for airline liaison officers explicitly included efforts to keep recognized Afghan refugees from leaving the region. One of the goals was "an information campaign, in particular for Afghan refugees in Pakistan and in Iran, to advise on migration options and to warn against the consequences of illegally entering Member States, of unlawful employment and of using facilitators to gain entry to the EU."[60] Liaison officers do not keep statistics on how often intercepted passengers appeal for asylum or how often agents make referrals.[61] Liaison officers are not trained to screen asylum seekers and have an incentive not to provoke the host country government by declaring one of its nationals to be an asylum seeker. In practice, there is no provision for asylum seekers without a visa to fly legally to their destination.

Britain has directly screened passengers abroad with the explicit goal of rooting out asylum applicants. The number of Roma with Czech nationality seeking asylum in the UK rose from 515 in 1998 to 1,200 in 2000. The government called them "bogus asylum seekers," even as it recognized that discrimination against Roma was prevalent in the Czech Republic and granted asylum to 6% of Roma claimants in early 2001. To avoid imposing visa controls on all Czech nationals, which would upset the broader bilateral relationship, the UK negotiated an agreement to station British officers at the Prague airport in 2001. The officers denied boarding to anyone who said they intended to ask for asylum or whom the officers believed intended to ask for asylum. The policy reduced the number of Czech nationals seeking asylum in the UK from 200 in the three weeks before the operation to 20 in the following three weeks. An appeals court and the House of Lords ruled that the non-refoulement provisions of the 1951 Refugee Convention did not apply to individuals who were still in their country of nationality, though the House of Lords did hold that the system illegally discriminated against Roma by singling them out for interrogation.[62] The policy was partly constrained by a combination of scrutiny from a domestic court and the goal of maintaining positive relations between origin and destination countries. Direct screening of passengers by British agents abroad has been replaced with the standard system of carrier sanctions and liaisons that accomplish the same end.

Containment

The Dublin system since 1990 has established which member state is responsible for examining an asylum claim. Asylum seekers who file in another member state may be transferred to the "responsible member state," which pledges to accept their physical return. The system ostensibly was designed to end "asylum shopping" in which rejected applicants in one member state file a new claim in another and the "refugee in orbit" problem in which no state is responsible for the asylum seeker.[63] Asylum seekers who enter the EU irregularly in most cases are supposed to have their claims heard by the first member state they enter.[64] The Dublin system was intended to apply only to asylum applications made at the border or within the territory of a member state.[65] The EU recognizes that the non-refoulement provision applies to asylum seekers arriving at a border, even if members do not always actually follow the law.[66]

The Dublin system thus created buffers out of the states at the external borders of the EU, such as Italy, that cushioned states in the interior of Europe, such as Germany, which were major countries of asylum. The system incentivized member states at the external borders to avoid the costs of refugee status determination and accommodating recognized refugees by negotiating readmission agreements and building up buffer states outside the EU.[67] Germany supported the accession to the EU of Poland and other countries in Central and Eastern Europe, which then made them even thicker buffers under the Dublin transfer system. Combined with air carrier sanctions and visa restrictions, in theory this combination of policies cut off legal access to Germany by land or air for the vast majority of potential asylum seekers.[68] However, because the Dublin system did not work well in practice, Germany took a disproportionately high number of asylum seekers in the 1990s and 2000s compared with most European countries.[69]

Governments legally designate other countries as safe to allow deportations that on their face comply with the principle of non-refoulement. Two different ways of buffering are to designate safe countries as part of a reciprocal agreement, as among members of the Dublin system, or as safe third countries of transit outside Europe. Designating the country of origin as safe is a form of caging.

Safe Third Countries

The justification for safe designation policies is that the international asylum regime does not give a refugee the right to seek protection in any given country. If refugees are safe in a designated third country and then try to enter a new country of protection, returning them does not constitute refoulement. The UNHCR accepts the logic of safe third countries in theory, but the devil is in the details about whether asylum seekers are protected in a given context. The UNHCR rejects altogether the practice of designating specific countries of origin as safe because such a blanket designation undermines the principle that the facts of an individual's claim should be assessed.[70]

Denmark was the first country in Europe to adopt a safe third-country scheme, beginning in 1986.[71] The EU then spread these policies through the Dublin system. The Dublin system does not require the responsible member state to determine the merit of an asylum claim. The responsible state can instead return the asylum seeker to a "third state" that complies with the provisions of the 1951 Refugee Convention and its 1967 Protocol.[72] The London Resolutions (1992) stated that identifying a safe third country should precede the determination of whether the asylum application had merit. If a safe third country was identified, the asylum applicant should normally be returned to that country.[73] The London Resolutions moved the goal from using EU members at the external borders as buffers for states in the interior to containing even acknowledged refugees in one of the "safe" countries they passed through on their way to the EU.

Agreements between governments such as the London Resolutions are a kind of "escape to Europe" to avoid national political and judicial constraints. The British government pushed especially hard for EU-wide safe third-country rules. Chancellor Helmut Kohl used Germany's participation in the Dublin asylum system to justify reforms to Germany's Basic Law in 1993, specifically the inclusion of a safe third-country provision. Kohl claimed that a more restrictive German policy was necessary to bring Germany into line with the common European asylum policy. German judge Ralf Rothkegel acerbically described the idea of sending asylum seekers elsewhere for a decision as the "Pontius Pilate objection" to refugee status determination. Germany surrounded itself with either EU members or designated safe third countries with which it negotiated readmission agreements, including Romania (1992), Poland and Switzerland (1993), and Bulgaria and the Czech Republic (1995). These agreements created an incentive for those countries to keep out asylum seekers destined for Germany who would be returned to the transit country if they were rejected. States wanted to avoid becoming a "closed sack" that asylum seekers could enter but not leave.[74] Visa, safe third country, and readmission policies worked together in an architecture of repulsion.

The Dublin II directive elaborated the criteria for designating a safe third country. The state had to be party to the 1951 Refugee Convention, respect the principle of non-refoulement, prohibit deportations that would violate the Convention Against Torture, allow appeals for refugee status, and protect recognized refugees.[75] Examinations could be sped up, with fewer procedural rights, for applicants from safe third countries.[76] Applicants entering illegally from a "European safe third country" could be rejected without an examination of their case.[77] While the Dublin II directive established the legal grounds for creating a common EU list of safe third countries, the European Court of Justice annulled the provision because the Council had made rules outside its competence in the EU's division of powers.[78] Member state governments were authorized to create their own national lists and report them to the European Commission.[79] The ECJ thus temporarily placed a moderate check on efforts to Europeanize this technique of remote control. EU member states developed different lists of safe third countries.[80] In 2017, twelve EU countries (Austria, Bulgaria, Croatia, Cyprus, Germany, Hungary, Malta, Netherlands, Spain, Switzerland, and the UK) had some form of safe third country provision, as did candidate countries Serbia and Turkey.[81]

By the late 2000s, Greece had stopped functioning as an effective legal buffer for other European states. The Greek asylum system was obviously broken. A record of illegal pushbacks in which Greek authorities expel travelers without assessing whether they have valid protection claims, squalid detention centers, a first-instance asylum recognition rate of only 0.06% (compared to an average in the other major EU asylum seeker destinations of 36.2%), lack of an appeals process, and rampant corruption led the UNHCR to call on EU members to halt Dublin transfers to Greece. The governments of Sweden, Norway, and the Netherlands heeded the call.[82] The European Court of Human Rights then intervened in the landmark *M.S.S. v. Belgium and Greece* case brought by an Afghan asylum seeker. In 2008, an Afghan interpreter for NATO forces in Afghanistan fled Kabul. His first point of entry into the EU was Greece, where authorities entered his fingerprints into the common EU database for asylum seekers and irregular migrants. He then made his way to Belgium and applied for asylum based on a claim that he feared Taliban persecution of Afghans who had collaborated with NATO. The Belgian authorities sent him back to Greece under the Dublin transfer system. However, the European Court of Human Rights upheld his claim that Dublin transfers to Greece violated his rights because of the deficiencies in the Greek asylum system and the risk of chain refoulement.[83]

The theoretical lesson is that if buffer policies are too harsh and selectively violate European law, buffering breaks down. It is a constraint enhanced by the fact that in this case, Greece was a member of the EU. The supranational judiciary, support from some member state governments, and the suasion of the UNHCR were instrumental in blocking the transfers. None of these protections are absolute. The same court ruled in the *Ilias and Ahmed v. Hungary* (2017) case that two Bangladeshi nationals' rights had been violated when the Hungarian government expelled them to Serbia, which was on the Hungarian government's "safe third country list," without considering conditions in Serbia and the real risk of chain refoulement.[84] The Hungarian government led by Viktor Orbán routinely flouted EU law in its response to the 2015 European refugee crisis and in its broader move toward illiberal democracy. When the rule of law starts to break down *tout court*, institutional mechanisms that normally constrain states lose their effect.

Safe origins

The Dublin II directive in 2005 authorized a common list of "safe countries of origin" that would be used by all members of the Dublin system as well as national lists drawn up by member states.[85] Asylum applications from nationals of safe countries of origin, or stateless people who normally lived there, would be considered unfounded "on the basis of the rebuttable presumption of the safety of that country."[86] Rejected applicants from safe countries could be expelled faster. The criteria for designating a safe country of *origin* were more rigid than the criteria for designating a safe *third* country. The former included being democratic; a general, consistent pattern of no persecution; no torture, nor inhuman or degrading punishment; no threat of indiscriminate violence; no armed conflict; and effective remedies against rights violations.[87] EU officials informally considered seven African and three Latin American countries for a safe country of origin list.

The list was not motivated by an effort to identify the safest countries. According to a U.S. diplomatic cable, "Only countries with significant numbers of asylum seekers were reportedly considered for inclusion on the list."[88] Foreign policy interests and domestic politics shaped deliberations:

> Momentum is gaining to strike all Latin American countries off the list for political reasons. Countries not given the "seal of approval" of being selected for the list might complain about the omission, so it might be best to ignore

the whole region. As to the African candidates, the two EU heavyweights—France and Germany—are taking opposing sides. France is pushing hard for all seven to be included on the list because France receives the bulk of the claims from these countries. (For instance, over 90% of all asylum claims made by Malians in the EU are filed in France.) Germany, because of domestic politics, is questioning the African countries identified for inclusion on the list over the issue of female genital mutilation [FGM]. Since the Green party campaigned hard for Germany to consider gender and other related claims in deciding asylum requests, it does not want to include African countries on the list where FGM is practiced for cultural reasons.[89]

Statewatch, originally a British NGO that became a European-wide organization for monitoring civil liberties in 1991, obtained the records of EU discussions about the safe third-country list. It found "significant disagreement between the member states and concern over whether any of the seven African countries are 'safe.'"[90] Austria's discussion of the list of African countries exclusively centered on female genital mutilation. The Czech government reversed its position on several of the countries of origin without explanation. In the case of Senegal, the British government supported declaring it safe even though "due to the conflict in the Casamance region there will almost certainly be some applicants who have a valid claim to asylum." Germany supported designating Ghana as safe despite reporting cases of torture and arbitrary arrest and admitting that the responsible authorities "are only rarely investigated" and had never been convicted of human rights violations. Fourteen member states established lists of safe countries of origin by 2018. The lists were not consistent and changed frequently.[91]

The European Commission proposed a new regulation to establish a common list of safe countries of origin in September 2015. The Commission concluded that Albania, Bosnia and Herzegovina, the former Yugoslav Republic of Macedonia, Kosovo, Montenegro, Serbia and Turkey were safe countries of origin with low recognition rates for asylum applications by their nationals in the EU.[92] By mid-2016, it appeared likely that western Balkan countries would eventually become part of an EU-wide list of safe countries.[93] The European Council on Refugees and Exiles warned that even though a country may be considered generally free of persecution, minorities may still be targeted. Regardless of their legal merits, safe country lists are designed to cage potential asylum seekers in their places of origin so they will not even try to make protection claims in Europe.

Readmission Agreements

Without some form of readmission agreement, it is difficult or impossible for governments of destination countries to push back or deport asylum seekers. Readmission agreements typically bind governments to accept individuals expelled from each other's countries. Formal agreements are neither sufficient nor necessary for returns in practice. They are not sufficient because it is sometimes hard to prove which countries' migrants have transited, especially if travelers have destroyed their documents to impede return. Irregular migrants have used this technique at least since the 1940s, as outlined in chapter 2's discussion of Jews trying to reach Palestine. Biometric databases, such as the iris scans of 2.3 million refugees registered by the UNHCR in the Middle East, can be used to identify refugees who attempt to access benefits in other countries.[94] The same technology, if accessible to government agencies, could be used to identify a refugee's country of origin or transit countries where the person's eye was scanned to facilitate expulsion.

Readmission is generally contingent on the overall relationship between the destination country and the country of origin or transit and a willingness to put the agreements into practice. The political context matters more than the legal arrangement.[95] Formal readmission agreements are not necessary because many governments have signed quasi-secret memoranda of understanding or informal notes that achieve the same purpose, often without any kind of judicial or parliamentary oversight.[96] For example, Spain has memoranda of understanding with Ghana (2005), Senegal (2006), and Mali (2007) that facilitate readmission.[97]

Readmission agreements have multiple purposes beyond the externalization of borders. European governments have signed readmission agreements since the nineteenth century that only apply to each other's nationals. Later versions, beginning with a 1906 Dutch-German agreement, have tended to cover third-country nationals as well. Until the 1950s, the goal of these agreements was the readmission of specific types of undesired individuals such as extradited criminals. After World War II, the agreements became a tool for controlling migration flows more broadly.[98] Fifteen agreements were signed between 1950 and 1970 and three between 1970 and 1990. The number of "second generation" agreements aimed at controlling asylum seekers and unauthorized migrants increased quickly in Europe in the 1990s with the expansion of Schengen and the lifting of visa requirements between the EU and Central European countries.[99] Between 1990 and 2000, 302 agreements were signed, three-quarters of which were bilateral treaties. Within Europe, Germany led the way with agreements with Romania (1992),

Bulgaria (1992), Poland (1993), and the Czech Republic (1994). The German agreements prompted those states in turn to negotiate accords with their neighbors.[100] Spain became a model for formal agreements with African countries, beginning with Morocco (1992), Algeria (2002), Guinea-Bissau (2003), and Mauritania (2003).[101] Almost all the agreements were between destination countries and buffer states, rather than countries of origin. European governments signed the majority of the world's admission agreements by 2000, led by France with forty-four. By contrast, Canada signed twelve, Australia four, and the United States two.[102]

Readmission agreements between the EU and transit states have become increasingly common since the Schengen countries and Poland signed an accord in 1991.[103] The EU has tried to standardize and expand bilateral and EU-wide agreements. Its 2004 criteria for selecting countries was based on the degree of "migration pressure" and the "geographical position of countries, including considerations of regional coherence and neighborhood"—in other words, their position as migration buffers.[104] Russia and the Balkan countries have the most agreements with EU member states.[105] Russian ambassador to the EU Vladimir Chizhov called Russia the first line of defense for thwarting unauthorized movements to Europe.[106] Between 2002 and 2014, seventeen countries concluded readmission agreements with the EU, and the EU has negotiated with countries all over the world.[107] "Although these agreements are reciprocal in theory, it is clear that in practice they essentially serve the interests of the Community," European commissioner for Justice and Internal Affairs Franco Frattini told the French Senate in March 2006. "The successful conclusion of the negotiations depends therefore on the 'levers' or should I say 'carrots' that the Commission has at its disposal, in other words sufficiently strong incentives to obtain the cooperation of the third party in question."[108] By the 2000s, the EU was packaging readmission provisions into wide-ranging treaties with Central America (2003) and the Andean Community (2003) and making improved relationships and financial aid contingent on their inclusion. The EU's 2000 Cotonou Agreement for economic and development cooperation between the EU and 78 countries in the Asia, Caribbean, and Pacific Group of States included readmission rules, but non-EU countries successfully lobbied to keep out provisions regarding third-country national readmissions and irregular migration.[109] Countries outside the Global North are not simply passive actors. Even governments in asymmetric relationships have bargaining chips.

Transit countries create readmission agreements with an outer belt of countries in a game of "hot potato" stretching all the way from the Global North to the countries that produce refugees. For example, the EU signed a readmission agreement with Russia in 2006. Russia then negotiated readmission agreements with major source and transit countries, beginning in Central Asia, to allow chain deportation.[110] Similarly, the EU has a readmission agreement with Turkey, which in turn has readmission agreements with Syria, Russia, Uzbekistan, Egypt, and Nigeria.[111] Kazakhstan set up the framework for chain deportation preemptively by negotiating readmission agreements with Kyrgyzstan and Tajikistan with the hope of then gaining liberalized visas from Central European and Baltic states.[112]

Rights groups worry that non-refoulement provisions that should protect refugees are simply ignored when readmission agreements are signed with authoritarian countries.[113] In a typical example, after Spain returns migrants to Mauritania, the Mauritanian authorities summarily expel them outside any official procedure and without any opportunity for appeal.[114] There are also concerns that chain refoulement takes place even among democratic countries. For example, in August 2002, nineteen Guatemalans arrived at London's Heathrow Airport after stopovers in the United States and Spain. At Heathrow they expressed fear of persecution because of their political beliefs. British authorities returned them to Spain, where Spanish authorities returned them to Miami, where U.S. authorities returned them to Guatemala. None of the authorities ever attempted to determine if the asylum seekers had valid claims.[115] There are no systematic records kept of the chain refoulement that readmission agreements facilitate.[116]

Control Capacity

Powerful EU members led by Germany created the first migration buffers in Europe. In the early 1990s, the German government gave 120 million marks to Poland and 60 million marks to the Czech Republic for improved controls in the east.[117] Germany paid Romania to reduce the flow of Roma asylum seekers.[118] Bilateral agreements between individual member states and other countries, and a cascade of non-EU states in Europe following Germany's lead, spread buffers outward in the 1990s. The EU then began building up the borders of countries in the process of acceding to the Union. For example, the EU's Phare program paid for improvements to Poland's border infrastructure, hiring more guards and supplying digital equipment. The EU also channeled funds to its members on the periphery. Greece received more than €227 million to strengthen its borders and detention capacity and just over €12 million to support refugees between 2011 and 2013.[119] The EU has externalized its borders by building up the capacities of third countries that are not potential members.[120]

The Maastricht Treaty that established the EU in 1992 created a legal supranational framework to externalize Europe's borders. EU summits and meetings in Tampere (1999), Seville (2002), Thessaloniki (2003), The Hague (2004), and Brussels (2005) laid out increasingly elaborate plans for pushing Europe's borders outward, tying migration control to economic development abroad, and eventually achieving the full integration of immigration policy into EU foreign policy. The Seville Conclusions made improvements in broad EU third-country relationships contingent on their cooperation on migration control, thus embedding remote control of migration in the high politics of the EU.[121] Aspirational statements at the early meetings were followed by the allocation of significant funding, the pursuit of cooperative agreements with transit countries to establish migration buffer zones, and the establishment of Frontex as the EU's external border control agency in 2004.[122] Frontex commands few resources directly and mostly relies on the voluntary participation of member-state governments for its operations.[123] Still, its budget grew from €15.7 million in 2006 to €254 million in 2016.[124] By 2009, Frontex had signed cooperation agreements with a dozen third countries around its periphery and North America.[125] The EU folded Frontex into the European Border and Coast Guard in 2016 and authorized it to operate in neighboring third countries with their permission.[126]

By 2005, the EU had adopted the Global Approach to Migration and devoted an annual budget of €100 million for "migration management" outside EU borders.[127] Border assistance missions to neighboring states like Ukraine and Moldova trained officers and linked national migration databases to Frontex resources. Surveillance gear, document readers, communications equipment, vehicles, and CO_2 detectors to sniff human breath beefed up national capacity.[128] The EU financed "migrant accommodation centers" across the Ukraine and made its qualification for "good neighbor" status conditional on passing and implementing EU standards of border control, migration, and asylum.[129] The Aeneas program gave €120 million to countries that cooperated with Europe on migration control between 2004 and 2006. Most of the funding went to countries that had signed readmission agreements with the EU. The dominant focus was Africa, followed by Eastern Europe, Asia, and Latin America. The Thematic Programme for Migration and Asylum continued the goals of Aeneas with a €384 million budget from 2007 to 2013 to fund projects on remittances, diaspora-led development, "brain circulation" of highly skilled professionals, return and reintegration, and addressing the social consequences of outmigration.[130] The EU signed "mobility partnerships" with Cape Verde, Moldova, Georgia, Armenia, Morocco, Azerbaijan, Tunisia, Jordan, and Belarus.[131] These deals typically increased legal access to the EU for some of their citizens in exchange for upgrading screening of migrants' documents, training for border police, and readmission agreements.[132]

The EU-Africa Action Plan included a €1.8 billion fund for addressing root causes of irregular migration and displaced persons in Africa. The most important measure from the perspective of remote control was capacity building in African countries. These measures included supporting the drafting of new laws and institutions to control land, sea and air borders. The EU pledged to provide equipment, "anti-trafficking" training, and intelligence. Potential migrants were to be provided with access to credible information in their countries of origin about legal migration channels and the dangers of irregular migration. The language of the agreement propagated the false notion that irregular migrants could travel legally if they wished to, when in fact, for the vast majority of them, there was no legal avenue for their safe movement because the application processes described in the EU's plans did not actually exist for asylum seekers.[133]

States outside the EU often resist entreaties to become buffers. For example, Malian authorities rejected linking migration control to development assistance. Almost a quarter of Mali's population lives in other West African countries, and the Malian economy depends on skilled immigrant labor. The government wanted to preserve the intra-African mobility that drives its economy. As in countries of emigration such as Mexico, there is

FIGURE 8.2 Mediterranean and North Africa

also a significant counterhegemonic position toward France as the former colonizer. France retaliated against a perceived lack of Malian migration cooperation in 2008 by cutting its development aid.[134] Remote control is based on applying carrots and sticks in the buffers.

At a 2015 summit in the Maltese capital of Valletta, European and African leaders pledged to step up their cooperation to improve the management of migration flows.[135] The EU's "Better Migration Management" project, known as the Khartoum Process, similarly aims to manage the root causes of forced displacement and irregular flows in the Horn of Africa. Of the €40 million budget, €25 million was designated for migration-control capacity building. An internal document suggested that two of the risks of the program were the diversion of equipment and training for repressive aims and "criticism by NGOs and civil society for engaging with repressive governments on migration (particularly in Eritrea and Sudan)."[136] After the EU announced a €155 million package for Sudan in 2016, Amnesty International and the international press pointed out that the International Criminal Court issued an arrest warrant for Sudanese President Omar Hassan al Bashir in 2009 for war crimes and crimes against humanity committed during the ethnic cleansing campaign in Darfur. One of the major agencies of the Sudanese border control forces had a well-documented history of involvement in serious human rights violations.[137] Next door, the UN accused Eritrea's government of crimes against humanity in a detailed 2016 report.[138] Ninety percent of Eritreans seeking asylum in the EU in 2015 were granted some form of protection, the second-highest recognition rate for any nationality after Syrians.[139] The contradictions between a commitment to human rights and remote control of migration have sharpened as the effective frontiers of Europe push all the way back to the countries from which refugees flee. Transnational media, NGOs, and the various agencies of the UN highlight this tension.

Hard and Soft Caging

Military intervention is the hardest tool of caging. For example, the conflict in the former Yugoslavia in the 1990s led to efforts to keep potential refugees in their own countries. UN Security Council resolutions established six safe havens in 1993 to protect predominantly Muslim populations in Bosnia-Herzegovina from ethnic cleansing by Bosnian Serbs and authorized air strikes to protect UN peacekeepers guarding the zones.[140] These so-called safe zones have sometimes turned into deathtraps. In July 1995, Bosnian Serb forces drove out Dutch peacekeepers and murdered around 8,000

Muslim men and boys in what UN Secretary-General Kofi Annan later called the worst crime on European soil since World War II.[141] Subsequent military interventions in Kosovo and Libya were partly motivated to prevent deaths of civilians as well as prevent them from crossing the seas around Europe, as described in the following chapter.

Like Australia and the United States, the EU and its members wage publicity campaigns in countries of origin and transit in an attempt to deter people from leaving home. The European Council called for "information campaigns on the actual possibilities for legal immigration, and for the prevention of all forms of trafficking in human beings" in cooperation with countries of origin and transit in 1999.[142] In practice, many EU-financed awareness campaigns have been "limited to prevention of irregular migration."[143] Member states, such as the UK, have advertised on television, radio, and in newspaper ads in Pakistan, India, Vietnam, and northern France that urge potential irregular migrants not to try to come to the UK.[144] A Spanish campaign in Senegal launched in 2007 with the collaboration of Senegalese authorities and the IOM urges Senegalese, "Don't risk your life for nothing, you are part of Africa's future." The campaign cost almost €1 million to pay for radio, television, and newspaper ads. It included testimonials from friends and family of migrants who died trying to reach Spain.[145] Efforts at soft caging are relatively cheap. There is no evidence that they are effective.

Barbicans at the Gates

All EU member states have a special border procedure for asylum applications. A legal fiction at times has claimed that a foreigner at a border checkpoint or in an international airport transit area is not legally present in the state's territory.[146] For example, a 1945 French ordinance provided that foreigners in transit through an airport could be detained in a waiting zone and forcibly returned without any kind of official processing or appeal.[147] French authorities were not obligated under French law to examine asylum requests made in the international zone or to provide legal assistance or interpreters to asylum seekers. The Council of Europe denounced the technique of international zones as "a device to avoid obligations" in a nonbinding 1991 statement.[148]

In the landmark 1992 *Amuur v. France* case, the European Court of Human Rights constrained how European states can treat foreigners in the "anomalous zones" of airports.[149] Four Somali siblings—Mahad, Lahima, Abdelkader, and Mohammed Amuur—arrived at Paris-Orly on a flight from

Damascus in March 1992 and asked for asylum. They said they had fled Somalia after the overthrow of the president and the murder of several of their family members. French officials kept them in the international zone of the airport for twenty days until the minister of the interior refused them entry because their passports were falsified. The government forced the family back to Damascus, where the local UNHCR office recognized them as refugees.[150] The European Court of Human Rights ruled that the international zone was French territory where French law applied and that confining asylum seekers to the zone for long periods illegally deprived them of their liberty.[151] However, France continues to maintain a separate asylum regime in waiting zones. Asylum applicants at the airport are typically interviewed by phone to determine whether they have a well-founded claim. Half of the interviews in 2014 involved a translator on the conference call, which has raised questions about the reliability of the process. A catch-22 is that negative decisions can be appealed, but the appeals process typically takes longer than the maximum allowable stay of twenty-six days.[152] While the Strasbourg court limited the conditions inside the barbican, it remains a technique of control.

Britain, France, and Belgium have developed a unique set of "juxtaposed controls" of passengers crossing the English Channel by ferry or through the Chunnel. They are the terrestrial equivalent of the U.S. airport pre-clearance program, except that the juxtaposed controls are symmetrical in practice. The juxtaposed controls were imposed because the UK is not part of the Schengen free-movement zone. The Sangatte Protocol since 1993 has allowed British officials to carry out passport controls in a narrowly circumscribed zone on French territory. French officials do the same in Britain. Officials also have been authorized to carry out checks on board the Eurostar train. A similar agreement between the UK and Belgium went into effect in 1997. Ferry routes were covered by an agreement between France and the UK in 2003 and among France, Belgium, and the UK in 2004. The genesis of juxtaposed controls includes traveler convenience as well as an effort to crack down on irregular migration and to deter asylum seekers. Individuals denied entry are the responsibility of the government of the departure country. When British agents refuse entry in the control zone, there is no right of appeal in British courts, as there would be on British territory.[153] A representative of the British government openly stated in court in 2008 that juxtaposed controls target asylum seekers:

> When, for example, Colombia and Ecuador were included as visa States, this was directly in response to an increase in the number of those nationals

coming directly to the United Kingdom in order to apply for asylum. A similar aim is present in the juxtaposed controls in France, where asylum seekers are refused leave [permission] to enter.[154]

After juxtaposed controls began on the Eurostar, the number of unauthorized passengers arriving at Waterloo Station in London fell by 90%.[155] From 2002 to 2015, more than seventy migrants trying to reach the UK died in the French port of Calais, mostly in road or train accidents.[156]

The UNHCR has long insisted that even when confronted by a mass influx of asylum seekers, states must at least temporarily admit them and scrupulously observe the principle of non-refoulement, including "non-rejection at the frontier."[157] In practice, states have often shut their doors to asylum seekers and refused to hear their claims or pushed them back across the border. Spain and several Balkan states routinely pushed back asylum seekers and developed barbican spaces impossible to access during the 2010s.

Europe in North Africa

The Spanish government has played a leading role in shifting Europe's border control into Africa, beginning with Morocco.[158] Under Spanish pressure, Morocco criminalized irregular migration in 2003 and began joint naval patrols around the Straits of Gibraltar and the Canary Islands. The EU gave Morocco €67.6 million for border management between 2003 and 2010.[159] Morocco initially resisted full cooperation with both Spain and the EU. "Why should a country like Morocco, the last stop before 'the European Eldorado,' take all the responsibility?" asked Morocco's ambassador to the EU, Menouar Alem. "Would-be migrants to Europe reach Morocco after transiting many countries, some of which don't even have relations with the EU, so why should we take all the responsibility?"[160] For years, Brussels pressured the Moroccan government to tighten visa requirements for African countries, but Rabat demurred because of its broad interests in maintaining friendly relations throughout the continent.[161] Over the course of the 2000s, however, both formal and informal cooperation increased. In its Mobility Partnership, finally concluded with the EU in 2013 after more than a decade of talks, Morocco gained trade concessions; reduced fees for remittances and emigrant homeland investment; and negotiations on easing visas for Moroccans who were traveling for study, research, and business. In return, Rabat agreed to allow readmission, build up its border control capacity, and cooperate with Frontex and the European Asylum Support Office.[162]

Europe's territory begins in coastal North Africa where Morocco abuts the Spanish enclaves of Ceuta and Melilla. Portugal took Ceuta in 1415. Melilla fell to Spain in 1497. They were arguably Europe's first overseas colonies. Spain retained control of the territories when Morocco gained independence in 1956. The Moroccan government continues to claim sovereignty over the enclaves. During the mid-1990s, Ceuta and Melilla became a major route for Moroccans and others attempting to reach Europe. The EU paid most of the costs for Spain to build increasingly elaborate fences, initially modeled on U.S. border fences with Mexico.[163] By 2006, a triple fence up to six-meters high encircled the enclaves. Around 2,000 police and Spanish Guardia Civil officers manned their guard towers and monitored a dense array of motion sensors and infrared and video cameras. The measures were largely effective at deflecting irregular migration to the Canary Islands, and, once that route closed, to departure points further south in Mauritania and Senegal.

The Moroccan government objected to the fences, which were built several meters inside Spanish territory, but in practice used extreme coercion to prevent unauthorized crossings into the enclaves. In 2005, hundreds of migrants tried to cross in several major incidents. At least thirteen migrants

FIGURE 8.3 Spanish guards face African migrants attempting to scale the fence at the border between Morocco and the North African Spanish enclave of Melilla on April 3, 2014. The Spanish government announced in 2014 that one must cross all three of the fences to have entered Spanish territory. Photo by Alexander Koerner/ Getty Images.

died between August and October after border guards opened fire with live ammunition and heavy rubber bullets. Spanish and Moroccan authorities blamed each other for the deaths.[164] On October 7, two days after the worst incident, Moroccan authorities rounded up 800 sub-Saharan Africans, including children and pregnant women, and abandoned them in the desert between Morocco and Algeria without food or water. By the time a delegation from Doctors Without Borders found the group, twenty-four were dead.[165] Morocco added 9,000 migration control agents, improved its border control capacities, detained asylum seekers in camps, and stopped issuing identification documents to refugees recognized by the local UNHCR office.[166] There is evidence that, informally, Moroccan guards also destroyed documents issued to asylum seekers by UNHCR.[167] The EU gave Morocco €40 million to dig a trench around the enclaves, build detention centers, and otherwise deter irregular migration.[168]After a new migration and asylum law was adopted in 2013, Moroccan authorities bused detained foreigners to cities far from the Spanish enclaves rather than leaving them in the desert.[169]

The Spanish government continued to push back migrants at the fences, often violently, without giving them any opportunity to ask for asylum. Spain summarily expelled 324 sub-Saharan Africans in 2014 who had crossed at least one, and sometimes all three, of the fences.[170] On February 6, 2014, a group attempted to swim from Moroccan territory to Ceuta. At least fourteen people drowned as Guardia Civil officers fired rubber bullets and tear gas to keep them away. Spanish authorities summarily expelled the twenty-three survivors who reached the beach. According to the minister of the interior's new justification, previously unpublicized but supposedly in effect since 2005, one must cross all three fences to have entered Spanish territory.[171] A Melilla court rejected the argument that the area between the fences is somehow not Spanish territory but the court's decision did not change the government's policy.[172]

Moroccan and Spanish forces cooperate in practice even though their formal readmission agreement is almost never applied.[173] For example, on March 28, 2014, video obtained by the Spanish NGO Prodein showed a group of sub-Saharan Africans sitting on top of the first fence in broad daylight. Armed Moroccan guards enter the strip between the Spanish fences, apparently at the invitation of the Spanish guards, and beat a supine man before dragging him and others back to the Moroccan side.[174] Another video filmed on October 15, 2014, begins with a group of two dozen sub-Saharan African men sitting on the middle fence six meters in the air. Masked Guardia Civil officers in riot gear throw up scaling ladders on both sides and beat the African men with their batons. Some of the migrants do not comply with orders to come down, though none resist violently. Guards beat one of them until he falls several meters to the ground. Five Guardia Civil officers drag his apparently unconscious body along a path between the fences as an ambulance slowly cruises past. No one gives him medical aid. The guards carry the body through a sally port and dump him on the Moroccan side.[175]

Spain's 2009 Asylum Law provides that "illegal entry into Spanish territory may not be penalized when it has been done by someone who is eligible to become a beneficiary of international protection."[176] If refugees are forced back to an unsafe country, pushbacks constitute refoulement. Even if the country of return is generally considered safe, according to international norms, "it is generally accepted that asylum seekers must always be allowed the possibility to rebut the supposed safety of the country concerned."[177] To provide a thin legal cover for the pushbacks, in March 2015, a new category of border rejections (*rechazos*) was added to the special migration regime for Ceuta and Melilla for foreigners who were turned back at the fences.[178] While the law stipulated that the "rejections" were to take place in compliance with international norms, in practice, violent pushbacks even of those who cross all three fences have continued. Spain's national ombudsman, seventy-seven Spanish NGOs, the European Council on Refugee and Exiles, Amnesty International, the Committee Against Torture, and the Council of Europe's commissioner for human rights condemned the pushbacks.[179]

The Strasbourg court ruled in 2017 that the Spanish pushbacks violated the provisions in the European Convention on Human Rights against collective expulsion and the right to an effective remedy. The case was brought by two men from the Ivory Coast and Mali who had joined approximately seventy-five others to climb the fences in Melilla in August 2014. Rocks thrown by the Moroccan border guards knocked the Ivorian men off the fence into Spanish territory. Spanish guards violently and summarily expelled the entire group to Morocco without any attempt to identify them or hear an asylum appeal. The court ruled that it did not have to determine whether the border crossing point was on Spanish territory because the men had clearly been under the continuous and exclusive control of Spanish guards and thus under Spain's jurisdiction. The court cited video evidence and the written reports of the UNHCR and NGOs in determining that the men's rights had been violated, thus highlighting the interaction between journalists, rights organizations, and the judiciary in constraining state practices.[180]

At the same time that the Spanish government announced the special regime of border rejections, it stated that it would accept asylum claims in Ceuta and Melilla at border-crossing offices established at the entrance to each enclave in March 2015. In reality, Moroccan border guards controlled access to the office and systematically refused to allow sub-Saharan Africans without visas to exit Morocco and approach the office. They sometimes allowed Syrians, Algerians, and Moroccans to pass. Anyone else seeking protection had no way of legally reaching the enclaves to file a claim. Even the route for Syrians became much more difficult after neighboring Algeria imposed visas on Syrians in December 2014, thus cutting off their access to Morocco. Not a single asylum application had been processed by October 2017 at the Ceuta border post. At the Melilla post, only 219 applications were filed in the first nine months of 2017.[181]

For those who have managed to apply for asylum in Ceuta and Melilla, the enclaves themselves become a buffer between the Spanish mainland and Africa. Spanish authorities carry out identification checks and restrict free mobility on ferry services between the enclaves and the Spanish mainland in an exception to the general rule of free movement in the Schengen zone. Asylum seekers in Ceuta and Melilla are issued a document that only lets them move about within the enclave. Holders cannot travel to the Spanish mainland unless they receive asylum or the government authorizes a special transfer.[182] The October 2017 decision by the European Court of Human Rights placed some limits on barbican strategies but did not eliminate them altogether.

Barring the Balkans

During the Syrian civil war that began in 2011, several governments in the Balkans established special rules at their gates to reduce access by asylum seekers. Designated barbican spaces, illegal pushbacks, increased border fortifications, and capacity building of buffer states combined enforcement at the border and remote control.

The Bulgarian government claimed that asylum seekers were welcome to apply at border-crossing checkpoints. Yet the Turkish government did not allow travelers without proper papers to exit Turkish crossing points to reach the Bulgarian posts. The procedure to ask for asylum at the border was therefore illusory. Those who crossed without papers faced fencing manned by border guards supplemented with Frontex-coordinated teams from other EU member states. Mauled by police dogs and robbed and beaten by officers, many of those who managed to make it across were pushed back into Turkey.[183] Sixteen-year-old Hamdast from Afghanistan described to Human Rights Watch what happened after he crossed from Turkey into Bulgaria with forty-seven others:

They made us stand in a line. They made us take off our trousers down to our knees and searched us to see if we had money. There were five police officers. They took 200 euros from me. They also took food and my phone. I had new boots, the policeman liked them and took them as well. My bag, which had been full, was given back to me empty . . . One officer hit me on the face with a tree branch because I talked . . . Then police trucks came and took all of us to the Turkish border and the police kicked each of us while making us cross into Turkey.[184]

The combination of illegal pushbacks and restricted access to a post where it was only hypothetically possible to ask for asylum redirected asylum seekers toward other countries.

A 600-kilometer gap in the Schengen zone between Greece and Hungary turned the western Balkan states into a unique buffer inside Europe during the Syrian civil war. Few asylum seekers wished to stay in Greece given the country's low asylum-recognition rate, wretched conditions in winter camps, and high unemployment. They preferred to reach countries in northwestern Europe, such as Germany and Sweden, with more welcoming policies and opportunities to make a living. The lack of effective buffering by Greece and these push-and-pull factors sent people north to seek protection. The shortest route lay through Macedonia and Serbia. In January 2014, Serbia and the EU began negotiating an accession agreement, which required Serbia to improve its asylum reception facilities and to harmonize its laws of migration and asylum with EU directives. The EU gave Serbia €45 million in migration-related aid between 2001 and 2014, half of which financed controls, surveillance, databases, and border guard training. The EU financed a similar package for Macedonia. Serbian border police worked with Hungarian, Austrian, and German police on the border with Hungary in operations coordinated by Frontex. NGOs collected extensive evidence of chain pushbacks from Serbia into Macedonia and Macedonia into Greece. Border guards often beat migrants and ignored formal readmission procedures.[185]

During the height of the Syrian/European refugee crisis in 2015, the Hungarian government built a 175-kilometer razor-wire fence along the entire length of its border with Serbia and another barrier along its 348-kilometer border with Croatia. Hungarian authorities routinely and often violently pushed back migrants without hearing asylum claims. In one highly publicized incident, police deployed tear gas, pepper gas, batons, and water cannons against migrants attempting to tear their way through the fence.[186] Legal entries to apply for asylum were limited to twenty to thirty people a day at two squalid transit camps outside the border fence, and, beginning in January 2018, only one person a day was allowed to enter.[187] The Hungarian government set up "pre-transit zones," a unique version of the barbican, located on Serbian and Hungarian territory, but which the Hungarian authorities declared "no man's land." Asylum seekers had to wait in the pre-transit zone before accessing the transit zone. By late 2016, asylum seekers had to register first on the Serbian side and could no longer wait in the pre-transit zone. The European Court of Human Rights ruled in 2017 that the detention of two Bangladeshi nationals for three weeks in the transit zone without access to their lawyer was an illegal deprivation of liberty, and that their expulsion to Serbia put them at risk of chain refoulement.[188]

A July 2016 law allowed pushbacks of people caught as deep as eight kilometers inside Hungary. In March 2017, the Orbán government's amendment of the "state of crisis due to mass migration" law legalized pushbacks throughout the country's territory. Nearly 40,000 people were pushed back or denied access at the border by the end of 2017. One of them, Shahzad Khurram, a Pakistani citizen, entered Hungary and asked for asylum in August 2016. Hungarian police ignored the asylum claim and summarily expelled him back to Serbia. His case was pending in the European Court of Human Rights as of 2018, along with that of an Iranian citizen who had converted to Christianity and who suffered the same treatment from Hungarian police in September 2016.[189] Human Rights Watch gathered evidence of pushbacks from Croatia in 2016 as well.[190] Buffers and the barbican essentially closed access to asylum.

The European Commission initiated an "infringement procedure" against Hungary in December 2015 for violating EU asylum law. One of the bases of the EU claim was that the special transit zones at the border and the restriction of access to those zones violated asylum seekers' rights. The infringement claim was active as of 2018 and could be sent to the European Court of Justice for adjudication. If the Hungarian government were to refuse to comply with the court's decision, the European Commission could eventually impose financial penalties on Hungary.[191] However, the slow pace of EU complaints suggests that EU law and the ECJ are not robust checks on the barbican strategy of its members, notwithstanding the success of the European Court of Human Rights in putting a check on conditions inside airport transit zones. The strong territorial rights of personhood in the European Convention on Human Rights are vulnerable when the rule of law is systematically being undermined by an increasingly authoritarian government such as Prime Minister Orbán's.

Conclusion

The European project of reducing mobility controls between members while strengthening the external borders and then shifting control outward is unique. The individual pieces of the remote control strategies themselves are common, with the exception of Frontex, which does not have parallels in the North American or Australian cases. Restrictive visa policies, carrier sanctions, liaison officers posted abroad, readmission agreements, publicity campaigns trying to convince potential migrants to stay in place, safe third- and origin-country agreements, and agreements on which country is responsible for hearing asylum claims can all be found in some form in the other contexts. What is unusual are the supranational factors that promote or restrain these policies and the many pathways that they develop.

The escape to Europe thesis explains many early episodes of remote control as governments of member states found a venue for policymaking that was more isolated from the national judiciaries, rights groups, foreign ministries, and political cultures that had frustrated their control agenda. Governments of every political stripe have participated in the intensification and maintenance of remote controls. EU institutions did not directly coordinate all instances of these policies. In the 1990s, for example, non-EU members' independent adjustment to early movers like Germany created an outward ripple of remote control, but there are also many examples of collective policymaking that quickly spread controls among member states and then outward as they become a condition of joining the Union. The ubiquity of policies rooted in law, regulations, or formal agreement with other states—around readmission, visas, carrier sanctions, safe third countries, and safe countries of origin—is a result of Europeanization.

Europeanization also includes built-in constraints. The supranational institutions such as the European Parliament and even the European Commission have been more likely to take human rights considerations seriously in their approach toward migration and asylum. Much of the systematic monitoring of violations of asylum rights takes place with funding from the Asylum, Migration, and Integration Fund of the EU as well as private foundations such as the European Programme for Integration and Migration.[192] The European Court of Human Rights has placed some limits on procedures in barbican spaces such as airport transit zones and the forced return of asylum seekers to "safe third countries." The following chapter shows how the Strasbourg court has limited maritime interceptions on the high seas and the indirect way that transnational civil society and the UNHCR have modestly constrained buffering by monitoring activities financed by European countries.

CHAPTER 9 | The Euro-Moat

WIDE IS THE MOAT around Europe. It stretches as far as the coast of West Africa, where a Finnish aircraft surveilling Senegalese waters directs an Italian ship to intercept migrants below. Frontex is charged with coordinating controls over the EU's external borders. Since 2006 it has organized maritime interceptions by member states in operations named after a pantheon of figures from Greek mythology: Operation Hera between the Canary Islands and the west coast of Africa; Agios, Minerva, and Indalo in the western Mediterranean; Nautilus and Hermes in the Central Mediterranean; and Poseidon in the Aegean.

Patrolling the moat is tightly linked to buffering. European governments pressure African coastal states to keep irregular migrants from disembarking and to readmit those intercepted at sea. The weakness of coastal states' control capacity has then led European governments to drive further inland and build expanding rings of land buffers around the moat. The modest constraints on Europe's moat strategy are the supranational judiciary and monitoring of conditions at sea and in coastal buffer states by NGOs, investigative journalists, and the UNHCR.

Guantanamito

Operation Hera II was the first Frontex maritime interception effort and a template for others to follow. Spain, Portugal, Italy, and Finland deployed their militaries thousands of kilometers from home waters to intercept irregular migrants who were trying to reach the Canary Islands in small boats called *cayucos*. With the cooperation of the Senegalese and Mauritanian governments, European navies intercepted the *cayucos* in the African countries' territorial waters and pushed them back to the coast. Irregular arrivals in the Canary Islands fell from 31,700 in 2006 to 2,200 in 2009. Thousands are estimated to have died at sea. Most were seeking a better livelihood, but 2.6% of arrivals between 2006 and 2008 asked for asylum.[1]

Mauritania became a buffer for Spain 850 kilometers from the closest Spanish island. Since 2006, around 250 Spanish police and Guardia Civil officers in Nouadhibou and Nouakchott have conducted joint patrols in Mauritanian harbors and along its coast. In practice, this usually means that Mauritanian officials act as ship-riders on Spanish vessels to give Spanish authorities legal cover for interception in Mauritanian territorial waters or its contiguous zone. Mauritania accepts the return of migrants intercepted by Spanish forces up to twenty-four nautical miles from the coast. Senegal permits returns from up to 200 nautical miles offshore. According to Spanish authorities, the arrangement "allows a Spanish police officer acting in that third country to work as if he were in Spain."[2]

Frontex does not have legal agreements allowing interdictions in third countries. Its Operation Seahorse in the territorial waters of third countries falls under Spanish memoranda of understanding with West African countries. Informal memoranda allow governments to avoid public scrutiny or inputs from civil society.[3] Madrid's informal bilateral agreements and EU piggybacking on Spanish deals invert the escape to Europe thesis. In this instance, formal EU agreements would be subject to greater scrutiny from European advocacy networks and EU institutions. Shifting the policy down to the Spanish level allows Europe to "escape" to the more flexible and less monitored policies of the member state.

Establishing who has jurisdiction over people intercepted at sea has been a source of contention. On January 31, 2007, the cargo ship *Marine I* sent out a distress call as it capsized in international waters with 369 African and Asian passengers on board. A Spanish tug rescued the ship and towed it to the Mauritanian coast. After a week-long negotiation, Mauritania allowed the passengers to disembark under Spanish police control in return for Spain's payment of €650,000 and a promise to cover the cost of deportations. Spanish police established the identity of seventy of the passengers and transferred them to the Canary Islands to initiate asylum claims. Another group was held by Spanish police at an abandoned fish-processing plant in Mauritania. A local NGO brought a complaint against the Spanish government on behalf of the detainees at the plant. The UN Committee Against Torture held that the detainees in Mauritania were subject to Spanish jurisdiction because Spain "maintained control over the persons on board the *Marine I* from the time the vessel was rescued and throughout the identification and repatriation process." While the complaint in *Marine I* failed because the organization filing it did not have legal standing, the case helped establish the principle of extraterritorial jurisdiction in which states exercise control outside their territories over specific individuals.[4]

Passengers later intercepted off Mauritania were taken without any humanitarian protection screening to an empty school in Nouadhibou known informally as *Guantanamito* (Little Guantanamo). The "welcome center" also housed irregular migrants plucked off the streets as they awaited deportation to Mali or Senegal. A confidential 2009 U.S. diplomatic cable reported that Mauritanian authorities were rounding up migrants and expelling them to satisfy a "numbers game." The expulsions demonstrated Mauritania's commitment to control, which kept the training and cooperation money flowing from Spain. Mauritanian authorities then allowed the same migrants to return to Mauritania a few days later.[5] Expulsions included recognized refugees and asylum seekers.[6]

The extraordinary cooperation between Spain and Mauritania was made possible in part because there is very little migration of Mauritanians to Spain.[7] Thus, the Mauritanian authorities did not face the same sensitivity to foreign violations of their sovereignty and cooperation as governments of countries that are both transit and sending states, such as Morocco and Mexico. The Senegalese government agreed to repatriations from the Canary Islands "only under condition of extreme discretion by the Spanish," according to a confidential U.S. diplomatic cable. In return for readmitting its nationals and letting Spain patrol its territorial waters, Senegal received a USD$26 million line of credit from Spain. A village chief in an isolated area of Senegal told diplomats, "If you want to stop our young people from jumping into boats, you'd better give us more aid."[8]

Having apparently closed the Atlantic route, Madrid and Brussels caged irregular migrants in the sub-Saharan band of Mauritania, Senegal, Mali, and Niger.[9] Spain has also pushed farther by signing migration cooperation agreements with Gambia (2006), Guinea (2006), and Cape Verde (2007).[10] As a Guardia Civil officer explained to researchers in 2012, "since we cannot get the necessary cooperation of North African states to stop irregular migration we will cut off the routes" further south.[11] After Spain reduced its aid to Mauritania in 2009, the EU continued to finance migration controls, including forty-seven new border posts with Mali and Senegal and equipment for biometric identification checks and electronic databases.[12] European border control has pushed south through the Atlantic and across the Sahel.

The Albanian Model

While Spain and Frontex extended Europe's borders into West Africa, the Italian government pioneered pushbacks in the Adriatic. As on land, "pushbacks" refer to a government forcing travelers away from its sea borders without assessing whether they have valid protection claims. Putting any kind of migrant at risk by pushing a boat back out to sea when it is in danger of sinking violates the law of the sea's mandate to rescue people in distress, as discussed in chapter 3.

The Italian government's attempts to stop Albanians from crossing the Adriatic in the 1990s created a model for much larger Italian deployments a decade later in the Central Mediterranean. Around 20,000 Albanians fled to Italy after the fall of communism in 1991. Albania's financial collapse and widespread violence in 1997 generated a second flow. An exchange of letters between the Italian and Albanian governments on March 25, 1997, authorized the summary expulsion of Albanians who had reached Italy. The agreement allowed Italian "assistance for the control and containment at sea of Albanian clandestine expatriations," including boats passing through Albanian territorial or international waters, and "redirecting their course to Albanian ports." In return, Italy provided Albania with financial, police, and humanitarian assistance. [13] Three days later, the UN approved a Security Council resolution authorizing an Italian-led international protection mission to facilitate humanitarian assistance in Albania. The main unwritten goal was to prevent refugees from reaching Europe. [14]

The night that the Security Council authorized Italy's mission, the Italian navy intercepted the *Kater i Radës* in Albanian waters heading west toward Italy. After a pursuit through the night, a 1,285-ton Italian corvette collided with the 56-ton *Kater i Radës* and sent the smaller boat to the bottom of the sea, losing 81 of its 120 passengers. A third of the dead were children. Sixteen survivors sued the Italian government in the European Court of Human Rights. The court dismissed their claim because they had not exhausted their legal remedies in the Italian judicial system. An Italian court later convicted both the Italian and Albanian captains of manslaughter. [15] The Italian navy and Guardia di Finanza continued to patrol in Albanian waters, installed a radar station on Albanian soil, trained Albanian border guards, and provided motorboats for Albanian patrols until 2009, more than a decade after the original crisis had ended. The Italian Ministry of the Interior later described cooperation with Albania as a successful model for agreements with Libya in the 2000s. [16]

From Libya to Lampedusa

The Italian island of Lampedusa lies just 290 kilometers north of Libya. Rome and Brussels have spent years trying to turn Libya into a buffer state to deter maritime departures to Lampedusa. At the same time, Libya's well-known record of sponsoring terrorism in the 1980s and its dreadful human rights record have given European courts and civil society arguments to hinder, but not stop, the harshest impulses of European governments.

The UN imposed sanctions on Libya in 1992 to force it to hand over two Libyan men for trial in the 1988 bombing of a Pan Am 747 over Lockerbie, Scotland. The sanctions were not formally lifted until 2004, but that did not stop the Libyan and Italian governments from signing a 2000 accord to fight terrorism, organized crime, drug trafficking, and illegal immigration, with an emphasis on the last category.[17] In November 2002, the European Council announced it was essential to begin cooperating with Libya on migration control.[18] According to a 2004 U.S. diplomatic cable, "Libya's promise to help prevent clandestine migration was the dominant factor in the EU's preliminary decision on September 22 to lift economic sanctions on the former pariah."[19] The lifting of sanctions allowed Rome to give Tripoli dual-use equipment to control irregular migration, including military vehicles and boats, in addition to the cameras, night vision scopes, document -forgery detection kits, and other gear it had already donated. The Italian company Finmeccanica, whose controlling shareholder is the Italian government, sold Libya ten helicopters in 2006 with the stated objective of securing Libya's borders and coast.[20] Italy's "humanitarian support" included donations of 500 lifebuoys, 500 lifejackets, and "1,000 sacks for corpses transport."[21] As anthropologist Maurizio Albahari notes, "Italian and EU authorities have long expected migrant deaths."[22]

In 2004, Italian Prime Minister Silvio Berlusconi met twice with Brotherly Leader and Guide of the Revolution Muammar Gaddafi. The date of their second meeting was declared a "day of friendship" to bury the bitter memories of Italy's colonial occupation. The Italian government agreed to finance deportation flights of thousands of unauthorized migrants from Libya to their countries of origin. The repatriations included Eritreans and Sudanese, at a time when practically all those nationals reaching Europe were granted asylum, which suggests that they were refouled in violation of international law. Rome helped pay for the construction of detention camps at Garyan, Sabha, and Kufra. Italian officers trained their Libyan colleagues how to detect forged documents, scuba dive, and speak Italian.[23] In the fall of 2004,

Italy deported 1,400 recent maritime arrivals from Lampedusa to Libya and paid for the chain refoulement of Egyptians from Italy to Egypt via Libya.[24] The European Parliament, Council of Europe, and UNHCR condemned the mass expulsions, which took place in a context of murky asylum procedures in Italy. Rome defended its practice by claiming that each individual was given the opportunity to explain his or her situation before being deported, thus implicitly recognizing that deportation without providing an opportunity to ask for asylum would be illegitimate.[25] The new center-left administration of Romano Prodi quietly stopped the deportation flights to Libya in 2006, but the asylum system was not fundamentally reformed.[26] United States diplomats who visited Lampedusa in May 2009 concluded in a cable to Washington, "It is likely that some bona fide refugees will be unable to have asylum claims processed."[27] Indeed, of the three-quarters of arrivals in Lampedusa in 2008 who applied for asylum, half were given some form of protection.[28]

The intergovernmental side of the EU was eager to join Italy in making Libya a buffer state. In June 2005, the EU Justice and Home Affairs Council called for migration control cooperation with Libya, including maritime interdiction, stationing EU immigration liaison officers in Libyan airports and seaports, and training Libyan migration police.[29] The EU paid €10 million for joint EU-Libyan maritime patrols, checkpoints on Libya's southern desert borders, and repatriations from Libya.[30] While the EU's 2004 Hague Programme sought cooperation with transit countries only if they observed their obligations under the 1951 Refugee Convention, the 2005 EU Summit in Brussels jettisoned these conditions and urged cooperation on migration management with Libya, Morocco, and Algeria.[31] According to Libyan law, "the Jamahiriya supports the oppressed and the defenders on the road to freedom and they should not abandon the refuges and their protection."[32] However, Libya is not a party to the 1951 Refugee Convention or its 1967 Protocol. A 2004 EU Commission technical mission report concluded, "there is no form of asylum procedure" and "in practice no refugee policy exists."[33]

Tripoli and Rome signed a "technical agreement" on migration control in December 2007. Calling the agreement "technical" avoided a parliamentary debate in Italy and public scrutiny.[34] After Berlusconi took power again in 2008, he signed a formal agreement with Gaddafi that included cooperation on migration control in Libyan and international waters. Italy and the EU would split the costs equally. Italy would invest USD$5 billion in infrastructure projects in Libya over twenty-five years, including a €300 million surveillance system for Libya's southern borders, as reparations for abuses Italy committed during its colonial rule. The two countries would jointly operate patrols in Libyan and international waters on six boats provided by Italy.[35] Elsewhere in the region, Algeria agreed to readmit migrants returned by Italy. Tunisia pledged to deter irregular maritime departures in return for Italian support for its security forces and increased development aid.[36] Rome defended its cooperation with North African governments as a legitimate effort to stop illegal migration and denied that stopping refugees was a goal, even though in 2008, more than a third of sea arrivals in Italy received some form of protection.[37]

The Italian government began a new policy of pushbacks in 2009 that openly challenged the principle of non-refoulement on the high seas. On May 6, Italian ships intercepted about 200 migrants on three vessels in international waters thirty-five nautical miles south of Lampedusa. Officials confiscated the migrants' belongings, including UNHCR certificates showing that some were recognized refugees. After the Italian crew assured the passengers they were being taken to Italy, the ship sailed in the opposite direction.[38] A photographer recorded Italian officers carrying protesting passengers off the boat onto the dock in Tripoli, where they were handed over to Libyan authorities. During the first week of the interdiction program, over 500 migrants were summarily returned to Libya. They were detained, often beaten, and then dumped in the desert near the Sudanese border.[39] Government officials and NGOs were aware at the time of widespread rape, beatings, and other abuses in Libyan detention camps.[40]

Frontex joined the chase at sea. On June 18, a German helicopter operating under the aegis of Operation Nautilus IV coordinated the Italian Coast Guard's interception of a boat carrying seventy-five migrants near Lampedusa. The Italian Coast Guard then handed them over to a Libyan patrol boat.[41] Irregular maritime arrivals from Libya fell 90% between summer 2008 and summer 2009.[42] The UNHCR and rights groups argued that pushbacks on the high seas were illegal. The EU Commission asked the Italian government for more information. "The case-law of the ECHR provides that acts carried out on the high seas by a State vessel constitute cases of extraterritorial jurisdiction and may engage the responsibility of the State concerned," stated the Commission.[43] Under EU and international pressure, Rome stopped the open pushbacks in November 2009.

A landmark ruling from the European Court of Human Rights in the 2012 *Hirsi Jamma and Others v. Italy* case then held that states intercepting travelers on the high seas may have extraterritorial jurisdiction and are obliged to follow the principle of non-refoulement. Twenty-four-year-old Hirsi Jamaa, ten other Somalis, and thirteen Eritreans were among those returned by Italy on the first day of the operation on May 9, 2009. They sued the Italian government for violating the bans on torture, inhuman or degrading treatment or punishment (Article 3), and collective expulsion (Article 4) in the European Convention on Human Rights. The Italian government maintained that the returns took place during a search and rescue operation, rather than a police action, and thus it had never exercised "absolute and exclusive control" over the plaintiffs. Without exercising that control, Italy did not have jurisdiction, and the convention did not apply. The European Court of Human Rights unanimously rejected Rome's reasoning. The court ruled that while jurisdiction is normally defined by a state's territory, there are exceptions. "Italy cannot circumvent its 'jurisdiction' under the Convention by describing the events in issue as rescue operations on the high seas," the court ruled.[44]

The court extensively cited reports from transnational rights organizations, the UNHCR, and the U.S. State Department in its finding that the returns constituted refoulement. "As regards the general situation in a particular country, the Court has often attached importance to the information contained in recent reports from independent international human rights protection associations such as Amnesty International, or governmental sources," the court noted. It cited Human Rights Watch and UNHCR reports in noting that "individuals forcibly repatriated to Eritrea face being tortured and detained in inhuman conditions merely for having left the country irregularly."[45] Among the most damning facts establishing that refugees had been refouled was that the UNHCR office in Tripoli recognized seventy-three of those returned to Libya as refugees, including Hirsi Jamaa and thirteen other plaintiffs. Five of the returnees reached Italy on a later trip and were granted asylum.

EU regulations issued in 2010 prohibited refoulement during all Frontex operations at sea, including handing intercepted passengers over to a state that practiced refoulement.[46] Supranational courts are not the only European institutions that constrained the remote control policies of its members. In this instance, an intergovernmental institution, the European Council, did the same, though it was following the precedent of the European Court of Human Rights in the *Hirsi* case and the EU Commission's 2009 inquiry. The European Parliament successfully sued to have the Council Decision of April 26, 2010, annulled because it had not followed proper procedures for making EU law.[47]

However, a new regulation issued May 15, 2014, instated an even stronger version of non-refoulement that specifically referred to compliance with European Court of Human Rights case law and a prohibition on using third countries to circumvent legal obligations.[48] Legal scholar Maarten den Heijer notes that the 2014 regulations still allowed naval forces to force ships carrying migrants away from the territorial sea or contiguous zone, did not clarify how to deal with coastal member states with inadequate asylum procedures, did not guarantee that migrants would be able to understand where they were being taken, did not provide a right of appeal against return to a third country, and did not address the issue of interdictions in the territorial waters of third countries.[49] Nonetheless, the regulations showed how far the EU had moved from open pushbacks to a ban on refoulement on the high seas.

The bilateral agreements between Italy and Libya were suspended in 2011 during the Libyan civil war and NATO intervention that ousted Gaddafi. France and the UK, which were instrumental in promoting the military intervention, were explicitly motivated in large part by the fear that continued civil war would push refugees into Europe. French President Sarkozy warned on March 11 that 200,000 people had already fled from Libya and unless conditions improved, "they would not have a choice" and would cross the Mediterranean. The French government stressed that it would "show a very great firmness with regard to illegal immigration." Restoring order in Libya was essential not only to contain Libyans but also to rebuild Libya as a transit buffer. "Libya is the funnel of Africa: countries like Liberia, Somalia, and Eritrea have flows of illegal immigration that pass through Libya; it is a true risk for Europe," said Minister for European Affairs Laurent Wauquiez. British Prime Minister David Cameron similarly argued that Britain could not accept "a failed pariah state on Europe's southern border" that would threaten British security and "push people across the Mediterranean."[50] Ironically, NATO bombing in which Italy played a leading role destroyed two of the Libyan Coast Guard's six coastal patrol vessels that had been used to intercept migrants.[51]

Between 2014 and 2016, more than half a million migrants, primarily from sub-Saharan Africa, arrived in Italy from North Africa.[52] In June 2015, the EU militarized remote control by launching a naval mission in the waters between North Africa and Italy with the declared goal of disrupting people smuggling. The EU Naval Force Mediterranean had mandates for three phases. The first phase focused on gathering information and patrolling, the second on seizing smuggling vessels, and the third on their destruction. The legal basis for the operation was strengthened by UN Security Council Resolution 2240 that granted UN member states authorization to inspect vessels suspected of migrant smuggling on the high seas off Libya for one year. As of April 2017, the force had destroyed more than 400 boats, turned over more than 100 suspected smugglers to Italian prosecutors, and rescued more than 35,000 migrants.[53] Leaked internal documents from EU defense chiefs reveal the tension between the legal and humanitarian obligations to rescue and the primary mission focused on stopping boats and deterring migrants:

> [T]he information strategy should avoid suggesting that the focus is to rescue migrants at sea but emphasise that the aim of the operation is to disrupt the migrants smuggling business model. By doing so the operation will indirectly contribute to reduce loss of life at sea. The target audience should include Libya and North African regional neighbours.[54]

Two legal considerations posed a challenge to the third phase of operations in Libyan territorial waters. First, an invitation by the fragile Libyan government that controlled only a fraction of Libya's territory and another UN Security Council resolution were necessary. In lieu of immediate action inside Libyan waters, it focused on building up Libya as a buffer.[55] "Through the capability and capacity building of the Libyan Navy and Coastguard, the EU will be able to offer the Libyan authorities something in exchange for their cooperation in tackling the irregular migration issue, which could help secure their invitation to operate inside their territory," the official assessment of the second phase explained.[56]

Following the 2011 war, the EU spent €26 million a year training hundreds of Libyan migration control officers.[57] The European Council announced in February 2017 that it would spend €200 million in North Africa, primarily Libya, to increase national migration control capacity building efforts.[58] The Libyan and Italian governments signed another memorandum of understanding to control irregular migration, including control over Libya's southern desert borders. The agreement promised financing from Italy and the EU and delivery of ten patrol boats to the Libyan Coast Guard.[59] EU heads of state pledged to enhance Libya's "border management capacity" with the standard array of buffering measures supported with priority access to €200 in 2017.[60] Meanwhile, the UNHCR trained Libyan Coast Guard personnel in human rights and refugee law.[61] In May 2017, NGOs involved in rescuing migrants at sea observed Libyan Coast Guard officers firing shots at an Italian vessel transporting rescued migrants in international waters. Monitoring of open radio channels revealed that the Libyan Coast Guard apparently mistook the Italian ship for a migrant smuggling boat.[62] Rome was financing an agency willing to kill people traveling across the straits without visas.

FIGURE 9.1 A Libyan coast guardsman stands on a boat filled with 147 visa-less passengers intercepted off the coast of Libya on June 27, 2017. The Italian government provides equipment, training, and funding to the Libyan Coast Guard and pays private militias to prevent asylum seekers and other migrants from reaching the territorial waters of European countries. Photo by Taha Jawashi/AFP/Getty Images.

A leaked January 2017 report from the EU's European External Action Service reported that the Libyan Government of National Accord did not have full control over Libya's territory or even its own security services.[63] An unspecified number of staff at the Department for Combating Irregular Migration were "involved with militias." The government could not keep track of the number of detained migrants. "Detention centres are also under the control of militias with serious human rights violations being frequently reported," the report stated.[64] Similarly, a panel of experts reporting to the UN Security Council in June 2017 found that smugglers, the Department to Counter Illegal Migration, and the Libyan Coast Guard were involved in abuses against migrants "including executions, torture and deprivation of food, water and access to sanitation."[65] A UN support mission in Libya reported in December 2016,

> Migrants, as well as representatives of international non-governmental organizations that carry out search and rescue operations, have also recounted dangerous, life-threatening interceptions by armed men believed to be from the Libyan coastguard. After interception, migrants are often beaten, robbed

and taken to detention centres or private houses and farms, where they are subjected to forced labour, rape and other sexual violence.[66]

A sudden drop in the number of sea arrivals in Italy in summer 2017 prompted independent investigators to figure out the cause. They determined that the Italian government was secretly paying the same Libyan militias who had been smuggling migrants to illegally detain them in "makeshift dungeons" outside the formal detention center network.[67] The Libyan government's detentions were no better. As Amnesty International summarized, up to 20,000 migrants "were held in horrific conditions of extreme overcrowding, lacking access to medical care and adequate nutrition, and systematically subjected to torture and other ill-treatment, including sexual violence, severe beatings and extortion."[68] Contracting out migration control to militias and the Libyan government reduced movement across the Mediterranean. It remains an open question as of this writing whether public knowledge of these details in Europe will generate effective pressure for reform, but without such knowledge, no pressure would exist.

"Crimes of Peace"

The law of the sea requires all shipmasters to help people in distress if it is possible to safely render aid.[69] Yet disputes over the obligations of coastal states have contributed to dangers at sea. The Italian and Maltese governments disagree about who is responsible for endangered migrants in the enormous Maltese search and rescue (SAR) area, which envelops the Italian island of Lampedusa, and in the SAR area of Libya, which has not always had a functioning government. The Italian government maintains that rescued passengers should disembark in the country responsible for the SAR area, while Malta argues that they should disembark in the nearest safe port. Most attempts to cross the Mediterranean involve boats that are dangerously overweight. Italy regards overloaded vessels to inherently be in distress. For Malta, to be considered in distress the vessel must be sinking.[70]

The dangerous absurdity of disputes about responsibility was highlighted in the 2007 tuna net incident. Twenty-seven migrants from a dozen African countries left Libya in a wooden dingy. A week later, they encountered a Maltese fishing trawler. None of the African men could swim, but with their own dingy taking on water, they climbed onto a floating fishing net pulled by the trawler. They clung to the net for three days while the Libyan, Maltese, and Italian governments argued over which government was responsible for their rescue. Eventually an Italian ship rescued the men.[71]

It is impossible to know how many deaths have been caused by governments trying to evade their responsibility to rescue, but leaks reported by journalists provide a window into the human costs. In October 2013, a ship sank 100 kilometers south of Lampedusa in the Maltese SAR with the loss of 268 Syrian refugees, including sixty children. Four years later, the Italian magazine *L'Espresso* published transcripts of leaked tapes recording phone conversations between Italian and Maltese SAR officials. The tapes revealed that Italian authorities knew five hours before the ship sank that it was taking on water. Rome initially refused to mobilize an Italian military vessel just thirty-seven kilometers away. As an Italian Coast Guard official explained to a Maltese officer, Rome wanted to keep its vessel in place "to spot new targets" and because using it to rescue the Syrians would make Italian authorities "in charge of transfer to the nearest coast." Only after a Maltese aircraft verified that the Syrians' ship was completely capsized did Italian officials send their ship to pick up the survivors and corpses.[72]

Remote control at sea also subverts the legal obligation and maritime norm for civilians to render aid. In the 2004 *Cap Anamur* case, the Italian government prosecuted three members of a German relief organization for rescuing thirty-seven migrants in the Mediterranean. In 2007, a group of seven Tunisian fishermen were arrested after rescuing passengers from a deflating rubber dingy and taking them to Lampedusa. Although both groups were acquitted, the UNHCR cautioned that penalizing Good Samaritans would have a chilling effect on the willingness of mariners to assist migrants in distress.[73]

Some of the clearest evidence that policies of coastal states incentivize mariners to ignore people in danger emerged in the 2011 "boat left-to-die" incident. During the Libyan civil war, opposition militias often targeted sub-Saharan Africans based on rumors that they were pro-Gaddafi mercenaries. On March 26, seventy-two sub-Saharan passengers left Tripoli headed for Italy in a seven-meter inflatable rubber dingy. Like many vessels, the overcrowded dingy carried insufficient water, food, and fuel. The captain eventually used a satellite phone to make a distress call to an Eritrean priest living in Rome, who then informed the Italian SAR center of the situation. The Straits of Sicily is one of the world's busiest waterways and was closely surveilled by NATO's Operation Unified Protector during its intervention in the Libyan civil war. A military helicopter quickly flew over the dingy and hovered as its crew dropped packets of cookies and water and gave hand signals for the people in the dingy to wait. The helicopter flew away and never returned. After ten days, with half the passengers already dead, a large naval vessel sailed close enough that the survivors could see sailors photographing them. The ship sailed away and never returned. The crew of two fishing boats then spotted the drifting dingy but refused to help. Two weeks later, the dingy washed up on the rocks in Libya. Eleven of the seventy-two passengers were still alive. Two quickly succumbed. The nine survivors eventually left Libya. As of 2012, five had been granted asylum or recognized as refugees, including one Eritrean and four Ethiopians. The asylum claims for the four who managed to reach Europe were still pending.[74]

The "boat left-to-die" saga was not an isolated incident. In August 2014, the SAR center in Rome sent out a call to seventy-six ships asking them to render aid to a nearby migrant vessel in distress. Within one minute, seventy of the ships had turned off their radar signals to become invisible.[75] Punitive policies have even limited civilians' willingness to recover cadavers. An Italian man fishing off Sicily in 1996 recovered a drowned body and brought it back to the village of Portopalo, where he informed local officials. He lost weeks of work, which was his family's only livelihood, as police interrogated him and impounded his fishing boat. Meanwhile, other villagers pulling in their nets found dozens of corpses and piles of clothing from the wreck of the F-174 that had sunk with 283 South Asian passengers on board. A fisherman explained the lesson drawn from the incident. "When, toward the end of 1996, we noticed all those corpses, there was no need to reach any explicit agreement between us fishermen. We all knew that if we reported our findings, the whole fleet would be forced to stop. We just couldn't afford it." At first the fishermen were traumatized. As the months passed, "those who initially vomited at the scene did not get upset any longer," Maurizio Albahari reported. "Corpses were routinely tossed back into the sea, and the authorities never alerted."[76]

More than 26,500 migrants died at Europe's external borders between 2000 and the first half of 2016.[77] Researchers have found a strong correlation between the intensity of EU maritime interdiction operations, as measured by budgets and days of active operations, and numbers of boat losses between 2006 and 2013.[78] "Thousands of deaths in the Mediterranean, over two decades, are not misfortunate accidents, inevitable fatalities, acts of God or of nature. They are crimes of peace," charges Albahari.[79] Among the most notorious incidents, a boat off Lampedusa sank on October 3, 2013. Italian authorities awarded honorary Italian citizenship and a state funeral to the more than 350 people who died. The 155 Eritrean survivors were charged with illegal entry and detained.[80] The symbolic welcome for the dead and criminalization of the living underscored that policies are often motivated by public relations performances aimed at diverse domestic and international audiences. A message upholding the value of human life, in this case costless because the lives have already been lost, coincides with a message that sovereign borders will be firmly defended.

The legal obligation to rescue coexists uneasily with the coercive goal of interdicting migrants. All major maritime interception operations have included search and rescue components. The operation that most explicitly and successfully emphasized search and rescue was Italy's *Mare Nostrum* policy developed in response to the October 2013 sinkings. In 2014, the British government called for an end to *Mare Nostrum*, claiming that the promise of rescue was incentivizing migrants to make dangerous sea journeys and indirectly contributing to deaths at sea. Columnist Dan Hodges skewered the logic in an essay titled "Drown an Immigrant to Save an Immigrant" that began with his take on the government's position:

> We understand that by withdrawing this rescue cover we will be leaving innocent children, women and men to drown who we would otherwise have saved. But eventually word will get around the war-torn communities of Syria and Libya and the other unstable nations of the region that we are indeed leaving innocent children, women and men to drown. And when it does, they will think twice about making the journey. And so eventually, over time, more lives will be saved.

Hodges then outlined his own position:

> There may well be a "pull" factor motivating some of these refugees. But I would guess there is also possibly a "push factor" at play here as well. I'm not sure about you, but if I were planning to load my children, my parents and my grandparents onto some rickety raft with a view to sailing it 1,500 miles across the shark-infested waters of the Mediterranean, I'd have to have a pretty good reason. And it would have to be better than a forlorn hope a random Italian coastguard cutter might spot me and haul me aboard.

Three-quarters of all irregular maritime arrivals in Europe in 2015 were Syrian, Afghan, or Iraqi. Ninety-seven percent of Syrians, 67% of Afghans, and 86% of Iraqis who reached Europe were granted asylum.[81] Not everyone arriving by sea without a visa had a valid protection claim, but statistics collected by the very governments trying to keep them out show that the vast majority were refugees.

Nongovernmental organizations have increasingly become involved in rescuing migrants at sea between Libya and Italy. In 2014, NGOs were

FIGURE 9.2 A migrant is rescued from the Mediterranean some twenty nautical miles north of Libya by a member of Proactiva Open Arms on October 3, 2016. The Italian government tries to prevent NGOs from conducting rescue operations in the Mediterranean. Photo by Aris Messinis /AFP/ Getty Images.

rescuing 0.9% of the total, but by the first quarter of 2017, they were rescuing 35%—more than all the Italian agencies combined. Malta-based Migrant Offshore Aid Station began conducting private search and rescue operations off Libya in 2014 and was joined by Doctors Without Borders, Jugend Rettet, Life Boat, Proactiva Open Arms, Save the Children, Sea-Eye, Sea-Watch, and SOS Mediterranee.[82] In addition to the thirteen vessels on station by 2016, Sea-Watch deployed a reconnaissance aircraft that its organizers said "will be able to observe the Med more closely and might be able to document human rights abuse." A Doctors Without Borders representative told sociologist Paolo Cuttitta, "It is useful to have someone playing the watchdog role in international waters."[83] In 2017, the Italian government, with the approval of the EU, tried to restrict the activities of nine NGOs rescuing migrants at sea by drafting a code of conduct that would bar them from Italian ports if they did not comply. The rules included allowing police on board to search for traffickers and bans on making phone calls or transferring migrants from one ship to another.[84] By June 2018 the newly elected populist government's interior minister, Matteo Salvini, refused to allow NGO ships transporting rescued migrants to dock at Italian ports.[85] Restricting NGO operations at sea put blinders on the watchdogs.

Closing the Aegean

The unfriendly relationship between Athens and Ankara has long limited the efficacy of remote controls. Their lack of cooperation was highlighted in multiple incidents in 2009, when Frontex aircraft ostensibly flying over Greek islands were warned by Turkish radar operators that they were in Turkish airspace and would be intercepted by Turkish fighter planes if they did not change course.[86] Although Greece and Turkey signed a readmission agreement in 2001, Turkish authorities historically have not accepted most returns.

As a result, Greek authorities have simply pushed migrants back under cover of darkness or operations at sea.[87] Pushbacks of anyone risks refoulement, and pushbacks of Syrians during the civil war almost certainly constituted refoulement. Every year between 2012 and 2016, independent rights organizations documented routine pushbacks from Greece into Turkey.[88] In a typical investigation of practices along the border between the two countries, Amnesty International reported the testimony of a nineteen-year-old Syrian man detained on the Greek side of the Evros River:

> At nightfall, hooded men with no insignia on their uniforms loaded us all in a big van and took us to the river bank. Using a small wooden boat they took us all across the river to Turkey. They slapped anyone who was slow.[89]

Nighttime pushbacks on the Evros, the construction of a fence on the short land border between Greece and Turkey, and enhanced cooperation with Bulgaria and Turkey on their land border diverted flows to the sea route between Turkey and Greece.[90]

Many Greek islands are so close to the Turkish mainland that there are no international waters between them. When migrants are intercepted by the Greek Coast Guard, they are already in Greek waters. Greek authorities have experimented with various strategies to push migrants back into Turkish jurisdiction. A Greek official speaking under condition of anonymity explained how pushbacks from Greek islands work in practice:

> If [the migrants] don't damage their boats to such an extent that they're unusable—a mistake on their part—then we put them back on the boats and bring them back to the Turkish coast or to an uninhabited island. This is not official policy—of course not—the Turkish authorities must not know. So either we drag people out of our waters in their boat, or we bring them and their boats on board of the patrol ship and drive them into Turkish waters,

where we launch their boat and put the people back on . . . Everything occurs at night. Who can define where the sea border runs? It's a ping [pong] game: The Greeks send the irregular migrants to Turkey and Turkey sends the boat back to the Greek side; in the process people die and ships go down.[91]

Another technique is to prevent a boat with migrants from reaching the shore by aggressively maneuvering in a way that threatens capsize. The migrant boats are heavily overloaded; the risk is real. A Greek Coast Guard official described the technique to a German NGO. "We drive very close to the boats and put the headlights on, to see who is there," he said. "Of course they are not going to turn around voluntarily because they want to come here." The solution is encirclement. "[We] simply drive around them, create waves and give the people a fright—as though telling them, 'we decide what goes on here —go away!' "[92] The encirclement strategy avoids the practical and legal implications of transferring passengers at sea, while using the threat of capsize and drowning as a deterrent. Officials are aware that these policies are illegal and would be perceived in many quarters as illegitimate, which is why they typically take place at night or far out to sea where the perpetrators are not easily observed.

Unilateral border controls on the Greek side have proved ineffective despite these abuses, which has prompted EU efforts to cooperate more closely with Turkey as a coastal buffer state. The EU recognized Turkey as a candidate country for full membership in 1999 and discussed its visa liberalization in 2013, but the question of whether Turkey will eventually become part of the EU is far less certain than it has been for other candidate states. There are asymmetries between Turkey and the EU, but with 75 million inhabitants and a status as a regional power, Turkey is not as easily pressured as weaker or less strategically situated states like Albania and Mauritania.[93]

Pressure from the EU has cross-cutting effects on controlling asylum seekers. On the one hand, Brussels tries to convince Ankara to act coercively as a buffer. Turkish citizens' visa-free access to Europe is contingent on Ankara discouraging clandestine transit and cooperating with Frontex, EU immigration liaison officers, and Greek and Bulgarian border guards.[94] On the other hand, the EU urges Turkey to adopt a rights-based approach and align its migration control and asylum laws with the EU *acquis*. EU officials began training Turkish officials in asylum screening in 1999. The Law on Foreigners and International Protection adopted in April 2013 formalized de facto "temporary protection" for most Syrian refugees. One condition of EU visa liberalization for Turks is that Turkey provide assistance and protection to asylum seekers.[95] An emphasis on human rights discourages refoulement and the deadliest control measures, though it is also a way to encourage the containment of refugees who are granted some sort of humanitarian protection.[96] Ankara's hand in these negotiations strengthened over time as most European politicians grew desperate to stop the entrance of refugees and irregular migrants.

Transit countries have incentives to maintain cross-border mobility even in the face of external pressure to become more restrictive. The Turkish government expanded its ambitions to become a regional power beginning in the early 2000s. Open visa policies facilitated growing trade and transportation links, including the spectacular expansion of Turkish Airlines to fly to more countries than any other airline in the world.[97] Ankara abolished visa requirements with Syria, Albania, Libya, Tajikistan, Azerbaijan, Lebanon, and Saudi Arabia in 2009 and agreed to visa-free travel with Iran and Russia.[98] Turkey increasingly became a potential conduit for migrants, including asylum seekers, not only from its neighbors but also from East Africa and Central Asia. At the same time, the EU expected Turkey to impose visa requirements on countries blacklisted by the EU, including Syria, Jordan, and Lebanon.[99] The Turkish solution to the quandary of maintaining an open visa policy while controlling irregular migration was to negotiate readmission agreements so that unwanted migrants could be expelled. Turkey signed readmission agreements with Greece (2001), Syria (2003), Romania (2004), Kyrgyzstan (2004), Ukraine (2005), and Russia (2011), and opened discussions with several other countries.[100]

Turkey was deeply affected by the refugee crises in neighboring Syria and Iraq. By 2018, Ankara had registered over 3.5 million of the 5.6 million Syrian refugees uprooted by the conflict, more than any other country in the region and more than twice as many as all European countries combined.[101] In addition to being a major host country, Turkey's position at Syria's northern border made it the first country of transit for Syrian refugees on their way to Europe.[102] Refugees from the Middle East traveled from Turkey to Greece via the Aegean Sea (the eastern Mediterranean route) and continued their journey through Macedonia, Serbia, Hungary, and Austria (the western Balkan route) before reaching Germany or Sweden. In 2015 alone, over 850,000 refugees entered Greece from Turkey, more than through any other route.[103]

In August 2015, Germany's center-right chancellor Angela Merkel suspended, for Syrian nationals, the Dublin procedure of returning asylum seekers to the first country in which they entered the EU. This was a major shift from Germany's policies since the early 1990s of turning EU member states at the external border of the EU into buffers for Germany.

The episode appeared to be an ad hoc response to the public revulsion around the drowning of the Syrian boy Alan Kurdi on a Turkish beach and Merkel's humanitarian ideology derived from her upbringing as the daughter of a Lutheran pastor. The suspension was highly controversial in Germany and met with a polarized response. Crowds of German citizens carrying stuffed animals for the children welcomed refugees at train stations at the same time as a backlash against refugees, and against Muslims in particular, built on the far right. The easing of remote control was short-lived. Merkel took the lead in negotiating a deal between the EU and Turkey to assist more Syrian refugees in Turkey and cage them there so they would not reach Europe.[104]

The European Council announced a joint action plan with Turkey in October 2015 that included funds to improve the living conditions of Syrian refugees in Turkey and increase buffering measures.[105] The Turkish side guaranteed that refugees would be registered and have access to public services. The EU committed to informing refugees about legal avenues to the EU (though these are all but foreclosed for most asylum seekers) and to contribute to strengthening the Turkish Coast Guard, deploying a Frontex liaison officer to Turkey, and cooperating on joint returns. Ankara pledged to increase the interception capacities of its Coast Guard, prevent irregular migration across land borders with Bulgaria and Greece, and crack down on smuggling networks. Turkey would accelerate readmission in line with the 2013 EU-Turkey agreement that was signed parallel to the launch of the dialogue to ease visa requirements for Turks traveling to the EU.[106] The joint action plan was activated at a meeting between EU and Turkish leaders the following month that included EU promises to give Turkey €3 billion, revitalize the accession talks, and accelerate visa liberalization.

EU-Turkey summit meetings in March 2016 agreed to give Turkey an additional €3 billion and return to Turkey "all new irregular migrants crossing from Turkey into Greek islands as from 20 March 2016 (as a) temporary and extraordinary measure which is necessary to end the human suffering and restore public order." [107] The agreement specified that migrants were "irregular" if they did not apply for asylum in Greece or if their asylum applications were rejected by Greek authorities. The governments agreed that "for every Syrian being returned to Turkey from Greek islands, another Syrian will be resettled from Turkey to the EU." However, this mechanism on paper was limited to the resettlement of around 72,000 refugees. In practice, only 3,098 Syrians were resettled from Turkey to the EU between April 2016 and February 2017.[108] Arrivals of irregular migrants in Greece dropped by 97% after the agreement went into effect.[109]

The UNHCR, the Council of Europe's commissioner for human rights, and numerous NGOs strongly criticized the EU-Turkey agreement. Two elements of the deal were especially controversial— the possibility of illegal mass expulsions and whether Turkey could be considered "safe" for return.[110] EU regulations require that for a country to be considered a "European safe third country," it must have "ratified and observe the provisions of the Geneva Convention without any geographical limitations."[111] Along with Madagascar, Turkey is one of only two countries to maintain the 1951 Convention's geographical limitation on the definition of refugees, which restricts the category to Europeans.[112] The Turkish government said it would lift the geographic limitation when its accession to the EU was completely negotiated, a fair burden-sharing arrangement between the EU and Turkey was in place, and Turkey had the necessary infrastructure for mass asylum. Apart from Bulgaria, no EU country had ever considered Turkey part of a national list of safe countries of origin.[113]

The argument that Turkey was a "European safe third country" became even harder to make after Turkey informed the Council of Europe in July 2016 of its decision to "temporarily suspend" its commitments under the European Convention on Human Rights.[114] To be considered a "first country of asylum" under EU regulations is a slightly lower bar that requires a working asylum system and sufficient protection. Human Rights Watch argued these requirements were not met from 2015 to 2017 in Turkey and reported instances of Turkish border guards shooting at Syrians attempting to enter Turkey and pushing some back without any legal process. Non-Syrians returned from Greece to Turkey were rarely able to apply for asylum or access lawyers to work on their case.[115]

The UNHCR distanced itself from the EU-Turkey agreement and suspended its operations on the Greek islands.[116] Likewise, Doctors Without Borders suspended its activities on the same day to "not allow our assistance to be instrumentalized for a mass expulsion operation."[117] The long-term enforcement and consequences of the EU-Turkey deal became even more uncertain following the Turkish military coup in July 2016 and imposition of martial law. A suit by three asylum seekers in Greece asking for an annulment of the 2016 EU-Turkey agreement was thrown out of the General Court of the EU based on the logic that it did not have jurisdiction because the agreement was not a formal treaty.[118] If sustained, this logic would provide an easy way for governments to work around EU law by simply creating memoranda of understanding rather than formal treaties. Many remote control techniques are designed to evade the spirit of the law while narrowly complying with the letter.

In the face of continued flows in the eastern Mediterranean, German Chancellor Angela Merkel and Turkish Prime Minister Ahmet Davutoğlu announced in February 2016 that they would seek NATO's support to combat migrant smuggling.[119] The NATO umbrella provided a mechanism for Turkey, as a NATO member, to cooperate with European governments. Although Greece is a member of both NATO and the EU, Greek authorities were initially reluctant to agree to NATO involvement in the Aegean Sea, given potential infringements of Greek sovereignty.[120] Ships from Germany, Greece, the United States, Turkey, Poland, UK, Canada, the Netherlands, and France had participated in the mission in the Aegean by summer 2016. The operational area for the deployment was initially limited to international waters but was extended to the territorial waters of Greece and Turkey in early March 2016. Greek and Turkish vessels only operated within their own territorial waters to avoid confrontations. NATO stated that the people it intercepted who came via Turkey would be returned.[121]

Concerns about a military response to refugee flows have been voiced from legal, humanitarian, and utilitarian standpoints. While from legal and humanitarian perspectives, the operation raised questions about refoulement and refugees' access to safety in Europe, others criticized the NATO operation for being ineffectual. According to the Greek government, NATO vessels only identified a fraction of the boats carrying migrants to Greece and merely redirected flows to different destinations within Greece. Daily maritime arrivals in Greece fell after the NATO mission launch, but there was a much larger immediate downturn after the EU-Turkey agreement of March 26, 2016.[122] The main factor determining the efficacy of remote controls in the Turkish-Greek sea corridor has been whether the EU can dangle enough carrots for the Turkish government to cooperate.

Offshore Processing

The idea of sending people seeking asylum in the EU somewhere else to assess their claim has been proposed numerous times since the 1980s. The Danish government submitted an unsuccessful draft resolution to the UN General Assembly in 1986 to create regional refugee processing centers where asylum seekers could be returned.[123] In 1993, the Dutch government proposed that the Intergovernmental Consultations on Migration, Asylum and Refugees (IGC) consider the possibility of sending all asylum seekers back to reception centers in their region of origin to process claims.[124] The IGC is a policy forum for rich democracies in Europe, North America, and

Australia founded by the UNHCR in 1985 and later dubbed by its critics as "the spearhead of Fortress Europe."[125]

The IGC's reports rejected the option of exclusively examining asylum claims in offshore centers. The biggest practical obstacle was the avoidance of creating a new pull factor that would draw potential asylum seekers to such camps. Politically, the proposal would require unprecedented coordination among the host and sponsoring states, UNHCR, and other actors. The major humanitarian and legal obstacles were how to protect the safety of asylum seekers in the centers, avoid refoulement, and establish which government was legally responsible for protection. The IGC considered other models of "protected areas" where refugees could be processed.[126] It took the U.S. processing of Haitians in Guantanamo as a partly successful model, though one difficult to repeat elsewhere due to the unique legal status of Guantanamo, the U.S. military's unusually high capacity for logistics and detention, and the possibility of intercepting asylum seekers before they reached U.S. territory. The report emphasized the need for "financial or political inducements, such as development assistance" to convince host countries for offshore processing to cooperate.[127] The original Dutch proposal and the IGC linked the safe third-country concept to offshore processing. Alternative models such as protection in a designated zone in the country of origin might be possible in some circumstances but were inherently messier given greater problems of potential refoulement and providing protection.[128]

The Danish government took up the idea of offshore processing again in 2001 and circulated favorable reports on U.S. interdiction of Haitians and Australia's "Pacific Solution," discussed in chapter 10, as potential models. The most prominent push began two years later when British Prime Minister Tony Blair proposed that the EU develop safe havens outside its borders to process asylum seekers. Blair had promised to cut the number of applications of asylum seekers in half. The proposal broadly mirrored earlier versions but differed in its sustained effort to use the full force of the EU. In keeping with the "escape to Europe" thesis, the British government tried to solve its perceived problem of too many asylum seekers in Britain by Europeanizing the issue. Blair's Liberal government proposed that centers in Albania and Croatia screen potential refugees for the entire EU. The Danish, Dutch, Italian, and Spanish governments supported the British proposal.[129]

The governments of Sweden, France, Belgium, and, initially, Germany, opposed the British position. The basic practical, political, humanitarian, and legal questions that had plagued earlier proposals remained unanswered. The Croatian government said it was insulted by the plan. Albania lacked an asylum system.[130] "We are against any sort of system that would deny people the right to apply for asylum in the country they have sought refuge in," announced Jan Karlsson, the Swedish minister of immigration.[131] As a supranational institution, the EU Commission enjoys a greater degree of independence from populist demands for restriction. Its report analyzing the British proposal suggested that offshore processing would be effective as a complement to rather than as a substitute for the asylum system, and that the EU should help strengthen safe environments in third countries by encouraging them to create asylum systems and sign readmission agreements. Several techniques of remote control were closely bundled together. On the other hand, the Commission pointed out that offshore processing was likely to be successful only if there was a workable model in which at least some recognized refugees would be resettled in the EU and its members agreed to share responsibility for that resettlement.[132] Hostility to offshore processing originated in opposite motivations: fears that it would violate the rights of asylum seekers, and fears that it would force European states to accept the resettlement of unwanted refugees in a responsibility-sharing scheme.[133]

The center-left German government reversed its position on offshore processing during 2004 and 2005. Interior Minister Otto Schily proposed that asylum seekers be intercepted in the Mediterranean and returned to EU-financed camps in North Africa. Schily's plan was the most restrictive in that EU states would then only accept some fraction of the recognized refugees on a voluntary basis. The UNHCR, numerous NGOs, and the Swedish and Finnish governments strongly opposed Schily's proposal and questioned whether camps in North Africa could be considered safe. The Italian government supported setting up screening camps in Libya, but all the governments in North Africa rejected the plan, which they feared would act as a magnet for asylum seekers. The Austrian government, which had supported extraterritorial processing since 1998, suggested extending the model to the EU's land borders in the east with an eye toward processing Chechens in camps set up in the Ukraine. Baltic states receiving asylum seekers from Chechnya applauded the proposal, but it was quickly rejected by the Ukrainian government.[134]

The idea of offshoring the detention and screening of asylum seekers intercepted at sea was raised again every year from 2015 to 2018. The Italian government called for refugee processing centers to be set up in Niger, Tunisia, and Sudan. Hungarian President Viktor Orbán suggested the EU build "a large refugee city" in Libya to process claims, an idea rejected by Libyan authorities, who did not even control their own country, as "very far removed from the reality on the ground." In the plan designed by Interior Minister Thomas de Maiziere, "People who are rescued in the Mediterranean should be brought back to safe accommodation facilities in northern Africa" and then those with recognized protection needs resettled in Europe by country quotas.[135]

Variations of offshore-processing plans include the selection of asylum seekers in transit countries. The Austrian government proposed that Niger and Jordan process applicants for asylum in the EU and take responsibility for applicants rejected in Europe whose countries of origin would not accept them. French President Emmanuel Macron proposed "hotspots" in Libya to process asylum seekers bound for Europe. Programs put into practice have been extremely limited. For example, a few hundred asylum seekers living in camps in Libya have been pre-selected by the UNHCR and flown directly to Italy or to Niger for asylum interviews with French officials. In effect, these are nano-scale refugee resettlement programs. In 2016 and 2017, the Italian "humanitarian corridor" program funded by church organizations involved the pre-selection of around 850 Iraqis and Syrians in Lebanon by private organizations, a security screening conducted by Italian officials in Beirut, and then flights to Italy where they made formal asylum claims. All the initial arrivals were granted asylum or some form of humanitarian protection. The program operated similarly to refugee resettlement, except there was an added layer of uncertainty for those seeking protection because the official asylum screening took place in Italy and participants could be rejected and deported at that stage. A smaller Italian program operated in Ethiopia and Morocco.[136] Resettlements by the UNHCR in European countries were limited to 11,175 in 2015, rising to 26,400 in 2017. The vast majority were Syrians.[137] These programs point to the feasibility of providing legal pathways to protection, but unless they are scaled up, their main function is to provide a public relations opportunity for states to bolster their humanitarian bona fides at minimal cost. The strong focus of European governments remains remote control that keeps most asylum seekers from accessing protection while accepting a token number of refugees to tout as proof of their virtue.

On some accounts, geography as well as bilateral relations constrained EU options. A U.S. State Department analysis observed that one of the obstacles to extraterritorial processing was that "no EU Member State possesses a territory in the vicinity which is outside its immigration laws (similar to those used by the U.S. and Australia in deterring dangerous, unauthorized maritime crossings)."[138] Governments can change a territory's legal status, however. While the indefinite leased status of the U.S. naval base at Guantanamo Bay is truly unique, why did Greece, Italy, or Spain not follow the Australian model discussed in chapter 10 and "excise" one of their islands, turning Lesbos, Lampedusa, or Cabrera into a barbican detention camp like Australia's Christmas Island? The European supranational courts would presumably have blocked such a naked effort to remove a European territory from the space where its asylum laws applied. Offshoring proposals continued to fail as of 2018, not because of geography, but because of strongly divergent views within the EU, the legal constraints of a supranational system, and the unwillingness of transit states to cooperate.

Conclusion

Maritime interception is only effective if there is somewhere to take people intercepted at sea. The idea of offshore processing has been floated in Europe since the 1980s but none of its many problems has been resolved as of this writing. The main institutional barrier is not that European governments lack access to a territory where they could assess asylum claims in an enclosed environment with fewer rights. Such a territorial designation could simply be invented, as the Australian example of "excision" in the following chapter shows. The main obstacle is a strong supranational judiciary that monitors strong rights of territorial personhood and has increasingly suggested that state control over individuals outside its territory incurs their obligation to respect the rights of the persons under their control.

In lieu of offshore processing, European governments collaborate with coastal states to prevent departures and accept readmission of people intercepted at sea. This kind of buffering has often involved collaboration with authoritarian states or even militias selling their services to the highest bidder. Both severely abuse migrants and ignore international norms around asylum. However, the EU has been caught in a net of its own weaving. It works to increase the capacity of the UNHCR to develop offices in countries such as Libya as part of the EU's "Global Approach to Migration."[39] Those same offices then became witness to the abuses of migrants, including recognized refugees, in the countries of transit. The direct statements of the UNHCR usually pull their punches, but their findings reverberate in the world's press, supranational European courts, and among sympathetic constituencies in the policymaking world and broader public.

Civil society organizations that were originally formed as national organizations have followed the EU in expanding to include nodes in multiple EU countries and in Brussels. These organizations are then following the EU in moving beyond Europe's borders as well. Monitoring of conditions in buffer states produces evidence that the courts then rely on when blocking refoulement. Remote control is moderately constrained by a chain of unintended consequences. Even where the priority is control, its pairing with rights-based institutions extends the contradictions of the two goals into spaces further and further afield. It is no longer possible to claim, "We did not know what was happening." The left hand of Europe is taking notes that record the actions of the right.

| Stopping the Refugee Boats

AN EXCEPTIONALLY THICK AERIAL dome, wide maritime borders, and the absence of a land border enable a high level of migration control in Australia. Most of the few people asking for asylum arrive by air, but like most other countries of the Global North, maritime arrivals generate the political heat. For several decades the government's options were self-limited by foreign policy interests that favored asylum seekers from current or former allied countries, from Chinese in the 1940s to South Vietnamese in the 1970s; the desire to project abroad an image of Australia as a humanitarian country moving away from its overtly racist white Australia immigration policy; and interpretations of international law that interceptions of asylum seekers at sea were illegitimate. These constraints generally collapsed by the 2000s as a domestic political consensus arose in the leadership of the major parties around a strict deterrent policy. The strategy is built on buffers in Indonesia and Papua New Guinea, the idiosyncratic construction of legal barbicans by redefining rights in particular Australian territories, aggressive interceptions of visa-less travelers in the moat, and caging maritime asylum seekers in other countries' territories where most have been determined to be refugees by the UNHCR definition.

In general, Australia enjoys a regional hegemony that allows it to push boats back into Indonesian territorial waters and pay the governments of Papua New Guinea and tiny Nauru to conduct offshore processing. Australia's judicial system has weak rights of territorial personhood and shows little deference to international law. Of the four major cases in this volume, Australian courts limit remote control strategies the least. The only current modest limitations on Canberra's remote controls derive from reliance on other governments to do the work of buffering and caging and scrutiny by civil

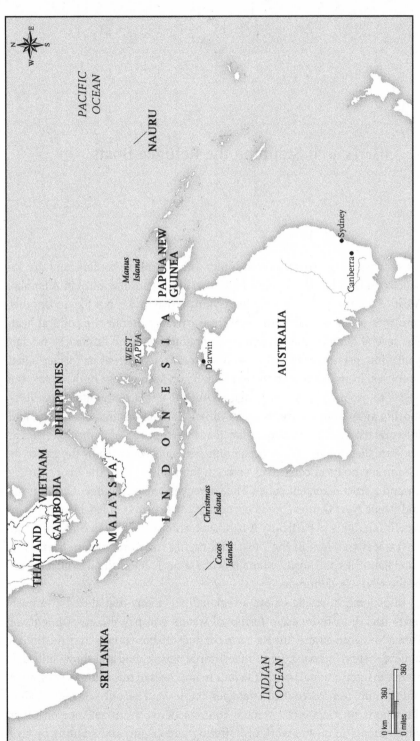

FIGURE 10.1 Australia and Southeast Asia

society. Cooperation with the major transit country of Indonesia is shaped by the broader quality of the binational relationship. A network of Australian civil society actors—journalists, activists, and NGOs—is periodically able to reveal shocking and arguably illegal practices at sea and offshore.

Australia's Dome

As in the United States, the Australian government has built its aerial dome using a familiar set of techniques that were originally based on regulating passenger ships in the nineteenth century and then extended to airlines and airports around the world. The colony of Victoria introduced shipping sanctions to limit Chinese immigration in 1855. General shipping sanctions for inadmissible passengers were added in 1905, four years after Australia federated.[1] The carrier sanctions regime for airlines disembarking passengers without proper documents began in 1958 and was tightened in 1966, 1979, and 1980.[2]

Since 1979, Australia has had a universal visa policy that requires visas or electronic travel authorizations of all nationalities. All but New Zealanders are required to obtain permission in advance.[3] Canberra began deploying airline liaison officers to enforce visa policies remotely in 1989 in a network that grew to 147 migration officers in forty overseas locations. Their job is to deter irregular migrants, including asylum seekers, from ever reaching Australian airports.[4] The Advance Passenger Processing system since 2005 has required airlines to confirm that all passengers bound for Australia have a visa and to share their information with immigration officials in advance.[5] The 1958 Migration Act defines *traveling to* Australia without a visa as unlawful, thus appearing to define an activity outside Australian territory as illegal, while insisting that non-refoulement provisions do not apply outside Australian territory.[6] Through this legal trick, the Australian government exercises extraterritorial control without incurring extraterritorial obligations.

Most asylum seekers arrive by air, including 60% of the nearly 120,000 asylum applicants between 2001 and 2014.[7] Unlike a trickle of asylum seekers landing at airports amid millions of other travelers, asylum seekers on boats are pictured as a "desperate horde" or an "invasion."[8] Almost 1,200 boats carrying around 70,000 asylum seekers without visas arrived in Australia between 1976 and 2016.[9] Ironically, asylum seekers arriving irregularly by sea historically have had a much higher recognition rate than those who arrive by air with visas. In the 2000s, the recognition rate for maritime arrivals ranged from 70% to 97% each year, while the rate for air arrivals was about 20%.

As migration researcher Khaled Koser summarizes, "arguably Australia is worrying about the wrong asylum seekers. Whereas the majority of those arriving by boat are refugees, the majority of those arriving by air are not."[10]

Analysts have explained the intense political attention to asylum seekers in Australia as the result of two major factors. The first explanation is an historical aversion to spontaneous arrivals built by a century of strict immigration control enabled by Australia's isolated geography. The second explanation is that asylum policy is a way for left-leaning governments to distract populist white anxieties about the large percentage of immigrants from non-European origins and a multiculturalist accommodation of Australia's diverse populations, and for conservative governments to draw on those fears without explicitly using racial categories.[11] Whether the government is right or left, the accreted policies of enhanced remote control look similar.

The self-governing colonies that formed Australia were among the world's pioneers in designing restrictions against Chinese. When the colonies federated in 1901, some of Australia's first laws banned the immigration of Chinese and Pacific Islanders. The composition of immigration to Australia shifted after World War II from overwhelming origins in the British Isles to encompass Southern Europe and the Middle East. The end of the "White Australia" policy in 1973 opened the door to Asia.[12] By 2016, the foreign-born share of the population reached 28%.[13] The appearance of the One Nation party led by Pauline Hanson brought expressions of xenophobia from the margins into mainstream debate. "I believe we are in danger of being swamped by Asians," Hanson told Parliament in September 1996.[14] By the 2000s, a harsh asylum policy built around mandatory detention of asylum seekers who arrived by air and a range of efforts to deter maritime arrivals became a near-consensus that cut across major party lines.

Early Maritime Arrivals

Few asylum seekers attempted to reach Australia by sea until the 1970s. During World War II, fourteen Chinese seamen arrived and were eventually allowed to stay as a "wartime legacy" of Australia's alliance with China against Japan. In July 1959, the Australian government rebuffed a U.S. request to give political asylum to recently exiled Cuban president Fulgencio Batista, including a proposal in which Batista would simply arrive in an Australian port on a "round the world cruise" and ask for a visa.[15] A handful of stowaways from the People's Republic of China were deported in the early

1960s, though five were allowed to stay in 1962 after they expressed fear of being repatriated.[16]

Eight "raft men" from West Papua became the first group of asylum seekers to arrive in Australia by sea in their own craft when they landed on Moa Island in February 1969. Alexander Toembay and seven others asked for protection from political persecution in West Papua, which had recently been annexed by Indonesia. At the time, the U.S. ambassador to Indonesia was confidentially warning Washington, "Military repression has stimulated fears and rumors of intended genocide" among the population in West Papua.[17] Under an implied Australian threat to deport the raft men by force, the men agreed to be flown to the Australian-controlled territory of Papua and New Guinea for their asylum claims to be heard. The territory's administrator rejected their claim and argued that the men were responsible for their own predicament. If only they would cast aside their "anti-Indonesian attitudes" and "unwillingness to adapt to the regime," they could return to West Papua without "danger of loss of life or serious loss of liberty."[18] The raft men were deported. Asylum seekers did not arrive by sea again until after the Indochinese War in the mid-1970s. Australia acceded to the 1967 Protocol in 1973, but in practice it rarely granted political asylum. Instead, Canberra applied "humanitarian considerations" when deciding whether asylum seekers could stay, which in the government's view, "had the advantage of being flexible."[19]

From Toleration to Deportation

Less than three weeks after communist forces took Saigon in April 1975, the Australian Department of Labor and Immigration held an interagency meeting "to consider contingency planning in case sea craft carrying South Vietnamese . . . should arrive in Australian waters or make landfall on the Australian coast without approval."[20] The report produced from the meeting recommended against trying to prevent Vietnamese refugees from landing. The authors concluded that such a move would violate Australia's international legal obligations. It would likely incur a backlash from an Australian public that would sympathize with refugees fleeing from Australia's fallen ally. More than 500 Australian soldiers had died fighting on the South Vietnamese side during the war.[21] Labor Prime Minister Gough Whitlam decided to let Vietnamese passengers and crew disembark in custody.[22]

A year later, twenty-five-year-old Lam Binh, his brother, and three friends sailed into Darwin on a wooden fishing boat. Australia was not their original destination. With a page torn from a school atlas as their chart, they aimed to reach the United States via Guam or the U.S. base at Subic Bay in the Philippines. A chance encounter with a civilian Australian ship captain in Malaysia convinced them that Australia was closer, friendlier, and that they would be allowed to land under Australian law. "Okay," said Lam Binh. "We'll go to Australia."[23] The five men were issued temporary visas on landing and soon adjusted to permanent residency without any political fuss. A few more boats made the 3,500-kilometer journey. The political climate remained largely welcoming over the next year. Foreign Minister Andrew Peacock publicly rejected the idea of attempting to stop maritime arrivals.[24] "Is there an Australian federal leader prepared to risk the national and international outcry by sending out the Navy physically to turn back the fleet of small boats?" journalist Bruce Wilson asked rhetorically in an editorial:

> I should not like to be the Australian politician or diplomat trying to explain to Australians and the world, how, on the one hand, we saw it necessary to help anti-communist Vietnam fight a civil war, while on the other hand we refuse to accept anti-communist Vietnamese as refugees from those same countries.[25]

The international image of Australia as a humanitarian country and bulwark against international communism, and an understanding that vessels could not legally be intercepted in international waters, made stopping the boats unthinkable. A 1979 Cabinet memo lamented, "International law in general, would not allow Australia to legislate to restrict or prohibit the movement of refugee vessels on the high seas, except in the circumstances provided in Article 24 of the 1958 Geneva Convention on the Territorial Sea and the Contiguous Zone."[26]

The lack of a truly global refugee regime meant that Australia was not initially buffered from Indochinese refugees by its neighbors in Southeast Asia. The governments of many countries in the region that were not signatories to the Refugee Convention or its Protocol often pushed back boats carrying Indochinese. For example, in November 1978, the Thai government announced that Thailand would not accept refugee arrivals and that unseaworthy boats would be repaired and then pushed back out to sea. Malaysian officials called the refugees "scum, garbage, and residue" and threatened to shoot maritime arrivals on sight. The Malaysian military fired across the bows of boats attempting to approach its shores to keep them away. In February 1979, about a quarter of boats that tried to land on Malaysian shores were towed back to international waters. By mid-1979, the Malaysian navy towed back 80% of arriving boats. The Indonesian government tried to prevent refugee boats from landing unless they were continuing to Australia after repairs and taking on supplies. Many refugees responded by destroying their boats on the beach so they could not be towed back out to sea. When Britain signed the 1951 Refugee Convention, it included a reservation that the Convention did not apply to its colonies, such as Hong Kong.[27] In February 1979, a freighter called the *Skyluck* with 2,700 Vietnamese aboard entered the harbor of the British colony of Hong Kong, where the authorities refused to allow the ship to land. It rode at anchor for five months before the crew ran her aground to ensure that the refugees would be taken ashore, where they were placed in detention camps until they could be resettled.[28]

Australia's remote control options were limited because unlike most other communist countries, the Vietnamese government did not try to prevent its nationals from leaving. Officials extorted hundreds of millions of dollars' worth of gold as a condition of departure, particularly from persecuted ethnic Chinese. [29] As the CIA analyzed the situation, exit was a political escape valve as well, similar to the Cuban government's episodic relaxation of exit controls described in chapter 6.

> The Indochina states show little sign of embarrassment about the large numbers of people who choose to leave, and in the case of Vietnam they encourage them. Despite the fact that many who leave Vietnam are people whose skills are badly needed by the new regime, most officials apparently prefer to rid themselves of potential malcontents rather than hope to convert them.[30]

The boat exodus became an international humanitarian crisis as passengers drowned or were killed. Between 1980 and 1982, 80 to 90% of refugee boats arriving in Thailand and Malaysia had been attacked by pirates. A 1983 CIA report estimated that 100,000 to 140,000 Vietnamese had died at sea.[31]

In 1978 President Jimmy Carter ordered U.S. ships to pick up Vietnamese people at sea and take them to offshore-processing stations like the U.S. territory of Guam. All of the Vietnamese who wanted to reach the United States were resettled, unlike later offshore-processing schemes based on selection and a message of deterrence.[32] Private ship captains who encountered boats in danger were obligated to rescue the passengers, but their status afterward was often uncertain because of the mismatch between obligations of rescue and admission in what James Pugash called "the dilemma of the sea refugee." As Pugash explained, "The plight of the Vietnam refugee draws the two principles together into the Catch 22 of the law of the sea. The shipmaster of a freighter in waters off Indochina is obligated to rescue Vietnamese sea refugees, but no nation is bound to take the refugees once they have been rescued."[33]

A group of French intellectuals that included Jean-Paul Sartre launched *Un bateau pour le Vietnam*, an operation using a repurposed freighter to rescue Indochinese refugees at sea in the 1970s and 1980s.[34] Inspired by the French effort, German Emergency Doctors (GED) formed in 1979. Its flagship *Cap Anamur* and sister ships began rescuing more than 10,000 "boat people" in 1980 and taking them to Germany, which accepted them until 1982 because the ships were flagged in Germany. Other aid agencies carried out maritime rescue operations, including World Vision and Food for the Hungry.[35] These efforts became the model for NGO ships operating in the Mediterranean in the 2010s discussed in the previous chapter.

Over 2,000 Indochinese asylum seekers arrived in Australia by sea from 1976 to 1981.[36] By the election of 1977, the boats were becoming a domestic political issue, prompting the conservative government of Malcom Fraser to consider various options to deter new arrivals and process those who came. Canberra announced that Indochinese who arrived after March 1978 would have to apply for refugee status on arrival and would no longer be immediately accepted as permanent residents. The process was intended to maintain Australia's international obligations while assuaging a public that was growing hostile to Indochinese arrivals.[37] Australian officials explicitly modeled the new policy on Canada's refugee status determination system. Conditions in countries of origin would be assessed with guidance from the Department of Foreign Affairs, UNHCR, and organizations such as Amnesty International. Canberra agreed to allow asylum applicants to be given advice by their own attorneys in these proceedings, even though "difficulties were foreseen in the proposed procedures breeding a new race of 'immigration lawyers,' marked by their skill in delaying official procedures by exploiting appeal mechanisms and in other ways obstructing fair determination by the committee."[38] Once asylum seekers reached Australian territory, the government decided that its harshest options were limited by the presence of legal advocates and foreign policy interests.

Fraser's solution was to ask governments in the region to detain vessels of asylum seekers in transit and process them in those countries. In the absence of a repatriation option and the refusal of Southeast Asian countries to accept refugee settlement, international agreements set up a system to manage the outflow. In July 1979, the Vietnamese government agreed to suspend spontaneous departures and create an "Organized Departure Plan" for resettlement. The Malaysian, Thai, and other Southeast Asian governments agreed to allow temporary asylum while the U.S., Australian, Canadian, French, and other governments promised to permanently resettle refugees from camps in Southeast Asia.[39] The use of remote islands in the Pacific for first-asylum processing was pioneered by Indonesia on Natuna and the Anambas Islands and in the Philippines on Palawan Island.[40] In 1979 Canberra began paying for the UNHCR to process Vietnamese refugees in Indonesia. After the Vietnamese government agreed to place a moratorium on boat departures, the numbers of people leaving Vietnam fell sharply. Cooperation with the government producing the refugees accomplished what buffering strategies could only partly achieve.[41] The willingness of multiple resettlement countries to give the refugees permanent protection after buffer countries temporarily housed them created a system of unprecedented interstate collaboration.

A short-lived barbican strategy provided a back-up layer of control. The Cabinet had rejected an initial plan before the Organized Departure Plan went into effect to create a barbican on land where "boat people" could be held under a special regime. According to a confidential 1979 Cabinet memo contemplating how to stop "refugee boats," which showed the government considered Vietnamese to be refugees, "[a]nother option to be considered is the establishment of a large detention centre in Darwin to accommodate boat people without a future obligation by Australia to accept them for permanent residence or to consider their claims for refugee status."[42] While the plan was rejected, the Australian Parliament tightened restrictions with a temporary 1980 law that prohibited maritime arrivals from disembarking without permits, thus creating a barbican in the territorial waters of Australian ports.[43] The rationale behind the temporary restrictions was laid out in a proposal by M. J. R. MacKellar, minister for immigration and ethnic affairs, the previous year. Limiting the period of "special circumstances" that restrictive laws were in effect "would provide flexibility, and help defuse public criticism."[44] The last boat to arrive in the first wave from Indochina sailed into Darwin with 146 people in October 1981. The passengers were deported to Taiwan and Hong Kong.[45]

No more boats arrived until eight years later, when twenty-six Cambodians seeking protection landed in 1989, followed by vessels from China and Vietnam. The passengers encountered a more hostile reception than those who arrived in the 1970s. Asylum seekers from Cambodia were eventually allowed to settle in Australia on the condition that they briefly return to Cambodia and then come back to Australia. The logic of a quick "touchback" was awkward given that the purpose of asylum is to protect people who cannot safely return to their country of origin. The reason for this oxymoronic policy was to demonstrate symbolically that Cambodia was safe. Cambodia's peace plan was considered a major Australian foreign policy success, and the government did not want to suggest that Cambodia was unstable.[46]

Vietnamese asylum seekers, most of who had previously been resettled in China, arrived in northern Australia by small boats in the 1990s. The acceptance of asylum seekers from Vietnam risked politically undermining the regional Comprehensive Plan of Action adopted in 1989, under which Australia resettled 19,000 Indochinese.[47] Yet as in the 1970s, the government announced that it could not stop asylum seekers in international waters.[48] A 1995 memorandum of understanding between Australia and China laid the groundwork for the return of more than 1,000 of the roughly 2,500 who had arrived in forty boats since 1989. Canberra's responses to the episodic arrivals of Indochinese asylum seekers by sea followed a bumpy line of generally becoming more restrictive.

By the late 1990s, the composition of maritime arrivals shifted away from Indochina and toward the Middle East and South Asia. Between 1999 and 2000, protection visas for irregular maritime arrivals were granted to 100% of Sri Lankans, 99% of Afghans, 98% of Iraqis, and 27% of Iranians.[49] The number of irregular maritime arrivals reached a new high of 5,516 in 2001. Although arguably a modest number compared with a permanent immigrant inflow of 92,000 the previous year, irregular maritime arrivals soon became a defining issue in national politics.

Elusive Solutions

The Australian territory of Christmas Island lies more than 1,500 kilometers northwest of the mainland but just 325 kilometers south of Indonesia—within three day's sail for small boats. On August 26, 2001, Australia's search and rescue command broadcast a call requesting any nearby ships to assist a wooden fishing boat in distress 140 kilometers north of Christmas Island. The Norwegian container ship *MV Tampa* rescued the 433 passengers, who were mostly Afghan asylum seekers from the persecuted Hazara ethnic minority. Australian authorities asked Captain Arne Rinnan to take the passengers to Indonesia because the rescue took place within Indonesia's search and rescue area. As Rinnan steered toward Indonesia, several Afghans threatened to commit suicide unless they were taken to Christmas Island. Rinnan turned the ship around, prompting Prime Minister Howard to announce that they would not be allowed to land. He would "draw a line on what is increasingly becoming an uncontrollable number of illegal arrivals in this country." The *Tampa* anchored in the contiguous zone off Christmas

Island for five days amid a growing humanitarian crisis on a ship that was only licensed to carry forty people. Fifteen of the passengers fell unconscious. Rinnan finally issued a distress call and sailed into Australian territorial waters, where Australian special forces boarded the *Tampa* and took control. When the Norwegian ambassador inspected the ship on August 30, passengers presented him with a note asking for asylum in Australia. Given that 99% of Afghans recently seeking asylum in Australia had been given protection, it was obvious that most would be recognized as refugees if given the chance to present their claim.[50]

The Migration Act of 1958 gave the government the authority to board ships carrying passengers intending to land and to bring them to the onshore "migration zone" for detention. The law was murky about the legal status and rights of people who were within Australian territorial waters but outside the migration zone. On August 29, Howard tried to rush the Border Protection Bill through parliament. The bill authorized the government to retroactively invalidate applications for protection visas made on board ships in Australian territorial waters, expel ships from those waters, and constrain the courts from reviewing the executive's decisions. The House of Representatives passed the bill, but the Senate rejected it on August 30.[51]

Howard tried to find other countries that would take responsibility for the asylum seekers. The governments of Indonesia, East Timor, Fiji, and Tuvalu refused.[52] Had all other governments refused to cooperate, Australia might have been forced to accept the *Tampa* passengers to avoid their obvious refoulement. On September 1, Howard announced that New Zealand would accept 150 asylum seekers and the rest would be taken to the Republic of Nauru for refugee status determination at Australia's expense. Those processed on Nauru who made successful claims would be resettled in Australia or other countries.[53] The *Tampa* passengers were transferred to an Australian troopship for passage by sea to Papua New Guinea (PNG) and then by air to New Zealand or Nauru. As they sailed for PNG, the Federal Court of Australia ruled that the Afghans had been unlawfully detained by the Australian government and that they should be returned to the Australian mainland and released. The Full Federal Court overturned the ruling based on the logic that the executive branch had the authority under the constitution to prevent landings of asylum seekers.[54] Parliament then passed a law that validated the government's earlier actions against the *Tampa* passengers.[55]

With a reelection campaign looming, the Howard government institutionalized its response to the *Tampa* incident in what became known as the "Pacific Solution." Its three major components were a barbican strategy of redefining rights in particular territories through "excision," a moat strategy of interception at sea, and a caging strategy of offshore processing of irregular maritime arrivals seeking protection. While the details of each component changed over time, the constant was that Australia's limited judicial oversight and regional hegemony enabled a robust architecture to repel asylum seekers.

Excisions

The uniquely Australian concept of "excision" created barbicans of legally defined spaces. Parliament passed bills in September 2001 that categorized several Australian islands in the Indian Ocean—Christmas, Ashmore, Cartier, and Cocos—as "excised offshore places." Anyone who arrived there by sea without papers was deemed "an offshore entry person" who was excluded from applying for a visa, including a humanitarian protection visa. Offshore entry persons were subject to removal to a "declared country" such as PNG or Nauru for processing unless they received a special exemption from the immigration minister.[56] The territorial excision only applied to migration law and did not affect Australian sovereignty over the spaces or the rights within them of Australian citizens or foreigners already holding visas.[57]

The goal of excision was to create a domestic legal mechanism to prevent maritime asylum seekers from applying for protection, while complying with the government's recognition of its non-refoulement obligations in the 1951 Refugee Convention. "Any asylum seekers on vessels that enter Australian territorial waters engage Australia's non-refoulement obligation under Article 33 of the Refugees Convention," read a 2002 directive. Like the U.S. government since 1992, the Australian government claimed that the Refugee Convention did not apply to its activities outside its territory.[58] The implication is that people intercepted in international waters could be refouled. For those who enter Australian territorial waters, the only way to meet the non-refoulement obligation is by offshore processing in a country that credibly appears to avoid refouling refugees. Many legal scholars point out that the basic design of the Pacific Solution at best violates the spirit of the Refugee Convention. Legal scholar Claire Inder calls it a "highly disingenuous approach to legality itself, placing form above substance."[59]

The excised spaces of Australia's barbicans proliferated over the decade with some setbacks before the Labor Party fell into line with conservative approaches. Opposition in the Senate blocked the Howard government's bills in 2002 that would have excised several thousand small reefs, sandbars, and islands close to the northern half of the Australian mainland.[60] The Howard government pushed through regulations that excised these same areas in 2005.[61] The following year, the Howard government proposed a bill that would have redefined some air travel as sea travel. In the tortured logic of the bill,

> [t]he Bill will also deem certain air arrivals to be entry by sea so the persons will be subject to the new regime. Persons who travel most of the way to Australia by sea but travel the last leg by air, before entering (on or after 13 April 2006) and who become unlawful on entry, will be taken to have entered Australia by sea. These are basically situations where persons are airlifted into Australia at the end of their sea journey.[62]

The bill would have excised "the entire Australian mainland" from the migration zone as well, but the Senate once again blocked it based on strong opposition from Labor and even some members of Parliament in the conservative Liberal/National coalition government.

Parliament finally excised the entire mainland in 2013 with support from Labor as well as the conservative coalition.[63] The idiosyncratic language of "excising the mainland" is misleading in that the bill did not create a migration zone separate from the mainland and the islands, which together constitute Australia's territory. Rather, the 2006 bill and 2013 law distinguished between how irregular migrants anywhere in Australia's territory would be treated depending on their mode of transport on arrival. Those who arrived by air were detained but could apply for asylum in Australia and appeal a rejected application. Irregular maritime arrivals could not apply for asylum in Australia without the express permission of the Minister for Immigration.

Even during the 2007 to 2012 period, when asylum seekers could present claims on Christmas Island, they did not have equal access to the courts for the normal review of decisions on whether to grant them protection.[64] The so-called Indian Ocean Solution turned Christmas Island into the barbican par excellence. The department of immigration processed asylum cases outside the migration statute and without the possibility of appeals to the Refugee Review Tribunal or Administrative Appeals Tribunal. An immigration official decided whether an application had merit using nonbinding "guidelines" based on international and Australian law. The "Independent Merits Review" of rejected applications consisted of a private contractor from a company, such as the Wizard People, examining the file and then making a nonbinding recommendation to the immigration department. Access to lawyers was deliberately restricted by holding asylum seekers in a remote location hundreds of kilometers from Australia's cities. In November 2010, the High Court ruled in the Plaintiff M61 case that screening on Christmas Island must take place within the binding framework of the domestic statute and that rejected applicants must have access to judicial review. The court did not require equivalent offshore and onshore procedures, but it reigned in a highly discretionary system.[65]

The stain of arriving by sea without a visa marked an individual even if she traveled to parts of Australia that had not yet been excised. The 2002 directive stated that unauthorized arrivals seeking protection who entered Australia at an excised place like Christmas Island, or who were taken to an offshore processing center like Nauru and subsequently brought to mainland Australia as "transitory persons," were to be processed according to the offshore system.[66] This provision allows people being processed offshore to be brought to Australia for advanced medical care and then sent back to the offshore detention centers without having the opportunity to apply for protection in Australia. They traveled inside a legal bubble that sustained the fiction that they had not officially entered Australia, even if they were physically present in Australia for years.

In the face of suits in the High Court against the return to Manus and Nauru of people brought to the Australian mainland for medical treatment or to give birth, an internal e-mail in the immigration department revealed the suit was "likely to cause problems with being able to remove transitory persons" and it was "therefore important to return as many transitory persons as we can, as soon as possible."[67] The conservative Abbot government began taking detainees on Nauru who required medical care to Papua New Guinea, rather than the far better facilities in Australia, to prevent the patient detainees from becoming part of the social movement to stay in Australia.[68]

An activist organization called GetUp! organized a campaign in 2016 to allow 267 "transitory" asylum seekers, including thirty-seven babies born in Australia to mothers who had been detained in the offshore-processing centers, to stay in Australia despite the unfavorable M68 ruling.[69] Churches around the country invoked the medieval tradition of sanctuary to shelter asylum seekers. As of February 2017, more than 300 detainees from Nauru and Manus were in Australia for medical treatment or a family member's treatment.[70] In a minor victory for the detainees and their allies in civil society, the government allowed some of them to be placed in "community detention" rather than a jail-like facility. All of them were still "detained" for the purposes of their visas and could be sent offshore at the immigration minister's discretion.[71]

Patrolling the Moat

Maritime interceptions are only effective if there is a barbican where intercepted passengers can be taken, a foreign country that can be coerced or paid to accept offshore processing, or a foreign country of embarkation that will either accept or be unable to prevent returns. Australia's interceptions evolved through four stages.

- Pacific Solution I (September 2001 to 2007). Interception and transfer to Manus and Nauru. A few boats were turned back to Indonesia under Operation Relex and Operation Relex II.
- Indian Ocean Solution (2008 to July 2012). Interception and transfer to Christmas Island.
- Pacific Solution II (August 2012 to August 2013). Interception and transfer to Manus and Nauru.
- Operation Sovereign Borders (September 2013; continuing in 2018). Most boats were turned back to their country of embarkation.

During the Pacific Solution I from 2001 to 2007, Australian forces intercepted 1,637 asylum seekers in the contiguous zone and transported them to Nauru or Manus for processing. Australian vessels towed back five other boats to Indonesian waters without conducting any protection screening and without any readmission agreement with the Indonesian government.[72] The government defended these interceptions not only as a deterrent measure but also as a necessary step to prevent deaths at sea. Nearly 1,500 people drowned en route to Australia between 2000 and 2014.[73] As in Europe and the United States, humanitarianism was used to justify stricter controls.

Prime Minister Kevin Rudd dismantled the Pacific Solution after winning the 2007 election. The new Labor government decried Howard's approach that had brought "great shame on Australia," whose "international reputation was tarnished."[74] The remaining asylum seekers on Nauru were transported to Australia in February 2008. Rudd announced that asylum claims of future irregular boat arrivals in excised offshore places would be processed in a detention center on Christmas Island in what became known as the Indian Ocean Solution.[75] As the number of arrivals on Christmas increased, the facility became overcrowded, and it became public knowledge that processing on Christmas was five times more expensive than on the mainland.

When Julia Gillard unseated fellow Labor member Rudd to become prime minister in June 2010, she unsuccessfully tried to convince other countries in the region to conduct offshore processing. East Timor refused. The Malaysian government agreed. Under the terms of the Malaysian Solution announced in May 2011, 800 irregular maritime asylum seekers would be transferred to Malaysia for processing. In return, Australia would resettle 4,000 refugees already in Malaysia.[76] Malaysia was not party to the 1951 Refugee Convention or its Protocol. In a rare moment of the Australian courts constraining the executive's remote control policies, the High Court declared the Malaysian Solution invalid. It ruled that offshore-processing countries must offer "effective protection" for asylum seekers equivalent to the system in Australia and that the agreement did not adequately protect unaccompanied children who were legally the wards of the Australian immigration minister.[77]

With the Malaysian Solution blocked by the courts and 278 boats carrying more than 17,000 people arriving in 2012, the Gillard government reintroduced a revised version of the Pacific Solution in August. Like the earlier version, interdicted asylum seekers were sent to Manus and Nauru under the Pacific Solution II. Asylum seekers found to be refugees would be resettled in Australia, albeit with delays of many years linked to the fiction that there was an orderly queue in which the irregular arrivals could have waited.[78] While awaiting resettlement, the refugees would remain held in detention.

Kevin Rudd took his political vengeance on Gillard in June 2013 and ousted her to regain his post as prime minister. Rudd continued to send irregular maritime arrivals to Manus and Nauru. The most consequential change came in July when he announced that "asylum seekers who come here by boat without a visa will *never* be settled in Australia."[79] Previous versions of the Pacific Solution had always included the possibility that at least some recognized refugees would be allowed to permanently settle in Australia.

Rudd's second government was short-lived as a Liberal/National coalition brought Prime Minister Tony Abbott to power in 2013 on the backs of his campaign pledge to "stop the boats." Abbott's Operation Sovereign Borders was built around secret maritime operations, pushbacks to Indonesia, and collaboration with Indonesian authorities to prevent boats from leaving. The Australian government claimed that even basic details about maritime interceptions must be kept confidential to protect national security and to prevent people smugglers from adapting to new enforcement strategies.[80]

Independent news media revealed why the government's policies were so secretive. The *Guardian* reported in 2013 that the immigration minister had explicitly authorized the defense force chief to pushback boats with asylum seekers to Indonesia. In a subsequent freedom of information case hearing, the head of Operation Sovereign Borders acknowledged ongoing incursions into Indonesian waters to carry out the turnbacks.[81] It was later revealed that Australian authorities were intercepting boats with asylum seekers, destroying their vessels, and placing them in lifeboats with instructions and only enough fuel to return to Indonesia. The passengers were not screened for protection claims, and their phones were confiscated so they could not film what was happening.[82]

Negative press attention and an effort to avoid the diplomatic irritant with Indonesia prompted the Australian government to try to disguise the craft used for turning back asylum seekers. The *Guardian* reported in March 2015 that the government had paid millions of dollars to a factory in Vietnam to build wooden vessels painted to look like fishing boats. In May 2015, a ship with sixty-five asylum seekers left Indonesia bound for New Zealand. Australian vessels intercepted the asylum seekers twice. The second time, Australian officials came aboard and paid the crew US$32,000 in cash to take the asylum seekers back to Indonesia on two faux fishing boats. One boat ran out of fuel. The passengers crammed onto the second boat, which eventually struck a reef on the Indonesian coast. The Australian immigration and foreign ministers denied the mounting evidence that the Australian government had paid the crew to turn back the asylum seekers, but Abbott refused to confirm or deny whether payments had been made.[83] The government turned back twenty-nine boats between 2013 and 2016.[84]

While Indonesia is only three day's sail from Christmas Island, the passage from Sri Lanka takes two weeks. Many asylum seekers making the long trip are from the persecuted Tamil minority or Sinhalese suspected of collaborating with Tamil rebels. Australia and Sri Lanka signed a memorandum of understanding in 2009 to combat people smuggling, facilitate extradition, and conduct a publicity campaign to warn Sri Lankan citizens of the dangers of smuggling people by sea.[85] In July 2014, Australian forces intercepted a boat with forty-one Sri Lankans and conducted a quick asylum screening process at sea. The details remain shrouded in secrecy, but the process reportedly involved asking the asylum seekers just four questions by teleconference with an immigration official on the mainland: name, nationality, country of embarkation, and reason for leaving. By contrast, interviews for Vietnamese "boat people" arriving in 1979 had included forty-nine questions.[86] Two Sri Lankan men later recounted that the interview took place on an open deck, noisy with wind and machinery, over a satellite phone line that kept cutting out. The immigration department rejected all claims and turned the passengers over to the Sri Lankan navy to face charges of illegal exit punishable by two years in prison. One repatriated man later told a journalist that Sri Lankan interrogators warned him that because the international media was watching, "[w]e can't do anything [to you now]. But all of you; we will see you again." Nine of the forty-one repatriated asylum seekers later fled to Nepal. Just six months after being rejected at sea by the Australian "enhanced screening" process, the UNHCR office in Nepal officially recognized the nine as refugees.[87] Independent researchers have gathered evidence suggesting the torture of some asylum seekers repatriated to Sri Lanka.[88]

The same summer, Australian forces intercepted another boat in the contiguous zone off Christmas Island that carried 157 Tamil asylum seekers. Officials held the passengers at sea for a month while attempting to negotiate their return with the Indian government. India was their point of departure, but Indian authorities refused to readmit them. The Australian government eventually transferred the Tamil passengers to Australia's Cocos Islands in the excised area, then a detention facility in Western Australia, and finally to Nauru for processing. In response to a suit by one of the Tamil men, the High Court ruled four to three in *CPCF v. Minister for Immigration and Border Protection* that the government's actions were legal under domestic law. The court did not address whether the actions complied with international law.[89] Australian courts have given the government wide latitude to exercise remote controls at sea.

Thirty-eight Sri Lankans on a boat intercepted in November 2014 were briefly screened at sea as well.[90] One was taken for offshore processing, while the rest were returned to the custody of the Sri Lankan navy. In 2015, ninety-two intercepted Vietnamese asylum seekers on two boats were taken back to Vietnam after "enhanced screening." One of the Vietnamese women, Tran Thi Thanh Loan, later said that no one in her group spoke English and no translation was provided. They did not realize they were being repatriated until they reached a Vietnamese port. Two years later, she and several others reached Indonesian waters and were recognized by the UNHCR as refugees.[91] The Australian and Vietnamese governments signed a memorandum of understanding to repatriate Vietnamese asylum seekers detained at sea in December 2016.[92]

From the onset of Operation Sovereign Borders in September 2013 to January 2017, 740 people were returned at sea after an "on-water assessment process."[93] "Turnbacks" to Indonesia and "takebacks" to Sri Lanka and Vietnam may violate the non-refoulement provisions of international law and the law of the sea's obligations to take people rescued at sea to a place of safety.[94] It has been difficult for legal advocates to force the courts to consider the issue, however, because potential plaintiffs are usually sent back quickly and secretly. The government hides basic details of its operations even after the fact in a strategy to avoid judicial or parliamentary oversight.

Operation Sovereign Borders is costly but effective in its stated goals. A 2016 study estimated that policies of interception, offshore processing, and mandatory immigration detention cost AUD$9.6 billion between 2013 and 2016.[95] Operation Sovereign Borders succeeded at stopping people from reaching Australia by sea to ask for protection. After a record high of 300 boats with 20,587 passengers arrived in 2013, only one boat arrived in 2014, and none for the next four years.[96]

Caging Offshore

Australia did not invent offshore detention for refugees. Recall from chapter 2 that the Australian government in 1940 rebuffed a British proposal to transfer Jews whom the British navy had intercepted trying to reach Palestine. The Howard government was directly inspired by the sustained U.S. example of Guantanamo.[97] An even closer cognate was the Clinton administration's asylum screenings of Haitians on ships in Jamaican waters in 1994, and its unimplemented agreements to temporarily house asylees in several countries around the Caribbean until they could be resettled elsewhere (see chapter 5). The Australian model remains unusual because processing takes place in another sovereign state (rather than a liminal barbican territory like the U.S. base at Guantanamo), it takes place in a country through which asylum seekers have not passed (unlike in many buffer states), and extraterritorial processing is the cornerstone of a sustained, large-scale asylum regime.[98] Australia's regional hegemony allows it to buy legal and political cover for its remote control activities from third countries. Nauru and Manus are the two main sites.

Nauru

Fewer than 10,000 people live on Nauru—the world's smallest island state just a tenth the size of Washington, DC. The Micronesian island lies just below the equator 3,000 kilometers northeast of Australia. Formerly named Pleasant Island, Nauru has been highly dependent on Australia for more than a century beginning with its annexation in World War I. Australia later administered Nauru under a League of Nations mandate and as a United Nations Trust Territory until independence in 1968. The destruction of the island's ecology from mining phosphate for the cotrustees of Australia, New Zealand, and the UK was so extensive that the Australian government seriously considered resettling the entire Nauruan population to Australia in the 1960s. The plan fell apart over the Nauruan leadership's demands for sovereignty over an Australian island in the state of Queensland.[99] After a boom that briefly made it the richest democracy in the world on a per capita basis, the exhaustion of phosphate mining left Nauru with a GDP of just AUD$29.5 million in 2000 and heavily reliant on Australia.[100] Australia's overseas development aid budget for Nauru rose from AUD$3.1 million in 2000–2001 to AUD$22.2 million after the bilateral memorandum of understanding to process the *Tampa* asylum seekers in 2001. From FY2001 to FY2016, the Australian government gave Nauru nearly AUD$400 million in aid.[101]

Nauru was not a party to the 1951 Refugee Convention until June 2011.[102] The UNHCR initially conducted the screenings on Nauru in 2001 but withdrew, leaving Australian officials from the department of immigration to process refugee claims in another sovereign country.[103] A senior officer from the same department reviewed rejected applications. Unlike asylum seekers onshore, asylum seekers whose applications were processed offshore did not have access to lawyers or the right to appeal to the Refugee Review Tribunal. Since 2012, officials from Nauru have been responsible for refugee status determination.[104] The Australian federal police provided security for the processing center on Nauru along with the Nauruan police and a private contractor. Journalists, lawyers, and civil society organizations were rarely allowed to visit the island to observe conditions or assist detainees.[105] An application for a journalist visa cost AUD$8,000—"non-refundable should your application be unsuccessful." In practice, visas were almost always denied.[106] My queries to Nauruan authorities in 2017 about the possibility of visiting Nauru were never answered. As on Manus, private contractors are required to sign nondisclosure agreements. One of the plain goals of offshore processing is to restrict the judiciary and civil society from pushing back against the exercise of executive power.

Detainees, the few journalists who found a way to enter Nauru, former staff members, and leaked internal documents report that processing-center staff systemically mistreated its residents.[107] More than 2,000 incident reports written by staff at the private detention center organized and financed by the Australian government were leaked to the *Guardian* and published as the Nauru Files. The reports detailed a litany of child abuse, detainees exchanging sex with guards for favors like longer showers, and sexual assaults on young women.[108] Many lost hope of ever being resettled and lived in a state of heightened uncertainty. "Self-harm and suicide attempts increase steadily after six months in detention," said Dr. Peter Young, the former director of mental health for the Australian government's immigrant detention system. "This is driven by hopelessness which is known to be the strongest predictor of suicide."[109] Children have stitched their lips together, slit their wrists, and eaten detergent to try to end their lives.[110]

Many of the detainees on Nauru were not locked up in the two processing centers. In October 2015, the Nauruan government announced that asylum seekers and recognized refugees would be released into the community. The evident goal was to undercut the standing of the plaintiff in the M68 case, in which a detainee sued the Australian government for its offshore-processing system, by creating the pretense that no one was detained on Nauru. Given that the entire island is so small and asylum seekers and refugees are not allowed to leave unless they submit to repatriation, in practice they were still held against their will.[111] Most child refugees or asylum seekers did not attend school in Nauru because they fear being bullied by local children and teachers. According to the UNHCR, police did not investigate persistent physical attacks by locals. The government of Nauru expelled the chief justice, magistrate, and police commissioner, all of whom were Australian citizens serving on Nauru, in 2014. The move essentially eliminated the judiciary and left people seeking protection further exposed.[112] A process putatively designed to determine whether the detainees were fleeing persecution in their home countries exposed them to new forms of persecution on Pleasant Island.[113]

Manus

Australia has a long history of intervention in Papua New Guinea as well. Australia administered PNG from 1905 to its independence in 1975. It receives more Australian foreign aid than any other country— more than AUD$7 billion between 2001 and 2016.[114] Unlike Nauru, the level of aid remained similar before and after PNG began processing asylum seekers on Australia's behalf in 2001 at a detention center on Manus Island.[115] Papua New Guinea's population of 7.5 million and USD$16 billion economy make it less dependent on Australia than tiny Nauru. Papua New Guinea has been a party to the Refugee Convention and the 1967 Protocol since 1986, though it signed with many formal reservations that gutted refugees' rights. Officers from PNG began refugee status determination hearings after a year of training by Australian officials. The UNHCR gave advice on individual cases to compensate for a pattern of ad hoc decisions and deficiencies. As on Nauru, asylum seekers did not have access to legal representation. Advocacy organizations and journalists were rarely allowed to visit Manus.[116]

The Howard government shut down the center on Manus in 2004 as interceptions reduced maritime arrivals and opposition grew in Australia as a reaction to reports of the poor health of the detainees and the high financial costs of the program.[117] After the Malaysia Solution was blocked by the High Court, the Gillard government resumed operations on Manus in 2012. The Australian government transferred many asylum seekers from Christmas Island to Manus, but there was not enough room for all of them. Among the selection criteria for who was transferred was that no children younger than seven should be sent to Manus because they could not be safely inoculated against the Japanese encephalitis that posed a risk on the island. The director of offshore processing and transfers told an Australian Human Rights Commission inquiry that he was instructed by the department of immigration to select children for transfer who were at least seven, but who looked as young as possible. The goal was to deter future asylum seekers from attempting the crossing by showing the world that the government was prepared to detain even young children.[118]

Independent researchers painstakingly gleaned information about conditions on Manus, which were broadly similar to treatment in the centers on Nauru. In one case, a twenty-four-year-old Iranian detainee named Hamid Khazaei developed a leg infection. Without proper medical treatment, the infection spread, and he died of blood poisoning two weeks later after a delayed evacuation to Brisbane.[119] At the request of his family, Khazaei's organs were removed for donation to people in Australia.[120] A second detainee died during an assault on the compound by PNG security forces. As on Nauru, asylum seekers and refugees faced an increasingly hostile backlash from the local population. In August 2016, 103 current and former staff at the centers on Nauru and Manus called for the camps to be closed and for the detainees to be brought to Australia.[121]

In June 2015, the conservative government in Australia passed a bill with full support from Labor to fund offshore processing. The law declared that the Australian government could take "any action in relation to the arrangement or the regional processing functions" of its policies on PNG and Nauru. The provisions retroactively applied to August 2012 to encompass the entire period since the Liberal government of Julia Gillard reinstated offshore processing.[122] The breathtaking scope of the law highlighted the extreme constraints that the executive and Parliament could impose on the courts as an avenue for redress. The High Court ruled in the Plaintiff M68 case in 2016 that the Australian government had the legal authority to participate in the detention of asylum seekers on Nauru.[123] In June 2017, the Australian government settled a class action suit brought by almost 2,000 asylum seekers who alleged they had been illegally detained in dangerous and harmful conditions on Manus Island. The government agreed to pay more than AUD$70 million to settle the suit and avoid an embarrassing trial.[124]

The UNHCR warned of the dangers of refoulement for asylum seekers so dispirited by the conditions of their detention, and the long delays in processing and resettlement, that they would agree to an unsafe return to their countries of origin.[125] The PNG Supreme Court ruled in *Namah v. Pato* in 2016 that the detention of asylum seekers and refugees violated PNG's constitutional guarantee of the right to liberty and that the conditions of the facilities violated their rights and dignity. The court held that both the PNG and Australian governments comply with their ruling to close the detention facility. Many detainees refused to leave the detention facility, but security forces forcibly evicted them in November 2017 and transferred them to three new centers where they waited in limbo as of 2018.[126]

Waiting for Resettlement

What was the result of the processing on Nauru and Manus? The six-year Pacific Solution I cost the Australian government AUD$1 billion to transport, house, and process asylum seekers.[127] Just one year of the Pacific Solution II to operate the Manus and Nauru detention centers cost AUD$1.24 billion.[128] Each year Australian taxpayers spent AUD$573,000 (USD$419,425) per processed person for their operations on Manus and Nauru.[129]

During the Pacific Solution I, 70% of the 1,637 people taken there were recognized as refugees. Australia eventually resettled 705, New Zealand accepted 401, and a total of 47 went to Sweden, Canada, Denmark, and Norway.[130] Australian forces took 3,127 people to Manus and Nauru from July 2013 to March 2017 during the Pacific Solution II. Forty-two percent were Iranian. The other major nationalities, after the stateless, were Pakistani, Afghan, Sri Lankan, Iraq, Somali, Bangladeshi, and Sudanese. Of those brought to Nauru by early 2017, no one's refugee claim was rejected, 1,014 were determined to be refugees, and 456 were still being processed. Of those brought to Manus, 707 were determined to be refugees, 224 claims were rejected, and 81 had departed or died without their application being processed.[131] Most people intercepted at sea, and then detained for years on remote islands in precarious conditions at a tremendous cost, were refugees.

Since Rudd's vow in 2013 that asylum seekers arriving by sea would never be allowed to resettle in Australia, successive governments have made the same pledge and struggled to find alternative destinations. In April 2007, Washington and Canberra announced an informal agreement for the annual reciprocal exchange of up to 200 refugees held at Guantanamo and

200 held on Nauru. The plan became known as the "Atlantic Solution." The Guantanamo detainees were primarily Haitian and Cuban. The details of the agreement, such as the fate of anyone who declined to be resettled across the planet from their intended destination, were not released. However, after Rudd ended the Pacific Solution, the Burmese refugees who were slated to be resettled in the United States were brought to Australia instead. The fact that the agreement was negotiated between the Australian and U.S. governments plainly showed that Canberra, not the government of Nauru, exercised control over the asylum seekers, notwithstanding official Australian claims to the contrary.[132]

A September 2014 agreement between Canberra and Phnom Penh stipulated that recognized refugees who had been screened in Nauru would be voluntarily resettled in Cambodia, subject to various conditions, with the costs paid by Australia. Canberra pledged up to AUD$15.5 million in resettlement aid and an additional AUD$40 million in development aid to close the deal. Only seven refugees took the offer. Three Iranians and a Burmese man eventually decided to leave Cambodia and return to their countries of origin, leaving just three refugees in the Cambodian program in 2017.[133] The Turnbull government did not accept an offer from New Zealand to annually resettle 150 refugees from the offshore-processing centers, based on the argument that Australia "will not undertake activities that could be used by people smugglers as marketing opportunities" for resettlement to New Zealand.[134] Presumably the Turnbull government did not consider the prospect of resettling in Cambodia to present such a marketing opportunity.

In September 2016, Turnbull's government announced that it would resettle an undefined number of Salvadoran, Guatemalan, and Honduran refugees from a U.S.-financed project in Costa Rica. United States officials prescreened the Central Americans in their countries, and then the UNHCR screened them more thoroughly in Costa Rica for potential resettlement under a "protection transfer agreement." Most were fleeing gang violence.[135] Unlike the detainees on Manus and Nauru, the Central Americans were never intercepted. In November, the Obama administration agreed to accept up to 1,250 recognized refugees on Manus and Nauru for resettlement in the United States. "It wasn't a people swap deal," claimed Immigration Minister Peter Dutton, but the arrangements were clearly linked. The governments have insisted on keeping the text of the agreement secret.[136]

After Donald Trump assumed the presidency in January 2017, he held a phone conversation with Turnbull in which Turnbull sought assurance that Trump would honor the agreement. Trump berated Turnbull, abruptly ended the call, and tweeted that night, "Do you believe it? The Obama Administration agreed to take thousands of illegal immigrants from Australia. Why? I will study this dumb deal!"[137] By February 2018, only 169 refugees had been resettled in the United States.[138] According to the Australian immigration department, rejected applicants could settle on Nauru for up to twenty years, be permanently resettled in Cambodia, or settle in PNG.[139] Swapping refugees to countries half a planet away from their intended destination, where they did not have any family ties, was aimed at deterring others from attempting to reach sanctuary, while still allowing the governments to say that they had met the legal obligations of non-refoulement.

Containment

As in North America and Europe, strategies of buffering and caging are part of the Australian toolkit. Canberra has cooperated with the Sri Lankan government at least since 2012 to disrupt departures and interdict boats leaving the island. Canberra provided the Sri Lankan navy with two patrol vessels in 2014, along with surveillance and electronic equipment. The purpose of these donations was explicitly to prohibit people smuggling and illegal exit, which includes the departure of Tamils seeking asylum from their persecution at the hands of Sri Lankan authorities.[140] It is difficult for Canberra to try to cage other asylum seekers at home, however, in part because of difficult relationships with countries of origin that are wracked by the conflicts that propel refugees to leave. Australia participated in the 1991 and 2003 U.S.-led invasions of Iraq, and its military continued to fight the Islamic State in Iraq in the 2010s. Australian forces have fought in Afghanistan since October 2001 in what has become the longest war in Australian history.[141]

"No way"

The softest form of caging—publicity campaigns aimed at encouraging refugees to stay home—have been deployed by the department of immigration since 1994, when it carried out a TV and radio campaign in China.[142] Among the many video clips aimed at asylum seekers trying to reach Australia by sea is a gruesome dramatization of what it feels like to drown. The view jerks between menacing grey skies and roiling green water. Amid the sound of retching and gurgling, a final blast of underwater bubbles fades to black.[143]

One of the main publicity targets is the Shiite Dari-speaking Hazara minority in Afghanistan who fled to Pakistan. In the aftermath of a 2011 suicide bombing of a Shiite rally in Quetta that killed forty-two people, photographs circulated showing a billboard hanging over the blood-soaked square. The billboard pictured the interception of a leaky fishing boat and a warning in Dari not to come to Australia illegally.[144] The immigration department released a similar AUD$20 million multimedia campaign in 2014.[145] Its signature poster featured a fishing boat tossed by dark waves under storm clouds. A red slash across a map of Australia made it clear that entry was denied. General Angus Campbell, commander of Operation Sovereign Borders, stood in camouflaged fatigues in front of the poster in a video message. "If you come to Australia illegally by boat, there is *no way* you will *ever* make Australia home,"[146] he warned emphatically. The video was released in twelve languages, including Arabic, Dari, and Vietnamese. An eighteen-page graphic novel depicted the travails of a Central Asian man who paid a scowling smuggler for a miserable sea voyage, only to be intercepted and sent to an island shanty town where he sank into depression yearning for home. The campaign continued in 2015 with an AUD$4 million televised drama commissioned to show the perils of the journey. The plan was to show the drama in Syria, Iraq, Afghanistan, and transit countries.[147] The immigration department also advertised its message on Facebook and Google AdWords.[148]

I asked two Pakistani asylum seekers in Australia who had arrived by boat via Christmas Island if they had seen the publicity campaign before they left. "There is only electricity for one hour a day," one explained. "We don't have time for the Internet. We're busy. We're farmers." The idea that an advertisement would deter them from leaving when suicide bombers were targeting their people brought a rare burst of laughter to what was otherwise another spirit-crushing day of detention.[149]

Regional Buffers

Canberra cooperates with the governments of other countries in the region to keep asylum seekers in transit from even attempting to cross the natural moat. As in Europe and North America, Australia has used the concept of "safe third country" to bottle up asylum seekers in transit or to justify their deportation. A 1994 law established a safe-third country provision to prevent Vietnamese who had been recognized as refugees in China from obtaining protection visas in Australia.[150] The Federal Court ruled in 1998 that an asylum seeker sent back to a third country where he had "effective protection" was not refouled, though legal scholar Susan Kneebone describes "a fairly minimal test of safe third country" in determining Australia's protection obligations.[151] In 1999, the Border Protection Legislation Amendment Act wrote a broadened safe third-country provision into the migration statute.[152] The government justified offshore processing through the Pacific Solution by claiming that it took place in safe third countries, but it deviated from the EU model of safe third countries by sending asylum seekers to countries they had never transited and to whom they had no previous connection.[153]

Papua New Guinea functions as a buffer state as well as offshore-processing cage. A 2003 agreement treats PNG as a safe third country. Persons who have been in PNG more than a week and then cross to Australia are not eligible to file an asylum claim. The agreement is reciprocal but clearly targets would-be asylum seekers passing through PNG, whose government is required to hear the asylum claims and provide protection for recognized refugees. The safe third-country agreement was first invoked in 2006 to return three men from West Papua, Indonesia, who passed through PNG en route to Australia's Boigu Island to ask for asylum.[154] The IOM provides services for deported irregular migrants in PNG and organizes their repatriation with Australian funding. Australian migration liaisons are stationed at the Port Moresby airport. Canberra also has built up the capacity of migration enforcement by training PNG authorities and has conducted joint patrols in the Torres Strait between the two countries.

Indonesia is the principal country of irregular transit. The Australian government tried to make it a migration buffer and cage for asylum seekers from Indochina beginning in 1979 and from a much larger set of countries since the late 1990s. Cooperation around buffering has included making Indonesian migration laws more restrictive, strengthening its enforcement and refugee status determination capacity, and direct action by Australian agents inside Indonesian territory. Indonesia joined the Convention Against Torture, which contains a provision banning refoulement to countries where an individual will be tortured, in 1998. It has not signed the 1951 Refugee Convention, so the UNHCR conducts refugee status determinations. As of 2009, the Australian government accepted about a third of the refugees for resettlement.

The IOM focuses more on migration management than the UNHCR, which has a more rights-based approach. The IOM has been active in Indonesia with Australian financing since 2000. Recognized refugees are placed in facilities operated by the IOM while they await resettlement. Rejected applicants either voluntarily repatriate with the assistance of the IOM, stay in facilities operated by the IOM, or are released in Indonesia.[155] The agency runs workshops on border security and discourages locals from participating in the clandestine migration business. In one publicity campaign, the IOM convened religious leaders to write sermon booklets about the evils of people smuggling, which the IOM then published. The biblical story of Judas selling out Jesus for thirty pieces of silver was the basis of one of the sermons. "Let us not become like Judas who was looking for his personal gain over the wellbeing of common interest," the sermon read. "Remember that helping to smuggle illegal migrants is wrong. God bless. Amen."[156]

Unlike in major transit countries such as Mexico, Turkey, and Morocco, the issue of transit migration through Indonesia is not linked to emigration. Few Indonesians seek to migrate to Australia. As in the other cases, however, the extent to which the Indonesian government is willing to act as a buffer is contingent on the broader quality of bilateral ties. Relations improved significantly in the early 2000s.[157] Australia and Indonesia co-chaired the Bali Process that began in 2002 as a regional forum to combat people smuggling. The 2006 Lombok Treaty between Australia and Indonesia included a provision to cooperate against people smuggling, which under Australian pressure, was criminalized in 2011.[158] A July 2013 decree required Iranians to obtain a visa in advance, a measure requested by Australia and squarely aimed at Iranians passing through Indonesia bound for Australia to ask for asylum.[159]

As a confidential U.S. State Department cable summarized in 2009, "[Prime Minister] Rudd is putting a lot of faith in Indonesia to stop the flow of boats."[160] Canberra funded deportations, new police posts in coastal areas, a computerized border-crossing alert system, and patrol boats and aircraft. Australian federal police trained their Indonesian counterparts, offered intelligence, and provided interpreters to interview suspected smugglers and witnesses. Australian officials offered cash to Indonesian officials to induce them to keep vessels from leaving. In return, the Indonesian police and navy routinely arrested migrants bound for Australia. The United States was a quiet partner that provided intelligence used to track smugglers. Indonesian authorities arrested 359 people smugglers between 2007 and 2013, though in practice, police were often bribed to allow irregular migrants to pass. Jakarta and Canberra maintained a joint secretive "People Smuggling Disruption Program" that between September 2013 and January 2017 purported to have disrupted sixty-five smuggling ventures.[161]

One low-cost solution has been for police to infiltrate smuggling rings and sabotage the motors of boats used to transport asylum seekers. According to anthropologist Antje Missbach, "there are strong indications that Indonesia has tolerated the campaigns of Australian intelligence agencies to disrupt and sabotage asylum seeker boats before they leave Indonesia."[162] In 2013, the incoming center-right coalition government announced a plan to buy boats

FIGURE 10.2 Indonesian police officers escort asylum seekers to a local marine police station in Surabaya, East Java, after they were taken from a troubled boat adrift in heavy seas off Indonesia while trying to reach Australia on July 29, 2012. The Australian government uses Indonesia as a buffer state to deter departures of asylum seekers bound for Australia. Photo by AP, Trisnadi.

from Indonesian fishermen that might otherwise be used by smugglers. The plan was widely mocked as the "buy the boats" policy in a play on Tony Abbott's "stop the boats" pledge.[163]

Cooperation with Indonesia on buffering is sometimes constrained by bilateral tensions. In 2006, Australia granted asylum to forty-two West Papuan independence activists. Jakarta recalled its ambassador from Canberra in protest.[164] Relations eventually improved but worsened again during the October 2009 *Ocean Viking* saga when Australian authorities intercepted a boat that had broken down in Indonesia's search and rescue area with seventy-eight Tamil asylum seekers aboard. The Australian customs vessel *Ocean Viking* rescued the Tamils and brought them to the coast of Indonesia, whose government agreed to allow their return.[165] The asylum seekers refused to disembark for a month until Canberra agreed that recognized refugees would be resettled, after being detained and processed at an Australian-built detention center in Tanjung Pinang.[166] President Susilo Bambang Yudhoyono then abruptly cancelled a planned trip to Australia. One theory for the cancellation was that Prime Minister Rudd's "megaphone diplomacy" of loudly discussing the *Ocean Viking* issue created domestic political problems for the Indonesian president. "The Indonesian public don't want to be a dumping ground for what they perceive is Australia's problem," a U.S. State Department report concluded.[167] Bilateral relations recovered and then weakened again during Abbott's tenure, when the public learned that the Australian intelligence service had been intercepting mobile phone calls involving Yudhoyono and his wife and closest associates. Abbot publicly and stridently discussed remote control measures involving Indonesia, and Australian forces towed boats with asylum seekers back into Indonesian waters at least five times from December 2013 to January 2014. In retaliation either for the intrusions themselves or for the embarrassment of becoming public knowledge, Jakarta temporarily suspended its cooperation on deterring departures.[168]

Indonesia is not Nauru. Cooperation with Jakarta was more effective when the Australian government insisted that Indonesia was an equal partner, while funding the UNHCR and IOM operations in Indonesia in a micro-version of the "grand compromise" between the Global North and Global South. *Grosso modo*, the Indonesian government seems willing to acquiesce in remote control measures quietly sponsored by the Australian government, but it does not have the political will or immediate capacity to take more proactive measures. Like several other major transit countries that lie at the gateway to the Global North, Indonesia is a middle-income country with a large population that cannot simply be forced to do the bidding of a richer neighbor hoping to keep out unwanted asylum seekers.

Limited Constraints

The Australian judiciary has been unusually weak in constraining the remote control actions of the executive and parliament. Like the United States, Australian courts have largely ignored international jurisprudence around refugee law.[169] As Hilary Charlesworth and her colleagues summarized,

The Australian judiciary's approach to international law manifests a range of

> anxieties, some implicit and some articulated. They include the preservation
> of the separation of powers through maintaining the distinctiveness of the ju-
> dicial from the political sphere; the fear of opening the floodgates to litiga-
> tion; the sense that the use of international norms will cause instability in
> the Australian legal system; and the idea that international law is essentially
> un-Australian.[170]

Australia differs from the United States in that its constitution does not include a bill of rights, nor does it have a Canadian-style rights charter or belong to supranational arrangements like the EU that incorporated the European Convention on Human Rights. The weakness of rights of territorial personhood has allowed the Australian executive and Parliament to create highly discretionary policies and to reduce judicial autonomy in decisions around immigration and refugee law.[171] For example, the 2013 Migration Amendment does not allow normal judicial review of decisions about humanitarian visas for irregular maritime arrivals.[172] The Maritime Powers Act (2013) provides that the government's detention powers are not invalidated by a failure to consider Australia's international obligations, defective consideration of those obligations, or an exercise of the power that is inconsistent with those obligations."[173] Such measures are designed to prevent lawsuits from challenging the policies of turn-backs and cursory screenings at sea for violating international law against refoulement.[174] The consistent assault on the judiciary's oversight also means that territoriality has become less important over the course of the various versions of the Pacific Solution. Once asylum seekers are marked with the scarlet letter of irregular maritime arrival, the government allows them to be physically present on Australian territory while making transportation connections, for temporary detention, or for medical treatment. By contrast, as chapter 5 describes, the U.S. government goes to great lengths to keep aircraft transferring potential asylum seekers from even landing on the runway of a U.S. territory for refueling.

Foreign relations have presented only modest obstacles to the most punitive Australian policies. Australia has numerous bilateral agreements with countries to cooperate against people smuggling or to readmit rejected migrants. As one immigration official said, "We'll work with everybody and anybody who can help."[175] The biggest practical constraints have been the vagaries of the bilateral relationship with Indonesia, by far the most important transit state for maritime arrivals. Preventing that transit is embedded in a complex relationship that has hindered migration control when the broader relationship sours, but which thus far has rebounded quickly. In Indonesia, the government is sensitive to international criticism of its human rights record dealing with transit migration, which is publicized by media and NGOs such as Human Rights Watch.[176] No leader wants to appear to be a foreign lackey. The result is to make such cooperation secret. The risks of relying on foreign governments to host offshore-processing centers was highlighted to a greater degree by the PNG Supreme Court's 2016 ruling that the Manus detainees must be released. However, the availability of Nauru as a remote client state continues to give the Australian government options.

International branding has only slightly restrained Canberra's activities. One of the reasons that the Australian government accepted the first wave of Vietnamese asylum seekers in the 1970s was that a harsh response would risk Australia's reputation in the region. "As a large, underpopulated 'white' country Australia would be especially vulnerable to international criticism if we failed to respond in a humane manner to the arrival of boat refugees from Asia on Australian territory," a Cabinet memo explained.[177] Yet the Australian model of denying access to asylum has been praised by some leaders in Europe as a model worthy of emulation, rather than the object of reprobation.[178] Several of Australia's neighbors in the region, including Malaysia, Indonesia, and Thailand have a history of pushbacks of Indochinese refugees in the 1970s and 1980s and of Rohingya fleeing Burma in the 2010s.[179] Many other governments in the region cannot credibly claim to do any better.

One of the stronger constraints on Australia's policies is its civil society organizations devoted to investigating and publicizing the conditions on Manus and Nauru. It is difficult to assess the counterfactual of how much worse conditions might be in the absence of such watchdogs, but the extreme degree to which the governments of Australia, PNG, and Nauru attempt to squelch civil society monitoring suggests that their activities matter. For example, in June 2014, immigration minister Scott Morrison referred ten contractors from Save the Children, who had been providing support for detainees on Nauru, to the Australian federal police for investigation under an anti-whistleblowing law. The government later dropped the accusations after a public outcry.[180] The Australian federal police also launched a major investigation into Dr. Peter Young, who directed mental health services for the private company contracted to provide medical treatment for detainees in Australia's offshore and onshore centers, after he criticized the official polices. Dr. Young publicly claimed that cruel detention conditions were deliberately created to deter other asylum seekers and to coerce detainees to repatriate. "The harmfulness is a 'designed-in' feature," he said. "You can't allow transparency, if what you're trying to do is inflict suffering. Secrecy is necessary because these places are designed to damage."[181] The 2015 Australian Border Force Act passed with bipartisan support to make disclosing "protected information," including disclosures by private contractors working on Manus and Nauru, punishable by two years in prison. After a group of doctors sued, an amendment created a blanket exemption for health professionals.[182]

A vibrant set of organizations including the Refugee Council of Australia, the Australian Refugee Action Network, Amnesty International, and academic institutions regularly produce reports that attempt to break through the secret barriers around government policies.[183] Their public outreach activities, such as an annual protest on Palm Sunday, draw attention to policies that would otherwise be even more ignored by the public. While the dominant framing of refugee issues is largely negative at the national level, some media outlets have periodically penetrated the veil of secrecy around interception and offshore processing. The Nauruan and Australian governments have made it all but impossible for journalists and lawyers to visit Nauru, but a few reporters have been able to enter, including one in disguise, to report on conditions.[184] The Australian Broadcasting Corporation's program *Four Corners* in October 2016 smuggled footage out of Nauru depicting the grim life of the more than 100 refugee children held there. *The Guardian* has played a leading role in uncovering both conditions on Nauru and maritime interception activities. The Australian federal police have used warrantless searches of journalist Paul Farrell's telecommunications metadata to track down his sources on asylum policies in an apparent effort to restrict the flow of such information.[185]

At the same time, mobile phone technologies have made it possible for asylum seekers to share information with the world about their conditions. Protests and strikes in Nauru, Manus, and Indonesian centers have drawn public attention to the desperation of asylum seekers and refugees endlessly awaiting resettlement.[186] Behrouz Boochani, a Kurdish Iranian journalist detained on Manus, wrote a book and published articles in major international media. His Twitter feed carried a constant stream of updates, and he was able to call into conferences on the Australian mainland to discuss his experiences. He even filmed a documentary with a mobile phone entitled *Chauka, Please Tell Us the Time* that was presented at the Sydney Film Festival.[187] The hermetic seal around the islands of detention sometimes fails and information leaks out.

Conclusion

The Australian government wants potential asylum seekers to know that conditions are harsh so they will be deterred from coming. Policymakers want the Australian public to know that it is taking a firm stand against irregular arrivals. On the other hand, Australia's international brand as a progressive liberal democracy is weakened by policies that are too callous. Distinct messages about the policies and attempts to reach different audiences with different messages are probably beyond a government's capacity to fine-tune. Videos intended for Hazaras in Pakistan end up on the website of the *Guardian*.

Secrecy encourages abuse. Lack of oversight from courts, media, and civil society; paying private contractors and weak foreign governments to surveil and punish; and refusing to respond to parliamentary inquiries about operations at sea can be expected to systemically undermine the rule of law and foster brutality more than intended by even the most cynical democratic government. Revelations about these policies then generate pressure for reforms that are difficult to accomplish when the basis of the policies is that even recognized refugees will be denied sanctuary in Australia if they try to come by sea.

| Protecting Access to Sanctuary

Sunlight is said to be the best of disinfectants.

—U.S. Supreme Court Justice Louis Brandeis, 1914

PERSECUTED PEOPLE SEEKING ASYLUM must first reach a territory where they can make a claim. Governments of countries in the Global North try to evade the spirit of refugee protection laws, while plausibly complying with their letter, by keeping asylum seekers away from their borders using techniques of remote control. Legal scholars have rightly criticized the "hyper-legal" logic of these policies. The fact that so many people who are able to evade the deadly barriers have successfully gained asylum highlights that these policies deliberately prevent refugees from reaching sanctuary. The reluctance of governments to rescue drowning refugees at the conclusion of the Mare Nostrum program in the Mediterranean in 2014 encapsulates the basic logic of remote control of people seeking asylum. Leaders in the Global North know people are dying. As long as government agents and refugees are not situated in a common physical space, governments deny responsibility. By cracking down on NGOs at sea, governments ensure that even private actors are not in a position to render aid or to force the state to activate norms of rescue and sanctuary.

The "Hippocratic Bubble"

Establishing whether a policy is legal is an important benchmark for its legitimacy and a way to hold governments accountable for principles to which they have agreed.[1] Questioning legality is necessary but insufficient. The question should not just be whether a policy is legal, but also whether it is good. Humanitarianism—the imperative of compassionate action across social boundaries—provides a moral framework for measuring whether a policy is good. At its core is a Golden Rule mandate to treat others as one would wish to be treated. What rules would you make, if you were under what the philosopher John Rawls called "a veil of ignorance," and did not know in advance of making the rules where you would fall in the social order?[2] If you did not know if you would be born in a safe or war-torn country, or if you would be a citizen of a free society or a persecuted minority, what asylum policies would you design?

The rise of long-distance humanitarianism since the Enlightenment, particularly around the anti-slavery movement in the nineteenth century, eroded the importance of shared space as a condition for humanitarian action. Long-distance humanitarians attempt to alleviate the suffering of others even across great geographic and social distances.[3] At the same time, contemporary philosophers and political theorists debate whether we have greater obligations toward protecting people who share our physical space. Michael Walzer argues that the positive act of turning away people in need of refuge is worse than the negative act of ignoring people suffering at a distance. Alexander Betts and Paul Collier reply that to favor the person who can reach the physical space of refuge is unfair to those who do not have the resources to move. I would argue that given that granting protection is not inherently a zero-sum game, the harm of refoulement into the hands of persecutors is greater than the harm of unequal treatment of the persecuted.[4]

Regardless of where one stands on the ethical debate, psychologists have shown that people are more likely to mobilize around saving the lives of identifiable individuals in close proximity.[5] Remote control policies by design or effect thwart that humanitarian impulse. Like nation-states, medical institutions can evade their obligations by repelling those in need from entering shared spaces. Sociologist Alejandro Portes describes how U.S. hospitals often deliberately create obstacles between sick people seeking health care and the doctors who have taken the Hippocratic Oath to render aid. Only patients with the resources and insurance to get past a hospital's clerical gatekeepers and physical barriers surrounding the examination room can put themselves in a space where the doctor's norm to render aid is activated. This "Hippocratic bubble" is created by the same logic of controlling space that puts up barriers to keep out asylum seekers.[6] Ironically, the healing temple where Hippocrates founded modern medicine stands on the Greek island of Kos across the water from the beach where Alan Kurdi's body washed up in 2015. The world's collective failure to shelter refugees from the Syrian civil war produced its most visible icon of despair when a toddler died at the edge of the Hippocratic bubble.

Legal scholars are often skeptical of humanitarianism, and a clear-eyed view of humanitarianism's limits is warranted. Coercive policies, from military interventions in countries of origin to interceptions at sea, have been justified by policymakers who cite the humanitarian principle of saving lives, even as these same policies sometimes kill or put lives at risk. Humanitarianism can be paternalistic. Paradoxically, it can dehumanize refugees by reducing them to objects of pity. Unlike a rights-based regime, humanitarianism is discretionary. It can generate fickle policies that change in the face of compassion fatigue and resistance from other quarters. Humanitarianism only provides vague standards, unlike the specific rights and obligations found in the law.[7] Like the law, humanitarianism is an insufficient basis for protecting refugees.

When it comes to remote control of asylum seekers, however, it is the diffuse quality of humanitarianism that makes it so potentially powerful. Regardless of whether a given technique of remote control sustains scrutiny in court, the cumulative effect of these policies shocks the conscience. Keeping refugees at a distance is a public relations scheme to render them invisible so their plight can be ignored. It is a strategy to evade legal obligations that have developed over the last century as well as humanitarian norms that have evolved over millennia. Hyper-legal evasions of the spirit of the law may succeed at complying with the letter, but they are still accountable to norms.[8] The simplicity of the Golden Rule provides a standard easily understood by the public, unlike the arcane details of the latest version of the Dublin regulations. The norms cannot be evaded so easily because they focus attention on the effects of a whole architecture of repulsion rather than a technical, legal analysis of one of its many elements.

Whither Deterrence?

Remote control policies have become widespread across the Global North. Legal scholars Thomas Gammeltoft-Hansen and Nikolas Tan argue that the "deterrence paradigm is not sustainable in the long term, or even perhaps in the medium term" because of its economic costs, lack of effectiveness, and legal challenges.[9] Gammeltoft-Hansen and James Hathaway's pathbreaking jurisprudential work argues that remote control measures will be increasingly limited by legal doctrines that recognize a state's jurisdiction over a person outside its territory when a state takes effective control over that person, the concept of more than one state sharing jurisdiction when they take joint action, and a state's liability for deputizing other governments or nonstate actors to do its bidding.[10]

When Law Matters

These pages have shown that the efficacy of legal challenges varies by the type of remote control and type of legal system in each context. Even when the courts strike down specific policies, they can unintentionally encourage further externalization by keeping asylum seekers outside a state's obvious control. Civic institutions and international relations place additional limits on some of the policies and explain much of the variation that exists across cases. The evidence suggests that the basic structure of the deterrence paradigm is likely to be sustained, but a long-running contest played out across domestic and transnational fields of politics, law, and media may be able to dull the elements of deterrence that most blatantly violate legal and humanitarian principles.

Research dominated by legal experts not surprisingly emphasizes the constraints on government policies imposed by international treaties, customary law, supranational law, domestic statutes, and case law. Most scholars develop jurisprudential arguments about how those laws should be interpreted.[11] At an empirical level, there is much variation across time, country, and technique of control in the extent to which state action is constrained by the courts. Only particular kinds of judicial systems strongly constrain policies. Among the cases studied in this volume, the combination of strong foundational rights of territorial personhood and a judicial tradition of drawing directly on international law is only found in the two supranational European courts. The Strasbourg court has become a much greater check on the remote control policies of the EU and its member states since theories were elaborated in the late 1990s that explained Europeanization as a way for member-state executive branches to create stricter controls than they could accomplish on their own.[12] Supranational courts have primarily constrained intercepting asylum seekers on the high seas, using unsafe third countries as destinations for deportations, and limiting rights of asylum seekers in barbican spaces.

Academic arguments about the strong constraints of the courts that were developed in the European context in the 2000s do not always travel well to Australia and the United States, where the courts have long showed much greater deference to the executive on admissions policy.[13] The most obvious U.S. difference with the EU and Canada is a U.S. pattern of disregarding international law, highlighted by the U.S. Supreme Court decision in 1993 that U.S. immigration law and the Refugee Convention and its Protocol do not apply on the high seas.[14] On the other hand, the U.S. and Canadian courts have strong rights of territorial personhood that modestly limit the use of fictive "barbican" strategies at the margins of the territory. Compared to Australia, the United States is more firmly embedded in a liberal legal regime with a constitutional bill of rights, muscular judicial review, and the legacy of the civil rights movement of the 1960s that has left a robust infrastructure of advocates specializing in impact litigation.[15] Australia's judicial system has the weakest rights of territorial personhood and shows little deference to international law. The Australian government is willing to transfer detainees offshore via the Australian mainland or take them to the mainland periodically because there are not strong rights of territorial personhood for courts to draw on to allow an effective asylum claim. Of all the cases in this volume, Australian courts consequently limit remote control strategies the least.

An underappreciated deterrent on remote control policies is domestic and transnational civil society. These expanding institutions are important because they are able to attack some remote control policies on humanitarian as well as legal grounds. As Zucker and Zucker recognized in the United States, "The greatest victories of the pressure groups in the area of asylum have been won in the courts, not in the Congress." Most of the victories were for asylum seekers who reached U.S. territory.[16] Groups of activists and their congressional allies have had modest and temporary successes in modifying U.S. remote control policy, including resettlement to the U.S. mainland in 1993 of HIV-positive Haitians who had been held at Guantanamo, the temporary suspension of Haitian repatriation in March 1994, and the resettlement of Cubans held at Guantanamo to the U.S. mainland in 1995.[17] A potential hazard of putting too many eggs in the basket of "cause lawyering" is that litigation narrows the focus of a social movement and makes it susceptible to a loss of momentum in the face of repeated defeats in the courts.[18] Integrated advocacy that combines legal action with civil society efforts built up over the course of decades is more effective and enduring.[19]

Integrated Advocacy

The constraints of courts and transnational advocacy work together. In one legal mechanism, court cases draw from expert knowledge developed by transnational advocates and rights-oriented government agencies. For example, the landmark 2012 *Hirsi* decision cited reports on conditions in Libya, Somalia, and Eritrea from the UNHCR, Amnesty International,

Human Rights Watch, the U.S. State Department, and the Council of Europe's Committee for the Prevention of Torture.[20] It may be possible to establish legal liability for states that sponsor remote control activities outside of their jurisdictions or direct control if the government is "aware that its contributions will lead to a breach of international law."[21] Researchers can make a broader range of government officials aware of these effects, and, most importantly, publicize that knowledge so that governments cannot credibly feign ignorance.

Feedback loops channel information between the legal process and the production of knowledge by refugee advocates. For example, legal advocates use court cases to force governments to reveal details about their policies, which then become part of the public record. The direction of feedback can also operate from the political to the legal. In a political effort to show their humanitarian concern for refugees and to establish "safe third countries" to which asylum seekers can be returned, countries in the Global North fund the activities of the UNHCR in buffer states. Reports by the UNHCR, or by NGOs promoted by the UNHCR, are sometimes used in both political and legal settings to argue against those buffering strategies. Expert knowledge by organizations on the ground can trickle up into official reporting on human rights abuses. For example, NGOs' reports on rights abuses of refugees and other migrants in places such as Mauritania and Morocco are favorably cited in confidential U.S. diplomatic cables.[22] Such reports are sometimes used as part of the decision-making by other government actors. For instance, in a discussion of safe third countries in 2004, the European Council "provided references to material upon which the member states could base their decisions. The majority of this material consisted of U.S. State Department Reports, although some Amnesty International and UN Committee Against Torture reports were also included."[23]

Transnational advocates have a constraining effect through a humanitarian publicity mechanism as human rights organizations and investigative journalists increasingly reach beyond state borders to highlight the secret practices and effects of remote control policies. They amplify each other in conjunction with actors such as the UNHCR and organs within governments that monitor human rights violations at home and abroad. Remote control strategies that violate humanitarian norms, such as paying and training undemocratic buffer states to carry out abusive policies, are less effective when their secret violence becomes public knowledge. The humanitarian mechanism operates in the public sphere and can be a complement to legal strategies.

Civil Society

Populist media whip up sentiment against asylum seekers, which in turn undergirds stricter remote control measures. At the same time, investigative journalism shines a light on conditions in buffer states and the moat that make visible the human costs of these policies. If one of the lessons of cognitive psychology is that people are moved by stories about identifiable individuals, then journalistic reports play an important role in facilitating humanitarian stances toward asylum seekers by showing the negative consequences of remote control policies on particular people, even at a distance, which counters state strategies of keeping asylum seekers out of sight and out of mind. On the other hand, an endless montage of photos showing faceless bodies on crowded boats or hiking through the wilderness can generate a narrative of invasion rather than empathy.[24]

Civil society can have an especially strong influence in buffer zones where a catch-22 ensnares rich democracies that try to use transit states as buffers. For buffering to be effective, the governments must support various enforcement policies. If those policies are known to be too ruthless, the buffering becomes illegitimate. The result is buffering policies that are much harsher in practice than in the law on the books. This catch-22 provides opportunities for civil society actors to undermine buffering of refugees by publicizing abuses. Their political allies in destination countries make buffering contingent on the maintenance of human rights norms. NGOs monitor governments for compliance with domestic and international law. They send researchers on fact-finding trips to transit countries and work with local partners. Their reports are routinely picked up and disseminated in major media outlets. Activists are following states in pushing their activities beyond national borders.

Academic studies by scholars such as Gammeltoft-Hansen and Hathaway are "piercing the corporate veil of internationalized migration control arrangements."[25] One area where scholarly studies can make a contribution that complements research focused on the present is explaining policies of remote control as they have developed over longer time frames. Governments often develop restrictive policies during episodes framed as exceptional crises and then institutionalize those policies.[26] Independent researchers can show the extent to which "crises" are really novel or acute, as opposed to recurring or even chronic, and sound a warning against panicked reactions that create lasting harm.

Foreign Relations

An analysis of foreign relations is necessary to understand the remote control options of destination country governments. The willingness of transit and origin states to cooperate with the Global North on mobility controls, such as restricting exit and allowing readmission, is contingent on their position in the hierarchy of sovereignty, the broader state of their relations, and their domestic messages and international branding. Remote control is linked to other interests in ways that can inhibit even powerful destination states from simply imposing their will on weaker states.[27] Transit states share a similar dilemma as states in the Global North that seek on the one hand to control who enters, while on the other hand, to enjoy the rewards of cross-border trade and migration, including flows with other countries in the Global South. Where there are no buffers between countries of origin and destination, such as in the Cuba-U.S. corridor, states of origin can more easily demand legal access for at least some of their citizens as a condition of allowing readmission. Europeanization has cross-cutting effects because so many actors are involved at different levels of governance. The two European supranational courts constrain refoulement at sea and the use of special barbican zones, while the European Council in particular enables remote control policies built around the dome and buffer.

The Dome

The extent to which governments can freely practice remote control varies by the type of policy. The least constrained remote control policies involve the dome, and the most constrained involve the barbican. The dome is the least subject to constraints because it has been normalized through more than a century of construction, its effects are mostly invisible, its practices take place extremely far from the territory of rich destination states, and plausible alternative narratives of security and anti-trafficking displace concerns about shutting off refugees' access to sanctuary.

The origins of the dome have nothing to do with refugees. The dome was originally created by governments of settler societies in the nineteenth century to select immigrants regardless of their motivations to move. The de facto deputizing of private transport companies to screen travelers (so that the companies can avoid sanctions) and visa requirements seem natural because they have been imposed for a century or more. These activities take place outside the state's sovereign territory, with the arguable exception of visa issuance at consulates, where the doctrine of "consular nonreviewability" prevents judicial oversight of visa officers' decisions in almost all cases.[28]

Since visas were widely imposed in World War I, they have become part of a securitized mobility regime that was later strengthened by controls to prevent skyjackings and the movement of terrorists. Even though the chances of an asylum seeker committing a terrorist act are infinitesimally small,[29] the narrative that these controls are necessary to protect security provides a plausible alternative to the narrative that the controls deliberately or in effect prevent asylum seekers from seeking safety. People smugglers whom asylum seekers contract to circumvent border controls are easily villainized and deliberately conflated with traffickers who use coercion to sell human bodies. Even if the public accepts that the people being smuggled are refugees, smugglers can be blamed for deaths and abuses rather than the government policies that leave refugees seeking safety with few choices. As shown in chapter 2, governments have honed the technique of blaming smugglers at least since British authorities castigated them for arranging the passage of European Jews to Palestine during World War II. For all these reasons, it is difficult for the media, NGOs, or legal advocates to press the case in the public sphere and courts that there is a fundamental problem with the application of the visa regime.

The Moat

As long as maritime interceptions take place in the territorial waters of a destination country, rights of non-refoulement in domestic and international law are generally observed in the Global North. In remote areas or under cover of darkness, refoulement or dangerous interception techniques that in practice push back boats by making their passengers fear for their lives have been extensively documented in places like Greece, but they are probably the exception. There are more varied limitations on the high seas. The European Court of Human Rights strongly constrains the activities of its signatory members, including all the EU countries. The U.S. government stands out for openly rejecting the near global consensus that refoulement in international waters is illegal, although the executive exercised some self-restraint by conducting cursory asylum screenings at sea at least through the Obama administration. By any legal standard, the "shout test" is inadequate, but the fact that it exists at all suggests that international norms, if not international law, minimally constrain state action. A similar argument applies to the euphemistic "enhanced screening" of asylum seekers at sea by Australian authorities.

It is expensive, technically difficult, and legally challenging for civil society and journalists to monitor government activities on the high seas. The presence of NGO vessels in the Mediterranean during the mid-2010s has raised public attention about these activities, which is why governments tried so hard to shut them down. Journalistic reports that track down asylum seekers who have been subjected to procedures at sea are one of the few sources of information about secretive practices. It is difficult to argue the counterfactual of what state policies would be in the absence of this monitoring, but the fact that governments try so hard to avoid it suggests that it is having some effect.

Buffers

Legal scholars have elaborated concepts of extraterritorial jurisdiction and shared jurisdiction to lay a basis in law for holding governments accountable for their activities in buffer states.[30] This is vital intellectual work that may lead to changes in practice, but political constraints on the Global North's remote control efforts are greater than legal constraints alone. Political constraints operate through two major mechanisms—liberalism and linkages to other issues.

The first political constraint is embedded liberalism. Even restrictionist governments in liberal states need to create at least the chimera of compliance with rights norms in the buffer, including the right to apply for asylum. Using buffer states effectively requires not only the cooperation of those governments but also cooperation in such a way that human rights abuses are not too openly egregious. The fundamental collision of rights and coercion in the Global North that prompts its governments to push border control outward continues in buffer countries. In Mexico, the government's solution to this issue has been to pass laws that on their face respect the human rights of asylum seekers and transit migrants but in reality treat them much more severely. Effective buffering inherently relies on secrecy that advocates and investigative journalists attempt to penetrate and publicize. The presence of the UNHCR and IOM in buffer countries has cross-cutting effects that on the one hand increase the capacity for strategies that contain potential migrants to the Global North, but which also raise global awareness about rights abuses that then limit destination-state supports for the buffers and their willingness to deport asylum seekers there. Rights-minded agencies and politicians within the governments of countries in the Global North sometimes make their buffering training and aid conditional on respect for human rights norms, which creates the potential for reducing buffering techniques that violates those rights.

A second major mechanism that limits many buffer states from simply doing the bidding of the Global North is the linkage between transit migration through the buffer and other forms of mobility. In many countries, such as the major North American gateway of Mexico and major European gateways of Turkey and Morocco, transit migration through the buffer is tightly linked to emigration from the buffer to the Global North. All these buffer countries have openly or secretly tried to gain greater access for their citizens to their rich neighbors in return for cracking down on people in transit. However, restrictionists in the Global North often want to limit immigration from the buffer countries as well, which retards collaboration. Not all major buffers are also countries of mass emigration. Indonesia, the major maritime transit gateway to Australia, is the source of little emigration to Australia. Many other countries are leery of cracking down on transit migration because they have commercial, migratory, and familial interests in maintaining ties with their neighbors further south. Thus, countries from Mali to Turkey have resisted simply doing the EU's bidding to restrict transit because they have core interests built around other kinds of mobility.

Caging

As with buffers, the presence of the UNHCR and NGOs in caging areas has cross-cutting effects. They increase the capacity to contain potential asylum seekers from reaching the Global North, but they also raise global awareness about rights abuses that then limit destination states' willingness to deport asylum seekers there, or at least the willingness of the courts to allow deportation. Caging in offshore-processing areas, such as Nauru and Manus Island, creates international reputational costs when cruel conditions are exposed by whistleblowers, NGOs, and media. When the cage is the country of origin, containment policies become even more awkward because one of the long-standing uses of refugee and asylum policy is to shame governments of countries of origin whose citizens have voted with their feet by leaving.[31] There is a domestic and international political price for openly cooperating with persecutors. The U.S.-Cuban case illustrates that when the relationship between the governments of the countries of origin and destination is hostile, the origin country can use the threat of outflows of refugees to gain more leverage in the broader relationship.

Barbicans

The courts have only sometimes been able to curb the use of barbican spaces. The greatest limits have been in Europe following the 1992 *Amuur* case, although this restraint should not be overstated. All EU member states have special asylum procedures in the transit zones of their airports. The European Court of Human Rights decision in 2017 may constrain the legal fictions used by the Spanish government to conduct mass expulsions from the fenced zone around the Spanish enclaves of Ceuta and Melilla. As of this writing, it is not clear if there will be any remedy in the Hungarian border area where the government of Viktor Orbán explicitly attempted to keep asylum seekers from access to full rights in designated spaces. The Australian courts did not block excision but eventually reigned in differential processing on Christmas Island. In the United States, the courts have limited the executive's attempts to carve out exceptions for people arriving on U.S. beaches while generally upholding the restrictive asylum-processing regime on Guantanamo. Processing on Guantanamo as well as on Tinian in the 1990s revealed modest self-limitations by the executive rather than sharp constraints imposed by courts.

Conclusion

In a speech to the European Parliament in 2014, Pope Francis called for a humanitarian response to people attempting to reach Europe by sea. "We cannot allow the Mediterranean to become a vast cemetery!" he said. "The boats landing daily on the shores of Europe are filled with men and women who need acceptance and assistance."[32] Yet the Mediterranean continues to be a cemetery without graves. Since the 1930s it has swallowed Jews fleeing Nazi Germany, Eritreans and Ethiopians, Somalis and Syrians, and Palestinians fleeing Israel's cage around Gaza. Buffering and interception takes place at sea, in Central American jungles, and deserts from Sonora to the Sahara. Agents deploy remote controls in the world's cities every day, in plain sight or out of view, at airport check-in counters and consulates.

Across the planet, the pages of history bleed with the memory of refugees turned back to their persecutors. Systematically closing access to sanctuary violates the humanitarian principles that motivate the spirit of the laws obliging governments to protect refugees from forced return. It is unrealistic to ask the courts to be the sole guarantors of effective protection. A robust civil society of monitoring organizations, investigative journalists, legal advocates, scholars, and engaged citizens must guard the paths to refuge from the duplicitous attempts to close them.

NOTES

Chapter 1

1. Ulrich Sinn, "Greek Sanctuaries as Places of Refuge," in *Greek Sanctuaries: New Approaches*, edited by Nanno Marinatos and Robin Hägg (London: Routledge, 1993), pp. 70–73; Benjamin Gray, "Exile, Refuge and the Greek Polis: Between Justice and Humanity," *Journal of Refugee Studies 30*, no. 2 (2016): pp. 190–219; Kent J. Rigsby, *Asylia: Territorial Inviolability in the Hellenistic World* (Berkeley: University of California Press, 1997), p. 110.

2. Paul Behrens, "The Law of Diplomatic Asylum: A Contextual Approach," *Michigan Journal of International Law 35* (2013): pp. 319–367.

3. Claire Higgins, "Humanitarian Corridors: Safe Passage but Only for a Few," Andrew and Renata Kaldor Centre for International Refugee Law, 2017, http://www.kaldorcentre.unsw.edu.au/publication/humanitarian-corridors.

4. "For the first time, U.S. resettles fewer refugees than the rest of the world," Pew Research Center, July 5, 2018, http://www.pewresearch.org/fact-tank/2018/07/05/for-the-first-time-u-s-resettles-fewer-refugees-than-the-rest-of-the-world/.

5. "Canada Denies Alan Kurdi's Family Applied for Asylum," *BBC News*, September 3, 2015, http://www.bbc.com/news/world-us-canada-34142695; "Relatives of Drowned Syrian Boy Alan Kurdi Land in Canada to Start New Life," *The Guardian*, December 28, 2015, https://www.theguardian.com/world/2015/dec/29/relatives-of-drowned-syrian-boy-alan-kurdi-land-in-canada-to-start-new-life; Bryan Walsh, "Alan Kurdi's Story: Behind the Most Heartbreaking Photo of 2015," *Time*, December 29, 2015, http://time.com/4162306/alan-kurdi-syria-drowned-boy-refugee-crisis/.

6. Chad C. Haddal, "Refugee and Asylum-Seeker Inflows in the United States and Other OECD Member States," Congressional Research Service, January 6, 2009; "Global Trends in Forced Displacement in 2016," UNHCR, June 19, 2017, http://www.unhcr.org/en-us/statistics/unhcrstats/5943e8a34/global-trends-forced-displacement-2016.html, pp. 27, 45.

7. "Global North" is a simplified term for the world's rich countries that are mostly, but not exclusively, concentrated in the Northern Hemisphere and roughly correspond to the membership of the Organisation for Economic Co-operation and

Development. The exceptions are its two middle-income members—Turkey and Mexico, which are considered here as gateways to the Global North.

8. Art. 33, 1951 Convention Relating to the Status of Refugees.

9. Guy S. Goodwin-Gil and Jane McAdam, *The Refugee in International Law* (New York: Oxford University Press, 2007), ch. 6.

10. UNHCR Population Statistics, UNHCR, http://popstats.unhcr.org/en/asylum_seekers.

11. Reece Jones, *Violent Borders: Refugees and the Right to Move* (London: Verso, 2016).

12. Aristide Zolberg, "The Archaeology of 'Remote Control,'" in *Migration Control in the North Atlantic World: The Evolution of State Practices in Europe and the United States from the French Revolution to the Inter-War Period*, edited by Andreas Fahrmeir, Olivier Faron, and Patrick Weil (New York: Berghahn Books, 2003), pp. 195–222.

13. James C. Hathaway, "The Emerging Politics of Non-Entrée," *Refugees 91* (1992): pp. 40–41; See also Gil Loescher, "Refugees and the Asylum Dilemma in the West," in *Refugees and the Asylum Dilemma in the West*, edited by Gil Loescher (University Park: Pennsylvania State University Press, 1992), pp. 2–3.

14. Virginie Guiraudon and Gallya Lahav, "A Reappraisal of the State Sovereignty Debate: The Case of Migration Control," *Comparative Political Studies 33*, no. 2 (2000): pp. 163–195; Matthew Gibney, "A Thousand Little Guantanamos: Western States and Measures to Prevent the Arrival of Refugees," in *Displacement, Asylum, Migration: The Oxford Amnesty Lectures 2004*, edited by Kate E. Tunstall (New York: Oxford University Press, 2006), pp. 139–169; Rens van Munster and Steven Sterkx, "Governing Mobility: The Externalization of European Migration Policy and the Boundaries of the European Union," in *European Research Reloaded: Cooperation and Integration among Europeanized States*, edited by Ronald Holzhacker and Markus Haverland (The Netherlands: Springer, 2006); Elspeth Guild and Didier Bigo, "The Transformation of European Border Controls," in *Extraterritorial Immigration Control: Legal Challenges*, edited by Ryan Bernard and Valsamis Mitsilegas (Leiden: Martinus Nijhoff, 2010), pp. 257–280; Jennifer Hyndman and Alison Mountz, "Another Brick in the Wall? Neo-*Refoulement* and the Externalization of Asylum by Australia and Europe," *Government and Opposition 43*, no. 2 (2008): pp. 249–269.

15. Bernard Ryan, "Extraterritorial Immigration Controls: What Role for Legal Guarantees?" In *Extraterritorial Immigration Control: Legal Challenges*, edited by Bernard Ryan and Valsamis Mitsilegas (Leiden: Martinus Nijhoff, 2010), p. 10.

16. Gregor Noll, *Negotiating Asylum: The EU acquis, Extraterritorial Protection and the Common Market of Deflection* (The Hague: Martinus Nijhoff, 2000), p. 179; Bernd Kasparek, "Borders and Populations in Flux: Frontex's Place in the European Union's Migration Management," in *The Politics of International Migration Management*, edited by Martin Geiger and Antoine Pécoud (New York: Palgrave Macmillan, 2010), p. 128.

17. Bruce Finley, "U.S. Takes Border War on the Road," *Denver Post*, December 19, 2004.

18. Anna Pratt, *Securing Borders: Detention and Deportation in Canada* (Vancouver: UBC Press, 2005), p. 201.

19. "Australian Border Force—Who We Are," Australian Government Department of Immigration and Border Protection, http://www.border.gov.au/australian-border-force-abf/who-we-are.

20. Zolberg, "The Archaeology of 'Remote Control.'"

21. Erika Feller, "Refugees Are Not Migrants," *Refugee Survey Quarterly* 24, no. 4 (2005): pp. 27-35.

22. David Scott FitzGerald and Rawan Arar, "The Sociology of Refugee Migration," *Annual Review of Sociology 44* (2018): pp. 387–406.

23. Claire Inder, "International Refugee Law, 'Hyper-Legalism' and Migration Management: The Pacific Solution," in *The Politics of International Migration Management*, edited by Martin Geiger and Antoine Pécoud (New York: Palgrave Macmillan, 2010), p. 221; Zoltán I. Búzás, "Evading International Law: How Agents Comply with the Letter of the Law but Violate Its Purpose," *European Journal of International Relations* 23, no. 4(2016): pp. 857–883.

24. Elizabeth G. Ferris, *The Politics of Protection: The Limits of Humanitarian Action* (Washington DC: Brookings Institution Press, 2011).

25. Liisa H. Malkki, "Refugees and Exile: From 'Refugee Studies' to the National Order of Things," *Annual Review of Anthropology 24* (1995): pp. 495–523.

26. Mariano-Florentino Cuéllar, "Refugee Security and the Organizational Logic of Legal Mandates," *Georgetown Journal of International Law 37* (2005): pp. 583–723; Bhupinder S. Chimni, "The Geopolitics of Refugee Studies: A View from the South," *Journal of Refugee Studies 11*, no. 4 (1998): pp. 350–374.

27. "Contributions to UNHCR—2017," UNHCR, http://www.unhcr.org/5954c4257.html.

28. Andrew Shacknove, "From Asylum to Containment," *International Journal of Refugee Law 5*, no. 4 (1993): pp. 516–533.

29. Jennifer Hyndman, "Preventive, Palliative, or Punitive? Safe Spaces in Bosnia-Herzegovina, Somalia, and Sri Lanka," *Journal of Refugee Studies 16*, no. 2 (2003): p. 177.

30. Cécile Dubernet, *The International Containment of Displaced Persons: Humanitarian Spaces without Exit* (Aldershot: Ashgate, 2001); Jason W. Davidson, "France, Britain and the Intervention in Libya: An Integrated Analysis," *Cambridge Review of International Affairs 26*, no. 2 (2013): pp. 310–329.

31. John C. Torpey, *The Invention of the Passport: Surveillance, Citizenship and the State* (Cambridge: Cambridge University Press, 2000).

32. Mathias Czaika, Hein de Haas, and María Villares-Varela, "The Global Evolution of Travel Visa Regimes," International Migration Institute Working Papers no. 134, University of Oxford, 2017, p. 24.

33. "Henley & Partners Passport Index 2018," Henley & Partners and the International Air Transport Association, 2018, https://www.henleypassportindex.com/assets/PI_2018_INFOGRAPHS_GLOBAL_180709.pdf; "Global Trends in Forced Displacement in 2017," UNHCR, June 25, 2018, http://www.unhcr.org/5b27be547.pdf.

34. Sophie Scholten, *The Privatisation of Immigration Control through Carrier Sanctions: The Role of Private Transport Companies in Dutch and British Immigration Control* (Leiden: Brill Nijhoff, 2015), pp. 93–94; "The Protocol against the Smuggling

of Migrants by Land, Sea and Air, Supplementing the United Nations Convention against Transnational Organized Crime," November 15, 2000, *United Nations Treaty Series*, vol. 2241, no. 39574, p. 507, Art. 11, https://treaties.un.org/doc/Publication/UNTS/Volume%202241/v2241.pdf.

35. In maritime law, "international waters" are divided into "the high seas" over which no state has claim, the "Economic Exclusion Zone" that extends up to 200 nautical miles from shore, and the "contiguous zone" that extends up to twenty-four nautical miles from shore. Much U.S. maritime interception policy conflates all three of these categories as the "high seas." See Azadeh Dastyari, *United States Migrant Interdiction and the Detention of Refugees in Guantánamo Bay* (Cambridge: Cambridge University Press, 2015), p. 61.

36. Tally Kritzman-Amir and Thomas Spijkerboer, "On the Morality and Legality of Borders: Border Politics and Asylum Seekers," *Harvard Human Rights Journal 26* (2013): pp. 1–38.

37. *Amuur v. France*, 17/1995/523/609, European Court of Human Rights (1996).

38. *Yang v. Maugans* 68 F.3d 1540 (1995).

39. Àngels Piñol, "Fernández defiende los 'rechazos en frontera' y el uso de gas pimienta," *El País*, May 5, 2014, http://ccaa.elpais.com/ccaa/2014/05/05/catalunya/1399287834_937254.html.

40. *Hernandez v. Mesa*, 582 U.S. ____ (2017), https://www.supremecourt.gov/oral_arguments/argument_transcripts/2016/15-118_3e04.pdf.

41. Taylor Dolven, "Over the Line: What Happens When U.S. Border Patrol Kills—in Mexico?" *Vice News*, June 9, 2017, https://news.vice.com/story/what-happens-when-u-s-border-patrol-kills-in-mexico.

42. The selection of appropriate units of analysis in comparisons involving Europe is uniquely difficult because of the EU's supranational character. Jurisdiction over different kinds of mobility policies is shared between individual member states and the EU in ways that shift over time. Some policies vary among EU members, and the composition of the EU itself has changed. Given this distribution of jurisdictional competence, an individual EU member state cannot be compared to a non-member as if they were exactly comparable units. Thus, following Wimmer and Glick Schiller's prescription against the "methodological nationalism" of assuming the nation-state is the natural unit of analysis and Beine et al.'s operationalization of this mandate in studies of immigration policy, the EU is generally treated here as a unit of analysis, while still attending to variation and disputes within the EU regarding asylum and control policies (Eiko R. Thielemann, "How Effective Are National and EU Policies in the Area of Forced Migration?" *Refugee Survey Quarterly* 31, no. 4 (2012): pp. 21–37; Andreas Wimmer and Nina Glick Schiller, "Methodological Nationalism, the Social Sciences, and the Study of Migration: An Essay in Historical Epistemology," *International Migration Review* 37, no. 3 (2003): pp. 576–610); Michel Beine et al.,"Comparing Immigration Policies: An Overview from the Impala Database," *International Migration Review* 50, no. 4 (2016): pp. 827–863).

43. Andrew Bennett and Colin Elman, "Case Study Methods in the International Relations Subfield," *Comparative Political Studies* 40, no. 2 (2007): pp. 170–95.

44. David Collier, "Understanding Process Tracing," *Political Science & Politics 44*, no. 4 (2011): pp. 823–30.

45. Torpey, *The Invention of the Passport*, pp. 4–5.

46. Phil Orchard, *A Right to Flee: Refugees, States, and the Construction of International Cooperation* (Cambridge: Cambridge University Press, 2014); Daniel Ghezelbash, *Refuge Lost: Asylum Law in an Interdependent World* (Cambridge: Cambridge University Press, 2018).

47. Guy S. Goodwin-Gill, "The Politics of Refugee Protection," *Refugee Survey Quarterly* 27, no. 1 (2008): pp. 8–23; David Scott FitzGerald and David Cook-Martín, *Culling the Masses: The Democratic Origins of Racist Immigration Policy in the Americas* (Cambridge, MA: Harvard University Press, 2014).

48. Matthew J. Gibney, *The Ethics and Politics of Asylum: Liberal Democracy and the Response To Refugees* (Cambridge: Cambridge University Press, 2004).

49. Valsamis Mitsilegas, "Extraterritorial Immigration Control in the 21st Century: The Individual and the State Transformed," in *Extraterritorial Immigration Control: Legal Challenge*, edited by Bernard Ryan and Valsamis Mitsilegas (Leiden: Martinus Nijhoff, 2010).

50. James F. Hollifield, "Migration and International Relations: Cooperation and Control in the European Community," *International Migration Review* 26, no. 2 (1992): pp. 568–595.

51. "Roma Refugees," *Toronto Star*, January 25, 2013, https://www.thestar.com/news/canada/2013/01/25/roma_refugees_canadian_billboards_in_hungary_warn_of_deportation.html.

52. Timothy J. Hatton, "Refugees and Asylum Seekers, the Crisis in Europe and the Future of Policy," *Economic Policy* 32 no. 91 (2017): p. 462.

53. Holly Ackerman, "The Balsero Phenomenon, 1991–1994," *Cuban Studies* 26 (1996): pp. 179–180.

54. Calculated from Table 12, "Report of the Expert Panel on Asylum Seekers 2012," Australian Government, August 2012, p. 98, http://artsonline.monash.edu.au/thebordercrossingobservatory/files/2015/03/expert_panel_on_asylum_seekers_full_report.pdf.

55. Phillip Connor, "Asylum Seeker Demography: Young and Male," Pew Research Center, Aug. 2, 2016, http://www.pewglobal.org/2016/08/02/4-asylum-seeker-demography-young-and-male/.

56. Andrew Shacknove, "From Asylum to Containment," *International Journal of Refugee Law* 5, no. 4 (1993): pp. 521–522.

57. Michael Collyer, Franck Düvell, and Hein Haas, "Critical Approaches to Transit Migration," *Population, Space and Place* 18, no. 4 (2012): pp. 407–414.

58. David A. Lake, *Hierarchy in International Relations* (Ithaca: Cornell University Press, 2009).

59. On evasion generally, see Búzás, "Evading International Law," p. 6.

Chapter 2

1. Thomas Gammeltoft-Hansen, *Access to Asylum: International Refugee Law and the Globalisation of Migration Control* (Cambridge: Cambridge University Press, 2011).

2. James C. Hathaway, *The Rights of Refugees under International Law* (Cambridge: Cambridge University Press, 2005), p. 337; cf. Ruben Zaiotti, ed.,

Externalizing Migration Management: Europe, North America and the Spread of Remote Control Practices (London: Routledge, 2016), pp. 17–20.

3. David Scott FitzGerald and David Cook-Martín, *Culling the Masses: The Democratic Origins of Racist Immigration Policy in the Americas* (Cambridge, MA: Harvard University Press, 2014).

4. Cf. Gammeltoft-Hansen, *Access to Asylum*, 61.

5. Cf. Matthew J. Gibney, *The Ethics and Politics of Asylum: Liberal Democracy and the Response to Refugees* (Cambridge: Cambridge University Press, 2004), p. 126; James C. Hathaway, "The Emerging Politics of Non-Entrée," *Refugees* 91 (1992): p. 41.

6. Linda Rabben, *Sanctuary and Asylum: A Social and Political History* (Seattle: University of Washington Press, 2016); Benjamin Gray, "Exile, Refuge and the Greek Polis: Between Justice and Humanity," *Journal of Refugee Studies* 30, no. 2 (2016): pp. 190–219.

7. 1793 France Const., Art. 120.

8. Phil Orchard, *A Right to Flee: Refugees, States, and the Construction of International Cooperation* (Cambridge: Cambridge University Press, 2014), pp. 99–100.

9. Peter Gatrell, *The Making of the Modern Refugee* (Oxford: Oxford University Press), pp. 21–84.

10. "Convention Relating to the International Status of Refugees," October 28, 1933, *League of Nations Treaty Series* 159, no. 3663, Art. 3; Guy S. Goodwin-Gil and Jane McAdam, *The Refugee In International Law* (New York: Oxford University Press, 2007), p. 202.

11. Gerald E. Dirks, *Canada's Refugee Policy: Indifference or Opportunism?* (Montreal: McGill-Queen's University Press, 1977), p. 58.

12. Aristide R. Zolberg, *A Nation by Design: Immigration Policy in the Fashioning of America* (Cambridge, MA: Harvard University Press, 2006), p. 285.

13. Judith Tydor Baumel, "The Jewish Refugee Children from Europe in the Eyes of the American Press and Public Opinion 1934–1945," *Holocaust and Genocide Studies* 5, no. 3 (1990): p. 299.

14. Read Lewis and Marian Schibsby, "Status of the Refugee under American Immigration Laws," *The Annals of the American Academy of Political and Social Science* 203, no. 1 (1939): p. 80.

15. Patricia Cohen, "In Old Files, Fading Hopes of Anne Frank's Family," *New York Times*, February 15, 2007.

16. Archivo Nacional de la República de Cuba, Presidencia 121, 79, "Informe sobre la protección a los inmigrantes judíos," Dr. Nicasio Silverio, Jefe Superior de Ciudadanía y Migración, October 26, 1938.

17. Irving M. Abella and Harold M. Troper, *None Is Too Many: Canada and the Jews of Europe, 1933–1948* (New York: Random House, 1983), p. 63; Richard Breitman and Allan J. Lichtman, *FDR and the Jews* (Cambridge, MA: Harvard University Press, 2013), p. 138; "Refugee Ship Idles off Florida Coast," *New York Times*, June 5, 1939.

18. Zaiotti, *Externalizing Migration Management*, 17.

19. Dalia Ofer, *Escaping the Holocaust: Illegal Immigration to the Land of Israel, 1939–1944* (New York: Oxford University Press, 1990), pp. 4, 319.

20. Ofer, *Escaping the Holocaust*, 10.

21. Ninian Stewart, *The Royal Navy and the Palestine Patrol* (Portland: Frank Cass, 2002), p. 9.

22. Stewart, *The Royal Navy*, 32.

23. "Jewish Illegal Immigration into Palestine. Memorandum prepared jointly by the Foreign Office and Colonial Office (confidential)," January 17, 1940, reproduced in Leni Yahil, "Select British Documents on the Illegal Immigration to Palestine (1939–1940)," *Yad Vashem Studies on the European Jewish Catastrophe and Resistance 10* (1974): p. 254.

24. "Jewish Illegal Immigration into Palestine," 259.

25. Letter of January 30, 1940 from Sd. N. S. Ronald to V. Jabotinsky, FO 371/25 238, reproduced in Yahil, "Select British Documents," 264.

26. Ofer, *Escaping the Holocaust*, 133, 353.

27. "Jewish Illegal Immigration into Palestine," 259; Ofer, *Escaping the Holocaust*, 45–47, 134–136; Yahil, "Select British Documents," 244–246.

28. "Jewish Illegal Immigration into Palestine," 259.

29. Edward Timms, "Remembering Refugees Lost at Sea: The *Struma*, the *Wilhelm Gustloff* and the *Cap Anamur*," in *For the Sake of Humanity*, edited by Alan Stephens and Raphael Walden (Leiden: Martinus Nijhoff, 2006), pp. 325–350.

30. Telegram of 18.12.1940, F.O. 371/25242, p. 220, reproduced in Yahil, "Select British Documents," 250.

31. Ofer, *Escaping the Holocaust*, 136.

32. Yahil, "Select British Documents," 283.

33. "Jewish Illegal Immigration into Palestine," 256–257.

34. Stewart, *The Royal Navy*, 31–36.

35. "400 Refugees, Barred by Palestine, Put Back to Sea in Small Ship," *Jewish Telegraphic Agency* 5, no. 116, April 23, 1939.

36. "Jewish Illegal Immigration into Palestine," 257.

37. Ofer, *Escaping the Holocaust*, 134, 136.

38. "Jewish Illegal Immigration into Palestine," 257.

39. "Refugees to Be Sent to British Colony," *The Palestine Post*, November 28, 1940, p. 1; Ofer, *Escaping the Holocaust*, 140.

40. Yahil, "Select British Documents," 248.

41. Klaus Neumann, *Across the Seas: Australia's Response to Refugees: A History* (Victoria: Black, 2015), pp. 63–64.

42. Cypher telegram of 17 Oct. 1940 from Governor of Mauritius to Secretary of State for Colonies, FO 371 25242, reproduced in Yahil, "Select British Documents," 270.

43. "Refugees to Be Sent to British Colony," 1; Ofer, *Escaping the Holocaust*, 140.

44. Geneviève Pitot, *The Mauritian Shekel: The Story of Jewish Detainees in Mauritius, 1940–1945* (Lanham: Rowman and Littlefield, 2000).

45. Stewart, *The Royal Navy*, 59, 64.

46. *Molvan v. Attorney-General for Palestine* [1948] AC 351.

47. Stewart, *The Royal Navy*, 90–91.

48. Stewart, *The Royal Navy*, 114, 155.

49. Steven Wagner, "British Intelligence and the 'Fifth' Occupying Power: The Secret Struggle to Prevent Jewish Illegal Immigration to Palestine," *Intelligence and National Security 29*, no. 5 (2014): p. 707.

50. Kim Salomon, *Refugees in the Cold War: Toward A New International Refugee Regime in the Early Postwar Era* (Lund: Lund University Press, 1991), p. 79.

51. "Palestine Issue Impairs US-UK Relations," CIA, October 31, 1947, https://www.cia.gov/library/readingroom/docs/CIA-RDP78-01617A005900020003-9.pdf.

52. *Molvan v. Attorney-General for Palestine* [1948] AC 351.

53. UN General Assembly, "Universal Declaration of Human Rights," December 10, 1948, Art. 14(1).

54. Guy S. Goodwin-Gill and Jane McAdam, *The Refugee in International Law* (New York: Oxford University Press, 2007), pp. 359, 363.

55. "Convention Relating to the Status of Refugees," July 28, 1951, *United Nations Treaty Series*, vol. 189, p. 137, Art. 1.

56. Spain is an outlier, which did not join until 1978 as part of the post-Franco transition to democracy.

57. Nehemiah Robinson, *Convention Relating to the Status of Refugees: Its History, Contents and Interpretation; A Commentary* (New York: Institute of Jewish Affairs, 1953), p. 163. See also Atle Grahl-Madsen, *The Status of Refugees in International Law*, vol. 2 (Leyden: A. W. Sijthoff, 1972).

58. Bill Frelick, "'Abundantly Clear': Refoulement," *Georgetown Immigration Law Journal* 19 (2004): p. 255; Maarten den Heijer, *Europe and Extraterritorial Asylum* (Oxford: Hart, 2012), pp. 138–139; Gammeltoft-Hansen, *Access to Asylum*, 47–59.

59. "Convention against Torture and Other Cruel, Inhuman or Degrading Treatment or Punishment," December 10, 1984, *United Nations Treaty Series*, vol. 1465, p. 85, Art. 3(1).

60. "General Comment No. 2: Implementation of Article 2 by State Parties," UN Committee Against Torture, CAT/C/GC/2, January 24, 2008, ¶7.

61. "Convention Relating to the Status of Refugees," Art. 31(1).

62. 1917 Immigration Act, 39 Stat. 877.

63. Tatiana Schaufuss, "The White Russian Refugees," *The Annals of the American Academy of Political and Social Science 203* (May 1939): p. 52.

64. 1948 Displaced Persons Act, Pub. L. No. 80-744, 62 Stat. 1009.

65. 1953 Refugee Relief Act, Pub. L. No. 83-203, 67 Stat. 40.0

66. Cuban Adjustment Act of 1966, Pub. L. No. 89-732, 80 Stat. 1161.

67. Indochina Migration and Refugee Assistance Act of 1975, Pub. L. No. 94-23, 89 Stat. 87. See Norman L. Zucker and Naomi Flink Zucker, *The Guarded Gate: The Reality of American Refugee Policy* (San Diego: Harcourt Brace Jovanovich, 1987); Carl J. Bon Tempo, *Americans at the Gate: The United States and Refugees during the Cold War* (Princeton: Princeton University Press, 2008).

68. 1965 Immigration and Nationality Act, Pub. L. No. 89-236, 79 Stat. 911.

69. Subversive Activities Control Act of 1950, Pub. L. No. 81-831, 64 Stat. 1010, §23.

70. 66 Stat. 214, §243(h).

71. 79 Stat. 918, §11(f).

72. 66 Stat. 214, §243(h); *INS v. Stevic*, 467 U.S. 407 (1984).

73. 66 Stat. 188, §212(d)(5). See Christopher T. Hanson, "Behind the Paper Curtain: Asylum Policy Versus Asylum Practice," *NYU Review of Law and Social Change 7*, no. 1 (1978): pp. 107–141.

74. 79 Stat. 913, §203(a)(7). See Gil Loescher and John A. Scanlan, *Calculated Kindness: Refugees and America's Half-open Door, 1945 to the Present* (New York: Free Press, 1986); see Zucker and Zucker, *The Guarded Gate*, Bon Tempo, *Americans at the Gate*, and María Cristina García, *The Refugee Challenge in Post-Cold War America* (New York: Oxford University Press, 2017) for the post–World War II history of U.S. policy.

75. *Attempted defection by Lithuanian Seaman Simas Kudirka: Hearings before the Subcommittee on State Department Organization and Foreign Operations of the Committee on Foreign Affairs, House of Representatives*, 91st Cong., 2nd Sess. (1971).

76. Richard K. Rein, "He Risked His Life to Leave Russia," *People*, October 13, 1980; Rebecca Hamlin and Philip E. Wolgin, "Symbolic Politics and Policy Feedback: The United Nations Protocol Relating to the Status of Refugees and American Refugee Policy in the Cold War," *International Migration Review* 46, no. 3 (2012): pp. 603–604.

77. Hamlin and Wolgin, "Symbolic Politics and Policy Feedback," 586–587.

78. *Matter of Dunar*, 14 I&N Dec. 310, 320 (BIA 1973).

79. Hamlin and Wolgin, "Symbolic Politics and Policy Feedback," 602.

80. 94 Stat. 105; 8 U.S.C. §1158.

81. 94 Stat. 107; *INS v. Stevic*, 467 U.S. 407, 408 (1984).

82. Hamlin and Wolgin, "Symbolic Politics and Policy Feedback," 615.

83. *Nishimura Ekiu v. United States*, 142 U.S. 651 (1892); *Chae Chan Ping v. United States* 130 U.S. 581 (1889); See Peter H. Schuck, "The Transformation of Immigration Law," *Columbia Law Review* 84, no. 1 (1984): pp. 1–90.

84. *Chehazeh v. Attorney General*, 666 F.3d 118, 145 (3d Cir. 2012).

85. Hiroshi Motomura, *Americans in Waiting: The Lost Story of Immigration and Citizenship in the United States* (New York: Oxford University Press, 2006).

86. Dirks, *Canada's Refugee Policy*, 156.

87. Dirks, *Canada's Refugee Policy*, 154, 180–182; Donald Galloway, *Essentials of Canadian Law: Immigration Law* (Concord, ON: Irwin Law, 1997), pp. 17–18; James C. Hathaway, "The Conundrum of Refugee Protection in Canada: From Control to Compliance to Collective Deterrence," *Journal of Policy History* 4, no. 1 (1992): pp. 71–92.

88. Aristide R. Zolberg, "Response to Crisis: Refugee Policy in the United States and Canada," in *Immigration, Language, and Ethnicity: Canada and the United States*, edited by Barry R. Chiswick (Washington, DC: AEI Press, 1992), pp. 65–66.

89. Galloway, *Essentials of Canadian Law*, 17–18; Dirks, *Canada's Refugee Policy*, 246.

90. Rebecca Hamlin, *Let Me Be a Refugee: Administrative Justice and the Politics of Asylum in the United States, Canada, and Australia* (New York: Oxford University Press, 2014), pp. 46–47.

91. *Singh v Canada (Minister of Employment and Immigration)*, [1985] 1 S.C.R. 177.

92. Meryll Dean and Miki Nagashima, "Sharing the Burden: The Role of Government and NGOs in Protecting and Providing for Asylum Seekers and Refugees in Japan," *Journal of Refugee Studies* 20, no. 3 (2007): pp. 481–508; Koichi Koizumi, "Refugee Policy Formation in Japan: Developments and Implications," *Journal of Refugee Studies* 5, no. 2 (1992): p. 123; Michael Strausz, "International Pressure and Domestic Precedent: Japan's Resettlement of Indochinese Refugees," *Asian Journal of Political Science* 20, no. 3 (2012): pp. 244–266; Sayuri Umeda, "Refugee Law and

Policy: Japan," The Law Library of Congress, 2016, https://www.loc.gov/law/help/refugee-law/japan.php#_ftn5.

93. Umeda, "Refugee Law and Policy: Japan,"

94. UNHCR Population Statistics, 2017, http://popstats.unhcr.org/en/asylum_seekers.

95. UNHCR Donor Profile, 2017, http://reporting.unhcr.org/donor-profiles.

96. In-seop Chung, "Korean Practice on Refugee Reception," *Seoul International Law Journal 16*, no. 1 (2009): pp. 197–222. [In Korean]

97. "[Statistics] Domestic Refugee Status (As of 12.31.2016)," Nancen: Refugee Human Rights Center, April 11, 2017, http://nancen.org/1598. [In Korean]

98. Jin-Heon Jung, "North Korean Migrants in South Korea: From Heroes to Burdens and First Unifiers," in *Multiethnic Korea? Multiculturalism, Migration, and Peoplehood Diversity in Contemporary Korea*, edited by J. Lie (Berkeley: Institute of East Asian Studies, University of California, Berkeley, 2014), pp. 142–164.

99. "South Korea Welcomes 30 Myanmar Refugees from Thailand," International Organization for Migration, July 28, 2017, https://www.iom.int/news/south-korea-welcomes-30-myanmar-refugees-thailand.

100. UNHCR Donor Profile, 2017, http://reporting.unhcr.org/donor-profiles.

101. Kristin Surak, "Convergence in Foreigners' Rights and Citizenship Policies? A Look at Japan," *International Migration Review 42*, no. 3 (2008): pp. 550–575.

102. Dong-Hoon Seol and John D. Skrentny, "Why Is There So Little Migrant Settlement in East Asia?" *International Migration Review 43*, no. 3 (2009): pp. 578–620.

103. Akashi Junichi, "Challenging Japans Refugee Policies," *Asian and Pacific Migration Journal 15*, no. 2 (2006): pp. 219–238.

104. Mariano-Florentino Cuéllar, "Refugee Security and the Organizational Logic of Legal Mandates," *Georgetown Journal of International Law 37* (2005): pp. 583–723.

105. "Transcript of Reagan's Speech at Air Base after His Visit to the Cemetery," *New York Times*, May 6, 1985, http://www.nytimes.com/1985/05/06/world/transcript-of-reagan-s-speech-at-air-base-after-his-visit-to-the-cemetery.html?pagewanted=all.

Chapter 3

1. Valsamis Mitsilegas, "Extraterritorial Immigration Control in the 21st Century: The Individual and the State Transformed," in *Extraterritorial Immigration Control: Legal Challenge*, edited by Bernard Ryan and Valsamis Mitsilegas (Leiden: Martinus Nijhoff, 2010), pp. 38–64; B. S. Chimni, "The Geopolitics of Refugee Studies: A View from the South," *Journal of Refugee Studies 11*, no. 4 (1998): pp. 350–374; Jennifer Hyndman and Alison Mountz, "Another Brick in the Wall? Neo-*Refoulement* and the Externalization of Asylum by Australia and Europe," *Government and Opposition 43*, no. 2 (2008): p. 253.

2. Phil Orchard, *A Right to Flee: Refugees, States, and the Construction of International Cooperation* (Cambridge: Cambridge University Press, 2014), p. 142.

3. "Hungarian Communist Agents Pose as Refugees," CIA, May 15, 1951, https://www.cia.gov/library/readingroom/docs/CIA-RDP80-00809A000600390323-0.pdf; "United States Escapee Program, Report to Operations Coordinating Board," Office for Refugees, Migration, and Voluntary Assistance, August 17, 1954, p. 16, https://www.cia.gov/library/readingroom/document/cia-rdp80-01065a000200040003-9.pdf.

4. "Convention Relating to the Status of Refugees," July 28, 1951, *United Nations Treaty Series*, vol. 189, p. 137, Art. 33 (2).

5. Alex Nowrasteh, "Terrorism and Immigration: A Risk Analysis," Cato Institute, September 13, 2016, https://object.cato.org/sites/cato.org/files/pubs/pdf/pa798_1_1.pdf.

6. Matt Schudel, "Omar Abdel Rahman, Imprisoned 'Blind Sheikh' Linked to Terrorist Efforts, Dies at 78," *Washington Post*, February 18, 2017, https://www.washingtonpost.com/world/omar-abdel-rahman-blind-sheik-convicted-in-1993-world-trade-center-attack-dies-at-78/2017/02/18/807c4f2c-f603-11e6-8d72-263470bf0401_story.html?utm_term=.bed5a73b6469.

7. Fred Burton, "U.S. Border Security: Looking North," *Stratfor*, May 6, 2006, https://www.stratfor.com/analysis/us-border-security-looking-north.

8. "Key Issues: Asylum and Security," Information Centre about Asylum and Refugees, December 2006, p. 1, http://icar.livingrefugeearchive.org/asylum%20and%20security.pdf.

9. Anthony Faiola and Souad Mekhennet, "Tracing the Path of Four Terrorists Sent to Europe by the Islamic State," *Washington Post*, April 22, 2016, https://www.washingtonpost.com/world/national-security/how-europes-migrant-crisis-became-an-opportunity-for-isis/2016/04/21/ec8a7231-062d-4185-bb27-cc7295d35415_story.html?utm_term=.a1c243e29c31.

10. "Global Study Shows Many around the World Uncomfortable with Levels of Immigration," Ipsos, August 10, 2016, https://www.ipsos.com/sites/default/files/migrations/en-uk/files/Assets/Docs/Polls/ipsos-global-advisor-immigration-and-refugees-2016-charts.pdf.

11. Liz Robbins and Miriam Jordan, "Apartments Are Stocked, Toys Donated. Only the Refugees Are Missing," *New York Times*, May 16, 2018; "For the first time, U.S. resettles fewer refugees than the rest of the world," Pew Research Center, July 5, 2018, http://www.pewresearch.org/fact-tank/2018/07/05/for-the-first-time-u-s-resettles-fewer-refugees-than-the-rest-of-the-world/.

12. *Trump v. Hawaii*, 585 U.S. (2018); Executive Order 13769, "Executive Order Protecting the Nation from Foreign Terrorist Entry into the United States," January 27, 2017; Executive Order 13780, "Executive Order Protecting the Nation from Foreign Terrorist Entry into the United States," March 6, 2017.

13. B. S. Chimni, "The Geopolitics of Refugee Studies: A View from the South," *Journal of Refugee Studies* 11, no. 4 (1998): pp. 350–374; Matthew Gibney, "A Thousand Little Guantanamos: Western States and Measures to Prevent the Arrival of Refugees," in *Displacement, Asylum, Migration: The Oxford Amnesty Lectures 2004*, edited by Kate E. Tunstall (New York: Oxford University Press, 2006), pp. 139–169. On the Cold War origins of the refugee regime, see Gil Loescher, *Beyond Charity: International Cooperation and the Global Refugee Crisis* (New York: Oxford University Press, 1993).

14. Kenneth W. Abbott, "International Relations Theory, International Law, and the Regime Governing Atrocities in Internal Conflicts," *The American Journal of International Law* 93, no. 2 (1999).

15. "Convention Relating to the Status of Refugees," July 28, 1951, *United Nations Treaty Series*, vol. 189, p. 137, Art. 1(B).

16. David Scott FitzGerald and David Cook-Martín, *Culling the Masses: The Democratic Origins of Racist Immigration Policy in the Americas* (Cambridge, MA: Harvard University Press, 2014); Laura Madokoro, *Elusive Refuge: Chinese Migrants in the Cold War* (Cambridge, MA: Harvard University Press, 2016).

17. Seth M. Holmes and Heide Castañeda, "Representing the 'European Refugee Crisis' in Germany and beyond: Deservingness and Difference, Life and Death," *American Ethnologist 43*, no. 1 (2016): pp. 12–24.

18. Myria Georgiou and Rafal Zaborowski, "Media Coverage of the 'Refugee Crisis': A Cross-European Perspective," *Council of Europe Report* (2017); Holmes and Castañeda, "Representing the 'European Refugee Crisis,'" 12–24.

19. Li Nguyen and Kerry McCallum, "Drowning in Our Own Home: A Metaphor-Led Discourse Analysis of Australian News Media Reporting on Maritime Asylum Seekers," *Communication Research and Practice 2*, no. 2 (2016): pp. 159–176.

20. Kerstin Lueck, Clemence Due, and Martha Augoustinos, "Neoliberalism and Nationalism: Representations of Asylum Seekers in the Australian Mainstream News Media," *Discourse & Society 26*, no. 5 (2015): pp. 608–629.

21. Cheryl M. R. Sulaiman-Hill et al., "Changing Images of Refugees: A Comparative Analysis of Australian and New Zealand Print Media 1998–2008," *Journal of Immigrant & Refugee Studies 9*, no. 4 (2011): pp. 345–366.

22. Augie Fleras, *Immigration Canada: Evolving Realities and Emerging Challenges in a Postnational World* (Vancouver: UBC Press, 2015); Victoria M. Esses, Stelian Medianu, and Andrea S. Lawson, "Uncertainty, Threat, and the Role of the Media in Promoting the Dehumanization of Immigrants and Refugees," *Journal of Social Issues 69*, no. 3 (2013) pp. 518–536.

23. "Convention Relating to the Status of Refugees," July 28, 1951, *United Nations Treaty Series*, vol. 189, p. 137, Art 31.

24. Costas Gabrielatos and Paul Baker, "Fleeing, Sneaking, Flooding a Corpus Analysis of Discursive Constructions of Refugees and Asylum Seekers in the UK Press, 1996–2005," *Journal of English Linguistics 36*, no. 1 (2008): pp. 5–38.

25. Matthew J. Gibney, *The Ethics and Politics of Asylum: Liberal Democracy and the Response to Refugees* (Cambridge: Cambridge University Press, 2004).

26. Jaya Ramji-Nogales, Andrew Ian Schoenholtz, and Philip G. Schrag, *Refugee Roulette: Disparities in Asylum Adjudication and Proposals for Reform* (New York: New York University Press, 2009).

27. U.S. Government Accountability Office (GAO), "U.S. Asylum System: Significant Variation Existed in Asylum Outcomes across Immigration Courts and Judges," September 2008, http://www.gao.gov/new.items/d08940.pdf; GAO, "Asylum: Variation Exists in Outcomes of Applications across Immigration Courts and Judges," November 2016, https://www.gao.gov/assets/690/680976.pdf. Defensive applicants are in deportation proceedings. Affirmative applicants are not in deportation proceedings and normally have one year within arriving in the United States to file for asylum.

28. James C. Hathaway, "The Emerging Politics of Non-Entrée," *Refugees 91* (1992): pp. 41; Gibney, *The Ethics and Politics of Asylum*, 126.

29. Gil Loescher, *The UNHCR and World Politics: A Perilous Path* (New York: Oxford University Press, 2001), p. 229.

30. See Merritt Roe Smith and Leo Marx, *Does Technology Drive History? The Dilemma of Technological Determinism* (Cambridge: MIT Press, 1994) on technological determinism.

31. My understanding of institutionalism is indebted to Rogers Brubaker, *Citizenship and Nationhood in France and Germany* (Cambridge, MA: Harvard University Press, 1992), Walter W. Paul and Paul DiMaggio, *The New Institutionalism in Organizational Analysis* (Chicago: University of Chicago Press, 1991), and Paul Pierson, *Politics in Time: History, Institutions, and Social Analysis* (Princeton: Princeton University Press, 2004). See the discussion of policy diffusion in David Cook-Martín and David Scott FitzGerald, "How Their Laws Affect Our Laws: Mechanisms of Immigration Policy Diffusion in the Americas, 1790–2010" *Law and Society Review* (2019, forthcoming).

32. John C. Torpey, *The Invention of the Passport: Surveillance, Citizenship and the State* (Cambridge: Cambridge University Press, 2000).

33. Rey Koslowski, "The International Travel Regimes," in *Global Mobility Regimes*, edited by Rey Koslowski (New York: Palgrave Macmillan, 2011), pp. 51–72.

34. Bernard Ryan, "Extraterritorial Immigration Controls: What Role for Legal Guarantees?" In *Extraterritorial Immigration Control: Legal Challenges*, edited by Bernard Ryan and Valsamis Mitsilegas (Leiden: Martinus Nijhoff, 2010) p. 5.

35. Orchard, *A Right to Flee*, 242.

36. Irial Glynn, *Asylum Policy, Boat People and Political Discourse: Boats, Votes and Asylum in Australia and Italy* (London: Palgrave Macmillan, 2016).

37. Maurizio Albahari, *Crimes of Peace: Mediterranean Migrations at the World's Deadliest Border* (Philadelphia: University of Pennsylvania Press, 2015), p. 71; Alison Mountz, *Seeking Asylum: Human Smuggling and Bureaucracy at the Border* (Minneapolis: University of Minnesota Press, 2010), p. xv.

38. "UNHCR Global Trends in Forced Displacement 2017, Annex Table 26," UNHCR, http://www.unhcr.org/statistics/17-WRD-tab_v3_external.zip.

39. Klaus Neumann, *Across the Seas: Australia's Response to Refugees: A History* (Victoria: Black, 2015), p. 276.

40. Susan Kneebone, ed., *Refugees, Asylum Seekers and the Rule of Law: Comparative Perspectives* (Cambridge: Cambridge University Press, 2009), p. 177.

41. Glynn, *Asylum Policy*, 132.

42. Ruben Zaiotti, ed., *Externalizing Migration Management: Europe, North America and the Spread of Remote Control Practices* (London: Routledge, 2016), p. 6.

43. Christina Boswell and Andrew Geddes, *Migration and Mobility in the European Union* (New York: Palgrave Macmillan, 2011).

44. Sabine Hess, "'We Are Facilitating States!' An Ethnographic Analysis of the ICMPD," in *The Politics of International Migration Management*, edited by Martin Geiger and Antoine Pécoud (New York: Palgrave Macmillan, 2010), pp. 96–118.

45. Heather Grabbe, "The Sharp Edges of Europe: Extending Schengen Eastwards," *International Affairs* 76, no. 3 (2000): pp. 528–529.

46. "Establishing a U.S.-EU Migration Dialogue," Wikleaks, November 24, 2009, https://wikileaks.org/plusd/cables/09BRUSSELS1584_a.html; FitzGerald and Cook-Martín, *Culling the Masses*. Daniel Ghezelbash, *Refuge Lost: Asylum Law in an Interdependent World* (Cambridge: Cambridge University Press, 2018).

47. Virginie Guiraudon and Gallya Lahav, "A Reappraisal of the State Sovereignty Debate: The Case of Migration Control," *Comparative Political Studies 33*, no. 2 (2000): p. 60.

48. Martin Geiger and Antoine Pécoud, "The Politics of International Migration Management," in *The Politics of International Migration Management*, edited by Martin Geiger and Antoine Pécoud (New York: Palgrave Macmillan, 2010), p. 5.

49. Douglas S. Massey et al., *Worlds in Motion: Understanding International Migration at the End of the Millennium* (New York: Oxford University Press, 1998), p. 290.

50. Wayne A. Cornelius et al., eds., *Controlling Immigration: A Global Perspective*, 2nd ed. (Stanford: Stanford University Press, 2004).

51. Saskia Sassen, *Globalization and Its Discontents* (New York: The New Press, 1998).

52. Guiraudon and Lahav, "A Reappraisal of the State Sovereignty Debate," 164; See also Rebecca Adler-Nissen and Thomas Gammeltoft-Hansen, "An Introduction to Sovereignty Games," in *Sovereignty Games: Instrumentalizing State Sovereignty in Europe and Beyond*, edited by Rebecca Adler-Nissen and Thomas Gammeltoft-Hansen (London: Palgrave Macmillan, 2008), p. 15.

53. Michelle Foster and Jason Pobjoy, "A Failed Case of Legal Exceptionalism? Refugee Status Determination in Australia's 'Excised' Territory," *International Journal of Refugee Law 23*, no. 4 (2011): pp. 583–631.

54. Guy S. Goodwin-Gill and Jane McAdam, *The Refugee in International Law* (New York: Oxford University Press, 2007), p. 390.

55. Thomas Gammeltoft-Hansen and James C. Hathaway, "Non-Refoulement in a World of Cooperative Deterrence," *Columbia Journal of Transnational Law 53* (2015): p. 235.

56. Stephen H. Legomsky, "Secondary Refugee Movements and the Return of Asylum Seekers to Third Countries: The Meaning of Effective Protection," *International Journal of Refugee Law 15*, no. 4 (2003): p. 568.

57. Maarten den Heijer, *Europe and Extraterritorial Asylum* (Oxford: Hart, 2012).

58. Hans J. Morgenthau, *Politics among Nations: The Struggle for Power and Peace*, 5th ed. (New York: Knopf, 1978), p. 560.

59. Eric A. Posner, *The Twilight of Human Rights Law* (New York: Oxford University Press, 2014), p. 7. For a vigorous and compelling rebuttal, see Kathryn Sikkink, *Evidence for Hope: Making Human Rights Work in the 21st Century* (Princeton: Princeton University Press, 2017).

60. Claire Inder, "International Refugee Law, 'Hyper-Legalism' and Migration Management: The Pacific Solution," in *The Politics of International Migration Management*, edited by Martin Geiger and Antoine Pécoud (New York: Palgrave Macmillan, 2010), p. 221; See also Guiraudon and Lahav, "A Reappraisal of the State Sovereignty Debate," 163–195; Hyndman and Mountz, "Another Brick in the Wall?," 249–269.

61. Neil Siegel, "Political Norms, Constitutional Conventions, and President Donald Trump," *Indiana Law Journal 93*, no. 1 (2018): pp. 177–205.

62. @realDonaldTrump Twitter feed, June 24, 2018, https://twitter.com/realdonaldtrump/status/1010900865602019329?lang=en.

63. Gammeltoft-Hansen and Hathaway, "Non-Refoulement in a World of Cooperative Deterrence," 235.

64. Thomas Gammeltoft-Hansen, *Access to Asylum: International Refugee Law and the Globalisation of Migration Control* (Cambridge: Cambridge University Press, 2011).

65. James F. Hollifield, "Migration and International Relations: Cooperation and Control in the European Community," *International Migration Review 26*, no. 2 (1992): pp. 568–595.

66. Christian Joppke, *Immigration and the Nation-State: The United States, Germany, and Great Britain* (New York: Oxford University Press, 1999); Christina Boswell and Andrew Geddes, *Migration and Mobility in the European Union* (New York: Palgrave Macmillan, 2011).

67. Yasemin N. Soysal, *Limits of Citizenship: Migrants and Postnational Membership in Europe* (Chicago: University of Chicago Press, 1994); David Jacobson, *Rights across Borders: Immigration and the Decline of Citizenship* (Baltimore: Johns Hopkins University Press, 1996).

68. Christian Joppke, "Immigration Challenges the Nation-State," in *Challenge to the Nation-State: Immigration in Western Europe and the United States*, edited by Christian Joppke (New York: Oxford University Press, 1998); Guiraudon and Lahav, "A Reappraisal of the State Sovereignty Debate," 163–195; Gary P. Freeman and Bob Birrell, "Divergent Paths of Immigration Politics in the United States and Australia," *Population and Development Review 27*, no. 3 (2001): pp. 525–551.

69. Rebecca Hamlin and Philip E. Wolgin, "Symbolic Politics and Policy Feedback: The United Nations Protocol Relating to the Status of Refugees and American Refugee Policy in the Cold War," *International Migration Review 46*, no. 3 (2012): pp. 619–620.

70. "Convention for the Unification of Certain Rules with Respect to Assistance and Salvage at Sea," September 23, 1910, 37 Stat. 1658. Art. 11; "International Convention for the Safety of Life at Sea," November 1, 1974, Ch. 5, Reg. 10; "International Convention on Maritime Search and Rescue," April 27, 1979; "Convention on the Law of the Sea," December 10, 1982, *United Nations Treaty Series*, vol. 1833, p. 3, Art. 98.

71. Guiraudon and Lahav, "A Reappraisal of the State Sovereignty Debate," 181.

72. Den Heijer, "Europe and Extraterritorial Asylum," 234–238, 242

73. "Convention on the Law of the Sea," December 10, 1982, *United Nations Treaty Series*, vol. 1833, p. 3, Art. 19 and 33.

74. Thomas C. Schelling, "The Life You Save May Be Your Own," in *Problems in Public Expenditure Analysis: Studies of Government Finance*, edited by Samuel B. Chase, Jr. (Washington, DC: Brookings Institution, 1968); Carlo Ginzburg, "Killing a Chinese Mandarin: The Moral Implications of Distance," *Critical Inquiry 21*, no. 1 (1994): pp. 46–60.

75. Peter Stamatov, "Activist Religion, Empire, and the Emergence of Modern Long-Distance Advocacy Networks," *American Sociological Review 75*, no. 4 (2010): pp. 607–628; Michael Barnett, *Empire of Humanity: A History of Humanitarianism* (Ithaca: Cornell University Press, 2011).

76. Margaret E. Keck and Kathryn Sikkink, *Activists Beyond Borders* (New York: Cornell University Press, 1998), p. 9.

77. Samuel Moyn, *The Last Utopia: Human Rights in History* (Cambridge, MA: Harvard University Press, 2010). Sikkink, *Evidence for Hope*, disputes Moyn's timing of the institutionalization of human rights but not the important role of NGOs.

78. See the general discussion in Keck and Sikkink, *Activists Beyond Borders*, 10, 16, 19, 21.

79. Keck and Sikkink, *Activists Beyond Borders*, 27–29.

80. On how branding has historically influenced U.S., Canadian, and Latin American immigration and refugee policies, see FitzGerald and Cook-Martín, *Culling the Masses*.

81. Guiraudon and Lahav, "A Reappraisal of the State Sovereignty Debate," 163–195.

82. "Obstacle Course to Europe: A Policy-made Humanitarian Crisis at EU Borders," Medecins Sans Frontieres, January 2016, http://www.msf.org/sites/msf.org/files/msf_obstacle_course_to_europe_0.pdf; Barnett, *Empire of Humanity*, 210–211.

83. Loescher, *The UNHCR and World Politics*.

84. "Funding UNHCR's Programmes," UNHCR, http://www.unhcr.org/4a2fb7a86.pdf; "Contributions to UNHCR, 2017," UNHCR, http://www.unhcr.org/5954c4257.html.

85. Gil Loescher, Alexander Betts, and James Milner, *The United Nations High Commissioner for Refugees (UNHCR): The Politics and Practice of Refugee Protection* (New York: Routledge, 2012), p. 94.

86. John Telford, "Evaluation of UNHCR's Role in Strengthening National NGOs," UNHCR Evaluation and Policy Analysis Unit, January 2001, http://www.unhcr.org/3b0a2a5512.pdf.

87. Susan Kneebone, "The Bali Process and Global Refugee Policy in the Asia–Pacific Region," *Journal of Refugee Studies 27*, no. 4 (2014): p. 610.

88. Peter Van Ham, "Place Branding: The State of the Art," *The Annals of the American Academy of Political and Social Science 616*, no. 1 (2008): pp. 126–149.

89. Stephen D. Krasner, "Compromising Westphalia," *International Security 20*, no. 3 (1995–1996): pp. 115–151,; David FitzGerald, "Citizenship à la Carte: Emigration and the Strengthening of the Sovereign State," in *Politics from Afar: Transnational Diasporas and Networks*, edited by Peter Mandaville and Terrence Lyons (New York: Columbia University Press, 2012).

90. David A. Lake, *Hierarchy in International Relations* (Cornell University Press, 2009).

91. James F. Hollifield, "The Emerging Migration State," *International Migration Review 38*, no. 3 (2004): p. 891.

Chapter 4

1. Emma Lazarus, "The New Colossus," (1883).

2. Christopher T. Hanson, "Behind the Paper Curtain: Asylum Policy Versus Asylum Practice," *NYU Review of Law and Social Change 7*, no. 1 (1978): p. 125.

3. Cited in Nevzat Soguk, *States and Strangers: Refugees and Displacements of Statecraft* (Minneapolis: University of Minnesota Press, 1999), p. 132.

4. Rey Koslowski, "The U.S. Visa Waiver Program and the Management of Mobility Across the Atlantic," in *Externalizing Migration Management: Europe,*

North America and the Spread of "Remote Control" Practices, edited by Ruben Zaiotti (London: Routledge, 2016), pp. 180–182.

5. Scott D. Watson, *The Securitization of Humanitarian Migration: Digging Moats and Sinking Boats* (New York: Routledge, 2009), pp. 121–125.

6. Anna Pratt, *Securing Borders: Detention and Deportation in Canada* (Vancouver: UBC Press, 2005), p. 99.

7. *Singh v Canada (Minister of Employment and Immigration)*, [1985] 1 S.C.R. 177.

8. Randy Lippert, "Canadian Refugee Determination and Advanced Liberal Government," *Canadian Journal of Law & Society 13*, no. 2 (1998): p. 192.

9. Mark B. Salter and Can E. Mutlu, "Asymmetric Borders: The Canada-Czech Republic 'Visa War' and the Question of Rights," *Centre for European Policy Studies Paper in Liberty and Security in Europe* (November 2010): pp. 2, 8, 11; Howard Adelman, "Canadian Borders and Immigration Post 9/11," *International Migration Review 36,* no. 1 (2002): p. 26.

10. "Asylum Claims from the Americas," Wikileaks, June 9, 2008, https://wikileaks.org/plusd/cables/08OTTAWA774_a.html; Liette Gilbert, "Visas as Technologies in the Externalization of Asylum Management: The Case of Canada's Entry Requirements for Mexican Nationals," in *Externalizing Migration Management: Europe, North America and the Spread of "Remote Control" Practices,* edited by Ruben Zaiotti (New York: Routledge, 2016), pp. 205–209, 213; Protecting Canada's Immigration System Act, 2012 S.C., c. 17; Ashifa Kassam, "Canada Prepares for Surge of Mexican Immigrants after Visa Lift and Trump Win," *The Guardian,* December 1, 2016, https://www.theguardian.com/world/2016/dec/01/canada-mexico-immigrants-visas-asylum-tourism.

11. "Department of Homeland Security Secretary Chertoff Maintains the Dialogue with Counterpart Deputy Prime Minister McLellan," Wikileaks, March 23, 2005, https://wikileaks.org/plusd/cables/05OTTAWA875_a.html.

12. "Ministers Hussen, Garneau and Goodale Provided an Update on Progress Regarding Asylum Seekers in Quebec and Announced New Outreach Initiatives in Nigeria," Government of Canada news release, May 7, 2018, https://www.canada.ca/en/immigration-refugees-citizenship/news/2018/05/ministers-hussen-garneau-and-goodale-provided-an-update-on-progress-regarding-asylum-seekers-in-quebec-and-announced-new-outreach-initiatives-in-ni.html; "Nigeria to Help Bust 'Myths' about Illegal Border Crossings into Canada," CBC News, May 18, 2018, http://www.cbc.ca/news/politics/hussen-nigeria-asylum-seekers-1.4668579.

13. *Testimony of Ms. Elizabeth A. Whitaker, Deputy Assistant Secretary for Mexico, Canada, and Public Diplomacy, Bureau of Western Hemisphere Affairs, U.S. Department of State: U.S.-Mexico Relations: Hearing before the Subcommittee on the Western Hemisphere of the Committee on International Relations, House of Representatives,* 109th Cong., 2nd Sess., April 26, 2006.

14. Ann Kimball, "The Transit State: A Comparative Analysis of Mexican and Moroccan Immigration Policies," Working Paper no. 150, Center for Comparative Immigration Studies, University of California, San Diego, 2007, p. 103.

15. "Lineamientos para tramites y procedimientos migratorios," *Diario Oficial de la Federación,* November 8, 2012, Art. 26.

16. Michael Flynn, "¿Dónde está LA FRONTERA?" *Bulletin of the Atomic Scientists* 58, no. 4 (2002): p. 29.

17. Manuel Ángel Castillo, "Las políticas hacia la migración centroamericana en países de origen, de destino y de tránsito," *Papeles de población 6* (2000): p. 145.

18. "Visit Nicaragua! No Visa Needed," Wikileaks, March 19, 2009, https://wikileaks.org/plusd/cables/09MANAGUA301_a.html.

19. Luisa Feline Freier, "A Reverse Migration Paradox? Policy Liberalisation and New South-South Migration to Latin America" (PhD diss., London School of Economics, 2016).

20. Ruben Zaiotti, ed. *Externalizing Migration Management: Europe, North America and the Spread of "Remote Control" Practices* (London: Routledge, 2016), and Georg Menz, "Neoliberalism, Privatisation and the Outsourcing of Migration Management: A Five Country Comparison," *Competition & Change 15*, no. 2 (2011): pp. 116–135; note 2 date carrier sanctions to the 1990s and 1902, respectively.

21. 1882 Immigration Act, 22 Stat. 215 §4.

22. 1891 Immigration Act, 26 Stat. 1086 §10; Torsten Feys, *The Battle for the Migrants: The Introduction of Steamshipping on the North Atlantic and Its Impact on the European Exodus* (St. John's: International Maritime Economic History Association, 2013), p. 228.

23. 43 Stat. 163 ¶16.

24. 8 U.S.C. §§1321–23.

25. Erika Feller, "Carrier Sanctions and International Law," *International Journal of Refugee Law 1*, no. 1 (1989): p. 52; Immigration Act 1976 as amended, §§86, 87, 93, 94, 99 (Can.); Bill C-55, An Act to Amend the Immigration Act of 1976, clause 22 (Can).

26. Bernard Ryan, "Extraterritorial Immigration Controls: What Role for Legal Guarantees?," in *Extraterritorial Immigration Control: Legal Challenges*, edited by Bernard Ryan and Valsamis Mitsilegas (Leiden: Martinus Nijhoff, 2010), p. 20.

27. Vic Satzewich, *Points of Entry: How Canada's Immigration Officers Decide Who Gets In* (Vancouver: UBC Press, 2015), p. 100.

28. Anna Pratt, *Securing Borders: Detention and Deportation in Canada* (Vancouver: UBC Press, 2005), p. 202.

29. "Alien Smuggling," Presidential Decision Directive/ NSC-9, June 18, 1993, p. 3.

30. Paul Behrens, "The Law of Diplomatic Asylum: A Contextual Approach," *Michigan Journal of International Law 35* (2013): pp. 319–367.

31. "2008–9 Departmental Performance Report," Canada Border Services Agency, https://www.tbs-sct.gc.ca/dpr-rmr/2008-2009/inst/bsf/bsf02-eng.asp.

32. "2000 Canada-United States Accord on Our Shared Border," Minister of Public Works and Government Services Canada, https://www.publicsafety.gc.ca/lbrr/archives/cn63684181-eng.pdf., p. 32.

33. Howard Adelman, "Canadian Borders and Immigration Post 9/11," *International Migration Review 36*, no. 1 (2002): pp. 15–28.

34. *Written Testimony of Alan D. Bersin, Assistant Secretary for International Affairs, U.S. Department of Homeland Security, before the House Committee on Foreign Affairs Subcommittee on the Western Hemisphere on "Potential Terrorist Threats: Border Security Challenges in Latin America and the Caribbean,"* 114th Cong., 2nd Sess. (March 22, 2016), pp. 2–3.

35. "2014 Beyond the Border Implementation Report to Leaders," The White House, 2015, https://obamawhitehouse.archives.gov/sites/default/files/docs/15-0745_btb_implementation_report_2014_-_final_03.20.15_v3_clean.pdf.

36. *Testimony of Michael Fisher, Chief United States Border Patrol U.S. Customs and Border Protection, DHS, before Subcommittee on Border, Maritime, and Global Counterterrorism of the Committee on Homeland Security, House of Representatives,* 111th Cong., 2nd Sess., July 22, 2010.

37. As of 2004, the "special interest countries" were Afghanistan, Kuwait, Somalia, Algeria, Lebanon, Sudan, Bahrain, Libya, Syria, Bangladesh, Malaysia, Tajikistan, Djibouti, Mauritania, Thailand, Egypt, Morocco, Tunisia, Eritrea, North Korea, Turkey, Indonesia, Oman, Turkmenistan, Iran, Pakistan, United Arab Emirates, Iraq, Philippines, Uzbekistan, Jordan, Qatar, Yemen, Kazakhstan, Saudi Arabia, and the Territories of Gaza and the West Bank (Doyle E. Amidon Jr., "U.S. Response to Special Interest Aliens, A Collaborative Effort," Strategy Research Project Report, U.S. Army War College, 2008, p. 1).

38. "DHS Secretary Chertoff in Mexico, February 15–16: Meetings with Interior, Treasury Officials," Wikileaks, February 26, 2007, https://wikileaks.org/plusd/cables/07mexico0965_a.html.

39. *Written Testimony of Alan D. Bersin,* March 22, 2016.

40. "Engaging the New Mexican Administration on Immigration and Border Security," Wikileaks, June 15, 2006, https://wikileaks.org/plusd/cables/06MEXICO3305_a.html.

41. *Written Testimony of Alan D. Bersin,* March 22, 2016, 6–8.

42. *Written Testimony of Alan D. Bersin,* March 22, 2016.

43. Thomas Gammeltoft-Hansen and Ninna Nyberg Sorensen, *The Migration Industry and the Commercialization of International Migration* (New York: Routledge, 2013).

44. Flynn, "¿Dónde está LA FRONTERA?," 25–35.

45. Martha Lorena Suazo, "Estudio Migratorio de Honduras," in *Estudio Comparativo de la Legislación y Políticas Migratorias en Centroamérica, México y República Dominicana,* edited by Gisele L. Bonnici and Elba Y. Coria (Guatemala City: Instituto Centroamericano de Estudios Sociales y Desarrollo, 2011).

46. Brook Larmer, "Smuggling People," *Newsweek,* March 16, 1997.

47. "Honduran Immigration: The Problems Persist, but with a Roadmap for Zelaya Administration to Reform," Wikileaks, February 13, 2006, https://wikileaks.org/plusd/cables/06TEGUCIGALPA268_a.html.

48. *Border Security and Deterring Illegal Entry into the United States: Hearing before the Subcommittee on Immigration and Claims of the Committee on the Judiciary, House of Representatives, Prepared Statement of Jonathan M. Winer, Deputy Assistant Secretary of State, Bureau of International Narcotics and Law Enforcement Affairs,* 105th Cong., 1st Sess., April 23, 1997; Guatemala passed anti-smuggling laws in 2015 ("The Blair House Communique: Joint Communique of the Presidents of El Salvador, Guatemala, and Honduras, and The Vice President of the United States of America in Relation to the Plan of the Alliance for Prosperity in the Northern Triangle," The White House Office of the Press Secretary,

February 24, 2016, https://www.whitehouse.gov/the-press-office/2016/02/25/blair-house-communique-joint-communique-presidents-el-salvador-guatemala.)

49. On mechanisms of policy diffusion, including leverage, see David Cook-Martín and David Scott FitzGerald, "How Their Laws Affect Our Laws: Mechanisms of Immigration Policy Diffusion in the Americas, 1790–2010" *Law and Society Review* (2019, forthcoming).

50. *Written Testimony of Alan D. Bersin*, March 22, 2016; U.S. Department of Homeland Security, *Yearbook of Immigration Statistics, 2002* (Washington, DC: U.S. Government Printing Office, 2003), table 20.

51. *Statement of Lev J. Kubiak, Assistant Director, International Operations, Homeland Security Investigations, U.S. Immigration and Customs Enforcement, Department of Homeland Security, Regarding a Hearing on "The Outer Ring of Border Security: DHS's International Security Programs" before the Subcommittee on Border and Maritime Security of the Committee on Homeland Security, House of Representatives*, 114th Cong., 1st Sess., June 2, 2015.

52. *Potential Terrorists Threats: Border Security Challenges in Latin America and the Caribbean: Hearing before the Subcommittee on the Western Hemisphere of the Committee on Foreign Affairs, House of Representatives, Statement of Lev J. Kubiak, Assistant Director for International Operations, Department of Homeland Security*, 114th Cong., 2nd Sess., March 22, 2016.

53. *Testimony of Deputy Assistant Secretary of State Juan Gonzalez before the House Foreign Affairs Subcommittee on the Western Hemisphere*, 114th Cong., 1st Sess., March 22, 2016, http://docs.house.gov/meetings/FA/FA07/20160322/104726/HHRG-114-FA07-Wstate-GonzalezJ-20160322.pdf.

54. Torsten Feys, "The Smuggling of 'Contraband Chinese' and the Other 'Chinese' from Europe: Comparing Trans-Pacific with Trans-Atlantic Illegal Migration to the US, 1875–1917," in *Tribute, Trade and Smuggling*, edited by Angela Schottenhammer (Wiesbaden: Otto Harrassowitz Verlag, 2014), p. 310.

55. Agreement on Air Transport Preclearance Between the Government of Canada and the Government of the United States of America, May 8, 1974, http://www.treaty-accord.gc.ca/text-texte.aspx?id=103842; Agreement on Air Transport Preclearance Between the Government of Canada and the Government of the United States of America, January 18, 2001, http://www.publications.gc.ca/site/eng/283432/publication.html; Mark B. Salter, "Governmentalities of an Airport: Heterotopia and Confession," *International Political Sociology* 1 (2007): p. 56.

56. Randy Lippert, "Canadian Refugee Determination and Advanced Liberal Government," *Canadian Journal of Law & Society* 13, no. 2 (1998): p. 195.

57. Preclearance Act, 2016, S.C. 2017, c. 27.

58. "Preclearance Overview," U.S. Customs and Border Protection 2016, https://www.cbp.gov/border-security/ports-entry/operations/preclearance.

59. Carlson, Kathryn, "Cancelled Air Canada Flight Causes Customs Confusion," *The Globe and Mail*, June 9, 2013.

60. "DHS Implementation of Executive Order #13769 'Protecting the Nation from Foreign Terrorist Entry Into the United States,' " Office of Inspector General, Department of Homeland Security, January 18, 2018, pp. 59–60. https://www.oig.dhs.gov/sites/default/files/assets/2018-01/OIG-18-37-Jan18.pdf.

61. Rebecca Adler-Nissen and Thomas Gammeltoft-Hansen, *Sovereignty Games: Instrumentalizing State Sovereignty in Europe and Beyond* (New York: Palgrave Macmillan, 2008).

62. *Matter of Kasinga*, 21 I. & N. 357 (BIA 1996); Karen Musalo, "A Short History of Gender Asylum in the United States: Resistance and Ambivalence May Very Slowly Be Inching Towards Recognition of Women's Claims," *Refugee Survey Quarterly 29*, no. 2 (2010). (Kassindja is often spelled Kasinga).

Chapter 5

1. Azadeh Dastyari, *United States Migrant Interdiction and the Detention of Refugees in Guantánamo Bay* (Cambridge: Cambridge University Press, 2015), p. 6.

2. Thomas Gammeltoft-Hansen, *Access to Asylum: International Refugee Law and the Globalisation of Migration Control* (Cambridge: Cambridge University Press, 2011), p. 75.

3. 1917 Immigration Act, Pub. L. No. 301, 39 Stat. 874, §1.

4. 1952 Immigration and Nationality Act, Pub. L. No. 82-414, 66 Stat. 163, §38.

5. Reagan expanded the U.S. territorial sea from three to twelve nautical miles in 1988 in keeping with the international norm (Proclamation No. 5928 reproduced in 103 Stat. 2981 (1989)); *Yang v. Maugans*, 68 F.3d 1540, 1548 (3d Cir. 1995).

6. Memorandum for John Harmon, Assistant Attorney General, Office of Legal Counsel, from David Crosland, Acting Commissioner, INS, *Re: Cases on Illegal Entry to Cubans in Boats* at 1 (May 6, 1980) cited in U.S. Department of Justice, Office of Legal Counsel, "Immigration Consequences of Undocumented Aliens' Arrival in United States Territorial Waters," Washington, DC, October 13, 1993.

7. Memorandum for Alan C. Nelson, Commissioner, INS, from Maurice C. Inman, Jr., General Counsel, INS, *Re: Interdiction of Aliens* (February 21, 1986) cited in U.S. Department of Justice, Office of Legal Counsel, "Immigration Consequences of Undocumented Aliens' Arrival in United States Territorial Waters," Washington, DC, October 13, 1993.

8. "Immigration Consequences of Undocumented Aliens' Arrival in United States Territorial Waters," U.S. Department of Justice, Office of Legal Counsel, Washington, DC, October 13, 1993, pp. 79, 83.

9. 110 Stat. 3009-546.

10. 66 Stat. 204, 8 U.S.C. §1251; *Landon v. Plasencia*, 459 U.S. 21, 26–27 (1982).

11. *Correa v. Thornburgh*, 901 F.2d 1166, 1171 n. 5 (2d Cir. 1990).

12. *Augustin v. Sava*, 735 F.2d 32, 36-37 (2d Cir. 1984).

13. Kendall Coffey, "The Due Process Right to Seek Asylum in the United States: The Immigration Dilemma and Constitutional Controversy," *Yale Law & Policy Review 19*, no. 2 (2001): p. 310; *Leng May Ma v. Barber*, 357 U.S. 185, 188 (1958).

14. *Matter of Pierre*, WL 29484 (BIA 1973).

15. Jason Dzubow, "Remembering the Golden Venture," *Asylumist*, June 6, 2010, http://www.asylumist.com/2010/06/06/remembering-the-golden-venture.

16. Mike Argento, "Golden Venture 20 Years Later: Many Lives Remain in Limbo," *York Daily Record*, May 31, 2013.

17. *Chen Zhou Chai v. J Carroll M.* 48 F. 3d 1331 (4th Cir. 1995). In the court's opinion, the INS had properly placed Chen into exclusion rather than deportation proceedings.

18. *Zhang v. Slattery* 55 F.3d 732, 754 (2d Cir. 1995); see also *Yang v. Maugans* 68 F.3d 1540 (1995).

19. *Zhang v. Slattery,* 55 F.3d 732, 755 (2d Cir. 1995).

20. *Yang v. Maugans* 68 F.3d 1540, 1553 (3rd Cir. 1995).

21. 8 CFR 235.3.

22. Stephen H. Legomsky, "The USA and the Caribbean Interdiction Program," *International Journal of Refugee Law 18,* no. 3–4 (2006): p. 694. Expedited removal was expanded in 2004 to include noncitizens apprehended within 100 miles of a land or sea border who had entered without inspection within the previous two weeks. In 2017, the Trump administration issued a memorandum that proposed to apply expedited removal throughout the country for those who had entered without inspection within the previous three months. See "Implementing the President's Border Security and Immigration Enforcement Improvement Policies," Department of Homeland Security, February 20, 2017, https://www.dhs.gov/sites/default/files/publications/17_0220_S1_Implementing-the-Presidents-Border-Security-Immigration-Enforcement-Improvement-Policies.pdf.

23. "Procedural Rights of Undocumented Aliens Interdicted in U.S. Internal Waters," U.S. Department of Justice, Office of Legal Counsel, November 21, 1996, pp. 382, 384.

24. *Fong Yue Ting v. United States,* 149 U.S. 698, 720(1893).

25. Alex Stepick, "Unintended Consequences: Rejecting Haitian Boat People and Destabilizing Duvalier," in *Western Hemisphere Immigration and United States Foreign Policy,* edited by Christopher Mitchell (University Park: Pennsylvania State University Press, 1992), p. 127; *Haitian Refugee Ctr. v. Civiletti,* 503 F. Supp. 442, 475 (S.D. Fla. 1980).

26. Stepick, "Unintended Consequences," 130–131.

27. Josh DeWind and David H. Kinley, III, *Aiding Migration: The Impact of International Development Assistance on Haiti* (Boulder: Westview Press, 1988), p. 30.

28. *Haitian Refugee Ctr. v. Civiletti,* 503 F. Supp. 442, 482 (S.D. Fla. 1980). See also Alex Stepick, "Haitian Boat People: A Study in the Conflicting Forces Shaping U.S. Immigration Policy," *Law and Contemporary Problems 45,* no. 2 (1982): p. 178.

29. Stepick, "Unintended Consequences," 139–141.

30. Proclamation No. 4865, "High Seas Interdiction of Illegal Aliens," September 29, 1981.

31. *United States as a Country of Mass First Asylum: Hearing before the Subcommittee on Immigration and Refugee Policy of the Senate Committee on the Judiciary,* 97th Cong., 1st Sess. (1981), p. 6. (Statement of Thomas O. Enders, Assistant Secretary of State for Inter-American Affairs.)

32. U.S. Department of Justice, "Proposed Interdiction of Haitian Flag Vessels," *Opinions of the Office of Legal Counsel,* vol. 5 (1981): p. 243.

33. Gregory Jaynes, "33 Haitians Drown as Boat Capsizes off Florida," *New York Times,* October 26, 1981.

34. 94 Stat. 105, 8 U.S.C. 1158(a).

35. Gary W. Palmer, "Guarding the Coast: Alien Migrant Interdiction Operations at Sea," *Connecticut Law Review 29* (1996): pp. 1565–1585.

36. The United States joined the 1967 Protocol in 1968; Refugee Act of 1980 codified at 8. U.S.C. §1253(h).

37. "Agreement between the United States of America and Haiti Effected by Exchange of Notes Signed at Port-au-Prince Sep. 23, 1981," 33 U.S.T. 3559, TIAS. No. 10,241.

38. Executive Order 12,324, "Interdiction of Illegal Aliens," September 29, 1981.

39. *Haitian Refugee Center, Inc. v. Baker.* 953 F.2d 1498 (11th Cir.), *cert denied,* 502 U.S. 1122 (1992); see also Palmer, "Guarding the Coast," 1575.

40. "Haitian Interdiction Case" (United States), Inter-American Commission on Human Rights, Report No. 51/96, Case 10.675, March 13, 1997, ¶128.

41. "INS Procedural Changes," U.S. Coast Guard Headquarters Telecommunications, March 13, 1991, http://www.cod.edu/people/faculty/yearman/FOIA/haitianrefugees/INS_interview_change.pdf.

42. *U.S. Human Rights Policy toward Haiti: Hearing before the Legislation and National Security Subcommittee of the Committee on Government Operations, House of Representatives,* 102nd Cong., 2nd Sess. (Statement of Harold J. Johnson, General Accounting Office), April 9, 1992, p. 7.

43. "Bodies on the Beach," *New York Times,* October 28, 1981.

44. *Haitian Refugee Center, Inc. v. Baker.* 953 F.2d 1498, 78–79, 97 (11th Cir. 1992).

45. *Haitian Refugee Center, Inc. v. Baker.* 953 F.2d 1498, 133 (11th Cir. 1992).

46. *Haitian Refugee Center, Inc. v. Baker.* 949 F.2d 1109 (11th Cir. 1991).

47. *Haitian Centers Council v. McNary,* No. 92 Civ. 1258 U.S. Dist. Lexis 8452, at *4 (E.D.N.Y. June 5, 1992).

48. "Haiti: Prospects for the Duvalier Regime," CIA Directorate of Intelligence, December 1982, https://www.cia.gov/library/readingroom/docs/CIA-RDP83S00855R000200100002-1.pdf; Stepick, "Unintended Consequences," 147–148.

49. "Haiti: Prospects for the Military Regime," CIA Directorate of Intelligence, October 17, 1988, https://www.cia.gov/library/readingroom/docs/CIA-RDP04T00990R000200140001-4.pdf; Stepick, "Unintended Consequences," 151.

50. "Policy Review Group Meeting on Haiti," National Security Council, December 10, 1987, p. 2, https://www.cia.gov/library/readingroom/docs/CIA-RDP89B00224R000401500003-4.pdf.

51. Cited in *Sale v. Haitian Centers Council, Inc.* 509 U. S. 155, 166 (1993); *U.S. Human Rights Policy toward Haiti: Hearing before the Legislation and National Security Subcommittee of the Committee on Government Operations, House of Representatives.* (Statement of Harold J. Johnson, General Accounting Office), April 9, 1992, p. 7.

52. Dastyari, *United States Migrant Interdiction,* 22.

53. *Haitian Centers Council, Inc. v. McNary* 969 F.2d 1326 (2d Cir. 1992).

54. Howard W. French, "Months of Terror Bring Rising Toll of Deaths in Haiti," *New York Times,* April 2, 1994.

55. Palmer, "Guarding the Coast," 1575. In June 1993, the U.S. government closed the Guantanamo Bay facility detaining Haitians and brought them to the United States to file asylum claims ("Haitian Interdiction Case" [United States], Inter-American

Commission on Human Rights, Report No. 51/96, Case 10.675, March 13, 1997, ¶¶59, 62.

56. Executive Order 12807, "Interdiction of Illegal Aliens," May 24, 1992.

57. Executive Order 12324, "Interdiction of Illegal Aliens," Sep. 29, 1981.

58. Executive Order 12807, "Interdiction of Illegal Aliens," May 24, 1992.

59. Victoria Clawson, Elizabeth Detweiler, and Laura Ho, "Litigating as Law Students: An Inside Look at Haitian Centers Council," *Yale Law Journal 103*, no. 8 (1994): p. 2345.

60. Harold Hongju Koh, "The 'Haiti Paradigm' in United States Human Rights Policy," *Yale Law Journal 103*, no. 8 (1994): p. 2396.

61. Koh, "The 'Haiti Paradigm,'" 2397.

62. Palmer, "Guarding the Coast," 1577.

63. "U.S. Sets Up Sea Barricade to Halt Haiti Refugees," *Los Angeles Times*, January 17, 1993.

64. Palmer, "Guarding the Coast," 1575; Robert B. Watts, "Caribbean Maritime Migration: Challenges for the New Millennium," *Homeland Security Affairs* (April 2008): p. 8.

65. *Sale v. Haitian Centers Council, Inc.* 509 U. S. 155, 162 (1993).

66. *Sale v. Haitian Centers Council, Inc.* 509 U. S. 155, 159–160 (1993).

67. *Sale v. Haitian Centers Council, Inc.* 509 U. S. 155, 183 (1993). Koh, "The 'Haiti Paradigm,'" 2419 points out a major problem with this logic. "It is nonsense to presume that treaty parties contract solely for domestic effect. Generally applied, such a presumption would permit the United States to commit genocide or torture on the high seas, notwithstanding the universal, peremptory prohibitions of the Genocide and Torture Conventions,"

68. *United States as a Country of Mass First Asylum: Hearing before the Subcommittee on Immigration and Refugee Policy of the Senate Committee on the Judiciary*, 97th Cong., 1st Sess. (1981), pp. 208–209. Letter from U.S. Department of Justice, Immigration and Naturalization Service to Hon. Edward M. Kennedy dated November 13, 1981.

69. "Haitian Interdiction Case" (United States), Inter-American Commission on Human Rights, Report No. 51/96, Case 10.675, March 13, 1997, ¶¶162–189.

70. See Stephen H. Legomsky, "The USA and the Caribbean Interdiction Program," *International Journal of Refugee Law 18*, no. 3–4 (2006): pp. 677–695 for a review.

71. Maarten den Heijer, *Europe and Extraterritorial Asylum* (Oxford: Hart, 2012). p. 311.

72. 8 U.S. Code §1324. *United States v. Delgado-Garcia*, 374 F. 3rd 1137 (DC Cir. 2004).

73. Koh, "The 'Haiti Paradigm,'" 2408.

74. Dastyari, *United States Migrant Interdiction*, 34.

75. Memorandum of understanding between the Government of the United States and the Government of Jamaica for the establishment within the Jamaican territorial sea and internal waters of a facility to process nationals of Haiti seeking refuge within or entry to the United States of America, entered into force 2 June 1994, KAV 3901, Temp State Dept No 94-153; Memorandum of understanding between the Government of the United Kingdom, the Government of the Turks and Caicos Islands, and the Government of the United States to establish in the Turks

and Caicos Islands a processing facility to determine the refugee status of boat people from Haiti, entered into force 18 June 1994, KAV xxxiii 3906, Temp State Dept No 94-158.

76. "U.S. Grants Asylum to 6 of 35 at Sea," Associated Press, June 18, 1994.

77. Michael Gordon, "In Shift, U.S. Will No Longer Admit Haitians at Sea," *New York Times*, July 6, 1994; "U.S. Policy on Haitian Boat People Appears Lost at Sea," *Interpreter Releases 71*, no. 26 (July 11, 1994): pp. 885–888.

78. Angus Francis, "Bringing Protection Home: Healing the Schism Between International Obligations and National Safeguards Created by Extraterritorial Processing," *International Journal of Refugee Law 20*, no. 2 (2008): p. 306.

79. Maria E. Sartori, "The Cuban Migration Dilemma: An Examination of the United States' Policy of Temporary Protection in Offshore Safe Havens," *Georgetown Immigration Law Journal 15* (2001): p. 329.

80. "Haitian Interdiction Case" (United States), Inter-American Commission on Human Rights, Report No. 51/96, Case 10.675, March 13, 1997, ¶¶64–65.

81. "No Port in a Storm: The Misguided Use of In-Country Refugee Processing in Haiti," Americas Watch, National Coalition for Haitian Refugees, and the Jesuit Refugee Service, vol. 5, no. 8, September 1983.

82. William J. Clinton, "Address to the Nation on Haiti," in *Public Papers of the Presidents of the United States: William J. Clinton, Book 2—August 1 to December 31, 1994* (Washington, DC: Government Printing Office), p. 1559.

83. Gil Loescher, Alexander Betts, and James Milner, *The United Nations High Commissioner for Refugees (UNHCR): The Politics and Practice of Refugee Protection* (New York: Routledge, 2012), p. 97.

84. Bill Frelick, "'Abundantly Clear': Refoulement," *Georgetown Immigration Law Journal 19* (Winter 2004): pp. 251–253.

85. Frelick, "'Abundantly Clear,'" 255.

86. Frelick, "'Abundantly Clear,'" 258.

87. "Haitian Interdiction Case," ¶120.

88. Rebecca Hamlin and Philip E. Wolgin, "Symbolic Politics and Policy Feedback: The United Nations Protocol Relating to the Status of Refugees and American Refugee Policy in the Cold War," *International Migration Review 46*, no. 3 (2012): p. 610.

89. "Advisory Opinion on the Extraterritorial Application of *Non-Refoulement* Obligations under the 1951 Convention Relating to the Status of Refugees and Its 1967 Protocol," UNHCR, January 26, 2007.

90. "U.S. Observations on UNHCR Advisory Opinion on Extraterritorial Application of Non-Refoulement Obligations," U.S. State Department, December 28, 2005, https://2001-2009.state.gov/s/l/2007/112631.htm.

91. Den Heijer, *Europe and Extraterritorial Asylum*, 143.

92. "General Comment No. 2: Implementation of Article 2 by State Parties," UN Committee Against Torture, CAT/C/GC/2, January 24, 2008, ¶7.

93. "List of Issues to Be Considered During the Examination of the Second Periodic Report of the United States of America: Response of the United States of America," U.S. Department of State, 2006, http://www.state.gov/j/drl/rls/68554.htm.

94. "Concluding Observations on the Third to Fifth Periodic Reports of United States of America," UN Committee Against Torture, CAT/C/USA/CO/3-5, November 20, 2014, ¶10, https://www.state.gov/documents/organization/234772.pdf.

95. Dastyari, *United States Migrant Interdiction*.

96. Frelick, "'Abundantly Clear,'" 245.

97. Frelick, "'Abundantly Clear,'" 246.

98. Dastyari, *United States Migrant Interdiction*, 140.

99. "Repatriation of 250 Haitian Migrants," Wikileaks, November 22, 2005, https://wikileaks.org/plusd/cables/05PORTAUPRINCE2871_a.html; Frelick, "'Abundantly Clear,'" 246; T. Alexander Aleinikoff, "Yale Law School *Sale* Symposium: International Protection Challenges Occasioned by Maritime Movement of Asylum Seekers," Opinio Juris, March 16, 2014, http://opiniojuris.org/2014/03/16/sale-symposium-international-protection-challenges-occasioned-maritime-movement-asylum-seekers/.

100. "Coast Guard Stops Haitian Migrant Surge, But Long Term Immigration Challenges Remain," Wikileaks, February 21, 2008, https://wikileaks.org/plusd/cables/08NASSAU160_a.html.

101. "Agreement between the Government of the United States of America and the Government of the Commonwealth of the Bahamas Concerning Cooperation in Maritime Law Enforcement," June 29, 2004, ¶16.

102. Aleinikoff, "Yale Law School *Sale* Symposium,"

103. "Mérida Initiative: The United States Has Provided Counternarcotics and Anticrime Support but Needs Better Performance Measures," GAO, July 21, 2010, p. 5.

104. "Congressional Budget Justification Department of State, Foreign Operations, and Related Programs, FY 2016," February 2, 2015, p. 360, http://www.state.gov/s/d/rm/rls/ebs/2016/pdf/index.htm.

105. "Dominican Illegals: USDOJ and USCG Action Request," Wikileaks, January 30, 2004, https://wikileaks.org/plusd/cables/04SANTODOMINGO594_a.html; Robert B. Watts, "Caribbean Maritime Migration: Challenges for the New Millennium," *Homeland Security Affairs* (April 2008): p. 6.

106. *Statement of Captain Anthony S. Tangeman on Coast Guard Migrant Interdiction Operations before the Subcommittee on Immigration and Claims of the Committee on the Judiciary, House of Representatives*, 106th Cong., 1st Sess., May 18, 1999, http://testimony.ost.dot.gov/test/pasttest/99test/Tangeman1.htm (accessed October, 27, 2016; access to the link was subsequently blocked.)

107. "Dominican Illegals: USDOJ and USCG Action Request," Wikileaks, January 30, 2004, https://wikileaks.org/plusd/cables/04SANTODOMINGO594_a.html.

108. Deborah Sontag, "Mexico's Position on Aliens Contradicted by Past Deeds," *New York Times*, July 15, 1993.

109. "Alien Smuggling," Presidential Decision Directive/ NSC-9, June 18, 1993, p. 1.

110. *Statement of Captain Anthony S. Tangeman*.

111. Dastyari, *United States Migrant Interdiction*, 141.

112. Anthony DePalma, "3 Ships Adrift in a Diplomatic Limbo," *New York Times*, July 1, 1993.

113. Sontag, "Mexico's Position on Aliens; "Alien Smuggling," Presidential Decision Directive/ NSC-9, June 18, 1993, p. 4.

114. William Claiborne, "U.S., Mexico End Impasse on Chinese," *Washington Post*, July 15, 1993.

115. "Recomendación 214-1993. Caso de la deportación de los inmigrantes de origen chino," Comisión Nacional de los Derechos Humanos, México, October 26, 1993.

116. "Organized Crime and Terrorist Activity in Mexico, 1999–2002," report prepared by the Federal Research Division, Library of Congress under an Interagency Agreement with the U.S. Government, February 2003, https://archive.org/stream/MexicoFOIA/Organized%20Crime%20and%20Terrorist%20Activity%20in%20Mexico,%201999-2002_djvu.txt.

117. Sontag, "Mexico's Position on Aliens."

118. Paul J. Smith, "Military Responses to the Global Migration Crisis: A Glimpse of Things to Come," *The Fletcher Forum of World Affairs 23* (1999): pp. 86–87.

119. "H.R.945—To Deny to Aliens the Opportunity to Apply for Asylum in Guam," https://www.congress.gov/bill/106th-congress/house-bill/945/all-actions-without-amendments.

120. 122 Stat. 754–876, § 702(a).

121. William Branigin, "Guam's Own 'China Beach,'" *Washington Post*, May 6, 1999.

122. "U.S. Immigration Law in the Commonwealth of the Northern Mariana Islands (CNMI)," USCIS, April 18, 2018, https://www.uscis.gov/laws/immigration-commonwealth-northern-mariana-islands-cnmi/us-immigration-law-commonwealth-northern-mariana-islands-cnmi.

123. Dirks, *Canada's Refugee Policy*, 166; Lynda Mannik, *Photography, Memory, and Refugee Identity: The Voyage of the SS Walnut, 1948* (Vancouver: University of British Columbia Press, 2013).

124. An Act to Amend the Immigration Act, 1976, Bill C-84, Senate Debates, September 16, 1987, p. 1848.

125. James C. Hathaway, "Postscript: Selective Concern: An Overview of Refugee Law in Canada," *McGill Law Journal 34* (1989): pp. 354–355; Act to Amend the Immigration Act, 1976 and the Criminal Code in consequence thereof, July 21, 1988. 8 (1.1).

126. Sharryn J. Aiken, "Of Gods and Monsters: National Security and Canadian Refugee Policy," *Revue québécoise de droit international 14*, no. 2 (2001): pp. 47–48.

127. Standing Committee on Citizenship and Immigration, Canada House of Commons, November 3, 1999, p. 1555, http://www.parl.gc.ca/HousePublications/Publication.aspx?Language=e&Mode=1&Parl=36&Ses=2&DocId=1039743&File=0.

128. Standing Committee on Citizenship and Immigration, Canada House of Commons, November 3, 1999, P. 1615, http://www.parl.gc.ca/HousePublications/Publication.aspx?Language=e&Mode=1&Parl=36&Ses=2&DocId=1039743&File=0.

129. Alison Mountz, *Seeking Asylum: Human Smuggling and Bureaucracy at the Border* (Minneapolis: University of Minnesota Press, 2010), p. xiv.

130. Mountz, *Seeking Asylum*, 15.

131. Scott D. Watson, *The Securitization of Humanitarian Migration: Digging Moats and Sinking Boats* (New York: Routledge, 2009), p. 142.

132. FitzGerald and Cook-Martín, *Culling the Masses*.

133. Guy S. Goodwin-Gill and Jane McAdam, *The Refugee in International Law* (New York: Oxford University Press, 2007).

Chapter 6

1. For the sociological history of Cuban migration to the United States, see Alejandro Portes and Alex Stepick, *City on the Edge: The Transformation of Miami* (Berkeley: University of California Press, 1993); Silvia Pedraza, *Political Disaffection in Cuba's Revolution and Exodus* (New York: Cambridge University Press, 2007); and Susan Eckstein, *The Immigrant Divide: How Cuban Americans Changed the US and Their Homeland* (New York: Routledge, 2009).

2. Jorge I. Domínguez, "Cooperating with the Enemy? US Immigration Policies toward Cuba," in *Western Hemisphere Immigration and United States Foreign Policy*, edited by Christopher Mitchell (University Park: Pennsylvania State University Press, 1992), pp. 31–32.

3. Josep M. Colomer, "Exit, Voice, and Hostility in Cuba," *International Migration Review 34*, no. 2 (2000): pp. 423–442.

4. David Scott FitzGerald and David Cook-Martín, *Culling the Masses: The Democratic Origins of Racist Immigration Policy in the Americas* (Cambridge, MA: Harvard University Press, 2014).

5. Domínguez, "Cooperating with the Enemy?," 69.

6. "The 'Other' Boatlift," U.S. Coast Guard, https://www.uscg.mil/history/uscghist/camarioca1965.asp.

7. "Castro's Aims Regarding the Future of U.S.-Cuban Relations," CIA Directorate of Intelligence, November 22, 1965, CIA-RDP79T00472A000600040007-5.pdf.

8. *Cuban Refugee Problem. Hearings before the Subcommittee to Investigate Problems Connected with Refugees and Escapees of the Committee on the Judiciary, United States Senate*, 89th Cong., 2nd Sess. (1966), p. 4.

9. Colomer, "Exit, Voice, and Hostility," 436; *United States Cuban Refugee Problem. Hearings*, 25.

10. Ruth Ellen Wasem, "Cuban Migration to the United States: Policy and Trends," Congressional Research Service, June 2, 2009, p. 2, https://fas.org/sgp/crs/row/R40566.pdf.

11. Wasem, "Cuban Migration," 1.

12. Domínguez, "Cooperating with the Enemy?," 67.

13. Domínguez, "Cooperating with the Enemy?," 43.

14. "Cuba: A Revolution's Discontent," CIA Directorate of Intelligence, May 1986, p. 3, https://www.cia.gov/library/readingroom/docs/CIA-RDP88T00768R000200220001-0.pdf.

15. "Meeting of the SIG/RP. Department of State Position Paper, Cuban Refugee Processing," U.S. Department of State, July 29, 1985, p. 2, https://www.cia.gov/library/readingroom/docs/CIA-RDP87M00539R000400520002-6.pdf.

16. Alex Larzelere, *The 1980 Cuban Boatlift* (Washington, DC: National Defense University Press, 1988), p. 133.

17. Domínguez, "Cooperating with the Enemy?," 62.

18. Larzelere, *The 1980 Cuban Boatlift*, 158-255.

19. "Memorandum for John Harmon, Assistant Attorney General, Office of Legal Counsel, from David Crosland, Acting Commissioner, INS," *Re: Cases on Illegal Entry to Cubans in Boats* at 1 (May 6, 1980) cited in "Immigration Consequences of Undocumented Aliens' Arrival in United States Territorial Waters," U.S. Department of Justice, Office of Legal Counsel, Washington, DC, October 13, 1993.

20. Larzelere, *The 1980 Cuban Boatlift*, 300–317.

21. *U.S. Refugee Programs, 1981: Hearing before the Committee on the Judiciary, United States Senate*, 96th Cong., 2nd Sess. (September 19, 1980), p. 26 (Statement of Attorney General Benjamin Civiletti).

22. "Cuba: The Mariel Experience," CIA National Foreign Assessment Center, October 31, 1980, pp. 1–2, https://www.cia.gov/library/readingroom/docs/CIA-RDP85T00287R000102500002-4.pdf; "Cuban Refugee Questions," CIA, February 25, 1982, https://www.cia.gov/library/readingroom/docs/CIA-RDP84B00049R000701760004-2.pdf.

23. Silvia Pedraza-Bailey, "Cuba's Exiles: Portrait of a Refugee Migration," *International Migration Review* 19 no. 1 (1985): pp. 22.

24. "Cuban Refugee Questions."

25. Larzelere, *The 1980 Cuban Boatlift*, 25, 133

26. "Cuba: The Mariel Experience," 2; "Cuba: Castro's May Day Speech," CIA National Foreign Assessment Center, May 13, 1983, p. 6, https://www.cia.gov/library/readingroom/docs/CIA-RDP85T00287R000101130002-6.pdf.

27. Domínguez, "Cooperating with the Enemy?," 47.

28. "Cuban Refugee Questions."

29. "Return to Cuba of Mariel Refugees Unfit for Release into U.S. Society. Memorandum to the Director of Central Intelligence from the Latin American Division," CIA, February 25, 1982, https://www.cia.gov/library/readingroom/docs/CIA-RDP84B00049R000701760005-1.pdf.

30. "Cuba-United States: Agreement on Immigration Procedures and the Return of Cuban Nationals. New York, Dec. 14, 1984," *International Legal Materials 24*, no. 1 (Jan. 1985): pp. 32–37.

31. Domínguez, "Cooperating with the Enemy?," 64.

32. "NSC Cuba Policy Review—Interagency Intelligence Assessment," National Security Council, 1982, p. 13.

33. "Suspension of Cuban Immigration," Presidential Proclamation 5517, August 22, 1986,https://www.cia.gov/library/readingroom/docs/CIA-RDP84B00049R000701890017-4.pdf.

34. Domínguez, "Cooperating with the Enemy?," 36.

35. "Border Patrol Strategic Plan 1994 and Beyond," U.S. Border Patrol, July 1994, p. 4, http://www.nnirr.org/drupal/sites/default/files/border-patrol-strategic-plan-1994-and-beyond.pdf; Ted Henken, "Balseros, Boteros, and El Bombo: Post-1994 Cuban Immigration to the United States and the Persistence of Special Treatment," *Latino Studies 3* (2005): p. 398.

36. Larry Nackerud et al., "The End of the Cuban Contradiction in U.S. Refugee Policy," *International Migration Review 33*, no. 1 (1999): p. 178; Colomer, "Exit, Voice, and Hostility," 438.

37. William M. LeoGrande, "From Havana to Miami: U.S. Cuba Policy as a Two-Level Game," *Journal of Interamerican Studies and World Affairs 40*, no. 1 (1998): pp. 76–77.

38. William J. Clinton, "The President's News Conference, August 19, 1994," in *Public Papers of the Presidents of the United States: William J. Clinton, Book 2—August 1 to December 31, 1994* (Washington, DC: Government Printing Office), pp. 1477–1484.

39. Robert B. Watts, "Caribbean Maritime Migration: Challenges for the New Millennium," *Homeland Security Affairs* (April 2008): p. 4.

40. "Cuba: U.S. Response to the 1994 Cuban Migration Crisis," U.S. General Accounting Office (GAO), 1995.

41. "U.S.–Cuba Joint Communiqué on Migration, New York City, September 9, 1994," *International Legal Materials 35* no. 2 (March 1996): pp. 328–329.

42. Wasem, "Cuban Migration," 13–14; "Refugee Admissions Program for Latin America and the Caribbean," U.S. Department of State, Population, Refugees, and Migration, May 23, 2014, http://www.state.gov/j/prm/releases/onepagers/228695.htm.

43. "14 November Repatriation of Cubans at Cabanas," Wikileaks, November 27, 2009, https://wikileaks.org/plusd/cables/09HAVANA709_a.html.

44. *Agreement between the United States and Cuba for the Lease of Lands for Coaling and Naval Stations*, February 23, 1903, Art. III, http://avalon.law.yale.edu/20th_century/dip_cuba002.asp; *Treaty between the United States of America and Cuba*, May 29, 1934, U.S.-Cuba. T.S. No. 866. http://avalon.law.yale.edu/20th_century/dip_cuba001.asp.

45. "Latin American Trends," CIA, January 15, 1975, p. 6, https://www.cia.gov/library/readingroom/docs/CIA-RDP79T00865A000100360002-1.pdf.

46. Maria E. Sartori, "The Cuban Migration Dilemma: An Examination of the United States' Policy of Temporary Protection in Offshore Safe Havens," *Georgetown Immigration Law Journal 15* (2001): p. 338.

47. Christopher T. Hanson, "Behind the Paper Curtain: Asylum Policy Versus Asylum Practice," *NYU Review of Law and Social Change 7*, no. 1 (1978): p. 125.

48. *United States as a Country of Mass First Asylum: Hearing before the Subcommittee on Immigration and Refugee Policy of the Senate Committee on the Judiciary*, 97th Cong., 1st Sess. (1981), pp. 106–107. (Statement of Hon. Robert McLory of Illinois.)

49. Gerald L. Neuman, "Anomalous Zones," *Stanford Law Review 48*, no. 5 (1996): p. 1228.

50. Azadeh Dastyari, "Refugees on Guantanamo Bay: A Blue Print for Australia's 'Pacific Solution'?" *Australian Quarterly 79*, no. 1 (2007): p. 104.

51. *Cuban Am. Bar Ass'n, Inc. v. Christopher*, 43 F.3d 1412, 1426 (11th Cir. 1995).

52. Nackerud et al., "The End of Cuban Contradiction," 179–180.

53. *Cuba-United States: Joint Statement on Normalization of Migration, Building on the Agreement of September 9, 1994*, May 2, 1995, http://www.presidency.ucsb.edu/ws/?pid=51305.

54. "Panama: Resettlement of Cuban Migrants Protected on Guantanamo," Wikileaks, June 24, 2008, https://wikileaks.org/plusd/cables/08PANAMA520_a.html.

55. "Request to Brazil to Resettle Cuban Migrants Protected on Guantanamo," Wikileaks, October 30, 2009, https://wikileaks.org/plusd/cables/09BRASILIA1276_a.html.

56. Azadeh Dastyari, *United States Migrant Interdiction and the Detention of Refugees in Guantánamo Bay* (Cambridge: Cambridge University Press, 2015), pp. 173–174.

57. Wasem, "Cuban Migration to the United States," p. 3.

58. "U.S. Army South Plays a Vital Role in Mass Migration Exercise," U.S. Army, March 10, 2015, https://www.army.mil/article/144159/us_army_south_plays_a_vital_role_in_mass_migration_exercise.

59. Curt Anderson, "If Cuban Migration Crisis Occurs Again, U.S. Ready," *Tampa Tribune*, April 10, 2005; "Mass Migration Annex to the State of Florida Comprehensive Emergency Management Plan," Florida State Emergency Response Team 2014, pp. 5–7, http://floridadisaster.org/documents/CEMP/2014/2014%20Hazard%20Annexes/MASS%20MIGRATION%20ANNEX.pdf.

60. "Cuba-US: Possible Pressure Tactics," CIA National Foreign Assessment Center, July 3, 1980, https://www.cia.gov/library/readingroom/docs/CIA-RDP85T00287R000101460002-0.pdf.

61. "Cuban Update: INS Issues Shipboard Processing Guidelines," *Interpreter Releases* 72, no. 40 (Oct. 16, 1995): p. 1407.

62. Perhaps because the wet foot, dry foot policy was derived from the combination of a statute, bilateral accord, and memorandum, there was considerable confusion about its terms. One mistaken view was that the policy was created by the 1994 bilateral accord, which in fact did not include the dry foot provision of the policy (e.g., Muzaffar Chisti and Sarah Pierce, "United States Abandons Its Harder Line on Haitian Migrants in the Face of Latest Natural Disaster," Migration Policy Institute, October 26, 2016, http://www.migrationpolicy.org/article/united-states-abandons-its-harder-line-haitian-migrants-face-latest-natural-disaster.). A second confusion was that the policy "effectively exempts U.S. territorial waters for asylum purposes" (Gammeltoft-Hansen, *Access to Asylum*, 115), when in fact shipboard screening took place in both U.S. territorial waters and on the high seas.

63. Dastyari, *United States Migrant Interdiction*, 5.

64. "Cuban, U.S. officials Conclude Immigration Talks," Agence France Press, December 14, 1999.

65. Clinton, "The President's News Conference," 1477–1484.

66. Lizette Alvarez, "In Quiet Policy Shift, INS Freeing Rafters Who Make It to U.S," *Miami Herald*, January 21, 1995.

67. Memorandum for all Regional Directors from Doris Meissner, Commissioner: "Eligibility for Permanent Residence under the Cuban Adjustment Act Despite Having Arrived Other than a Designated Port-of-Entry," April 19, 1999, https://www.uscis.gov/ilink/docView/AFM/HTML/AFM/0-0-0-1/0-0-0-26573/0-0-0-31937.html.

68. Henken, "Balseros, Boteros, and El Bombo," 404.

69. Henken, "Balseros, Boteros, and El Bombo," 403.

70. Henken, "Balseros, Boteros, and El Bombo," 403.

71. Mike Clary, "Coast Guard Forcibly Halts Cuban Refugees," *Los Angeles Times*, June 30, 1999, http://articles.latimes.com/1999/jun/30/news/mn-51562.

72. Dana Calvo, Louisa Yanez, and Tanya Weinberg, "Cubans Freed," *Sun-Sentinel*, July 1, 1999, http://articles.sun-sentinel.com/1999-07-01/news/9907010384_1_cuban-exiles-policy.

73. Lizette Alvarez, "In 2 Countries, 6-Year-Old Cuban Is Political Symbol, " *New York Times*, January 9, 2000, http://www.nytimes.com/2000/01/09/us/in-2-countries-6-year-old-cuban-is-political-symbol.html?_r=0.

74. Cited in *Movimiento Democracia Inc. et al. v. Johnson et al.*, 1:16-cv-21868, U.S. District Court for the Southern District of Florida, p. 6.

75. Associated Press, "15 Cubans Sent Home after Policy Dispute," *USA Today*, January 9, 2006, http://usatoday30.usatoday.com/news/nation/2006-01-09-cuban-policy_x.htm.

76. "Wet Foot Follies," *Chicago Tribune*, March 15, 2006, http://articles.chicagotribune.com/2006-03-15/news/0603150032_1_dry-foot-wet-foot-cubans.

77. Oscar Corral and Larry Lebowitz, "Cubans Sent Home; Picked Wrong Bridge," *Miami Herald*, January 10, 2006, http://www.latinamericanstudies.org/exile/bridge.htm.

78. Laura Wides-Muñoz, "Court Questions US Action That Turned Back 15 Cubans," *Boston Globe*, January 13, 2006, http://archive.boston.com/news/nation/articles/2006/01/13/court_questions_us_action_that_turned_back_15_cubans/.

79. *Movimiento Democracia, INC. v. Chertoff*, 417 F. Supp. 2d 1343 (Lexis 8637 [2006]), p. 1.

80. *Movimiento Democracia, INC. v. Chertoff*, p. 2.

81. *Movimiento Democracia, INC. v. Chertoff*, p. 16.

82. Madeline Bar Diaz, "Tired of Waiting, Returned Cubans Reach Keys Again," *South Florida Sun-Sentinel*, December 16, 2006, Broward Metro, A.1.

83. *Movimiento Democracia Inc. et al. v. Johnson et al.*

84. See *Haitian Refugee Ctr., Inc. v. Baker*, 953 F.2d 1498, 1508 (11th Cir. 1992) on the principle that aliens who have not entered do not have constitutional rights.

85. "Defendants' Notice to Court Regarding Status of Migrant Plaintiffs," June 30, 2016. U.S. District Court, Southern District of Florida, CASE NO. 16-21868-CIV-GAYLES, http://i2.cdn.turner.com/cnn/2016/images/06/30/statusofmigrants.pdf; Helen Davidson, "Australia Resettles Cuban Refugees Found Clinging to Lighthouse off Florida Keys," *The Guardian*, August 22, 2017, https://www.theguardian.com/australia-news/2017/aug/22/australia-resettles-cuban-refugees-found-clinging-to-lighthouse-off-florida-keys.

86. Barack Obama, "Statement by the President on Cuban Immigration Policy," The White House, January 12, 2017, https://obamawhitehouse.archives.gov/the-press-office/2017/01/12/statement-president-cuban-immigration-policy.

87. "Figures Show Dramatic Drop in Cuban Interdictions, Coast Guard Says," *The Sun-Sentinel*, May 16, 2017, http://www.sun-sentinel.com/news/florida/fl-reg-cuban-interdictions-20170516-story.html

88. Susan Gzesh, "So Close to the United States, So Far from God: Refugees and Asylees under Mexican Law," *World Refugee Survey* (1995): p. 36.

89. "Border Patrol Strategic Plan 1994 and Beyond," 4.

90. "Mexico Wrestling with Cuban Migration," Wikileaks, April 29, 2008, https://wikileaks.org/plusd/cables/08MEXICO1302_a.html.

91. "Illegal Migration from Cuba in Sharp Decline," Wikileaks, March 3, 2009, https://wikileaks.org/plusd/cables/09HAVANA142_a.html.

92. "Mexico Wrestling with Cuban Migration,"

93. "DHS Secretary Chertoff in Mexico," Wikileaks, February 26, 2007, https://wikileaks.org/plusd/cables/07MEXICO965_a.html.

94. "Implications for U.S. Of Possible Reform in Cuban Travel Regulations," Wikileaks, April 22, 2008, https://wikileaks.org/plusd/cables/08HAVANA335_a.html.

95. "Mexico-Cuba Talks Produce Little Movement on Repatriations," Wikileaks, June 16, 2008, https://wikileaks.org/plusd/cables/08MEXICO1839_a.html.

96. "Mexico Wrestling with Cuban Migration,"

97. "Mexico Wrestling with Cuban Migration"; "Mexico-Cuba Talks Produce Little Movement on Repatriations."

98. Ann Kimball, "The Transit State: A Comparative Analysis of Mexican and Moroccan Immigration Policies," Working Paper no. 150, Center for Comparative Immigration Studies, University of California, Sand Diego, 2007, pp. 103–104.

99. "Cuban-Mexican MOU on Migration," Wikileaks, October 20, 2008, https://wikileaks.org/plusd/cables/08MEXICO3102_a.html.

100. *Memorándum de Entendimiento entre el Gobierno de los Estados Unidos Mexicanos y el Gobierno de la República de Cuba para garantizar un flujo migratorio legal, ordenado y seguro entre ambos países* (2008).

101. "Cuban-Mexican MOU on Migration."

102. "Mexico Wrestling with Cuban Migration."

103. "Boletines Estadísticos 2001–2016," SEGOB, http://www.politicamigratoria.gob.mx/es_mx/SEGOB/Boletines_Estadisticos.

104. "Surge in Cuban Immigration to U.S. Continued through 2016," Pew Research Center 2017, http://www.pewresearch.org/fact-tank/2017/01/13/cuban-immigration-to-u-s-surges-as-relations-warm/.

105. *Written Testimony of Alan D. Bersin, Assistant Secretary for International Affairs and Chief Diplomatic Officer, Office of Policy U.S. Department of Homeland Security, before the House Committee on Foreign Affairs Subcommittee on the Western Hemisphere on "Potential Terrorist Threats: Border Security Challenges in Latin America and the Caribbean,"* 114th Cong., 2nd Sess., March 22, 2016.

106. "No More Cuban Rafters, Coast Guard Says," *Miami Herald*, May 12, 2017, http://www.miamiherald.com/news/nation-world/world/americas/cuba/article150184537.html

107. Ley no. 1312. Ley de Migración. Art. 2. *Gaceta Oficial*, no. 44, 16 de octubre de 2012, p. 1370.

108. Michael Clemens and Jennifer Hunt, "The Labor Market Effects of Refugee Waves: Reconciling Conflicting Results," Working Paper no. 455, Center for Global Development, July 2017, https://www.cgdev.org/sites/default/files/labor-market-effects-refugee-waves-reconciling-conflicting-results-July-revision.pdf.pdf.

Chapter 7

1. "U.S. Customs and Border Protection's Systemic Denial of Entry to Asylum Seekers at Ports of Entry on U.S.-Mexico Border," American Immigration Council,

January 13, 2017; "Crossing the Line: U.S. Border Agents Illegally Reject Asylum Seekers," Human Rights First, May 2017; "Audio Recording Reveals Border Agents Turning Back Asylum Seekers," Human Rights First, July 13, 2017, http://www.humanrightsfirst.org/press-release/audio-recording-reveals-border-agents-turning-back-asylum-seekers; Robert Moore, "Border Agents Are Using a New Weapon Against Asylum Seekers," *Texas Monthly*, June 2, 2018, https://www.texasmonthly.com/politics/immigrant-advocates-question-legality-of-latest-federal-tactics/.

2. "Remarks before the Tucson Committee on Foreign Relations by David T. Johnson, Assistant Secretary, Bureau of International Narcotics and Law Enforcement Affairs, Tucson, AZ. April 7, 2009," U.S. Department of State, http://www.state.gov/j/inl/rls/rm/121691.htm.

3. María Cristina García, *Seeking Refuge: Central American Migration to Mexico, the United States, and Canada* (Berkeley: University of California Press, 2006), p. 86.

4. Francis X. Clines, "Reagan Says His Opponents Risk Central American Influx," *New York Times*, June 21, 1983.

5. "Transcript of President's News Conference on his Proposal for Nicaragua," *New York Times*, April 5, 1985.

6. "Nicaragua: Prospects for a Refugee Exodus," CIA National Foreign Assessment Center, November 24, 1981, https://www.cia.gov/library/readingroom/docs/DOC_0000028335.pdf.

7. "White House Digest Paper re Central America: The Refugee Crisis," National Security Council, November 30, 1983, https://www.cia.gov/library/readingroom/docs/CIA-RDP10M02313R000100930005-3.pdf.

8. "Central America: The Refugee Dilemma," CIA Directorate of Intelligence, September 1, 1984, p. 5, https://www.cia.gov/library/readingroom/docs/CIA-RDP85S00315R000200080001-2.pdf.

9. Sergio Aguayo, *El Éxodo Centroamericano* (México: Dirección General de Publicaciones de la SEP, 1985) p. 70.

10. Sharon Stanton Russell, "Migration Patterns of U.S. Foreign Policy Interest," in *Threatened Peoples, Threatened Borders: World Migration Policy*, edited by Michael S. Teitelbaum and Myron Weiner (New York: Columbia University Press, 2002), p. 51.

11. García, *Seeking Refuge*, 92–93.

12. Scott D. Watson, *The Securitization of Humanitarian Migration: Digging Moats and Sinking Boats* (New York: Routledge, 2009), pp. 125–126; García, *Seeking Refuge*, 11, 129–130.

13. García, *Seeking Refuge*, 119, 129–130.

14. "Closing the Front Door on Refugees," Canadian Council for Refugees, December 2005, p. 2, http://ccrweb.ca/sites/ccrweb.ca/files/static-files/closingdoordec05.pdf.

15. Alison Mountz, *Seeking Asylum: Human Smuggling and Bureaucracy at the Border* (Minneapolis: University of Minnesota Press, 2010), p. 11.

16. Gerald L. Neuman, "Buffer Zones Against Refugees: Dublin, Schengen, and the German Asylum Amendment," *Virginia Journal of International Law 33*, 503 (1993).

17. Safe-Third Country Agreement 1988 (Bill C-55).

18. An Act to Amend the Immigration Act and Other Acts in Consequence Thereof (Bill C-86) 1992; see Mark Anthony Drumbl, "Canada's New Immigration Act: An Affront to the Charter and Canada's Collective Conscience?," *24 R.D.U.S.* 385 (1994).

19. 8 CFR 208.14 (e).

20. "Border Update—Canadian Immigration Digs out Old Regulation from the Mothballs," Wikileaks, February 14, 2003, https://wikileaks.org/plusd/cables/03MONTREAL204_a.html.

21. "UNHCR Monitoring Report, Canada-United States 'Safe Third Country Agreement, 29 December 2004–28 December 2005," UNHCR, June 1, 2006, pp. 10, 18, http://www.unhcr.org/en-us/protection/operations/455b2cca4/unhcr-monitoring-report-canada-united-states-safe-third-country-agreement.html.

22. "Agreement between the Government of Canada and the Government of the United States of America for Cooperation in the Examination of Refugee Status Claims from Nationals of Third Countries," December 5, 2002, https://www.canada.ca/en/immigration-refugees-citizenship/corporate/mandate/policies-operational-instructions-agreements/agreements/safe-third-country-agreement/final-text.html.

23. Efrat Arbel, "Shifting Borders and the Boundaries of Rights: Examining the Safe Third Country Agreement between Canada and the United States," *International Journal of Refugee Law 25*, no. 1 (2013): p. 2.

24. "U.S.-Canada Safe Third Country Agreement, Assessment Report," U.S. Citizenship and Immigration Services and Citizenship and Immigration Canada, November 16, 2006, ch. 4, 5, https://www.uscis.gov/unassigned/chapter-4-canada-chapter.

25. "2017 Asylum Claims," Immigration, Refugees and Citizenship Canada, Canada.ca., 2018, https://www.canada.ca/en/immigration-refugees-citizenship/services/refugees/asylum-claims-2017.html.

26. "Secretary Kelly's Statement on the Limited Extension of Haiti's Designation for Temporary Protected Status," Department of Homeland Security, May 22, 2017, https://www.dhs.gov/news/2017/05/22/secretary-kellys-statement-limited-extension-haitis-designation-temporary-protected; Brian MacQuarrie, "Fearing Deportation, Haitians Living in US Seek Refuge in Canada," *Boston Globe*, September 2, 2017, https://www.bostonglobe.com/metro/2017/09/02/fearing-deportation-haitians-living-seek-refuge-canada/DJbIoZNjge1yFU74ZxZsYL/story.html; "Canadian Officials in Nigeria Work with U.S. to Stem Asylum Seekers," Reuters, May 3, 2018, https://www.reuters.com/article/us-canada-immigration-border/canadian-officials-in-nigeria-work-with-u-s-to-stem-asylum-seekers-idUSKBN1I42LT.

27. This argument follows the work of Jeffrey G. Reitz, "The Distinctiveness of Canadian Immigration Experience," *Patterns of Prejudice 46*, no. 5 (2012): p. 531.

28. Edoardo Bazzaco, Mario Santiago Juárez, and Areli Palomo Contreras, *En tierra de nadie. El laberinto de la impunidad* (México: i(dh)eas, Litigio Estratégico en Derechos Humanos, 2011), p. 49; "México hace trabajo sucio de EU en migración: Castañeda," *La Jornada*, December 18, 2015.

29. Manuel Ángel Castillo and Mónica Toussaint, "Seguridad y migración en la frontera sur," in *Seguridad Nacional y Seguridad Interior*, edited by Arturo Alvarado and Mónica Serrano (México: El Colegio de México, 2010), p. 290. All translations are the author's unless otherwise noted.

30. Bill Frelick, "Running the Gauntlet: The Central American Journey in Mexico," *International Journal of Refugee Law 3*, no. 2 (1991): p. 213.

31. Ann Kimball, "The Transit State: A Comparative Analysis of Mexican and Moroccan Immigration Policies," Working Paper no. 150, Center for Comparative Immigration Studies, University of California, San Diego, 2007, p. 54.

32. Rodolfo Casillas, "Las rutas de los centroamericanos por México, Un ejercicio de caracterización, actores principales y complejidades," *Migración y Desarrollo 10* (2008): p. 163; Sonja Wolf, *Diagnóstico del Instituto Nacional de Migración* (México: El Instituto para la Seguridad y la Democracia, 2013), p. 260.

33. Kate Doyle, "Mexico's Southern Front: Guatemala and the Search for Security," National Security Archive, November 2, 2003, http://nsarchive.gwu.edu/NSAEBB/NSAEBB100/.

34. Kevin Hartigan, "Matching Humanitarian Norms with Cold, Hard Interests: The Making of Refugee Policies in Mexico and Honduras, 1980–89," *International Organization 46*, no. 3 (1992): pp. 709–730.

35. Hartigan, "Matching Humanitarian Norms."

36. "Mexico: Geographic Perspectives on the Strategic Southeast," CIA Directorate of Intelligence, June 1984, https://www.cia.gov/library/readingroom/docs/CIA-RDP85T00283R000600010003-8.pdf.

37. Doyle, "Mexico's Southern Front"; Archivo General de la Nación, SEDENA, Caja 19, expediente 62, hojas 605-625 reproduced at http://nsarchive.gwu.edu/NSAEBB/NSAEBB100/Doc17.pdf.

38. Manuel Ángel Castillo, "Mexico: Caught between the United States and Central America," Migration Policy Institute, April 1, 2006.

39. Castillo, "Mexico"; García, *Seeking Refuge*, 66; Jack Anderson, "Mexico's Hidden Tragedy," *Washington Post*, November 25, 1984, C7.

40. Hartigan, "Matching Humanitarian Norms," 725.

41. Aguayo, *El Éxodo Centroamericano*, 70.

42. See ch. 6 in David Scott FitzGerald and David Cook-Martín, *Culling the Masses: The Democratic Origins of Racist Immigration Policy in the Americas* (Cambridge, MA: Harvard University Press, 2014).

43. Hartigan, "Matching Humanitarian Norms," 721, 725, 729; García, *Seeking Refuge*, 46, 50.

44. Hartigan, "Matching Humanitarian Norms," 723.

45. Doyle, "Mexico's Southern Front."

46. Casillas, "Las rutas de los centroamericanos por México," 159–160.

47. Aguayo, *El Éxodo Centroamericano*, 113–114; García, *Seeking Refuge*, 68, 87.

48. "Central America: The Refugee Dilemma," CIA Directorate of Intelligence, September 1, 1984, p. 5, https://www.cia.gov/library/readingroom/docs/CIA-RDP85S00315R000200080001-2.pdf.

49. Joan Friedland and Jesús Rodríguez y Rodríguez, *Seeking Safe Ground: The Legal Situation of Central American Refugees in Mexico* (San Diego: Mexico-US Law Institute, University of San Diego Law School, 1987), p. 24.

50. Susan Gzesh, "So Close to the United States, So Far from God: Refugees and Asylees under Mexican Law," *World Refugee Survey* (1995): p. 34.

51. Rodolfo Casillas, "Migratory Policy in Mexico Regarding Central American Migratory Flows in the Current Context," *Estudios Internacionales 3*, no. 6 (1992): p. 76.

52. Aguayo, *El Éxodo Centroamericano*, 55–57.

53. Aguayo, *El Éxodo Centroamericano*, 45, 57, 60.

54. Friedland and Rodríguez y Rodríguez, *Seeking Safe Ground*, 50.

55. Aguayo, *El Éxodo Centroamericano*, 58.

56. Friedland and Rodríguez y Rodríguez, *Seeking Safe Ground*, 45, 49.

57. Aguayo, *El Éxodo Centroamericano*, 62.

58. García, *Seeking Refuge*, 157.

59. Bill Frelick, "Running the Gauntlet: The Central American Journey in Mexico," *International Journal of Refugee Law 3*, no. 2 (1991): pp. 211–212.

60. Alexander Betts, *Protection by Persuasion: International Cooperation in the Refugee Regime* (Ithaca: Cornell University Press, 2009).

61. Daniel Restrepo and Silva Mathema, "A Medium- and Long-Term Plan to Address the Central American Refugee Situation," Center for American Progress, 2016; Susanne Jonas and Néstor Rodríguez, *Guatemala-US Migration: Transforming Regions* (Austin: University of Texas Press, 2015); Maggie Morgan and Deborah E. Anker, "Obstacles to Entry for Central American Refugees in the US," in *States, the Law and Access to Refugee Protection*, edited by Maria O'Sullivan and Dallal Stevens (Oxford: Hart, 2017), p. 119.

62. "Border Patrol Strategic Plan: 1994 and Beyond," U.S. Border Patrol, 1994, p. 12.

63. *Common Enemy, Common Struggle: Progress in U.S.-Mexican Efforts to Defeat Organized Crime and Drug Trafficking. A Report to the Members of the Committee on Foreign Relations, U.S. Senate*, 111th Cong., 2nd Sess. (May 18, 2010), p. 8.

64. "Programa Especial de Migración 2014–2018," Secretaría de Gobernación, México, 2013, p. 45, http://www.gobernacion.gob.mx/es_mx/SEGOB/edicion_impresa_PEM.

65. "Presidential Certification Regarding the Provision of Documents to the House of Representatives under the Mexican Debt Disclosure Act of 1995," U.S. Department of Justice, June 28, 1996, https://www.justice.gov/file/20006/download.

66. "Working Group on Migration and Consular Affairs of the Mexico-United States Binational Commission, Joint Communiqué, Zacatecas," February 13–14, 1995, http://www.migracioninternacional.com/docum/index.html?buttonbot=gtfeb95i.html.

67. Gzesh, "So Close to the United States," 40.

68. Aristide R. Zolberg, *A Nation by Design: Immigration Policy in the Fashioning of America* (Cambridge, MA: Harvard University Press, 2006).

69. Rodolfo Casillas, "El Plan Sur de México y sus efectos sobre la migración internacional," *Ecuador Debate 56* (2002): p. 208.

70. Michael Flynn, "¿Dónde está LA FRONTERA?" *Bulletin of the Atomic Scientists 58*, no. 4 (2002); Felipe Jácome, "Trans-Mexican Migration: A Case of Structural Violence," Working Paper Series no. 2, Georgetown University Center for Latin American Studies, Washington, DC, 2008, p. 28.

71. "Chiapas: Mexico's Vulnerable Underbelly," Wikileaks, January 22, 2010, https://wikileaks.org/plusd/cables/10MEXICO69_a.html; INAMI 2005. Cited in Kimball, "The Transit State."

72. Chávez Rodríguez, "Asilo, refugio y otras formas de protección humanitaria en el México del siglo XXI," in *El Refugio de México*, edited by Katya Somohano and Pablo Yankelevich (Mexico City: Secretaría de Gobernación, 2011); Ernesto Rodríguez, Salvador Berumen, y Luis Felipe Ramos, "Migración centroamericana de tránsito irregular por México. Estimaciones y características generales," *Apuntes sobre migración*, México, Centro de Estudios Migratorios del INAMI; No. 01, julio 2011, p. 1.

73. James F. Hollifield, "The Emerging Migration State," *International Migration Review 38*, no. 3 (2004): pp. 885–912.

74. "Chiapas: Mexico's Vulnerable Underbelly."

75. Comments of Luis Ernesto Derbez to the Center for Strategic and International Studies, May 7, 2003, http://www.revistainterforum.com/espanol/articulos/061803soc_relaciones-us-mx.html.

76. Castillo and Toussaint, "Seguridad y migración en la frontera sur"; Alberto Cabezas, "México activa 'Plan Centinela' con medidas preventivas por guerra," Agencia EFE, 2003, http://www.nacion.com/ln_ee/2003/marzo/18/ultima-la19.html; M. Angeles Villarreal and Jennifer E. Lake, "Security and Prosperity Partnership of North America: An Overview and Selected Issues," Congressional Research Service, 2009; "Acuerdo por el que se reconoce al Instituto Nacional de Migración como Instancia de Seguridad Nacional," *Diario Oficial de la Federación*, May 18, 2005; Wolf, *Diagnóstico del Instituto Nacional de Migración*, 110–111; Adam Isacson, Maureen Meyer, and Gabriela Morales, "Mexico's Other Border: Security, Migration, and the Humanitarian Crisis at the Line with Central America," Washington Office on Latin America, 2014, p. 10; Francisco Alba and Manuel Ángel Castillo, "New Approaches to Migration Management in Mexico and Central America," Woodrow Wilson International Center for Scholars, 2012, p. 12.

77. "Country Reports on Terrorism 2004," U.S. Department of State Office of the Coordinator for Counterterrorism, April 2005.

78. "Engaging the New Mexican Administration on Immigration and Border Security," Wikileaks, June 15, 2006, https://wikileaks.org/plusd/cables/06MEXICO3305_a.html.

79. "DHS Secretary Chertoff in Mexico, February 15–16: Meetings with Interior, Treasury Officials," Wikileaks, February 26, 2007, https://wikileaks.org/plusd/cables/07mexico965_a.html.

80. George W. Grayson, "Mexico's Forgotten Southern Border," Center for Immigration Studies, 2002, p. 5; Clare Ribando Seelke and Kristin Finklea, "U.S.-Mexican Security Cooperation: The Mérida Initiative and Beyond," Congressional Research Service, 2016, p. 6.

81. *Testimony of Roberta S. Jacobson, Deputy Assistant Secretary, Bureau of Western Hemisphere Affairs, before the Western Hemisphere Subcommittee and the Homeland Security Border, Maritime, and Global Counterterrorism Subcommittee of the U.S. House of Representatives Committee on Foreign Affairs*, 111th Cong., 2nd Sess., May 27, 2010, http://www.state.gov/p/wha/rls/rm/2010/142297.htm.

82. Peter J. Meyer et al., "Unaccompanied Children from Central America: Foreign Policy Considerations," Congressional Research Service, April 11, 2016, pp. 8–9.

83. Quoted in "The Cost of Stemming the Tide: How Immigration Enforcement Practices in Southern Mexico Limit Migrant Children's Access to International Protection," Georgetown Law Human Rights Institute, 2015, p. 13.

84. María Eugenia Anguiano and Alma Trejo Peña, "Políticas de seguridad fronteriza y nuevas rutas de movilidad de migrantes mexicanos y guatemaltecos," LiminaR. Estudios Sociales y Humanísticos 5, no. 2 (2007): p. 50.

85. "Programa Especial de Migración 2014–2018," 43.

86. "Mérida Initiative Program Description Reference Document, Mexican Security Cooperation Plan," Department of State, 2008, Washington, DC: U.S. Government Printing Office.

87. Department of State, "Congressional Budget Justification. Department of State, Foreign Operations, and Related Programs, FY 2016," p. 436, https://www.state.gov/documents/organization/236395.pdf.

88. "Mérida Initiative Program Description Reference Document, Mexican Security Cooperation Plan," Department of State, 2008, Washington, DC: U.S. Government Printing Office.

89. Seelke and Finklea, "U.S.-Mexican Security Cooperation," 23.

90. "Mérida Initiative: The United States Has Provided Counternarcotics and Anticrime Support but Needs Better Performance Measures GAO-10-837," Government Accountability Office, 2010, pp. 8–9.

91. "HSI, Mexico Honor Graduates of Mexican Customs Investigator Training Program," ICE, March 21, 2014, https://www.ice.gov/news/releases/hsi-mexico-honor-graduates-mexican-customs-investigator-training-program.

92. Testimony of Allen Gina, Acting Assistant Commissioner, Office of Intelligence and Operations Coordination, U.S. Customs and Border Protection before House Homeland Security Committee: Subcommittee on Border, Maritime, and Global Counterterrorism and the House Foreign Affairs Committee Subcommittee on Western Hemisphere, 111th Cong., 2nd Sess., May 27, 2010.

93. "The Cost of Stemming the Tide," 17.

94. Maureen Meyer et al., "New Developments along Mexico's Southern Border," WOLA, 2014, http://www.wola.org/commentary/new_developments_along_mexico_s_southern_border.

95. Seelke and Finklea, "U.S.-Mexican Security Cooperation," 16.

96. "Remarks by President Obama and President Peña Nieto after Bilateral Meeting," White House Office of the Press Secretary, press release, January 6, 2015.

97. Testimony of Deputy Assistant Secretary of State Juan Gonzalez, March 22, 2016.

98. "Here Are All the Times Donald Trump Insulted Mexico," Time, Aug. 31, 2016, http://time.com/4473972/donald-trump-mexico-meeting-insult/.

99. @realDonaldTrump Twitter feed, April 2, 2018, https://twitter.com/realdonaldtrump/status/980762392303980544?lang=en.

100. @realDonaldTrump Twitter feed, April 23, 2018, https://twitter.com/realdonaldtrump/status/988415011382091776?lang=en.

101. "Último grupo de la caravana de migrantes centroamericanos cruza a EU," El Sol de Tijuana, May 4, 2018, https://www.elsoldetijuana.com.mx/mundo/

ultimo-grupo-de-la-caravana-de-migrantes-centroamericanos-cruza-a-eu-1662095. html; "US Stops Caravan of Central American Asylum Seekers," *The Guardian*, April 30, 2018; Adolfo Flores, "A Long Walk under the Lights," BuzzFeed, June 4, 2018, https://www.buzzfeed.com/adolfoflores/migrant-caravan-mexico-trump-asylum?utm_term=.gtMp8Q67G#.idMGkwvby.

102. Susan Gzesh, "So Close to the United States," 34; Ted Hesson, "Trump Blows Asylum Deal," Politico, April 19, 2018, https://www.politico.com/newsletters/morning-shift/2018/04/19/trump-blows-asylum-deal-176430.

103. "México no hará el trabajo sucio a EU contra migrantes: AMLO," *Proceso*, May 20, 2018, https://www.proceso.com.mx/535115/mexico-no-hara-el-trabajo-sucio-a-eu-contra-migrantes-amlo.

104. "Boletines Estadísticos 2001–2017," SEGOB, http://www.politicamigratoria. gob.mx/es_mx/SEGOB/Boletines_Estadisticos; Casillas, "Las rutas de los centroamericanos por México," 159.

105. "Encuesta Sobre Migración en la Frontera Sur de México," Informe Anual de Resultados, 2014, p. 41, https://www.colef.mx/emif/eng/resultados/informes/2014/ EMIF-ANUAL-SUR2014.pdf.

106. Susanne Jonas, "National Security, Regional Development, and Citizenship in U.S. Immigration Policy: Reflections from the Case of Central American Immigrants and Refugees," in *Free Markets, Open Societies, Closed Borders?: Trends in International Migration and Immigration Policy in the Americas*, edited by Max J. Castro (Coral Cables, FL: North-South Center Press, 1999), p. 180.

107. Gzesh, "So Close to the United States," 35; "Stop Illegal Aliens before They Reach the Homeland: Fund Latin American Repatriations of Third Country Nationals," Wikileaks, April 21, 2005, https://wikileaks.org/plusd/cables/ 05TEGUCIGALPA826_a.html.

108. "Stop Illegal Aliens before They Reach the Homeland: Fund Latin American Repatriations of Third Country Nationals," Wikileaks, April 21, 2005, https:// wikileaks.org/plusd/cables/05TEGUCIGALPA826_a.html.

109. Flynn, "¿Dónde está LA FRONTERA?," 29.

110. Gretchen Kuhner, "Detention of Asylum Seekers in Mexico," *Refuge: Canada's Journal of Refugees 20*, no. 3 (2002): p. 61; Flynn, "¿Dónde está LA FRONTERA?," 32.

111. Kuhner "Detention of Asylum Seekers," 64.

112. Flynn, "¿Dónde está LA FRONTERA?," 35.

113. "Honduran Ministers Demarched on Deportation Plan; GOH Supportive of U.S. Requests and Seeks DHS Assistance," Wikileaks, September 27, 2005, https:// wikileaks.org/plusd/cables/05TEGUCIGALPA1992_a.html; Grayson, "Mexico's Forgotten Southern Border," 4.

114. Olivia Ruiz, "Migration and Borders Present and Future Challenges," *Latin American Perspectives 33*, no. 2 (2006): pp. 50–51; *Memorándum de Entendimiento entre los Gobiernos de los Estados Unidos Mexicanos, de la República de El Salvador, de la República de Guatemala, de la República de Honduras y de la República de Nicaragua, para la Repatriación Digna, Ordenada, Ágil y Segura de Nacionales Centroamericanos Migrantes vía Terrestre*, Firmado en San Salvador el 5 de mayo de 2006; Wolf, *Diagnóstico del Instituto Nacional de Migración*, 358–360.

115. "Programa Especial de Migración 2014–2018," 45; *Written Testimony of Alan D. Bersin, Assistant Secretary for International Affairs and Chief Diplomatic Officer Office of Policy, DHS, before the House Committee On Foreign Affairs Subcommittee on the Western Hemisphere on "Potential Terrorist Threats: Border Security Challenges in Latin America and the Caribbean,"* March 22, 2016.

116. Interview with Yesenia Sánchez, Mexican government official, Tapachula, October 30, 2016; Isacson et al., "Mexico's Other Border," 9; "Meeting with Secretary Alejandro Poire, February 27, 2012," ICE Office of the Director Briefing Book, https://www.wola.org/files/120227_ICE.pdf; "U.S. Seeks Latin American Help Amid Rise in Asia, African migrants," Reuters, August 15, 2016, https://www.reuters.com/article/us-usa-immigration-mexico-exclusive/u-s-seeks-latin-american-help-amid-rise-in-asian-african-migrants-idUSKCN10R0DD.

117. Interview with Yesenia Sánchez, Tapachula, October 12, 2016.

118. *Testimony of Deputy Assistant Secretary of State Juan Gonzalez,* March 22, 2016.

119. "Guatemala/Mexico Border Issues," Wikileaks, December 27, 2004, https://wikileaks.org/plusd/cables/04GUATEMALA3270_a.html.

120. "Call on New Salvadoran Director of Migration," Wikileaks, June 16, 2009, https://wikileaks.org/plusd/cables/09SANSALVADOR550_a.html; "Guatemala/Mexico Border Issues."

121. Peter J. Meyer and Clare Ribando Seelke, "Central America Regional Security Initiative: Background and Policy Issue for Congress," Congressional Research Service, 2015, p. 17.

122. "Honduran Immigration: The Problems Persist, But with a Roadmap for Zelaya Administration to Reform," Wikileaks, February 13, 2006, https://wikileaks.org/plusd/cables/06TEGUCIGALPA268_a.html.

123. Meyer et al., "Unaccompanied Children," 9.

124. *Written Testimony of Alan D. Bersin,* March 22, 2016.

125. *Written Testimony of Alan D. Bersin,* March 22, 2016, 486.

126. "Congressional Budget Justification Department of State, Foreign Operations, and Related Programs, FY 2016," U.S. Department of State, February 2, 2015, p. 474, http://www.state.gov/s/d/rm/rls/ebs/2016/pdf/index.htm.

127. Interview, Tapachula, October 16, 2016; grammar lightly edited for clarity.

128. "United States Border Patrol Southwest Family Unit Subject and Unaccompanied Alien Children Apprehensions Fiscal Year 2016," U.S. Customs and Border Protection, October 18, 2016, https://www.cbp.gov/newsroom/stats/southwest-border-unaccompanied-children/fy-2016.

129. "H.R.2029—Consolidated Appropriations Act 2016," §7045, https://www.congress.gov/bill/114th-congress/house-bill/2029/text?q=%7B%22search%22%3A%5B%22%5C%22pl114-113%5C%22%22%5D%7D&resultIndex=1.

130. "Congressional Budget Justification Department of State, Foreign Operations, and Related Programs, FY 2016," February 2, 2015, p. 423, http://www.state.gov/s/d/rm/rls/ebs/2016/pdf/index.htm.

131. *Testimony of Deputy Assistant Secretary of State Juan Gonzalez,* March 22, 2016.

132. *Testimony of Michael Fisher, Chief United States Border Patrol U.S. Customs and Border Protection, Department of Homeland Security, before House Homeland Security Committee Subcommittee on Border, Maritime, and Global Counterterrorism,* 111th Cong.,

2nd Sess., July 22, 2010; see the posters at http://www.cbp.gov/border-security/human-trafficking/no-te-enga-241-es/print-ads and https://www.dvidshub.net/publication/749/no-mas-cruces-en-la-frontera#.VwamtKQgv8I.

133. "Plan of the Alliance for Prosperity in the Northern Triangle: A Road Map," Sep. 2014, p .9; P.L. 113-235, §7045 (a).

134. Roberto Dominguez and Martín Iñiguez Ramos, "The South/North Axis of Border Management in Mexico," in *Externalizing Migration Management: Europe, North America and the Spread of "Remote Control" Practices,* edited by Ruben Zaiotti (New York: Routledge, 2016), p. 232.

135. Mara Salvatrucha is a Salvadoran gang active in Central America, Mexico, and the United States. It preys on Central Americans in transit.

136. "La Bestia," YouTube, https://www.youtube.com/watch?v=IGimonYeqsk.

137. Jonathan T. Hiskey et al., "Understanding the Central American Refugee Crisis: Why They Are Fleeing and Why US Policies Are Failing to Deter Them," *American Immigration Council 1* (2016): pp. 1–2; The Canadian government funded a similar anti-snakehead publicity campaign in China in 2000; Mountz, *Seeking Asylum,* 47.

138. Meyer et al., "Unaccompanied Children," 24.

139. "U.S. to Admit More Central American Refugees," *New York Times,* July 26, 2016, https://www.nytimes.com/2016/07/27/us/politics/obama-refugees-central-america.html.

140. John Kerry, "Remarks on the U.S. Foreign Policy Agenda for 2016," National Defense University, January 13, 2016, http://www.state.gov/secretary/remarks/2016/01/251177.htm; Julia Preston, David M. Herszenhorn, and Michael D. Shear, "U.N. to Help U.S. Screen Central American Migrants," *New York Times,* January 12, 2016; Julie Hirschfeld Davis, "U.S. to Admit More Central American Refugees," *New York Times,* July 26, 2016; Meyer et al., "Unaccompanied Children," 9–10; "Termination of the Central American Minors Parole Program," *Federal Register* (82)157, August 16, 2017.

141. Gzesh, "So Close to the United States," 36.

142. "American Convention on Human rights 'Pact of San Jose, Costa Rica,'" 2014, https://www.oas.org/dil/treaties_B-32_American_Convention_on_Human_Rights.htm; Friedland and Rodríguez y Rodríguez, *Seeking Safe Ground,* 17.

143. Gzesh, "So Close to the United States," 36.

144. Jean-François Durieux, "Capturing the Central American Refugee Phenomenon: Refugee Law-Making in Mexico and Belize," *International Journal of Refugee Law 4,* no. 3 (1992): p. 310.

145. Gzesh, "So Close to the United States," 37.

146. García, *Seeking Refuge,* 77.

147. "Mexico Withdraws Reservations to Refugee and Stateless Conventions," UNHCR, February 11, 2014, http://www.unhcr.org/52fa05e79.html.

148. "Acuerdo por el que se emiten las Normas para el funcionamiento de las Estaciones Migratorias y Estancias Provisionales del Instituto Nacional de Migración," *Diario Oficial de la Federación,* November 8, 2012.

149. Centro de Derechos Humanos Fray Matías de Córdova, *Segundo informe sobre derechos humanos y condiciones de vida de las personas migrantes en el centro de*

detención de la ciudad de Tapachula, Chiapas (Tapachula, Chiapas: Centro de Derechos Humanos Fray Matías de Córdova, 2013), p. 21; Alba and Castillo, "New Approaches,"

150. "Ley de Migración," *Diario Oficial de la Federación*, May 25, 2011.

151. "Ley de Migración," 2011, Art. 76.

152. Art. 13, "Ley Sobre Refugiados y Protección Complementaria," *Diario Oficial de la Federación*, Jan. 27, 2011

153. Alba and Castillo "New Approaches," 18.

154. Bazzaco et al., *En tierra de nadie. El laberinto de la impunidad;* Wolf, *Diagnóstico del Instituto Nacional de Migración.*

155. Sin Fronteras, *Situación de los derechos humanos de las personas migrantes y solicitantes de asilo detenidas en las estaciones migratorias de México, 2007–2009* (México: Sin Fronteras, 2009), p. 26; Gabriela Díaz Prieto, *Operativos móviles de revisión migratoria en las carreteras de México* (Tijuana: El Colegio de la Frontera Norte, 2016).

156. "Overlooked, Under-Protected," Amnesty International, 2018, https://www.amnesty.org/download/Documents/AMR4176022018ENGLISH.PDF.

157. "Human Rights of Migrants and Other Persons in the Context of Human Mobility in Mexico," Inter-American Commission on Human Rights, 2013.

158. Comisión Nacional de los Derechos Humanos, *Informe especial sobre los casos de secuestro en contra de migrantes* (México: Comisión Nacional de los Derechos Humanos, 2009).

159. Comisión Nacional de los Derechos Humanos, *Informe especial sobre los casos de secuestro en contra de migrantes* (México: Comisión Nacional de los Derechos Humanos, 2011).

160. "Programa Especial de Migración 2014–2018," 51.

161. "Human Rights of Migrants," 90.

162. Art. 16. "Acuerdo por el que se emiten las normas para el funcionamiento de las estaciones migratorias del Instituto Nacional de Migración," *Diario Oficial de la Federación*, October 7, 2009.

163. Bazzaco et al., *En tierra de nadie,* 175.

164. "The Cost of Stemming the Tide," 16.

165. Wolf, *Diagnóstico del Instituto Nacional de Migración,* 333.

166. Calculated from *Boletines Estadísticos* 2003–2017, Secretaría de Gobernación.

167. Interview with Yesenia Sánchez, Tapachula, October 17, 2016; grammar lightly edited for clarity.

168. Interviews with Rev. Pat Murphy, director, Casa del Migrante, May 20, 2017; Marla Conrad, coordinator, Red Casas del Migrante y Centros de Derechos Humanos Zona Norte, Nogales February, 21, 2017; and Father Alvaro Salvador Gutierrez coordinator, Movilidad Humana de la Diócesis de Mexicali, February, 21, 2017.

169. "Estadísticas 2013–2017," Comisión Mexicana de Ayuda a Refugiados, https://www.gob.mx/cms/uploads/attachment/file/290340/ESTADISTICAS_2013_A_4TO_TRIMESTRE_2017.pd; Gabriela Díaz Prieto, "Familias centroamericanas migrantes en México," Instituto para las Mujeres en la Migración, Mexico City, 2017, http://familiascentroamericanasmigrantesenmexico.imumi.org/wp-content/uploads/2017/11/Familias-centroamericanas-completo.pdf.

170. Flynn, "¿Dónde está la FRONTERA?" 29–30; "U.S. Committee for Refugees World Refugee Survey 2002—Guatemala," U.S. Committee for Refugees and Immigrants, June 10, 2002.

171. "Illegal African Migration Poses Challenge to Panama," Wikileaks, December 10, 2009, https://wikileaks.org/plusd/cables/09PANAMA873_a.html.

172. Claire Inder, "International Refugee Law, 'Hyper-Legalism' and Migration Management: The Pacific Solution," in *The Politics of International Migration Management*, edited by Martin Geiger and Antoine Pécoud (New York: Palgrave Macmillan, 2010), p. 221.

Chapter 8

1. Maarten den Heijer, "Europe and Extraterritorial Asylum" (PhD dissertation, Institute of Immigration Law, Faculty of Law, Leiden University, 2011), p. 197.

2. Violeta Moreno-Lax, *Accessing Asylum in Europe: Extraterritorial Border Controls and Refugee Rights under EU Law* (Oxford University Press, 2017), p. 466.

3. Timothy J. Hatton, "Refugees and asylum seekers, the crisis in Europe and the future of policy," *Economic Policy 32* no. 91 (2017): p. 456

4. EU Commission 2007, "Study on the international law instruments in relation to illegal immigration by sea," Commission Staff Working Document. SEC (2007), p. 691, ¶4.2.2.10

5. See, for example, Will Worley, "Theresa May 'will campaign to leave the European Convention on Human Rights in 2020 election'," *The Independent*, December 29, 2016.

6. Ségolène Barbou des Places and Hélène Oger, "Making the European Migration Regime: Decoding Member States' Legal Strategies," *European Journal of Migration and Law 6*, no. 4 (2004): p. 356; Andrew Geddes, "International Migration and State Sovereignty in an Integrating Europe," *International Migration 39*, no. 6 (2001): p. 22; Virginie Guiraudon and Gallya Lahav, "A Reappraisal of the State Sovereignty Debate: The Case of Migration Control," *Comparative Political Studies 33*, no. 2 (2000): p. 182; Sandra Lavenex, "Shifting Up and Out: The Foreign Policy of European Immigration Control," *West European Politics 29*, no. 2 (2006): p. 330.

7. James Hampshire, "European Migration Governance Since the Lisbon Treaty: Introduction to the Special Issue," *Journal of Ethnic and Migration Studies 42*, no. 4 (2016): p. 542; Virginie Guiraudon, "The Constitution of a European Immigration Policy Domain: A Political Sociology Approach," *Journal of European Public Policy 10*, no. 2 (2003): p. 268; Heather Grabbe, "The Sharp Edges of Europe: Extending Schengen Eastwards," *International Affairs 76*, no. 3 (2000): p. 524.

8. Karin Fathimath Afeef, "The Politics of Extraterritorial Processing: Offshore Asylum Policies in Europe and the Pacific," Working Paper no. 36, Refugee Studies Centre, University of Oxford, 2006, p. 18.

9. Guiraudon and Lahav, "A Reappraisal," 169; *Case of Hirsi Jamaa and Others v. Italy*, no. 27765/09, ECtHR, 2012.

10. Helen Toner, "The Lisbon Treaty and the Future of European Immigration and Asylum Law," in *EU Migration Law: Legal Complexities and Political Rationales*, edited by Loic Azoulai and Karin De Vries (Oxford: Oxford University Press, 2014), p. 39.

11. Gregor Noll, *Negotiating Asylum: The EU acquis, Extraterritorial Protection and the Common Market of Deflection* (The Hague: Martinus Nijhoff, 2000), p. 442.

12. Thomas Gammeltoft-Hansen, *Access to Asylum: International Refugee Law and the Globalisation of Migration Control* (Cambridge: Cambridge University Press, 2011), p. 21; Maarten Den Heijer, *Europe and Extraterritorial Asylum* (Oxford: Hart, 2012).

13. Frank McNamara, "Member State Responsibility for Migration Control within Third States—Externalisation Revisited," *European Journal of Migration and Law 15* (2013): p. 334.

14. Afeef, *Politics of Extraterritorial Processing*, 14.

15. *T.I. v. UK*, no. 43844/98, ECtHR, 2000.

16. Lavenex, "Shifting Up and Out," 344.

17. Carl Levy, "Refugees, Europe, Camps/State of Exception: 'Into the Zone,' the European Union and Extraterritorial Processing of Migrants, Refugees, and Asylum-Seekers (Theories and Practice)," *Refugee Survey Quarterly 29*, no. 1 (2010): p. 113.

18. Guiraudon, "The Constitution," 277–278.

19. Richard Plender, "Recent Trends in National Immigration Control," *The International and Comparative Law Quarterly 35*, no. 3 (1986): pp. 531–566; Ingrid Boccardi, *Europe and Refugees: Towards an EU Aasylum Policy*, vol. 31 (The Hague: Kluwer Law International, 2002), p. 48.

20. The Benelux countries did the same over the course of the year and added several other refugee-producing countries—Afghanistan, Iraq, Iran, and Turkey (Boccardi, *Europe and Refugees*, 48).

21. *H.C. Hansard*, Vol. 112, col. 765, March 16, 1987, http://hansard. millbanksystems.com/commons/1987/mar/16/immigration-carriers-liability-bill#S6CV0112P0_19870316_HOC_383.

22. Sile Reynolds and Helen Muggeridge, "Remote Controls: How UK Border Controls are Endangering the Lives of Refugees," British Refugee Council, 2008, p. 25; Matthew Gibney, "A Thousand Little Guantanamos: Western States and Measures to Prevent the Arrival of Refugees," in *Displacement, Asylum, Migration: The Oxford Amnesty Lectures 2004*, edited by Kate E. Tunstall (New York: Oxford University Press, 2006), pp. 123, 159.

23. Reynolds and Muggeridge, "Remote Controls," 87, citing evidence by James Munro, Assistant Director of the Immigration Service to the High Court, *European Roma Rights Centre vs. Immigration Officer at Prague Airport*, August 10, 2002.

24. "ERRC Reaction to UK Reintroducing Visas for Slovak Citizens," ERRC, October 8, 1998, http://www.errc.org/article/errc-reaction-to-uk-reintroducing-visas-for-slovak-citizens/166; Grabbe, "The Sharp Edges," 528; Reynolds and Muggeridge, "Remote Controls," 26; Matthew E. Price, *Rethinking Asylum: History, Purpose, and Limits* (Cambridge: Cambridge University Press, 2009), p. 208.

25. Reynolds and Muggeridge, "Remote Controls," 26.

26. Price, *Rethinking Asylum*, 208.

27. See David Cook-Martín and David Scott FitzGerald, "How Their Laws Affect Our Laws: Mechanisms of Immigration Policy Diffusion in the Americas, 1790–2010," *Law and Society Review*, forthcoming, on mechanisms of policy diffusion.

28. Erika Feller, "Carrier Sanctions and International Law," *International Journal of Refugee Law 1*, no. 1 (1989): p. 50.

29. Strictly speaking, the lists refer to states, entities, special administrative regions, and territories rather than countries. Ireland and the UK are EU members but opted out of the common visa system and maintain their own lists. Iceland and Norway are not part of the EU, but they are part of the common visa system. The authority to create EU visa requirement and exemption lists is laid out in Treaty Establishing the European Community (1992), Art 100. For a detailed analysis of the Europeanization of visas, see Elspeth Guild, "The Border Abroad—Visas and Border Controls," in *In Search of Europe's Borders*, edited by Kees Groenendijk, Elspeth Guild, and Paul Minderhoud (The Hague: Kluwer Law International, 2003).

30. Grabbe, "The Sharp Edges," 533.

31. Council Regulation (EC) No 539/2001 of March 15, 2001; "Lists of third countries whose nationals must be in possession of a visa when crossing the external borders and of those whose nationals are exempt from that requirement," https://ec.europa.eu/home-affairs/sites/homeaffairs/files/what-we-do/policies/borders-and-visas/visa-policy/apply_for_a_visa/docs/visa_lists_en.pdf.

32. Guiraudon and Lahav, "A Reappraisal," 180.

33. Regulation (Ec) No 810/2009 of the European Parliament and of the Council of July 13, 2009 establishing a Community Code on Visas (Visa Code) (OJ L 243, 15.9.2009, Annex IV.

34. Council Regulation (EC) No 539/2001 of March 15, 2001, Annex II; "Lists of third countries whose nationals must be in possession of a visa when crossing the external borders and of those whose nationals are exempt from that requirement,"

35. See "EU Member States Granted Protection to More Than 330,000 Asylum Seekers in 2015," Eurostat Press Release, April 20, 2016, http://ec.europa.eu/eurostat/documents/2995521/7233417/3-20042016-AP-EN.pdf/.

36. Immigration Act 1971 Schedule 2, ¶8.

37. UK Immigration (Carriers Liability) Act 1987, §1(1).

38. *H.C. Hansard*, Vol. 112, col. 765, March 16, 1987, http://hansard.millbanksystems.com/commons/1987/mar/16/immigration-carriers-liability-bill#column_706.

39. *H.C. Hansard*, Vol. 112, col. 717, March 16, 1987, http://hansard.millbanksystems.com/commons/1987/mar/16/immigration-carriers-liability-bill#column_717.

40. *R v. Secretary of State for the Home Department, Ex parte Khalil Yassine, Rahma Yassime, Mohammad El-Nacher, Hicham Ali Hachem, Salam Bou Imad, Zouheir Bou Imad*, [1990] Imm AR 354, United Kingdom: High Court (England and Wales), 6 March 1990.

41. Matthew J. Gibney, *The Ethics and Politics of Asylum: Liberal Democracy and the Response to Refugees* (Cambridge: Cambridge University Press, 2004), p. 123.

42. Frances Nicholson, "Implementation of the Immigration (Carriers' Liability) Act 1987: Privatising Immigration Functions at the Expense of International Obligations?" *International & Comparative Law Quarterly 46*, no. 03 (1997): p. 591.

43. *European Roma Rights Centre and Others v. the Immigration Officer at Prague Airport and the Secretary of State for the Home Department*, §43 [2003] EWCA Civ 666.

44. *R v. Naillie; R v. Kanesarajah*, [1993] AC 674, [1993] 2 All ER 782, [1993] 2 WLR 927, [1993] Imm AR 462, United Kingdom: House of Lords (Judicial Committee), 26 May 1993.

45. Sophie Scholten, *The Privatisation of Immigration Control through Carrier Sanctions: The Role of Private Transport Companies in Dutch and British Immigration Control* (Leiden: Brill Nijhoff, 2015), pp. 3–4.

46. Loi du 15 decembre 1980 sur l'accès au territoire, le sejour; l'etablissement et l'eloignement des étrangers, §74, as amended in 1987; Danish Aliens Act as modified on December 17, 1987, Art. 59a.

47. *Schengen Implementation Agreement*, June 19, 1990, Art. 26; Sophie Scholten and Paul Minderhoud, "Regulating Immigration Control: Carrier Sanctions in the Netherlands," *European Journal of Migration and Law 10* (2008): pp. 127–128.

48. "Carriers' Liability," European Council on Refugees and Exiles, 1999, http://www.refworld.org/pdfid/3c02740b4.pdf.

49. Virginie Guiraudon, "Enlisting Third Parties in Border Control: A Comparative Study of Its Causes and Consequences," in *Borders and Security Governance: Managing Borders in a Globalised World*, edited by Marina Caparini and Otwin Marenin (Geneva: Geneva Centre for the Democratic Control of Armed Forces), p. 84.

50. *Schengen Implementation Agreement*, June 19, 1990, Art. 26; France, Law 92-190 of February 26, 1992, Art. 20a.

51. Den Heijer, "Europe and Extraterritorial Asylum," 186.

52. Tally Kritzman-Amir, "Privatization and Delegation of State Authority in Asylum Systems," *Law & Ethics of Human Rights 5*, no. 1 (2011): pp. 203–204.

53. Feller, "Carrier Sanctions," 58; den Heijer, "Europe and Extraterritorial Asylum," 184.

54. Feller, "Carrier Sanctions," 62; Decision No. VI/3 H 2728/87.

55. Gerald L. Neumann, "Buffer Zones against Refugees: Dublin, Schengen, and the German Asylum Amendment," *Virginia Journal of International Law 33* (1992): p. 521.

56. Guiraudon, "Enlisting Third Parties," 84.

57. Andrew Brouwer and Judith Kumin, "Interception and Asylum: When Migration Control and Human Rights Collide," *Refuge 21*, no. 4 (2003): p. 10.

58. The IATA/Control Authorities Working Group (IATA/CAWG) A Code of Conduct for Immigration Liaison Officers, October 2002, ¶ 2.3, http://www.icao.int/Meetings/FAL12/Documents/FAL.12.WP.040.att.1.en.pdf.

59. Morrison, *The Trafficking and Smuggling of Refugees*, 42.

60. Morrison, *The Trafficking and Smuggling of Refugees*, 54–59.

61. Brouwer and Kumin, "Interception and Asylum," 10–11; Reynolds and Muggeridge, "Remote Controls," 37.

62. *European Roma Rights Centre and Others v. the Immigration Officer at Prague Airport and the Secretary of State for the Home Department* [2003] EWCA Civ 666; *Regina v. Immigration Officer at Prague Airport and Another* [2004] UKHL 55.

63. The "Dublin II Regulation" set out the criteria for determining a single member state responsible for examining an asylum application (Council Regulation (EC) No 343/2003 of February 18, 2003). It was replaced by the "Dublin III Regulation" (Directive 2013/32/EU of the European Parliament and of the Council of June 26, 2013).

64. Convention determining the State Responsible for Examining Applications for Asylum Lodged in One of the Member States of the European Communities 1990 ("Dublin Convention") (97/C 254/01), Art. 6.

65. Den Heijer, "Europe and Extraterritorial Asylum," 214.

66. Gammeltoft-Hansen, *Access to Asylum*, 74.

67. Neumann, "Buffer Zones," 503–526.

68. Council of the European Union, Presidency Conclusions of the Seville European Council, June 21, 22, 2002, ¶33–36.

69. Sarah Collinson, "Visa Requirements, Carrier Sanctions, 'Safe Third Countries' and 'Readmission': The Development of an Asylum 'Buffer Zone' In Europe," *Transactions of the Institute of British Geographers 21*, no. 1 (1996): p. 84.

70. UNHCR EXCOM Conclusion No. 58(XL) "Problem of refugees and asylum-seekers who move in an irregular manner from a country in which they had already found protection" (1989). See Gil-Bazo 2015 for a legal analysis.

71. Matthew Hunt, "The Safe Country of Origin Concept in European Asylum Law: Past, Present and Future," *International Journal of Refugee Law 26*, no. 4 (2014): p. 504.

72. Convention determining the State responsible for examining applications for asylum lodged in one of the Member States of the European Communities 1990 ("Dublin Convention") (97/C 254/01) Art. 3(5).

73. Council Resolution of November 30, 1992 on a harmonized approach to questions concerning host third countries ("London Resolution"), November 30, 1992. The London Resolution usage of the term "host third country" is substantially the same as "safe third country."

74. Rosemary Byrne, Gregor Noll, and Jens Vedsted-Hansen, "Understanding Refugee Law in an Enlarged European Union," *European Journal of International Law 15*, no. 2 (2004): p. 360.

75. Council Directive 2005/85/EC of December 1, 2005 on minimum standards on procedures in Member States for granting and withdrawing refugee status, Art. 27.

76. Council Directive 2005/85/EC of December 1, 2005 on minimum standards on procedures in Member States for granting and withdrawing refugee status, Art. 23(4)(c).

77. Council Directive 2005/85/EC of December 1, 2005 on minimum standards on procedures in Member States for granting and withdrawing refugee status, Art. 36.

78. *European Parliament v. Council of the European Union*, C-133/06, 6 May 2008.

79. Directive 2013/32/EU of the European Parliament and of the Council of June 26, 2013 on common procedures for granting and withdrawing international protection, Art. 39(7).

80. "Refugee and Asylum-Seeker Inflows in the United States and Other OECD Member States," Congressional Research Service, 2009, p. 14, https://digital.library.unt.edu/ark:/67531/metadc813111/.

81. "Safe Country Concepts," Asylum Information Database, 2017, http://www.asylumineurope.org/comparator/asylum-procedure#safe-country-concepts.

82. "Greece: New Government Tackles Migration and Asylum Issues," Wikileaks, December 4, 2009, https://wikileaks.org/plusd/cables/09ATHENS1685_a.html;

"Observations on Greece as a Country of Asylum," UNHCR, 2009, http://www.refworld.org/pdfid/4b4b3fc82.pdf.

83. *M.S.S. v Belgium and Greece*, no. 30696/09, ECtHR, 2011.

84. *Ilias and Ahmed v. Hungary*, no. 47287/15, ECtHR, 2017.

85. Council Directive 2005/85/EC of December 1, 2005, Art. 29 & 30.

86. Council Directive 2005/85/EC of December 1, 2005, Art 23(4)(c); Recital 19.

87. Council Directive 2005/85/EC of December 1, 2005, Annex II.

88. "Migrant Camps in Libya/Ukraine: EU Debates Measures to Control International Migration," Wikileaks, September 28, 2004, https://wikileaks.org/plusd/cables/04BRUSSELS4151_a.html.

89. "Migrant Camps in Libya/Ukraine."

90. "EU Divided over List of 'Safe Countries or Origin,'" Statewatch, 2004, http://www.statewatch.org/news/2004/sep/safe-countries.pdf.

91. "Safe Countries of Origin—EMN Inform," European Migration Network, Brussels, 2018, http://emn.ie/files/p_201803140327442018_inform_safe_country_of_origin_14.03.2018.pdf.

92. European Commission. Proposal for a Regulation of the European Parliament and of the Council establishing an EU common list of safe countries of origin for the purposes of Directive 2013/32/EU of the European Parliament and of the Council on common procedures for granting and withdrawing international protection, and amending Directive 2013/32/EU, Pub. L. No. COM/2015/0452 (2016), http://eur-lex.europa.eu/legal-content/en/TXT/?uri=CELEX:52015PC0452.

93. Council of the European Union, "Outcome of the Council Meeting (3405th Meeting)," July 20, 2015, p. 10, http://www.consilium.europa.eu/media/22985/st11097en15.pdf.

94. "Iris Solution Helps Refugees Glimpse a Brighter Future," Planet Biometrics, Dec. 22, 2015, http://www.planetbiometrics.com/article-details/i/3923/desc/iris-solution-helps-refugees-glimpse-a-brighter-future/; "UN Uses IrisGuard EyePay Platform to Aid Vulnerable Refugees," IrisGuard press release, July 24, 2017, http://www.irisguard.com/index.php/news/index/2017/109.

95. Nils Coleman, *European Readmission Policy: Third Country Interests and Refugee Rights* (Leiden: Martinus Nijhoff, 2009), p. 318.

96. Sarah Wolff, "The Politics of Negotiating EU Readmission Agreements: Insights from Morocco and Turkey," in *Externalizing Migration Management: Europe, North America and the Spread of "Remote Control" Practices*, edited by Ruben Zaiotti (London: Routledge, 2016), p. 90.

97. "Los acuerdos bilaterales suscritos por España en materia migratoria con países del continente africano," Universidad de Granada, http://www.ugr.es/~redce/REDCE10/articulos/04MAsuncionAsinCabrera.htm.

98. Coleman, *European Readmission Policy*, 13–14.

99. Intergovernmental Consultations on Asylum, Refugee and Migration Policies in Europe, North America and Australia (IGC)," in *Report on Readmission Agreements* (Geneva: IGC, 1994), p. 2.

100. Collinson, "Visa Requirements," 85–87.

101. "Los acuerdos bilaterales suscritos por España en materia migratoria con países del continente africano."

102. IGC, *Report on Readmission Agreements* (Geneva: IGC, 2000), pp. 4, 39–40. Cf. Ruben Zaiotti, *Externalizing Migration Management: Europe, North America and the Spread of Remote Control Practices* (London: Routledge, 2016), p. 19.

103. The European Council endorsed the Schengen-Poland agreement as a model for bilateral agreements involving EU member states in 1994 (IGC, *Report on Readmission Agreement*, 21).

104. Coleman, *European Readmission Policy*, 147.

105. "Inventory of the Agreements Linked to Readmission," EUI, 2011, http://rsc.eui.eu/RDP/wp-content/uploads/2014/01/RAs-third-countries-with-EU-Member-States.jpg.

106. "Migration Management: Regional Approach for EU and Neighbors Proposed at Ministerial Conference," Wikileaks, February 9, 2006, https://wikileaks.org/plusd/cables/06BRUSSELS442_a.html.

107. European Council, Database of Treaties and Agreements, http://www.consilium.europa.eu/en/documents-publications/treaties-agreements/ (accessed September 24, 2018); Lavenex, "Shifting Up and Out," 347.

108. "Mauritania: 'Nobody Wants to Have Anything to Do with Us,'" AFR 38/001/2008, Amnesty International, 2008, p. 13, https://www.amnesty.org/download/Documents/AFR380012008ENGLISH.pdf.

109. Zaiotti, *Externalizing Migration Management*, 20.

110. Oleg Korneev and Andrey Leonov, "Eurasia and the Externalities of Border Control: Spillover Dynamics Of EU-Russia Cooperation on Migration," in *Externalizing Migration Management: Europe, North America and the Spread of "Remote Control" Practices*, edited by Ruben Zaiotti (London: Routledge, 2016), pp. 161–168.

111. Mehdi Rais, "European Union Readmission Agreements," *Forced Migration Review*, January 2016, p. 46.

112. Korneev and Leonov, "Eurasia and the Externalities of Border Control," 169.

113. Coleman, *European Readmission Policy*, 225.

114. "Mauritania," 24.

115. Stephen H. Legomsky, "Secondary Refugee Movements and the Return of Asylum Seekers to Third Countries: The Meaning of Effective Protection," *International Journal of Refugee Law* 15, no. 4 (2003): p. 584.

116. Carole Billet, "EC Readmission Agreements: A Prime Instrument of the External Dimension of the EU's Fight against Irregular Immigration. An Assessment after Ten Years of Practice," *European Journal of Migration and Law* 12, no. 1 (2010): pp. 45–79.

117. Gibney, *The Ethics and Politics of Asylum*, 103–104; IGC, *Report on Readmission Agreements*, 3.

118. Neuman, "Buffer Zones against Refugees," 514.

119. "Greece: Frontier of Hope and Fear," Amnesty International, 2014, p. 7.

120. Byrne et al., "Understanding Refugee Law,"

121. Coleman, *European Readmission Policy*, 132.

122. See Madeline Garlick, "The EU Discussions on Extraterritorial Processing: Solution or Conundrum?" *International Journal of Refugee Law* 18, no. 3-4 (2006): pp. 601–629, and Lavenex, "Shifting Up and Out" for reviews of each of these policy statements.

123. Bernd Kasparek, "Borders and Populations in Flux: Frontex's Place in the European Union's Migration Management," in *The Politics of International Migration Management*, edited by Martin Geiger and Antoine Pécoud (New York: Palgrave Macmillan 2010). Seline Trevisanut, "Which Borders for the EU Immigration Policy? Yardsticks of International Protection for EU Joint Borders Management," in *EU Migration Law: Legal Complexities and Political Rationales*, edited by Loic Azoulai and Karin De Vries (Oxford: Oxford University Press, 2014).

124. "Frontex Budget 2016," Frontex, http://frontex.europa.eu/assets/About_ Frontex/Governance_documents/Budget/Budget_2016.pdf.

125. "Beyond the Frontiers. Frontex: The First Five Years," Frontex, 2010, p .69.

126. Regulation (EU) 2016/1624 of the European Parliament and of the Council of 14 September 2016 on the European Border and Coast Guard and amending Regulation (EU) 2016/399 of the European Parliament and of the Council and repealing Regulation (EC) No 863/2007 of the European Parliament and of the Council, Council Regulation (EC) No 2007/2004 and Council Decision 2005/267/EC, Art. 54, https://eur-lex.europa.eu/legal-content/EN/TXT/?uri=CELEX%3A32016R1624.

127. "Migration Management: Regional Approach for EU and Neighbors Proposed at Ministerial Conference," Wikileaks, February 9, 2006, https://wikileaks.org/ plusd/cables/06BRUSSELS442_a.html; Presidency Conclusions, European Council Brussels, December 15 and 16, 2005, http://www.consilium.europa.eu/ueDocs/cms_ Data/docs/pressData/en/ec/87642.pdf.

128. Ivaylo Gatev, "Very Remote Control: Policing the Outer Perimeter of the Eastern Neighbourhood," in *The External Dimension of EU Justice and Home Affairs: Governance, Neighbours, Security*, edited by Thierry Balzacq (Houndmills: Palgrave Macmillan, 2009), pp. 212–217.

129. Gatev, "Very Remote Control," 222–223.

130. "Technical Assistance for Study on Concrete Results Obtained through Projects on Migration and Development Financed under AENEAS and the Thematic Programme for Migration and Asylum. Final Report," Framework Contract Commission, 2014, pp. 6, 9–10, https://ec.europa.eu/europeaid/sites/devco/files/ study-migration-and-development-20141031_en.pdf.

131. "Global Approach to Migration and Mobility," European Commission Migration and Home Affairs, http://ec.europa.eu/dgs/home-affairs/what-we-do/ policies/international-affairs/global-approach-to-migration/index_en.htm.

132. Stefan Brocza and Katharina Paulhart, "EU Mobility Partnerships: A Smart Instrument for the Externalization of Migration Control," *European Journal of Futures Research 3*, no. 15 (2015).

133. European Council, Valletta Summit Action Plan, November 11–12, 2015, http:// www.consilium.europa.eu/media/21839/action_plan_en.pdf.

134. Stephan Dünnwald, "Europe's Global Approach to Migration Management," in *Externalizing Migration Management: Europe, North America and the Spread of "Remote Control" Practices*, edited by Ruben Zaiotti (London: Routledge, 2016), pp. 118, 126–129.

135. Participants of the Valletta Summit on Migration, Political Declaration, Presented at the Valletta Summit on Migration, Valletta, 2015, http://www.consilium. europa.eu/en/meetings/international-summit/2015/11/FINAL_DECL_EN-(2)_pdf/.

136. The European Union Emergency Trust Fund for Stability and Addressing the Root Causes of Irregular Migration and Displaced Persons in Africa, Action Fiche for the implementation of the Horn of Africa Window T05—EUTF—HoA—REG—09, p. 9.

137. "Human Rights Impacts and Risks Associated with the Khartoum Process: Submission to the UK All-Party Parliamentary Group for Sudan and South Sudan," Amnesty International, October 2016.

138. "Detailed Findings of the Commission of Inquiry on Human Rights in Eritrea," Human Rights Council, 32nd session, June 8, 2016, http://www.ohchr.org/Documents/HRBodies/HRCouncil/CoIEritrea/A_HRC_32_CRP.1_read-only.pdf.

139. "EU Member States Granted Protection."

140. UN Security Council Resolutions 819 (April 16, 1993), 824 (May 6, 1993), and 836 (June 4, 1993).

141. SG/SM/9993, July 11, 2005, http://www.un.org/press/en/2005/sgsm9993.doc.htm.

142. Tampere European Council, October 15 and 16, 1999, Presidency Conclusions, ¶22.

143. "Technical Assistance," 6.

144. Reynolds and Muggeridge, "Remote Controls," 55.

145. Ana López-Sala, "Exploring Dissuasion as a (Geo)Political Instrument in Irregular Migration Control at the Southern Spanish Maritime Border," *Geopolitics* 20, no. 3 (2015): pp. 12–13.

146. Galina Cornelisse, "Territory, Procedures and Rights: Border Procedures in European Asylum Law," *Refugee Survey Quarterly* 35, no. 1 (2016): p. 74.

147. Guiraudon, "Enlisting Third Parties," 86.

148. Gerald L. Neuman, "Anomalous Zones," *Stanford Law Review* 48, no. 5 (1996): pp. 1833–1901.

149. Neuman, "Anomalous Zones."

150. *Amuur v. France*, no. 17/1995/523/609, ECtHR , 1996.

151. Judith Hippler Bello and Juliane Kokott, "Amuur v. France," *American Journal of International Law* 91, no. 1 (1997): pp. 147–152.

152. "Country Report: France," Asylum Information Database, December 2015; Tugba Basaran, "Legal Borders in Europe: The Waiting Zone," in *A Threat against Europe?*, edited by J. Peter Burgess and Serge Gutwirth (Brussels: Brussels University Press, 2011).

153. Gina Clayton, "The UK and Extraterritorial Immigration Control: Entry Clearance and Juxtaposed Control," in *Extraterritorial Immigration Control: Legal Challenges*, edited by Bernard Ryan and Valsamis Mitsilegas (Leiden: Brill, 2010), pp. 412–418.

154. Reynolds and Muggeridge, "Remote Controls," 87 citing evidence by James Munro, Assistant Director of the Immigration Service to the High Court, *European Roma Rights Centre vs Immigration Officer at Prague Airport*, August 10, 2002.

155. Clayton, "The UK and Extraterritorial Immigration Control," 417.

156. "Fatal Journeys," vol. 2, IOM, 2016, p. 11.

157. "Protection of Asylum-Seekers in Situations of Large-Scale Influx," UNHCR ExCom Conclusions no. 22 (XXXII) 1981, II. 2.

158. Dirk Godenau and Ana López-Sala, "Multi-layered Migration Deterrence and Technology in Spanish Maritime Border Management," *Journal of Borderlands Studies* 31, no. 2 (2016): pp. 151–169.

159. "Fear and Fences: Europe's Approach to Keeping Refugees at Bay," Amnesty International, 2015, p. 22.

160. "EU Readmission Agreements," European Policy Centre, March 21, 2012, http://www.epc.eu/pub_details.php?cat_id=6&pub_id=1435.

161. Wolff, "The Politics of Negotiating . . . ," 99.

162. Joint declaration establishing a Mobility Partnership between the Kingdom of Morocco and the European Union and its Member States, 6139/13, June 3, 2013.

163. Stefan Alscher, "Knocking at the Doors of 'Fortress Europe': Migration and Border Control in Southern Spain and Eastern Poland," Working Paper no. 126, Center for Comparative Immigration Studies, University of California, San Diego, 2005, p. 11; Peter Andreas, *Border Games: Policing the U.S.-Mexico Divide* (Ithaca: Cornell University Press, 2001).

164. "'Spain and Morocco' Failure to Protect the Rights of Migrants—Ceuta and Melilla One Year On," Amnesty International, October 30, 2006.

165. "S.O.S. Racismo 2006," *Informe Anual 2006*, Barcelona, Icaria Editorial, p. 116.

166. "Asylum Seekers Overwhelm UNHCR in Rabat," Wikileaks, January 3, 2006, https://wikileaks.org/plusd/cables/06RABAT2_a.html; Wolff, "The Politics of Negotiating," 98.

167. "'Spain and Morocco.'"

168. "Lampedusa and Melilla: Southern Frontier of Fortress Europe," European United Left/Nordic Green Left, Brussels, UUE/NGL, 2005.

169. "Fear and Fences," 31.

170. "Fear and Fences," 35.

171. Àngels Piñol, "Fernández defiende los 'rechazos en frontera' y el uso de gas pimienta," *El País*, May 5, 2014, http://ccaa.elpais.com/ccaa/2014/05/05/catalunya/1399287834_937254.html.

172. Gabriela Sánchez, "Imputado el coronel jefe de la Guardia Civil de Melilla por permitir las devoluciones en caliente," *eldiario.es*, September 15, 2014, http://www.eldiario.es/desalambre/Imputado-Guardia-Civil-Melilla-devoluciones_0_303070030.html.

173. Sánchez, "Imputado el coronel jefe."

174. "Vídeo: Una ONG denuncia la entrada de soldados marroquíes a España para deportar inmigrantes," *eldiario.es*, March 31, 2014, http://www.eldiario.es/desalambre/VIDEO-ONG-marroquies-territorio-inmigrantes_0_244625538.html.

175. "Video de Prodein sobre salto valla Melilla," Vimeo, October 15, 2014, https://vimeo.com/109123987.

176. "Ley 12/2009, de 30 de octubre, reguladora del derecho de asilo y de la protección subsidiaria," *Boletín Oficial del Estado* no. 263, sec 1. p. 90869, Art. 17(2)

177. Maarten den Heijer, "Europe and Extraterritorial Asylum" (PhD diss., Leiden University, 2011), pp. 255–256.

178. "Ley Orgánica 4/2015, de 30 de marzo, de protección de la seguridad ciudadana," *Boletín Oficial del Estado* no. 77, 31 de marzo de 2015, §I. p. 27242

179. "Spain: Legislation and Practice on Immigration and Asylum Must Adhere to Human Rights Standards," Council of Europe Commissioner for Human Rights, January 16, 2015, http://www.coe.int/be/web/commissioner/-/spain-legislation-and-practice-on-immigration-and-asylum-must-adhere-to-human-rights-standards; ECRE Weekly Bulletin, September 30, 2016, http://us1.campaign-archive1.com/?u=8 e3ebd297b1510becc6d6d690&id=7b2f301659#Ceuta; "Fear and Fences."

180. *N.D. and N.T. v. Spain*, no. 8675/15 and no. 8697/15, ECtHR, 2017.

181. "Refugees and Migrants in Spain: The Invisible Walls beyond the Southern Border," Spanish Refugee Aid Commission, 2017, pp. 23–25, https://www.cear.es/wp-content/uploads/2018/03/REPORT-MUROS-FRONTERA-SUR.pdf.

182. "Fear and Fences," 13, 22, 40; Ruben Andersson, *Illegality, Inc.: Clandestine Migration and the Business of Bordering Europe* (Berkeley: University of California Press, 2014), ch. 5.

183. "Containment Plan: Bulgaria's Pushbacks and Detentions of Syrian and Other Asylum Seekers and Migrants," Human Rights Watch, 2014, pp. 3, 25, https://www.hrw.org/report/2014/04/28/containment-plan/bulgarias-pushbacks-and-detention-syrian-and-other-asylum-seekers.

184. "Bulgaria: Pushbacks, Abuse at Borders," Human Rights Watch, January 20, 2016, https://www.hrw.org/news/2016/01/20/bulgaria-pushbacks-abuse-borders.

185. "Europe's Borderlands: Violations against Refugees and Migrants in Macedonia, Serbia and Hungary," Amnesty International, 2015, pp. 16, 65–66.

186. Rick Lyman and Helene Bienvenu, "Migrants Clash with Police in Hungary, as Others Enter Croatia," *New York Times*, September 16, 2015.

187. "Country Report: Hungary," Asylum Information Database, February 2018, pp. 17–19, http://www.asylumineurope.org/sites/default/files/report-download/aida_hu_2017update.pdf.

188. *Ilias and Ahmed v. Hungary*, no. 47287/15, ECtHR, 2017.

189. *Khurram v. Hungary*, no. 12625/17, ECtHR, 2017 and *H.K. v. Hungary*, no. 18531/17, ECtHR, 2017.

190. "Croatia: Asylum Seekers Forced Back to Serbia," Human Rights Watch, January 20, 2017, https://www.hrw.org/news/2017/01/20/croatia-asylum-seekers-forced-back-serbia.

191. "Migration: Commission Steps up Infringement Procedure against Hungary Concerning Its Asylum Law," European Commission Press Release Database, December 7, 2017, http://europa.eu/rapid/press-release_IP-17-5023_en.htm.

192. "About AIDA," Asylum Information Database, 2018, http://www.asylumineurope.org/about-aida.

Chapter 9

1. "Beyond the Frontiers. Frontex: The First Five Years," Frontex, 2010, pp. 34–37; Bernard Ryan, "Extraterritorial Immigration Controls: What Role for Legal Guarantees?," in *Extraterritorial Immigration Control: Legal Challenges*, edited by Bernard Ryan and Valsamis Mitsilegas (Leiden: Martinus Nijhoff, 2010), p. 34.

2. Maribel Casas-Cortes, Sebastian Cobarrubias, and John Pickles, "'Good Neighbours Make Good Fences': Seahorse Operations, Border Externalization and Extra-Territoriality," *European Urban and Regional Studies* 23, no. 3 (2014): pp. 5, 12.

3. Casas-Cortes et al., "'Good Neighbours Make Good Fences,'"12–13.

4. *J.H.A. v. Spain*, CAT/C/41/D/323/2007, UN Committee Against Torture, November 21, 2008.

5. "Long Detention Periods and Poor Conditions at the 'Mauritanian Guantanamo,'" Wikileaks, June 8, 2009, https://wikileaks.org/plusd/cables/09NOUAKCHOTT379_a.html.

6. "Mauritania: 'Nobody Wants to Have Anything to Do With Us,'" AFR 38/001/2008, Amnesty International, 2008, p. 3; Stephan Dünnwald, "Europe's Global Approach to Migration Management," in *Externalizing Migration Management: Europe, North America and the Spread of "Remote Control" Practices*, edited by Ruben Zaiotti (London: Routledge, 2016), p. 118.

7. Dünnwald, "Europe's Global Approach," 118–120.

8. "Senegal's Boat People: More Organized and Heading to America?," Wikileaks, July 5, 2006, https://wikileaks.org/plusd/cables/06DAKAR1588_a.html.

9. Valeria Bonavita, "The Externalization of Border Controls Towards the EU's Broader Neighbourhood," in *The European Union's Broader Neighbourhood: Challenges and Opportunities for Cooperation Beyond the European Neighbourhood Policy*, edited by Sieglinde Gstöhl and Erwan Lannon (London: Routledge, 2015), pp. 20–21.

10. "Los acuerdos bilaterales suscritos por España en materia migratoria con países del continente africano," Universidad de Granada, http://www.ugr.es/~redce/REDCE10/articulos/04MAsuncionAsinCabrera.htm.

11. Casas-Cortes et al., "'Good Neighbours Make Good Fences,'" 10.

12. "Mauritania," 3; Dünnwald, "Europe's Global Approach," 118.

13. Maurizio Albahari, *Crimes of Peace: Mediterranean Migrations at the World's Deadliest Border* (Philadelphia: University of Pennsylvania Press, 2015), p. 66.

14. UN Security Council Resolution 1101 (1997), March 28, 1997.

15. *Xhavara et. al v. Italy and Albania*, no. 39473/98, ECtHR, 2001; Albahari, *Crimes of Peace*, 66–69.

16. Albahari, *Crimes of Peace*, 71; Alessia di Pascale, "Migration Control at Sea: The Italian Case," in *Extraterritorial Immigration Control: Legal Challenges*, edited by Bernard Ryan and Valsamis Mitsilegas (Leiden: Martinus Nijhoff, 2010), p. 298.

17. "Technical Mission to Libya on Illegal Immigration, 27 Nov.–6 Dec. 2004. Report," European Commission, 2004, p. 45, http://www.statewatch.org/news/2005/may/eu-report-libya-ill-imm.pdf.

18. "Technical Mission to Libya on Illegal Immigration," 5.

19. "Migration Management: Regional Approach for EU and Neighbors Proposed at Ministerial Conference," Wikileaks, February 9, 2006, https://wikileaks.org/plusd/cables/06BRUSSELS442_a.html.

20. Albahari, *Crimes of Peace*, 83.

21. "Technical Mission to Libya on Illegal Immigration," 60–62.

22. Albahari, *Crimes of Peace*, 83.

23. "Technical Mission to Libya on Illegal Immigration," 63.

24. Guy S. Goodwin-Gil and Jane McAdam, *The Refugee in International Law* (New York: Oxford University Press, 2007), pp. 230–231.

25. Di Pascal, "Migration Control at Sea," 306.

26. Irial Glynn, *Asylum Policy, Boat People and Political Discourse: Boats, Votes and Asylum in Australia and Italy* (London: Palgrave Macmillan, 2016), pp. 142–144.

27. "Lampedusa," Wikileaks, May 22, 2009, https://wikileaks.org/plusd/cables/09NAPLES64_a.html.

28. Ryan, "Extraterritorial Immigration Controls," 31–32.

29. "Pushed Back, Pushed Around: Italy's Forced Return of Boat Migrants and Asylum Seekers, Libya's Mistreatment of Migrants and Asylum Seekers," Human Rights Watch, 2009, p. 31, https://www.hrw.org/report/2009/09/21/pushed-back-pushed-around/italys-forced-return-boat-migrants-and-asylum-seekers.

30. "Support to the Libyan Authorities to Enhance the Management of Borders and Migration Flows," European Union, 2010, http://ec.europa.eu/europeaid/documents/aap/2010/af_aap-spe_2010_lby_p2.pdf. See also Bonavita, "The Externalization of Border Controls," 26–27.

31. Den Heijer, "Europe and Extraterritorial Asylum," 179; Presidency Conclusions, European Council, Brussels, December 15 and 16, 2005, p. 9.

32. Law 20/1991, Art. 21 cited in "Technical Mission to Libya on Illegal Immigration," 13, http://www.statewatch.org/news/2005/may/eu-report-libya-ill-imm.pdf.

33. "Technical Mission to Libya on Illegal Immigration," 6, 52.

34. Albahari, *Crimes of Peace*, 84.

35. Natalino Ronzitti, "The Treaty on Friendship, Partnership and Cooperation between Italy and Libya: New Prospects for Cooperation in the Mediterranean?," *Bulletin of Italian Politics 1*, no. 1 (2009): pp. 125–133; Carl Levy, "Refugees, Europe, Camps/State of Exception: 'Into the Zone,' the European Union and Extraterritorial Processing of Migrants, Refugees, and Asylum-Seekers (Theories and Practice)," *Refugee Survey Quarterly 29*, no. 1 (2010): p. 113; *Case of Hirsi Jamaa and Others v. Italy*, no. 27765/09, ECtHR, 2012.

36. Glynn, *Asylum Policy*, 173; "Report to the Italian Government on the visit to Italy carried out by the European Committee for the Prevention of Torture and Inhuman or Degrading Treatment or Punishment (CPT) from 27 to 31 July 2009," European Committee for the Prevention of Torture and Inhuman or Degrading Treatment or Punishment, April 28, 2010, p. 13.

37. "UNHCR Deeply Concerned over Returns from Italy to Libya," UNHCR, May 7, 2007, http://www.unhcr.org/enus/news/press/2009/5/4a02d4546/unhcrdeeplyconcernedreturnsitalylibya.html.

38. *Hirsi Jamaa and Others v. Italy*, §104, no. 27765/09.

39. "Pushed Back, Pushed Around," 4, 23, 38–39, 70.

40. "Lampedusa," Wikileaks, May 22, 2009.

41. *Hirsi Jamaa and Others v. Italy*; "Pushed Back, Pushed Around," 37.

42. Ryan, "Extraterritorial Immigration Controls," 32.

43. Letter of July 15, 2009 from Mr Jacques Barrot, Vice-President of the European Commission, to the President of the European Parliament Committee on Civil Liberties, Justice and Home Affairs, cited in *Hirsi Jamaa and Others v. Italy*, §34.

44. *Hirsi Jamaa and Others v. Italy*, §79. .

45. *Hirsi Jamaa and Others v. Italy*, §150.

46. Council Decision of 26 April 2010 supplementing the Schengen Borders Code as regards the surveillance of the sea external borders in the context of operational cooperation coordinated by the European Agency for the Management of Operational Cooperation at the External Borders of the Member States of the European Union (2010/252/EU), Part 1. §1.2

47. Case C-355/10, EU Court of Justice, September 5, 2012.

48. Regulation (EU) No. 656/2014 of the European Parliament and of the Council of 15 May 2014 establishing rules for the surveillance of the external sea borders in the context of operational cooperation coordinated by the European Agency for the Management of Operational Cooperation at the External Borders of the Member States of the European Union, Recital 12–13.

49. Maarten Den Heijer, "Frontex and the Shifting Approaches to Boat Migration in the European Union: A Legal Analysis," in *Externalizing Migration Management: Europe, North America and the Spread of Remote Control Practices*, edited by Ruben Zaiotti (London: Routledge, 2016), pp. 60–62.

50. Jason W. Davidson, "France, Britain and the Intervention in Libya: an Integrated Analysis," *Cambridge Review of International Affairs 26*, no. 2 (2013): pp. 316, 323.

51. "EUBAM Libya Initial Mapping Report Executive Summary," European External Action Service, January 25, 2017, p. 43, http://statewatch.org/news/2017/feb/eu-eeas-libya-assessment-5616-17.pdf.

52. "A Perfect Storm: The Failure of European Policies in the Central Mediterranean," Amnesty International, 2017, p. 7, https://www.amnesty.org/download/Documents/EUR0366552017ENGLISH.PDF.

53. "Mission," Eunavfor Med, April 25, 2017, https://eeas.europa.eu/sites/eeas/files/april_2017_-_factsheet_on_eunavfor_med_mission_english.pdf.

54. "EU Defence Chiefs' Approved Plan for Military Intervention against 'Refugee Boats' in Libya and the Mediterranean," European Union Military Committee, May 15, 2015, p. 9, https://wikileaks.org/eu-military-refugees/EUMC.

55. Council Decision (CFSP) 2016/993, Council of the European Union, Pub. L. No. L 162/18 (2016), at Article 1 (3)(5), http://eur-lex.europa.eu/legal-content/EN/TXT/PDF/?uri=CELEX:32016D0993&from=EN.

56. Operation Commander Rear Admiral Enrico Credendino, EUNAVFOR MED—Op SOPHIA—Six Monthly Report 22 June–31 December 2015 (No. EEAS (2016) 126), Brussels: European External Action Service (EEAS), 2016, p. 20, https://migrantsatsea.files.wordpress.com/2016/02/eeas-2016-126.pdf.

57. "Mission Background," EU Integrated Border Assistance Mission in Libya, May 2015, http://www.eeas.europa.eu/archives/docs/csdp/missions-and-operations/eubam-libya/pdf/factsheet_eubam_libya_en.pdf.

58. "Malta Declaration by the Members of the European Council on the External Aspects of Migration: Addressing the Central Mediterranean Route," European Council, February 3, 2017, http://www.consilium.europa.eu/en/press/press-releases/2017/01/03-malta-declaration/.

59. "Memorandum d'intesa sulla cooperazione nel campo dello sviluppo, del contrasto all'immigrazione illegale, al traffico di esseri umani, al contrabbando e sul rafforzamento della sicurezza delle frontiere tra lo Stato della Libia e la Repubblica

Italiana," February 2, 2017, http://www.governo.it/sites/governoNEW.it/files/Libia.pdf.

60. "Malta Declaration by the Members of the European Council on the external aspects of migration: addressing the Central Mediterranean route," European Council, March 2, 2017, http://www.consilium.europa.eu/en/press/press-releases/2017/02/03-malta-declaration/.

61. "UNHCR Conducts Training on Refugee Law for Libyan Coastguard and Navy," UNHCR, February 1, 2017, http://data2.unhcr.org/en/news/15742.

62. "EU: Shifting Rescue to Libya Risks Lives: Italy Should Direct Safe Rescues," Human Rights Watch, June 19, 2017, https://www.hrw.org/news/2017/0 6/19/eu-shifting-rescue-libya-risks-lives.

63. "EUBAM Libya Initial Mapping Report Executive Summary," European External Action Service, January 25, 2017, p. 9, 15–17, http://statewatch.org/news/2017/feb/eu-eeas-libya-assessment-5616-17.pdf.

64. "EUBAM Libya Initial Mapping Report Executive Summary," European External Action Service, January 25, 2017, p. 38, http://statewatch.org/news/2017/feb/eu-eeas-libya-assessment-5616-17.pdf.

65. "Letter dated 1 June 2017 from the Panel of Experts on Libya established pursuant to resolution 1973 (2011) addressed to the President of the Security Council," UNSC, June 1, 2017, p. 21, http://undocs.org/S/2017/466.

66. Cited in "Letter dated 1 June 2017 from the Panel of Experts," 41–42.

67. Daniel Howden, "The Central Mediterranean: European Priorities, Libyan Realities," Refugees Deeply, October 2017, http://issues.newsdeeply.com/central-mediterranean-european-priorities-libyan-realities.

68. "Amnesty International Report 2017/2018," Amnesty International, p. 243, https://www.amnesty.org/en/countries/middle-east-and-north-africa/libya/report-libya/.

69. Albahari, *Crimes of Peace*.

70. Den Heijer, "Frontex and the Shifting Approaches," 64.

71. "Left at Sea Hanging on a Tuna Net," *BBC News*, September 10, 2007, http://news.bbc.co.uk/2/hi/programmes/panorama/6986062.stm.

72. Anna Momigliano, "Italian Forces Ignored a Sinking Ship Full of Syrian Refugees and Let More Than 250 Drown, Says Leaked Audio," *Washington Post*, May 9, 2017, https://www.washingtonpost.com/news/worldviews/wp/2017/05/09/italian-forces-ignored-a-sinking-ship-full-of-syrian-refugees-and-let-more-than-250-drown-says-leaked-audio/?utm_term=.88f350d5aa5e; Albahari, *Crimes of Peace*, 176–180.

73. "Italy Acquits Migrant Rescue Crew," *BBC News*, October 7, 2009, http://news.bbc.co.uk/go/pr/fr/-/2/hi/europe/8295727.stm; Albahari, *Crimes of Peace*, 101.

74. Tineke Strik, "Lives Lost in the Mediterranean Sea: Who Is Responsible?," Parliamentary Assembly of the Council of Europe, April 5, 2012.

75. Den Heijer, "Frontex and the Shifting Approaches," 63.

76. Albahari, *Crimes of Peace*, 100–101.

77. "Fatal Journeys, Tracking Lives Lost during Migration," vol. 1, IOM, 2014, p. 24; "Fatal Journeys, Tracking Lives Lost during Migration," vol. 2, IOM, 2016, p. 24; For various attempts to count the number of dead, see the "Deaths of the Borders of

Southern Europe" database at http://www.borderdeaths.org/, "The Migrants' Files" at http://www.themigrantsfiles.com/," and "The Fatal Policies of Fortress Europe" at http://www.unitedagainstracism.org/campaigns/refugee-campaign/fortress-europe/.

78. Keegan Williams and Alison Mountz, "Rising Tide: Analyzing the Relationship between Externalization and Migrant Death and Boat Losses," in *Externalizing Migration Management: Europe, North America and the Spread of "Remote Control" Practices*, edited by Ruben Zaiotti (London: Routledge, 2016), p. 43.

79. Albahari, *Crimes of Peace*, 21.

80. Nick Dines, Nicola Montagna, and Vincenzo Ruggiero, "Thinking Lampedusa: Border Construction, the Spectacle of Bare Life and the Productivity of Migrants," *Ethnic and Racial Studies 38*, no. 3 (2014): pp. 430–445.

81. "Fatal Journeys," vol. 2, IOM, p. 9; "Asylum Decisions in the EU," Eurostat, April, 20, 2016, http://ec.europa.eu/eurostat/documents/2995521/7233417/3-20042016-AP-EN.pdf/.

82. "A Perfect Storm."

83. Paolo Cuttitta, "Repoliticization through Search and Rescue? Humanitarian NGOs and Migration Management in the Central Mediterranean," *Geopolitics* (2017): pp. 9–10.

84. Crispian Balmer, "Italy Drafts Contested Code of Conduct for NGO Migrant Boats," *Reuters*, July 12, 2017, https://www.reuters.com/article/us-europe-migrants-ngos-idUSKBN19X2U1?utm_source=Refugees+Deeply&utm_campaign=c6e3641275EMAIL_CAMPAIGN_2017_07_14&utm_medium=email&utm_term=0_8b056c90e2-c6e3641275-117602093&mc_cid=c6e3641275&mc_eid=617fib37a5.

85. "Matteo Salvini: Italy's Ports Are Closed to Migrant Vessels," *Politico*, June 16, 2018, https://www.politico.eu/article/matteo-salvini-migration-italy-ports-closed-to-migrant-vessels/

86. "Frontex Presence Growing to Confront Greece's Migration Wave," Wikileaks, November 19, 2009, https://www.wikileaks.org/plusd/cables/09ATHENS1641_a.html.

87. "The Truth May Be Bitter but It Must Be Told: The Situation of Refugees in the Aegean and the Practices of the Greek Coast Guard," PRO ASYL, Frankfurt am Main, 2007, p. 26, https://www.proasyl.de/wp-content/uploads/2015/12/PRO_ASYL_Broschuere_Griechenland_Doku_Oktober_2007.pdf.

88. "Fear and Fences"; "The Truth May Be Bitter but It Must Be Told"; "Greece: Evidence Points to Illegal Forced Returns of Syrian Refugees to Turkey," Amnesty International, October 28, 2016.

89. "Greece: Frontier of Hope and Fear," Amnesty International, 2014, p. 13.

90. "Europe's Borderlands: Violations against Refugees and Migrants in Macedonia, Serbia and Hungary," Amnesty International, 2015, p. 63.

91. "The Truth May Be Bitter but It Must Be Told," 14–15.

92. "The Truth May Be Bitter but It Must Be Told," 14.

93. Ahmet Içduygu and Damla B. Aksel, "Two-to-Tango in Migration Diplomacy: Negotiating Readmission Agreement between the EU and Turkey," *European Journal of Migration and Law 16*, no. 3 (2014): pp. 337–363.

94. Sarah Wolff, "The Politics of Negotiating EU Readmission Agreements: Insights from Morocco and Turkey," in *Externalizing Migration Management: Europe, North America and the Spread of "Remote Control" Practices*, edited by Ruben Zaiotti (London: Routledge, 2016), p. 90.

95. John Morrison, "The Trafficking and Smuggling of Refugees: The End Game in European Asylum Policy?," UNHCR, 2000, p. 46; Cavidan Soykan, "Access to International Protection: Border Issues in Turkey," in *States, the Law and Access to Refugee Protection*, edited by Maria O'Sullivan and Dallal Stevens (Oxford: Hart Publishing, 2017), pp. 69–91.

96. Janja Vukašinović, "Illegal Migration in Turkey-EU Relations: An Issue of Political Bargaining or Political Cooperation?," *European Perspectives 3*, no. 2 (2011): p. 149.

97. "Turkish Airlines Becomes #1 in the World," *BusinessWire*, November 14, 2012, http://www.businesswire.com/news/home/20121114006447/en/Turkish-Airlines-1-World-Flying-Countries-Worldwide.

98. Wolff, "The Politics of Negotiating," 103.

99. Vukašinović, "Illegal Migration in Turkey-EU Relations," 158.

100. Wolff, "The Politics of Negotiating," 103–104.

101. "UNHCR Syria Regional Refugee Response," UNHCR, updated September 21, 2018, https://data2.unhcr.org/en/situations/syria.

102. Vukašinović, "Illegal Migration in Turkey-EU Relations," 147–167; Ahmet İçduygu, "Syrian Refugees in Turkey: The Long Road Ahead," Migration Policy Institute, April 2015, https://www.migrationpolicy.org/research/syrian-refugees-turkey-long-road-ahead.

103. "Migrants Detected Entering the EU Illegally, 2014–2015," *BBC*, March 2016, http://ichef-1.bbci.co.uk/news/624/cpsprodpb/11F0A/production/_88328437_migrant_routes_numbers_v9.png.

104. Joyce Marie Mushaben, "Angela Merkel's Leadership in the Refugee Crisis," *Current History 116*, no. 788 (2017): pp. 95–100.

105. "European Council Meeting (15 October 2015)—Conclusions (Vol. EUCO 26/15)," European Council, presented at the European Council meeting, Brussels, 2015, http://www.consilium.europa.eu/en/european-council/conclusions/.

106. "European Union—Turkey. Agreement between the European Union and the Republic of Turkey on the Readmission of Persons Residing without Authorisation," Pub. L. No. L 134/3 (2014), http://eur-lex.europa.eu/legal-content/EN/ALL/?uri=CELEX%3A22014A0507(01).

107. "EU-Turkey Statement, 18 March 2016," Participants of the EU–Turkey meeting, presented at the EU–Turkey meeting, March 18, 2016, http://www.consilium.europa.eu/press-releases-pdf/2016/3/40802210113_en.pdf.

108. "Relocation and Resettlement," European Commission press release, Feb. 8, 2017, http://europa.eu/rapid/press-release_IP-17-218_en.htm.

109. "Greece Data Snapshot—31 March 2016," UNHCR, March 31, 2016, http://data.unhcr.org/mediterranean/download.php?id=988; http://europa.eu/rapid/press-release_IP-17-1587_en.htm.

110. Nils Muižnieks, "Diese Pläne sind schlicht illegal," March 16, 2016, http://www.coe.int/en/web/commissioner/view/-/asset_publisher/ugj3i6qSEkhZ/content/diese-plane-sind-schlicht-illegal.

111. Article 33 (2) b-c of the Asylum Procedures Directive.

112. "States Parties to the 1951 Convention Relating to the Status of Refugees and the 1967 Protocol," UNHCR, April 2015, http://www.unhcr.org/protect/PROTECTION/3b73b0d63.pdf.

113. UN Treaty Collection, https://treaties.un.org/pages/ViewDetails.aspx?src=TREATY&mtdsg_no=V-5&chapter=5&lang=en; "Q&A: The EU-Turkey Deal on Migration and Refugees," Human Rights Watch, https://www.hrw.org/news/2016/03/03/qa-eu-turkey-deal-migration-and-refugees; "An EU 'Safe Countries of Origin' List," European Commission, http://ec.europa.eu/dgs/home-affairs/what-we-do/policies/european-agenda-migration/background-information/docs/2_eu_safe_countries_of_origin_en.pdf; "Common Asylum System at a Turning Point: Refugees Caught in Europe's Solidarity Crisis—Annual Report 2014/2015," Asylum Information Database, 2015, http://www.asylumineurope.org/sites/default/files/shadow-reports/aida_annualreport_2014-2015_0.pdf; Vukašinović, "Illegal Migration in Turkey-EU Relations," 157.

114. "Turkey Announces Decision to Suspend 'Temporarily' European Convention on Human Rights Commitments," Council of Europe, July 21, 2016, http://www.humanrightseurope.org/2016/07/turkey-announces-decision-to-temporarily-suspend-the-european-convention-on-human-rights/.

115. "Turkey/Syria: Border Guards Shoot, Block Fleeing Syrians," Human Rights Watch, February 3, 2018, https://www.hrw.org/news/2018/02/03/turkey-syria-border-guards-shoot-block-fleeing-syrians; "Post-Deportation Risks under the EU-Turkey Statement: What Happens after Readmission to Turkey?," European University Institute Migration Policy Centre Policy Brief, November 2017, http://cadmus.eui.eu/bitstream/handle/1814/49005/PB_2017_30_MPC.pdf?sequence=1&isAllowed=y.

116. Melissa Fleming, "UNHCR Redefines Role in Greece as EU-Turkey Deal Comes into Effect," March 22, 2016, http://www.unhcr.org/en-us/news/briefing/2016/3/56f10d049/unhcr-redefines-role-greece-eu-turkey-deal-comes-effect.html.

117. "Greece: MSF Ends Activities Inside the Lesvos 'Hotspot,'" Doctors Without Borders/Médecins Sans Frontières. March 22, 2016, http://www.msf.org/en/article/greece-msf-ends-activities-inside-lesvos-%E2%80%9Chotspot%E2%80%9D.

118. "Order of the General Court (First Chamber, Extended Composition)," InfoCuria—Case-law of the Court of Justice, February 28, 2017, http://curia.europa.eu/juris/document/document.jsf?text=&docid=188483&pageIndex=0&doclang=en&mode=lst&dir=&occ=first&part=1&cid=426840&utm_source=ECRE+Newsletters&utm_campaign=6f51494713-EMAIL_CAMPAIGN_2017_03_10&utm_medium=email&utm_term=0_3ec9497afd-6f51494713-422309169.

119. "Angela Merkel Offers Turkey Assistance for Border Region," German Federal Government, February 8, 2016, https://www.bundesregierung.de/Content/EN/Reiseberichte/2016/2016-02-08-merkel-ankara_en.html.

120. "Kammenos Sets out Conditions for NATO to Sweep Aegean," *Kathimerini* (English edition), February 11, 2016, http://www.ekathimerini.com/205872/article/ekathimerini/news/kammenos-sets-out-conditions-for-nato-to-sweep-aegean.

121. "French and Dutch Ships Join NATO's Deployment in the Aegean," NATO, March 18, 2016, http://www.mc.nato.int/PressReleases/Pages/French-and-Dutch-ships-join-NATO%E2%80%99s-deployment-in-the-Aegean.aspx; "Standing NATO Maritime Group 2 Expands Area of Activities," NATO, August 3, 2016, http://www.

mc.nato.int/PressReleases/Pages/Standing-NATO-Maritime-Group-2-expands-area-of-activities.aspx; Madeleine Moon, "Draft Report—NATO and the Future Role of Naval Power," NATO Parliamentary Assembly—Defense and Security Committee, 2016, p. 10; Jens Stoltenberg "Secretary General Stoltenberg's Opinion Piece—NATO and Europe's Refugee and Migrant Crisis," NATO, February 26, 2016, http://www.nato.int/cps/en/natohq/opinions_128645.htm.

122. Vassilis Nedos, "Athens Says Impact of NATO Patrols in Aegean Is Minimal," *Kathimerini* (English edition), April 16, 2016, http://www.ekathimerini.com/207999/article/ekathimerini/news/athens-says-impact-of-nato-patrols-in-aegean-is-minimal; "Greece Data Snapshot—09 June 2016," UNHCR, June 9, 2016.

123. Gregor Noll, "Visions of the Exceptional: Legal and Theoretical Issues Raised by Transit Processing Centres and Protection Zones," *European Journal of Migration and Law 5*, no. 3 (2003): pp. 311–312.

124. "Working Paper on Reception in the Region of Origin," IGC Secretariat, Geneva, 1994.

125. Sabine Hess, "'We Are Facilitating States!' An Ethnographic Analysis of the ICMPD," in *The Politics of International Migration Management*, edited by Martin Geiger and Antoine Pécoud (New York: Palgrave Macmillan, 2010), pp. 100–101.

126. "Reception in the Region of Origin: Draft Follow-up to the 1994 Working Paper," IGC Secretariat, Geneva, 1995, p. 7.

127. "Reception in the Region of Origin," 9.

128. "Working Paper on Reception in the Region of Origin," 1994, p. 52; "Reception in the Region of Origin: Draft follow-up to the 1994 Working Paper," IGC Secretariat, 1995, p. 11.

129. "Communication from the Commission to the Council and the European Parliament: Towards More accessible, Equitable and Managed Asylum Systems," COM (2003) 315; "Migrant Camps in Libya/Ukraine: EU Debates Measures to Control International Migration," Wikileaks, September 28, 2004, https://wikileaks.org/plusd/cables/04BRUSSELS4151_a.html; Noll, "Visions of the Exceptional," 304–306; Levy, "Refugees, Europe, Camps/State of Exception," 110.

130. "Migrant Camps in Libya/Ukraine," Wikileaks, September 28, 2004.

131. Levy, "Refugees, Europe, Camps/State of Exception," 110.

132. "Communication from the Commission to the Council and the European Parliament," 16–17.

133. Levy, "Refugees, Europe, Camps/State of Exception," 97.

134. "Migrant Camps in Libya/Ukraine," Wikileaks, September 28, 2004; Madeline Garlick, "The EU Discussions on Extraterritorial Processing: Solution or Conundrum?," *International Journal of Refugee Law 18*, no. 3–4 (2006): p. 619; Levy, "Refugees, Europe, Camps/State of Exception," 97.

135. "Libya Snubs EU Calls for Refugee Camps on Its Shores," *ahramonline*, October 6, 2016, http://english.ahram.org.eg/NewsContentP/2/245309/World/Libya-snubs-EU-calls-for-refugee-camps-on-its-shor.aspx; "Germany Proposes North Africa Centers for Rescued Mmigrants," *ekathimerini.com*, October 13, 2016, http://www.ekathimerini.com/212812/article/ekathimerini/news/germany-proposes-north-africa-centers-for-rescued-migrants,"

136. Austrian Defence Minister Eyes Plan to Overhaul EU Migrant Policy—Bild," *Reuters*, January 5, 2017, http://www.reuters.com/article/us-europe-migrants-austria/austrian-defense-minister-eyes-plan-to-overhaul-eu-migrant-policy-bild-idUSKBN14P2AS; "At French Outpost in African Migrant Hub, Asylum for a Select Few," *New York Times*, Feb. 25, 2018, https://www.nytimes.com/2018/02/25/world/africa/france-africa-migrants-asylum-niger.html; Claire Higgins, "Humanitarian Corridors: Safe Passage but Only for a Few," Andrew and Renata Kaldor Centre for International Refugee Law, 2017, http://www.kaldorcentre.unsw.edu.au/publication/humanitarian-corridors.

137. "Europe Resettlement," UNHCR, July 2017, https://data2.unhcr.org/ar/documents/download/60336; "Europe Key Data – 2017," UNHCR, March 2, 2018, https://data2.unhcr.org/en/documents/download/62326.

138. "Migrant Camps in Libya/Ukraine," Wikileaks, September 28, 2004.

139. Presidency Conclusions, European Council Brussels, December 15 and 16, 2005, p. 9.

Chapter 10

1. Asher Lazarus Hirsch, "The Borders beyond the Border: Australia's Extraterritorial Migration Controls," *Refugee Survey Quarterly 36*, no. 3 (2017): p. 60.

2. Erika Feller, "Carrier Sanctions and International Law," *International Journal of Refugee Law 1*, no. 1 (1989): p. 51; Migration Act 1958, as amended, §§ 11 (c), 23–24, 28–29, 36.

3. Hirsch, "The Borders beyond the Border," 60.

4. "Inquiry into the Integrity of Overseas Law Enforcement Operations: Response from the Department of Immigration and Citizenship," Parliamentary Joint Committee on the Australian Commission for Law Enforcement Integrity, 2012, p. 6.

5. Hirsch, "The Borders beyond the Border," 63.

6. Hirsch, "The Borders beyond the Border," 56–57. With enumerated exceptions, the Migration Act 1958, §42(1) states a "non-citizen must not travel to Australia without a visa that is in effect."

7. Author's calculations based on "Asylum Seekers and Refugees: What Are the Facts?," Parliament of Australia, March 2, 2015, http://www.aph.gov.au/About_Parliament/Parliamentary_Departments/Parliamentary_Library/pubs/rp/rp1415/AsylumFacts.

8. Anne McNevin, "The Liberal Paradox and the Politics of Asylum in Australia," *Australian Journal of Political Science 42*, no. 4 (2007): pp. 613, 622; Irial Glynn, *Asylum Policy, Boat People and Political Discourse: Boats, Votes and Asylum in Australia and Italy* (London: Palgrave Macmillan, 2016) pp. 88–89.

9. Calculated from table 2 in Janet Philips, "Boat Arrivals and Boat 'Turnbacks' in Australia since 1976: A Quick Guide to the Statistics," Parliament of Australia, January 17, 2017, http://www.aph.gov.au/About_Parliament/Parliamentary_Departments/Parliamentary_Library/pubs/rp/rp1617/Quick_Guides/BoatTurnbacks; figures from 1976 to 2008 include an unknown number of crew.

10. Khalid Koser, "Responding to Boat Arrivals in Australia: Time for a Reality Check," Lowy Institute for International Policy, Sydney, December 2010, p. 6.

11. McNevin, "The Liberal Paradox," 622; Glynn, *Asylum Policy,* 88–89.

12. James Jupp, *From White Australia to Woomera: The Story of Australian Immigration* (New York: Cambridge University Press, 2002).

13. "3412.0—Migration, Australia, 2015–16," Australian Bureau of Statistics, March 30, 2017, http://www.abs.gov.au/ausstats/abs@.nsf/mf/3412.0.

14. Glynn, *Asylum Policy*, 95, 149.

15. "Ex-President Batista," cablegram from Australian Embassy Washington, July 1, 1959; "Batista," cablegram from Australian Embassy Washington, July 7, 1959; National Archives of Australia (NAA), A1838; 1606/1 Part 1.

16. Laura Madokoro, *Elusive Refuge: Chinese Migrants in the Cold War* (Cambridge, MA: Harvard University Press, 2016), pp. 106–115.

17. "West Irian: The Nature of the Opposition," confidential airgram from U.S. Embassy in Djakarta, July 9, 1969, p. 4, https://nsarchive2.gwu.edu/NSAEBB/NSAEBB128/29.%20Airgram%20A-278%20from%20Jakarta%20to%20State%20Department,%20July%209,%201969.pdf.

18. Neumann, *Across the Seas*, 199–203.

19. "Political Asylum," memo no. 115, from D. F. De Stoop, Head, General Legal Section to Australian High Commission, Port Moresby, February 10, 1976, p. 3, NAA, A1838/393; 1601/1 Part 2.

20. Neumann, *Across the Seas*, 231–232.

21. Australian War Memorial, https://www.awm.gov.au/encyclopedia/war_casualties/.

22. "Contingency Planning-Unauthorized Arrival of Vietnamese," K. H. Rogers, First Assistant Secretary International Organisations and Protocol Division, to Mr. Feakes et al, July 3, 1975, NAA, A1838/393; 1601/1 Part 2.

23. Ron Sutton, "Anniversary of First Vietnam Boat Marked," *SBS*, April 27, 2011, http://www.sbs.com.au/news/article/2011/04/27/anniversary-first-vietnam-boat-marked.

24. Neumann, *Across the Seas*, 251, 288.

25. Quoted in Neumann, *Across the Seas*, 2–3.

26. "Cabinet Submission no. 3200, Legislation against Unauthorised Boat Arrivals," June 5, 1979, A1012, D/52 Part 1, NAA.

27. Madokoro, *Elusive Refuge*, 16

28. "Indochinese Refugees: The Continuing Exodus," CIA Directorate of Central Intelligence, June 1983, p. 4, https://www.cia.gov/library/readingroom/document/cia-rdp84s00558r000400020002-7.pdf; "Rising Tide of Indochinese Refugees," CIA National Foreign Assessment Center, December 7, 1978, p. 5, https://www.cia.gov/library/readingroom/document/cia-rdp80t00634a000500010024-5.pdf; Gil Loescher, *The UNHCR and World Politics: A Perilous Path* (New York: Oxford University Press, 2001), pp. 205–207.

29. "Vietnam's Refugee Machine," CIA National Foreign Assessment Center, 1975, p. iii, https://www.cia.gov/library/readingroom/docs/CIA-RDP80T00942A001200070001-3.pdf; "Indochinese Refugees: The Continuing Exodus," CIA Directorate of Central Intelligence, June 1983.

30. "Rising Tide of Indochinese Refugees," 9.

31. "Indochinese Refugees," 1, 26.

32. Norman L. Zucker and Naomi Flink Zucker, "From Immigration to Refugee Redefinition: A History of Refugee and Asylum Policy in the United States," *Journal of Policy History* 4, no. 1 (1992): p. 61.

33. James Z. Pugash, "The Dilemma of the Sea Refugee: Rescue Without Refuge," *Harvard International Law Journal 18*, no. 3 (1977): p. 578.

34. Sylvie Kauffmann, "Après le Vietnam en 1979, un bateau pour la Libye?," *Le Monde*, April 24, 2015, http://www.lemonde.fr/europe/article/2015/04/24/apres-le-vietnam-en-1979-un-bateau-pour-la-libye_4622412_3214.html.

35. Patrick Merziger, "The 'Radical Humanism' of 'Cap Anamur'/'German Emergency Doctors' in the 1980s: A Turning Point for the Idea, Practice and Policy of Humanitarian Aid," *European Review of History: Revue européenne d'histoire 23*, no. 1–2 (2016): pp. 171–192.

36. "Submission to the Joint Select Committee on Australia's Immigration Detention Network," September 2011, p. 167.

37. Claire Higgins, "Status Determination of Indochinese Boat Arrivals: A 'Balancing Act' in Australia," *Journal of Refugee Studies 30*, no. 1 (2017): p. 93.

38. "Standing Committee on Refugees, Second Meeting," October 20, 1977, Draft Report, p. 7, NAA, A1838, 1632/5/9/4/ Part 1.

39. Loescher, *The UNHCR and World Politics*, 207.

40. Loescher, *The UNHCR and World Politics*, 209.

41. "Submission to the Joint Select Committee on Australia's Immigration Detention Network," 167.

42. "Cabinet Submission no. 3200, Legislation against Unauthorised Boat Arrivals."

43. Immigration (Unauthorised Arrivals) Act 1980. The law was in effect until September 30, 1983 ("Submission to the Joint Select Committee on Australia's Immigration Detention Network," 168.)

44. "Cabinet Submission no. 3200, Legislation Against Unauthorised Boat Arrivals."

45. "Submission to the Joint Select Committee on Australia's Immigration Detention Network," 17.

46. "Asylum Procedures: Report on Policies and Practices in ICG Participating States 2009," Intergovernmental Consultations on Migration, Asylum and Refugees (IGC), 2009, p. 38, http://publications.iom.int/system/files/pdf/igc_asylumprocedures_2009_bluebook.pdf; Glynn, *Asylum Policy*, 98; Glenn Nicholls, "Unsettling Admissions: Asylum Seekers in Australia," *Journal of Refugee Studies 11*, no. 1 (1998): pp. 65–67; "Submission to the Joint Select Committee on Australia's Immigration Detention Network."

47. Susan Kneebone, ed., *Refugees, Asylum Seekers and the Rule of Law: Comparative Perspectives* (Cambridge: Cambridge University Press, 2009), pp. 175–176.

48. Scott D. Watson, *The Securitization of Humanitarian Migration: Digging Moats and Sinking Boats* (New York: Routledge, 2009), p. 94.

49. "Report of the Expert Panel on Asylum Seekers 2012," Australian Government, August 2012, p. 98, http://artsonline.monash.edu.au/thebordercrossingobservatory/files/2015/03/expert_panel_on_asylum_seekers_full_report.pdf.

50. Chantal Marie-Jeanne Bostock, "The International Legal Obligations Owed to the Asylum Seekers on the MV Tampa," *International Journal of Refugee Law 14*, no. 2/3 (2002): p. 299; "Report of the Expert Panel on Asylum Seekers," 98.

51. "Border Protection Bill 2001," Parliament of Australia, August 31, 2001, http://www.aph.gov.au/Parliamentary_Business/Bills_Legislation/bd/bd0102/02bd041.

52. Glynn, *Asylum Policy,* 127.

53. Bostock, "The International Legal Obligations"; Ernst Willheim, "MV Tampa: The Australian Response," *International Journal of Refugee Law* 15, no. 2 (2003): pp. 159–191; "Chapter 1—Border Protection: A New Regime," Parliament of Australia, http://www.aph.gov.au/Parliamentary_Business/Committees/Senate/Former_Committees/maritimeincident/report/c01; Kazimierz Bem et al., "A Price Too High: The Cost of Australia's Approach to Asylum Seekers," Just Australia and Oxfam Australia, 2007.

54. *Ruddock v. Vadarlis* [2001] FCA 1329.

55. Border Protection (Validation and Enforcement Powers) Act 2001, https://www.legislation.gov.au/Details/C2004A00886.

56. Claire Inder, "International Refugee Law, 'Hyper-Legalism' and Migration Management: The Pacific Solution," in *The Politics of International Migration Management,* edited by Martin Geiger and Antoine Pécoud (New York: Palgrave Macmillan, 2010), p. 226; Migration Amendment (Excision from Migration Zone) Bill, 2001 and The Migration Amendment (Excision from Migration Zone) (Consequential Provisions) Bill, 2001. One Nation MP Pauline Hanson first publicly proposed excision in an August 31, 2001, radio interview (McNevin, "The Liberal Paradox," 616–617).

57. "Excising Australia: Are We Really Shrinking?," Parliament of Australia, Department of Parliamentary Services Research Note no. 5, August 31, 2005, https://www.aph.gov.au/binaries/library/pubs/rn/2005-06/06rn05.pdf.

58. *CPCF v Minister for Immigration and Border Protection* [2015] HCA 1, §10.

59. Inder, "International Refugee Law," 231.

60. Migration Amendment Regulations 2002 (No. 4) 2002 No. 129, June 7, 2002; Migration Legislation Amendment (Further Border Protection Measures) Bill, 2002; "Excising Australia," Parliament of Australia, 2005.

61. Migration Amendment Regulations 2005 (No. 6) SLI 171.

62. Migration Amendment (Designated Unauthorised Arrivals) Bill, 2006. The April 2006 bill was a reaction to a March 2006 grant of protection visas to forty-two of forty-three West Papuan asylum seekers (Kneebone, *Refugees, Asylum Seekers and the Rule of Law,* 195).

63. "Federal Register of Legislation," Australian Government, https://www.legislation.gov.au/Details/C2013A00035/Html/Text#_Toc356901685; Karen Barlow, "Parliament Excises Mainland from Migration Zone," *ABC News,* May 16, 2013, http://www.abc.net.au/news/2013-05-16/parliament-excises-mainland-from-migration-zone/4693940.

64. "Excising Australia," Parliament of Australia, 2005.

65. *Plaintiff M61/2010E v. Commonwealth of Australia; Plaintiff M69 of 2010 v. Commonwealth of Australia* [2010] HCA 41, November 11, 2010; Michelle Foster and Jason Pobjoy, "A Failed Case of Legal Exceptionalism? Refugee Status Determination in Australia's 'Excised' Territory," *International Journal of Refugee Law* 23, no. 4 (2011): pp. 583–631.

66. "Onshore Protection Interim Procedures Advice No. 16," Onshore Protection Branch, September 2002, www.aph.gov.au/~/media/wopapub/senate/...ctte/.../sub118d_att_a_pdf.ashx.

67. Daniel Webb, "Let Them Stay Campaign a Success," *Law Institute Journal*, May 2, 2016, https://www.liv.asn.au/Staying-Informed/LIJ/LIJ/May-2016/Let-Them-Stay-campaign-a-success.

68. Madeline Gleeson, *Offshore: Behind the Wire on Manus and Nauru* (Sydney: NewSouth, 2016), p. 363.

69. *Plaintiff M68/2015 v. Minister for Immigration and Border Protection & Ors.*

70. "(AE17/185)—MIRPC—Medical Transfers to Australia—Programme 1.5: IMA Offshore Management," Immigration and Border Protection Portfolio, February 27, 2017, http://www.aph.gov.au/~/media/Committees/legcon_ctte/estimates/add_1617/DIBP/QoNs/AE17-185.pdf; "(AE17/199)—NRPC—Number in Australia seeking medical treatment—Programme 1.5: IMA Offshore Management," Immigration and Border Protection Portfolio, February 27, 2017, http://www.aph.gov.au/~/media/Committees/legcon_ctte/estimates/add_1617/DIBP/QoNs/AE17-199.pdf.

71. Michael Edwards, "Sanctuary Offered to Asylum Seekers Facing Removal to Offshore Detention by Churches across Australia," *ABC News*, February 3, 2016, http://www.abc.net.au/news/2016-02-04/churches-offer-sanctuary-to-asylum-seekers/7138484; Thomas Oriti, "Let Them Stay Labelled a Success, More Than Half of 267 Asylum Seekers in Community Detention," *ABC News*, April 1, 2016, http://www.abc.net.au/news/2016-04-02/let-them-stay-labelled-success-asylum-seeker-community-detention/7294456.

72. "Select Committee for an Inquiry into a Certain Maritime Incident," Commonwealth of Australia, 2002, p. 27, https://www.aph.gov.au/binaries/senate/committee/maritime_incident_ctte/report/report.pdf; Philips, "Boat Arrivals and Boat 'Turnbacks,'" 2017.

73. "Fatal Journeys: Tracking Lives Lost during Migration," IOM, 2014, p. 187.

74. Foster and Pobjoy, "A Failed Case of Legal Exceptionalism?," 589.

75. Janet Philips and Harriet Spinks, "Immigration Detention in Australia," Parliament of Australia, March 20, 2013, http://www.aph.gov.au/About_Parliament/Parliamentary_Departments/Parliamentary_Library/pubs/BN/2012-2013/Detention.

76. Glynn, *Asylum Policy*, 151; Foster and Pobjoy, "A Failed Case of Legal Exceptionalism?," 615.

77. *Plaintiff M70/2011 v. Minister for Immigration and Citizenship*; Sasha Lowes, "The Legality of Extraterritorial Processing of Asylum Claims: The Judgement of the High Court of Australia in the 'Malaysian Solution' Case," *Human Rights Law Review* 12, no. 1 (2012): pp. 169–182.

78. Antje Missbach, *Troubled Transit: Asylum Seekers Stuck in Indonesia* (Singapore: ISEAS-Yusof Ishak Institute, 2015), pp. 189–190.

79. Glynn, *Asylum Policy*, 159–160.

80. Gleeson, *Offshore*, 124.

81. Christopher Knaus, "Existence of 'Pivotal' Letter from Scott Morrison on Boat Turnbacks Revealed," *The Guardian*, November 28, 2016, https://www.theguardian.com/australia-news/2016/nov/28/existence-of-pivotal-letter-from-scott-morrison-on-boat-turnbacks-revealed.

82. Helen Davidson, "Fake Fishing Boats Used in Asylum Seeker Turnbacks Spotted off Cocos Islands," *The Guardian*, November 27, 2016, https://www.theguardian.com/australia-news/2016/nov/28/australia-still-using-fake-fishing-

boats-in-asylum-seeker-turnbacks; Ben Doherty and Helen Davidson, "Orange Lifeboats Used to Return Asylum Seekers to Be Replaced By 'Fishing Boats,'" *The Guardian*, March 5, 2015, https://www.theguardian.com/australia-news/2015/mar/05/orange-lifeboats-used-to-return-asylum-seekers-to-be-replaced-by-fishing-boats; Michael Bachelard, "Vomitous and Terrifying: The Lifeboats Used to Turn Back Asylum Seekers," *Sydney Morning Herald*, March 2, 2014, http://www.smh.com.au/national/vomitous-and-terrifying-the-lifeboats-used-to-turn-back-asylum-seekers-20140301-33t6s.html.

83. "By Hook or by Crook: Australia's Abuse of Asylum-Seekers at Sea," Amnesty International, October 28, 2015, https://www.amnesty.org/en/documents/ASA12/2576/2015/en/.

84. Philips, "Boat Arrivals and Boat 'Turnbacks,'" 2017.

85. "Australia Searches for Asylum Seeker Solution," Wikileaks, November 13, 2009, https://wikileaks.org/plusd/cables/09CANBERRA1006_a.html; "Australia-Indonesia: Moving beyond Asylum Seekers," Wikileaks, November 9, 2009, https://wikileaks.org/plusd/cables/09CANBERRA995_a.html.

86. "D.O.R.S. Committee Meeting 22 Feb. 1979," NAA, A1838, 1632/5/9/4 Part 1.

87. Maria O'Sullivan, "Interdiction and Screening of Asylum Seekers at Sea," in *States, the Law and Access to Refugee Protection: Fortresses and Fairness*, edited by Maria O'Sullivan and Dallal Stevens (Oxford: Hart, 2017), p. 103; David Corlett, "Sinhalese Asylum Seekers' On-water Claims Accepted by UN," *The Saturday Paper*, edition no. 45, January 31–February 6, 2015, https://www.thesaturdaypaper.com.au/news/politics/2015/01/31/sinhalese-asylum-seekers-water-claims-accepted-un/14226228001441.

88. "Failed Asylum Seekers: Sri Lanka," Edmund Rice Centre, August 21, 2014, https://d3n8a8pro7vhmx.cloudfront.net/erc/pages/41/attachments/original/1457429789/ERC_Interim_Research_Update_Returnees_to_Sri_Lanka_Aug2014.pdf?1457429789; "Sri Lanka: Australia Continues to Deport People to Danger," Edmund Rice Centre, May 5, 2015, https://d3n8a8pro7vhmx.cloudfront.net/erc/pages/41/attachments/original/1457429784/ERC_Interim_Research_Update_2_Returnees_to_Sri_Lanka_May2015.pdf?1457429784.

89. *CPCF v. Minister for Immigration and Border Protection* [2015] HCA 1.

90. Stephanie March, "Sri Lankan Asylum Seekers Facing Criminal Investigation after Being Handed Back by Australian Authorities," *ABC News*, July 7, 2014, http://www.abc.net.au/news/2014-07-07/morrison-confirms-sri-lankans-returned-after-interception/5575924; Paul Farrell, "Scott Morrison Confirms 37 Sri Lankan Asylum Seekers Were Handed Back," *The Guardian*, November 28, 2014, https://www.theguardian.com/australia-news/2014/nov/29/scott-morrison-confirms-37-sri-lankan-asylum-seekers-were-handed-back.

91. Shira Sebban, "Turned Back by Australia, Vietnamese Recognised as Refugees in Indonesia," *Brisbane Times*, June 12, 2017, http://www.brisbanetimes.com.au/world/turned-back-by-australia-vietnamese-recognised-as-refugees-in-indonesia-20170608-gwn475.html.

92. "Australia and Vietnam Further Cooperation to Stamp out People Smuggling," The Hon. Peter Dutton MP, Minister for Immigration and Border Protection,

December 12, 2016, http://www.minister.border.gov.au/peterdutton/Pages/Australia-and-Vietnam-further-cooperation-to-stamp-out-people-smuggling.aspx.

93. "Number of People Not Returned on the Basis of Non-Refoulement Obligations–Operation Sovereign Borders," Immigration and Border Protection Portfolio, February 27, 2017, http://www.aph.gov.au/~/media/Committees/legcon_ctte/estimates/add_1617/DIBP/QoNs/AE17-048.pdf.

94. "Turning Back Boats," UNSW Andrew & Renata Kaldor Centre for International Refugee Law, February 26, 2015, http://www.kaldorcentre.unsw.edu.au/publication/%E2%80%98turning-back-boats%E2%80%99.

95. *At What Cost? The Human, Economic and Strategic Cost of Australia's Asylum Seeker Policies and the Alternatives,* Save the Children Australia and UNICEF Australia, September 13, 2016, pp. 41–54, http://www.unicef.org.au/blog/september-2016/the-true-cost-of-australias-refugee-policies.

96. Philips, "Boat Arrivals and Boat 'Turnbacks,'" 2017. "Senate Legal and Constitutional Affairs Legislation Committee, Estimates," May 21 2018, p. 51, http://parlinfo.aph.gov.au/parlInfo/download/committees/estimate/0490c3ad-512d-453c-8526-3dff9705b43c/toc_pdf/Legal%20and%20Constitutional%20Affairs%20Legislation%20Committee_2018_05_21_6144.pdf;fileType=application%2Fpdf#search=%22committees/estimate/0490c3ad-512d-453c-8526-3dff9705b43c/0000%22.

97. Azadeh Dastyari, "Refugees on Guantanamo Bay: A Blue Print for Australia's 'Pacific Solution'?," *Australian Quarterly* 79, no. 1 (2007); Daniel Ghezelbash, *Refuge Lost: Asylum Law in an Interdependent World* (Cambridge: Cambridge University Press, 2018).

98. Azadeh Dastyari and Maria O'Sullivan, "Not for Export: The Failure of Australia's Extraterritorial Processing Regime in Papua New Guinea and the Decision of the PNG Supreme Court in Namah (2016)," *Monash University Law Review 42*, no. 2 (2016): pp. 310–311.

99. Neumann, *Across the Seas,* 182–186.

100. Calculated from "Nauru," UNdata, http://data.un.org/Data.aspx?q=Nauru&d=SNAAMA&f=grID%3A101%3BcurrID%3AUSD%3BpcFlag%3A1%3BcrID%3A520.

101. Calculated from "Aid Budget and Statistical Information," Australian Government, Department of Foreign Affairs and Trade, http://dfat.gov.au/aid/aid-budgets-statistics/Pages/default.aspx; 2012–13 to 2016–17 figures are budget estimates; "Nauru," World Bank, http://databank.worldbank.org/data/reports.aspx?source=2&country=NRU.

102. Inder, "International Refugee Law," See "Onshore Protection Interim Procedures Advice No. 16,"

103. Inder, "International Refugee Law," 228.

104. "Refugee Status Determination in Nauru," Andrew & Renata Kaldor Centre for International Refugee Law, January 2017, http://www.kaldorcentre.unsw.edu.au/sites/default/files/Factsheet_Offshore_processing_RSD_Nauru.pdf.

105. Gleeson, *Offshore,* 72.

106. "Visa Requirement," Government of the Republic of Nauru, http://www.naurugov.nr/about-nauru/visiting-nauru/visa-requirements.aspx.

107. Amy Nethery and Rosa Holman, "Secrecy and Human Rights Abuse in Australia's Offshore Immigration Detention Centres," *International Journal of Human Rights 20*, no. 7 (2016): pp. 1018–1038.

108. Nick Evershed et al., "The Nauru Files," *The Guardian*, https://www.theguardian.com/news/series/nauru-files.

109. Paul Farrell, Nick Evershed, and Helen Davidson, "The Nauru Files: Cache of 2,000 Leaked Reports Reveal Scale of Abuse of Children in Australian Offshore Detention," *The Guardian*, August 10, 2016, https://www.theguardian.com/australia-news/2016/aug/10/the-nauru-files-2000-leaked-reports-reveal-scale-of-abuse-of-children-in-australian-offshore-detention.

110. Gleeson, *Offshore*, 246.

111. "Island of Despair: Australia's 'Processing' of Refugees on Nauru," Amnesty International, 2016, https://www.amnesty.org/download/Documents/ASA1249342016ENGLISH.PDF; See also Azadeh Dastyari, *United States Migrant Interdiction and the Detention of Refugees in Guantánamo Bay* (Cambridge: Cambridge University Press, 2015) on legal aspects of processing.

112. Nethery and Holman, "Secrecy and Human Rights Abuse," 11.

113. "Island of Despair," 5.

114. Calculated from "Aid Budget and Statistical Information," Australian Government Department of Foreign Affairs and Trade. Figures are budget estimates.

115. Karin Fathimath Afeef, "The Politics of Extraterritorial Processing: Offshore Asylum Policies in Europe and the Pacific," Working Paper no. 36, Refugee Studies Centre, University of Oxford, 2006, p. 23.

116. Gleeson, *Offshore*, 42, 105; Savitri Taylor, "The Impact of Australian–PNG Border Management Co-operation on Refugee Protection," *Local-Global Journal 8* (2010): pp. 76–99.

117. Dastyari and O'Sullivan, "Not for Export," 314.

118. "National Inquiry into Children in Immigration Detention 2014," Sydney Public Hearing, July 31, 2014, pp. 7–8, https://www.humanrights.gov.au/sites/default/files/Mr%20Lake.pdf.

119. Stefan Armbruster, "Inquest Resumes into Manus Asylum Seeker Hamid Khazaei's Death," *SBS*, February 13, 2017, http://www.sbs.com.au/news/article/2017/02/10/inquest-resumes-manus-asylum-seeker-hamid-khazaeis-death.

120. Cameron Atfield, "Brain-dead Asylum Seeker Hamid Kehazaei's Organs to Be Donated," *The Sydney Morning Herald*, September 4, 2014, http://www.smh.com.au/federal-politics/political-news/braindead-asylum-seeker-hamid-kehazaeis-organs-to-be-donated-20140904-10cfzh.html.

121. "'This Is Critical': 103 Nauru and Manus Staff Speak Out—Their Letter in Full," *The Guardian*, August 16, 2016, https://www.theguardian.com/australia-news/2016/aug/17/this-is-critical-103-nauru-and-manus-staff-speak-out-their-letter-in-full.

122. Migration Amendment (Regional Processing Arrangements) Act 2015; Gleeson, *Offshore*, 363–364.

123. Gleeson, *Offshore*; *Plaintiff M68/2015 v. Minister for Immigration and Border Protection & Ors*.

124. Ben Doherty and Calla Wahlquist, "Government to Pay $70m Damages to 1,905 Manus Detainees in Class Action," *The Guardian*, June 13, 2017, https://www.theguardian.com/australia-news/2017/jun/14/government-to-pay-damages-to-manus-island-detainees-in-class-action.

125. Gleeson, *Offshore*, 84.

126. Dastyari and O'Sullivan, "Not for Export," 322–323; "Manus Island: Australia Abandons Refugees to a Life of Uncertainty and Peril," Amnesty International, February 1, 2018, https://www.amnesty.org/en/latest/news/2018/02/manus-island-australia-abandons-refugees-to-a-life-of-uncertainty-and-peril/

127. Glynn, *Asylum Policy,* 135.

128. Ben Doherty, "Australia's Offshore Detention Cost $1.2bn in 2014–15, Senate Estimates Told," *The Guardian,* December 8, 2015, https://www.theguardian.com/australia-news/2015/dec/09/offshore-detention-cost-12bn-senate-estimates-asylum-seekers-charter-flights.

129. "Island of Despair," 11.

130. "Report of the Expert Panel on Asylum Seekers 2012," Analysis & Policy Observatory, p. 131, http://apo.org.au/node/30608.

131. "(AE17/002)—US Resettlement Arrangement—Programme 1.5: IMA Offshore Management," Immigration and Border Protection Portfolio, February 27, 2017, www.aph.gov.au/~/media/Committees/legcon_ctte/estimates/add_1617/DIBP/QoNs/AE17-002.pdf; "(AE17/170)—IMA Offshore Management—Transferees Sent to Offshore Detention—Programme 1.5: IMA Offshore Management," Immigration and Border Protection Portfolio, February 27, 2017, http://www.aph.gov.au/~/media/Committees/legcon_ctte/estimates/add_1617/DIBP/QoNs/AE17-170.pdf; "(AE17/172)—IMA Offshore Management—Transferees Status—Programme 1.5: IMA Offshore Management," Immigration and Border Protection Portfolio, February 27, 2017, http://www.aph.gov.au/~/media/Committees/legcon_ctte/estimates/add_1617/DIBP/QoNs/AE17-172.pdf.

132. Kneebone, *Refugees, Asylum Seekers and the Rule of Law,* 197; Angus Francis, "Bringing Protection Home: Healing the Schism Between International Obligations and National Safeguards Created by Extraterritorial Processing," *International Journal of Refugee Law 20,* no. 2 (2008): p. 294.

133. "Memorandum of Understanding between the Government of the Kingdom of Cambodia and the Government of Australia, Relating to the Settlement of Refugees in Cambodia," National Legislative Bodies/ National Authorities, September 26, 2014, http://www.refworld.org/docid/5436588e4.html; Lindsay Murdoch, "Australia Transfers Seventh Refugee from Nauru to Cambodia under $55m Deal," *Sydney Morning Herald,* May 25, 2017, http://www.smh.com.au/world/australia-transfers-seventh-refugee-from-nauru-to-cambodia-under-55m-deal-20170525-gwczuu.html.

134. "(AE17/223)—Regional Cooperation—Offer from New Zealand—Programme 1.6: Regional Cooperation," Immigration and Border Protection Portfolio, February 27, 2017, http://www.aph.gov.au/~/media/Committees/legcon_ctte/estimates/add_1617/DIBP/QoNs/AE17-223.pdf.

135. Malcolm Turnbull, "Speech at President Obama's Leaders' Summit on Refugees," September 21, 2016, https://www.malcolmturnbull.com.au/media/speech-at-president-obamas-leaders-summit-on-refugees.

136. "Interview with Andrew Bold, Sky News," The Hon Peter Dutton MP Minister for Immigration and Border Protection, February 21, 2017, http://www.minister.border.gov.au/peterdutton/2017/Pages/interview-sky-news-21022017.aspx; Zoe Daniel and Stephanie March, "US Refugee Deal: Architect of Deal Says Arrangement Loosely Based on Australia 'Doing More,'" *ABC News,* March 21, 2017, http://www.

abc.net.au/news/2017-03-22/us-refugee-deal-architect-says-based-on-australia-doing-more/8375250; "(AE17/215)—US Manus and Nauru Refugee Deal—Signing of the Agreement—Programme 2.2: Migration," Immigration and Border Protection Portfolio, February 27, 2017, http://www.aph.gov.au/~/media/Committees/legcon_ctte/estimates/add_1617/DIBP/QoNs/AE17-215.pdf.

137. Greg Miller and Philip Rucker, "'This Was the Worst Call By Far': Trump Badgered, Bragged and Abruptly Ended Phone Call with Australian Leader," *Washington Post*, February 2, 2017, https://www.washingtonpost.com/world/national-security/no-gday-mate-on-call-with-australian-pm-trump-badgers-and-brags/2017/02/01/88a3bfb0-e8bf-11e6-80c2-30e57e57e05d_story.html?utm_term=.eeb17504b5a5.

138. "More Nauru Refugees Depart for US as Attack on Manus Provokes Panic," *The Guardian*, Feb. 17, 2018, https://www.theguardian.com/world/2018/feb/18/more-nauru-refugees-depart-for-us-as-attack-on-manus-provokes-panic.

139. "(AE17/213)—US Manus and Nauru Refugee Deal—Contingency Plans—Programme 2.2: Migration," Immigration and Border Protection Portfolio, February 27, 2017, http://www.aph.gov.au/~/media/Committees/legcon_ctte/estimates/add_1617/DIBP/QoNs/AE17-213.pdf.

140. Hirsch, "The Borders beyond the Border," 75.

141. "Australia's Military Involvement in Afghanistan Since 2001: A Chronology," Parliament of Australia, http://www.aph.gov.au/About_Parliament/Parliamentary_Departments/Parliamentary_Library/pubs/BN/1011/MilitaryInvolvementAfghanistan; "Iraq War," Lowy Institute, https://www.lowyinstitute.org/issues/iraq-war.

142. Josh Watkins, "Australia's Irregular Migration Information Campaigns: Border Externalization, Spatial Imaginaries, and Extraterritorial Subjugation," *Territory, Politics, Governance* 5, no. 3 (2017): pp. 282–303.

143. "Left Behind," an Australian Government Initiative (2010), https://www.youtube.com/watch?v=4MP5vsTJvaE.

144. Jane Hammond, "Refugee Leaky Boat Billboard Anger," *West Australian*, October 25, 2011, https://thewest.com.au/news/australia/refugee-leaky-boat-billboard-anger-ng-ya-143773.

145. Sarah Whyte, "It Costs $20 Million to Say: 'Don't Call Australia Home,'" *Sydney Morning Herald*, May 1, 2014, http://www.smh.com.au/federal-politics/political-news/it-costs-20-million-to-say-dont-call-australia-home-20140502-zr2ii.html.

146. "No Way. You Will Not Make Australia Home," *ABF TV*, YouTube, April 15, 2014, https://www.youtube.com/watch?v=rT12WH4a92w.

147. "Federal Government Funds TV Drama to Deter Asylum Seekers," *ABC News*, April 9, 2015, http://www.abc.net.au/lateline/content/2015/s4213714.htm.

148. "(AE17/110)—Advertising and Information Campaigns—Internal Product (DIBP)," Immigration and Border Protection Portfolio, February 27, 2017, http://www.aph.gov.au/~/media/Committees/legcon_ctte/estimates/add_1617/DIBP/QoNs/AE17-110.pdf.

149. Interview with author, Sydney, April 13, 2017.

150. Migration Legislation Amendment Act (No.4) 1994, No. 136, 1994—Schedule 1, http://www.austlii.edu.au/au/legis/cth/num_act/mlaa41994337/sch1.html. See the discussion in Francis, "Bringing Protection Home," 287.

151. *Minister for Immigration and Multicultural Affairs v Thiyagarajah* (1997) 80 FCR 543; *see* Kneebone, *Refugees, Asylum Seekers and the Rule of Law*, 203.

152. Border Protection Legislation Amendment Act 1999, no. 160, 1999, https://www.legislation.gov.au/Details/C2004A00551.

153. James C. Hathaway, *The Rights of Refugees under International Law* (Cambridge: Cambridge University Press, 2005), pp. 295–296.

154. Taylor, "The Impact of Australian–PNG."

155. "Indonesia Playing Key Role in Stopping Arrivals," Wikileaks, October 22, 2009, https://wikileaks.org/plusd/cables/09CANBERRA945_a.html.

156. Amy Nethery, Brynna Rafferty-Brown, and Savitri Taylor, "Exporting Detention: Australia-funded Immigration Detention in Indonesia," *Journal of Refugee Studies 26*, no. 1 (2013): p. 95; Missbach, *Troubled Transit*, 141–142.

157. "Australia-Indonesia: Moving beyond Asylum Seekers," Wikileaks, November 9, 2009, https://wikileaks.org/plusd/cables/09CANBERRA995_a.html.

158. "Agreement between Australia and the Republic of Indonesia on the Framework for Security Cooperation," Australian Treaty Series, November 13, 2006, Art. 3(7)a, http://www.austlii.edu.au/au/other/dfat/treaties/2008/3.html; Missbach, *Troubled Transit*, 160.

159. Missbach, *Troubled Transit*, 66.

160. "Indonesia Playing Key Role in Stopping Arrivals," Wikileaks, 2009.

161. "(AE17/001)—Smuggling Ventures—Operation Sovereign Borders," Immigration and Border Protection Portfolio, February 27, 2017, http://www.aph.gov.au/~/media/Committees/legcon_ctte/estimates/add_1617/DIBP/QoNs/AE17-001.pdf; "Eastern Indonesia: Afghans Bound for Australia Detained in West Timor," Wikileaks, June 3, 2008, https://wikileaks.org/plusd/cables/08SURABAYA68_a.html; "Indonesia Playing Key Role in Stopping Arrivals," Wikileaks, 2009; "As Migrant Flows Increase, GOI and Australia Cooperate on Ways to Deal with Situation," Wikileaks, October 28, 2009, https://wikileaks.org/plusd/cables/09JAKARTA1793_a.html; "Australia Searches for Asylum Seeker Solution," Wikileaks, November 13, 2009, https://wikileaks.org/plusd/cables/09CANBERRA1006_a.html; Missbach, *Troubled Transit*, 163–168; Hirsch, "The Borders beyond the Border," 74.

162. Missbach, *Troubled Transit*, 169, 180.

163. Jonathan Swan and Bianca Hall, "Scott Morrison Defiant on 'Crazy' Boat Buyback Policy," *Sydney Morning Herald*, September 2, 2013, http://www.smh.com.au/federal-politics/federal-election-2013/scott-morrison-defiant-on-crazy-boat-buyback-policy-20130902-2szsc.html.

164. Jennifer Hyndman and Alison Mountz, "Another Brick in the Wall? Neo-Refoulement and the Externalization of Asylum by Australia and Europe," *Government and Opposition 43*, no. 2 (2008): p. 261.

165. "Indonesia Playing Key Role in Stopping Arrivals."

166. All seventy-eight of the Ocean Viking refugees eventually were resettled in Canada, the United States, Norway, New Zealand, and Australia (Missbach, *Troubled Transit*, 53).

167. "Asylum-Seeker Stand-Off Solved but Rudd Under Pressure," Wikileaks, November 18, 2009, https://wikileaks.org/plusd/cables/09CANBERRA1011_a.html.

168. Missbach, *Troubled Transit*, 192–194.

169. Kneebone, *Refugees, Asylum Seekers and the Rule of Law*, 227; Dastyari and O´Sullivan, "Not for Export," 326.

170. Hilary Charlesworth et al., "Deep Anxieties: Australia and the International Legal Order," *The Sydney Law Review 25*, no. 4 (2003): p. 446.

171. Gary P. Freeman and Bob Birrell, "Divergent Paths of Immigration Politics in the United States and Australia," *Population and Development Review 27*, no. 3 (2001): pp. 525–551; Rebecca Hamlin, *Let Me Be a Refugee: Administrative Justice and the Politics of Asylum in the United States, Canada, and Australia* (New York: Oxford University Press, 2014).

172. "Federal Register of Legislation," Australian Government, https://www.legislation.gov.au/Details/C2013A00035/Html/Text#_Toc356901685.

173. Maritime Powers Act (2013) §§ 22A, 75A; Migration and Maritime Powers Legislation Amendment Act 2014; see Dastyari and O'Sullivan, "Not for Export," 322.

174. Peter Billings, "Operation Sovereign Borders and Interdiction at Sea: CPCF v Minister for Immigration and Border Protection," *Australian Journal of Administrative Law 23*, no. 1 (2016): pp. 93–94.

175. Hyndman and Mountz, "Another Brick in the Wall?," 261.

176. Missbach, *Troubled Transit*, 155.

177. Higgins, "Status Determination," 94.

178. Robyn Dixon, "Australia Closes the Door on Migrant Boats. Will It Be a Model for Europe?" *Los Angeles Times*, December 7, 2016, http://www.latimes.com/world/africa/la-fg-australia-refugees-protests-2016-story.html

179. "Turning Back Boats," Andrew & Renata Kaldor Centre for International Refugee Law Factsheet, 2017, http://www.kaldorcentre.unsw.edu.au/sites/default/files/Factsheet_Turning_Back_Boats.pdf.

180. Sarah Whyte, "Anti-whistleblowing Law Being Used to Pursue Save the Children Staff Used Only Twice in Five Years," *Sydney Morning Herald*, October 13, 2014, http://www.smh.com.au/federal-politics/political-news/antiwhistleblowing-law-being-used-to-pursue-save-the-children-staff-used-only-twice-in-five-years-20141013-1157jt.html.

181. Paul Ferrell, "Australian Police Accessed Phone Records of Asylum Whistleblower," *The Guardian*, May 23, 2016, https://www.theguardian.com/australia-news/2016/may/24/australian-police-accessed-phone-records-of-asylum-whistleblower; Ben Doherty, "Australia's offshore detention damages asylum seekers because it's supposed to, *The Guardian*, January 18, 2016, https://www.theguardian.com/australia-news/2016/jan/19/australias-offshore-detention-damages-asylum-seekers-because-its-supposed-to.

182. Bianca Hall, "'A Huge Win for Doctors': Turnbull Government Backs Down on Gag Laws for Doctors on Nauru and Manus," *Sydney Morning Herald*, October 20, 2016, http://www.smh.com.au/federal-politics/political-news/a-huge-win-for-doctors-turnbull-government-backs-down-on-gag-laws-for-doctors-on-nauru-and-manus-20161019-gs6ecs.html; "Determination of Immigration and Border Protection Workers—Amendment No. 1," Australian Government, Department of Immigration and Border Protection, September 30, 2016, https://www.border.gov.au/AccessandAccountability/Documents/determination-workers-c.pdf.

183. Jane McAdam and Fiona Chong, *Refugees: Why Seeking Asylum Is Legal and Australia's Policies Are Not* (Sydney: UNSW Press, 2014); Gleeson, *Offshore*.

184. Michael Gordon, *Freeing Ali: The Human Face of the Pacific Solution* (Sydney: University of New South Wales Press, 2005), p. 20.

185. Amada Meade, "Federal Police Admit Seeking Access to Reporter's Metadata without Warrant," *The Guardian*, April 13, 2016, https://www.theguardian.com/world/2016/apr/14/federal-police-admit-seeking-access-to-reporters-metadata-without-warrant.

186. Missbach, *Troubled Transit*, 56.

187. Behrouz Boochani, "This Is Manus Island. My Prison. My Torture. My Humiliation," *The Guardian*, February 18, 2016, https://www.theguardian.com/commentisfree/2016/feb/19/this-is-manus-island-my-prison-my-torture-my-humiliation; Eric Tlozek, "Iranian Refugee's Film Shot on Mobile Phone Shows Life Inside Manus Island Detention Centre," *ABC News*, April 2, 2017, http://www.abc.net.au/news/2017-04-03/refugees-film-shot-mobile-shows-life-inside-manus-island-centre/8411048.

Chapter 11

1. Thomas Gammeltoft-Hansen and James C. Hathaway, "Non-Refoulement in a World of Cooperative Deterrence," *Columbia Journal of Transnational Law 53*, no. 2 (2015): pp. 235–284.

2. John Rawls, *A Theory of Justice* (Cambridge, MA: Harvard University Press, 1971).

3. Peter Stamatov, *The Origins of Global Humanitarianism: Religion, Empires, and Advocacy* (Cambridge: Cambridge University Press, 2013).

4. Michael Walzer, *Spheres of Justice: A Defense of Pluralism and Equality* (New York: Basic Books, 1983); Alexander Betts and Paul Collier, *Refuge: Transforming a Broken Refugee System* (London: Penguin UK, 2017).

5. Thomas C. Schelling, "The Life You Save May Be Your Own," in *Problems in Public Expenditure Analysis: Studies of Government Finance*, edited by Samuel B. Chase, Jr. (Washington, DC: Brookings Institution, 1968).

6. Alejandro Portes, Patricia Fernández-Kelly, and Donald Light, "Life on the Edge: Immigrants Confront the American Health System," *Ethnic and Racial Studies 35*, no. 1 (2012): pp. 3–22.

7. David Kennedy, *The Dark Sides of Virtue: Reassessing International Humanitarianism* (Princeton: Princeton University Press, 2005); Michael Barnett, *Empire of Humanity: A History of Humanitarianism* (Ithaca: Cornell University Press, 2011), p. 19; Alexander T. Aleinikoff, "State-Centered Refugee Law: From Resettlement to Containment," *Michigan Journal of International Law 14* (1992): p. 134.

8. Zoltán I. Búzás, "Evading International Law: How Agents Comply with the Letter of the Law but Violate Its Purpose," *European Journal of International Relations* (2016): p. 6.

9. Thomas Gammeltoft-Hansen and Nikolas F. Tan, "The End of the Deterrence Paradigm? Future Directions for Global Refugee Policy," *Journal on Migration and Human Security 5*, no. 1 (2017): p. 45.

10. Gammeltoft-Hansen and Hathaway, "Non-Refoulement in a World of Cooperative Deterrence," 236.

11. For a compelling treatment of the EU case, see Violeta Moreno-Lax, *Accessing Asylum in Europe: Extraterritorial Border Controls and Refugee Rights under EU Law* (Oxford: Oxford University Press, 2017).

12. Virginie Guiraudon and Gallya Lahav, "A Reappraisal of the State Sovereignty Debate: The Case of Migration Control," *Comparative Political Studies 33*, no. 2 (2000): pp. 163–195.

13. See Susan Kneebone, ed., *Refugees, Asylum Seekers and the Rule of Law: Comparative Perspectives* (Cambridge: Cambridge University Press, 2009), and Rebecca Hamlin, *Let Me Be a Refugee: Administrative Justice and the Politics of Asylum in the United States, Canada, and Australia* (New York: Oxford University Press, 2014) on the deference of Australian courts.

14. *Sale v. Haitian Centers Council, Inc.* 509 U. S. 155 (1993).

15. Gary P. Freeman and Bob Birrell, "Divergent Paths of Immigration Politics in the United States and Australia," *Population and Development Review 27*, no. 3 (2001): p. 544.

16. Norman L. Zucker and Naomi Flink Zucker, "From Immigration to Refugee Redefinition: A History of Refugee and Asylum Policy in the United States," *Journal of Policy History 4*, no. 1 (1992): p. 67.

17. Azadeh Dastyari, *United States Migrant Interdiction and the Detention of Refugees in Guantánamo Bay* (Cambridge: Cambridge University Press, 2015), p. 58.

18. Austin Sarat and Stuart A. Scheingold, *Cause Lawyers and Social Movements* (Stanford: Stanford University Press, 2006), pp. 11–12.

19. David Cole, *Engines of Liberty: The Power of Citizen Activists to Make Constitutional Law* (New York: Basic Books, 2016).

20. *Hirsi Jamaa and Others v. Italy*, §104.

21. Gammeltoft-Hansen and Hathaway, "Non-Refoulement in a World of Cooperative Deterrence," 244.

22. E.g., "Long Detention Periods and Poor Conditions at the "Mauritanian Guantanamo," Wikileaks, June 8, 2009, https://wikileaks.org/plusd/cables/09NOUAKCHOTT379_a.html; "Asylum Seekers Overwhelm UNHCR in Rabat," Wikileaks, January 3, 2006, https://wikileaks.org/plusd/cables/06RABAT2_a.html.

23. "EU Divided over List of 'Safe Countries of Origin,'" Statewatch, 2004, http://www.statewatch.org/news/2004/sep/safe-countries.pdf.

24. Leo Chavez, *The Latino Threat: Constructing Immigrants, Citizens, and the Nation* (Stanford: Stanford University Press, 2013).

25. Gammeltoft-Hansen and Tan, "The End of the Deterrence Paradigm?," 41.

26. Alison Mountz, *Seeking Asylum: Human Smuggling and Bureaucracy at the Border* (Minneapolis: University of Minnesota Press, 2010); Phil Orchard, *A Right to Flee: Refugees, States, and the Construction of International Cooperation* (Cambridge: Cambridge University Press, 2014); Maurizio Albahari, *Crimes of Peace: Mediterranean Migrations at the World's Deadliest Border* (Philadelphia: University of Pennsylvania Press, 2015).

27. On refugee issue linkages generally, see Alexander Betts, *Forced Migration and Global Politics* (Oxford: Wiley-Blackwell, 2009), p. 94.

28. Donald S. Dobkin, "Challenging the Doctrine of Consular Nonreviewability in Immigration Cases," *Georgetown Immigration Law Journal 24* (2009): p. 113.

29. Alex Nowrasteh, "Terrorism and Immigration: A Risk Analysis," Cato Institute, September 13, 2016, https://object.cato.org/sites/cato.org/files/pubs/pdf/pa798_1_1.pdf.

30. Gammeltoft-Hansen and Hathaway, "Non-Refoulement in a World of Cooperative Deterrence."

31. Matthew E. Price, *Rethinking Asylum: History, Purpose, and Limits* (Cambridge: Cambridge University Press, 2009).

32. "Address of Pope Francis to the European Parliament," Vatican, November 25, 2014, http://w2.vatican.va/content/francesco/en/speeches/2014/november/documents/papa-francesco_20141125_strasburgo-parlamento-europeo.html.

architecture of protection, 7f, 5–6

architecture of repulsion

as settler society, 13–14
Southeast Asian buffers, 224–25
"White Australia" policy, 222
Australian Border Force, 4–5, 250

balsero crisis, 16–17, 109–11
barbicans. *See also* Christmas Island
  access to asylum and, 189
  in architecture of repulsion, 9
  in Australian territories, 219,
    227, 256–57
  of Balkan governments, 187
  description of, 9, 14
  of EU member states, 181–83, 187,
    189–91, 260
  "excision" concept of, 230
  maritime interceptions and, 233, 256
  in maritime remote control, 15
  in "Pacific Solution," 229–30
  "pre-transit zones" as, 188–89
  as remote control policy, 5–6, 264
al-Bashir, Omar Hassan, 180
Batista, Fulgencio, 222–23
Berlusconi, Silvio, 196–98
Bersin, Alan, 66, 139–40
Betts, Alexander, 254
Biometric Data Sharing, 65
Biometric Identification Transnational
    Migration Alert Program, 66, 146–47
Blackmun, Harry, 85
Blair, Tony, 214
Board of Immigration Appeals, 36, 73
Boochani, Behrouz, 251
"border dumping," 144
Border Patrol agents, 4
border/borders
  deterrence from crossing, 4–5
  "extraterritorialization" and, 10
  at foreign airports, 8
  internal displacement and, 3
  maritime borders, 8–9
  notion of, 4
  in U.S. Supreme Court cases, 10
  U.S.-Mexico border, 18–19
  visibility of, 4
Boughader Mucharrafille, Salim, 68

Brandeis, Louis, 253
Britain. *See* Palestine Patrol; United
    Kingdom
British Mandate (Mandate) (1920-1948),
    25, 28–30, 31–32
Brown, Simon, 166–67
buffers/buffer states. *See also specific
    countries*
  in architecture of repulsion, 8
  cost of repatriation, 144
  effectiveness of, 158
  human rights abuses and, 158–59
  legal structure of, 16
  of North America, 123–24
  as remote control policy, 262–63
Bush, George H. W., 81–82, 84
Bush, George W., 90

caging
  in architecture of repulsion, 6–7
  offshore claims processing, 16
  publicity campaign use and, 15–16
  as remote control policy, 263–64
Calderón, Felipe, 120, 139, 153
Camarioca boatlift, 103–4, 121–22
Cameron, David, 200
Campbell, Angus, 243–44
Canada
  admissions policies of, 256–57
  anti-emigration campaigns, 15–16
  asylum recognition rates, 3–4
  attitudes toward immigrants, 44–45
  Central American refugee
    acceptance, 126–27
  geographic isolation and, 14–15
  German Jewish refugees and, 22–23
  maritime asylum seekers in, 72, 96
  non-refoulement principle and,
    10–11, 97
  protections for asylum seekers, 14
  as Protocol signatory, 33, 37–38
  racist immigration policies, 44
  readmission agreements and, 16
  refugee resettlement in, 47
  remote control policies
    effectiveness, 16–17

Harper, Stephen, 60–61, 64–65
Hatchett, Joseph, 80
Hathaway, James, 4–5, 49, 255–56, 259
Heijer, Maarten den, 49, 85–86, 199–200
Hernández, Sergio, 10
Hippocratic bubble, 253–55
Hirsi Jamaa and Others v. Italy, 198–99, 257–58
Hodges, Dan, 206
Holland. *See* Dutch government
Howard, John, 228–30, 233, 237, 239–40
human rights. *See also* transnational advocacy
  abuses/violations of, 258, 262–63
  in civil societies, 259
  human rights law, 50
  human rights norms, 5–6
  international nongovernmental organizations, 53*t*
  remote controls and, 49–50
Human Rights Watch, 54, 153, 187, 189, 199, 212, 249, 257–58
human smuggling. *See* people-smuggling industry
humanitarian corridors, 2, 216
humanitarianism
  Australia and, 233
  Canada and, 37–38, 126–27
  diffuse quality of, 255
  discretionary quality of, 89
  human rights approaches and, 19–20, 22, 52
  limits of, 255
  Mariel boatlifts and, 106, 108
  as moral framework, 253–54
  multilateralism and, 98
  over long-distance, 254
  of refugee camps, 6
  security concerns and, 42
Hurd, Douglas, 166
Hussein, Saddam, 6–7
"hyper-legalism," 5–6, 77–79, 131, 157, 253, 255
hyper-territorialization

micro-distinctions in, 10
personhood and, 75–76
pushback(s) and, 123
in remote control system, 57
"wet foot, dry foot" policy, 102–3, 116, 118–19

Ilias and Ahmed v. Hungary, 173
Illegal Immigration Reform and Immigrant Responsibility Act (1996), 73
Immigration Act (1882), 63–64
Immigration Act (1917), 72
Immigration Act (1924), 63–64
Immigration Act (1976), 38
Immigration Act (UK; 1971), 166
Immigration and Nationality Act (INA) (1952), 35, 72
Immigration and Naturalization Service (INS), 64, 66–67, 72–73, 76, 79–80, 89, 92–93, 95, 115–16, 127
Immigration Reform and Control Act (1986), 136–37
"inadmissible aliens," 75
in-country processing, 87, 111
Inder, Claire, 5–6, 157, 230
Indian Ocean Solution, 231–32, 233
Indonesia. *See also* Christmas Island
  asylum in, 226–27, 229
  asylum seekers from, 223
  as buffer state, 247*f*, 219–21, 245–48, 249, 251, 263
  interceptions at sea, 219, 224–25, 233
  Operation Sovereign Borders and, 234–36
"information politics," 52–53, 54–55
Inter-American Commission on Human Rights, 85, 153–54
Intergovernmental Consultations on Migration, Asylum and Refugees (IGC), 48, 213–14
internally displaced persons, 3
international brand, 53–54, 56, 98, 126–27, 250, 251, 260
International Centre for Migration Policy Development, 48

Morocco, in European border control, 184f, 183–84, 187
Morrison, Scott, 250
Mountz, Alison, 98, 127
Moyn, Samuel, 52
M.S.S. v. Belgium and Greece, 172–73

Namah v. Pato, 241
National Institute of Migration (INAMI), 137–39
Nauru, 16, 219–21, 229, 230, 232–34, 236, 237–42, 248, 249–51
New York Times, 79, 81–82
New Zealand, geographic isolation and, 17
Nixon, Martha, 97
No Más Cruces (No More Crosses), 148–49
"no-fly lists," 64–65
Noll, Gregor, 161–62
"non-arrival measures," 4–5
non-*entrée*, emerging policies of, 4–5
nongovernmental organizations (NGOs), 11, 52, 54–55, 132–33. *See also* international nongovernmental organizations (INGOs) and advocacy groups
non-refoulement principle. *See also* Refugee Convention (1951); *specific countries*
  acceptance of, 3–4
  in asylum regime, 3
  catch 22 of, 9–10
  as human rights norm, 5–6
  legal recognition of, 17–18
  manipulation of territoriality and, 10
  maritime interception policies and, 18
  signatories to, 10–11
North American Free Trade Agreement (NAFTA), 137, 141–42

Obama, Barack, 64–65, 92, 118–19, 141, 150, 242, 261–62
Obama administration, 90, 118–19, 150
offshore processing. *See also* Australia
  caging and, 16

by Canadian government, 97
U.S. Coast Guard support for, 113–14
of Cuban migrants, 113
by EU governments, 163, 213–17
failed strategies, 11
in remote control system, 14
Operation Able Manner, 84
Operation Able Sentry, 90
Operation Able Vigil, 109–10
Operation Citadel, 68
Operation Coyote, 68
Operation Forerunner, 68
Operation Gatekeeper, 136–37
Operation Hold the Line, 136–37
Operation Lucero, 68
Operation Provide Comfort, 6–7, 15
Operation Sovereign Borders, 233, 234, 236–37, 243–44
Operation Uphold Democracy, 88
Operation Vigilant Sentry, 113–14
Orbán, Viktor, 173, 189–90, 215–16, 264
Organisation for Economic Co-operation and Development (OECD), 7–8
Ortega, Daniel, 63

Pacific Solution (Australian), 229–30, 233, 234, 241, 244–45, 249
Pacific Solution (U.S.), 92–95
Palermo Protocol (2000), 51–52
Palestine Patrol, 31f, 21–22, 25–32
Papua New Guinea (PNG). *See also* Manus; *Namah v. Pato*; Pacific Solution (Australian)
  as buffer state, 245
  relationship to Australia, 239
passports. *See also* airline liaison/liaison officers; carrier sanctions
  invention of, 12
  Palestine Patrol and, 25, 29
  in pre-clearance operations, 8
  Refugee Convention (1951) and, 34
  for refugees, 46–47
  requirement for, 59
  in system of remote control, 4
Patel, Kanu, 144–45

from Syrian civil war, 1–2
term usage, 5
remote control constraints
  foreign relations, 55–56
  law, 49–51
  transnational advocacy, 52–55
remote control, origins of
  Cold War and, 43–44
  explanations for, 41, 46–48
  media hostility/coverage, 44–45
  rights backlash in, 45
  securitization in, 42–43
  technological determinism in, 46
remote control/remote control policies
  border control measures as, 4
  concept of, 5
  effectiveness of, 16–17
  intensification/spread of, 12
  Palestine Patrol and, 25–32
  patterns of, 13–17
  proliferation explanations, 41
  secrecy/obfuscation and, 11–12
  similar concepts to, 4–5
  state control and, 12
  targets of, 5
  term usage, 4
Reno, Janet, 109–10
"Report to the Secretary on the
    Acquiescence of this Government
    in the Murder of the Jews," 42
Rinnan, Arne, 228–29
Robinson, Nehemiah, 33–34
Roosevelt, Franklin, 42
Rothkegel, Ralf, 171–72
Rudd, Kevin, 233–34, 241–42,
    246, 247–48

safe country of origin, 6–7, 48, 54–55,
    60–61, 163, 170–71, 173, 174–75, 179,
    181, 190, 212
safe havens, 6–7, 15, 89, 110, 180–81, 214
Safe Third Country Agreement, 130f
safe third country/countries
  Australian use of, 244–45
  designation of, 8, 16
  EU policies and, 48, 171–73, 174, 212, 214

in remote control system, 9–10
SS St. Louis and, 24–25
in T.I. v. UK case, 162–63
UNHCR reports on, 54–55
U.S./Canada agreement, 130f, 127–29
U.S./Mexican agreement, 142–43
Sale v. Haitian Centers Council, 84, 85–86,
    88–90, 93–94, 99–100
Salvini, Matteo, 206–7
sanctuary, 1, 5–6, 9–10, 19–20, 22–23,
    24–25, 40, 57, 58–59, 70, 87–88,
    96, 122, 232, 242–43, 252, 253,
    260, 264–65
Sangatte Protocol, 182
Sarkozy, Nicolas, 200
Sarokin, H. Lee, 74
Sartre, Jean-Paul, 226
Sassen, Saskia, 49
Schengen Implementation
    Agreement, 162f, 161, 167, 175–76,
    182, 187, 188
Schily, Otto, 215
search and rescue, 51, 105, 198–99,
    202–3, 206–7, 228–29, 247–48
securitization, 42–43, 48, 138–41
Security and Prosperity Partnership of
    North America, 138–39
Seol, Dong-Hoon, 39
settler societies, 13–14, 47, 260–61
shout test, 88–92, 261–62
Skrentny, John, 39
Smart Border Action Plan, 61
smuggling. See people-smuggling
    industry
South Korea, refugee policy in, 39–40
sovereignty, 55–56, 61, 65, 69–70, 81,
    84, 99–100, 111–12, 184, 194, 213,
    230, 237–38, 260
Spain, in European border control,
    184f, 183–87
Sri Lankan refugees, 96, 164, 166,
    235–36, 243
S.S. St. Louis, 24–25, 99
Statewatch (NGO), 174
Statue of Liberty, 58
Stuchiner, Jerry, 67

Printed in the USA/Agawam, MA
October 16, 2019

740592.005